DE GAULLE

DE GAULLE

THE MAN WHO DEFIED SIX US PRESIDENTS

DOUGLAS BOYD

First published 2013

The History Press
The Mill, Brimscombe Port
Stroud, Gloucestershire, GL5 2QG
www.thehistorypress.co.uk

© Douglas Boyd, 2013

The right of Douglas Boyd to be identified as the Author
of this work has been asserted in accordance with the
Copyright, Designs and Patents Act 1988.

British Library Cataloguing in Publication Data.
A catalogue record for this book is available from the British Library.

ISBN 978 0 7524 9700 6

Typesetting and origination by The History Press
Printed in Great Britain

CONTENTS

ACKNOWLEDGEMENTS

My thanks for help in researching this book are due to Monsieur Alexandre Cojannot, Conservateur du Patrimoine in the Archives of the Ministère des Affaires Etrangères in Paris; to fellow BBC pensioners Don Craven, Patrick Gerassi, Brian Johnson, Pierre Lesève and especially John Heuston for helping me correct many inaccuracies in previously published accounts of de Gaulle's early broadcasts from London; to John Yeowell for digging into his memories of serving in the Foreign Legion in 1940; to Louis Henry, who served with de Gaulle in Africa and Italy; to researcher extraordinaire Joan Goodbody in Washington, who unearthed for me documents for some reason not obtainable in Europe; and especially to the resources of the Fondation Charles de Gaulle in Paris.

In Washington, Alix Sundquist generously took the time to read the entire first draft and gave me the priceless benefit of her long years' experience in the US Foreign Service – including the three years when she was probably the most popular and effective US Consul-General ever – in Bordeaux. This should not be construed to mean that she in any way 'approved' the book, for we agreed to differ on a number of points.

At The History Press I would like to thank my commissioning editor Mark Beynon and Lindsey Smith for her eagle eye as senior editor, plus Emma Wiggin as proofreader. Also thanks to designers Martin Latham and Katie Beard.

With all their help, it follows that any remaining inaccuracies are mine.

ACRONYMS AND ABBREVIATIONS

ACC	Allied Co-ordination Committee
AFTAC	Air Force Tactival Application Centre
ALN	Armée de Libération Nationale
ALSOS	code name for US nuclear intelligence teams during Liberation
AMGOT	Allied Military Government of Occupied Territories
BCRA	Bureau Central de Renseignements et d'Action – Gaullist intelligence organisation in London
BST	British Summer Time
CEA	Commissariat à l'Energie Atomique
CFLN	Comité Français de Libération Nationale
CIA	Central Intelligence Agency
CNR	Conseil National de la Résistance
CRS	Compagnie Républicaine de Sécurité
DBLE	Demi-Brigade de la Légion Etrangère
Defcon	Defense Condition
DST	Direction de la Surveillance du Territoire
FFI	Forces Françaises de l'Intérieur
FLN	Front de Libération Nationale
FO	British Foreign Office
FTP	Franc-tireurs et Partisans – Communist Resistance organisation
GDR	German Democratic Republic
GPO	General Post Office – the British postal system
GPRF	Gouvernement Provisoire de le République Française
HUMINT	human intelligence, i.e. spies
ICBM	intercontinental ballistic missile
IRBM	intermediate-range ballistic missile
MAD	mutually assured destruction
MMFLA	Mission Militaire Française de Liaison Administrative
MRBM	medium-range ballistic missile
MRP	Mouvement Républicain Populaire
MUR	Mouvements Unis de la Résistance
NASA	National Aeronautics and Space Administration
NATO	North Atlantic Treaty Organization

N-PIC	National Photographic Interpretation Centre
NSA	National Security Agency
NSDM	National Security Decision Memorandum
OAS	Organisation Armée Secrète
OSS	Office of Strategic Services
PCF	Parti Communiste Français
REI	Régiment Etranger d'Infanterie
REP	Régiment Etranger de Parachutistes
RPF	Rassemblement du Peuple Français
SAC	Strategic Air Command
SACEUR	Senior American Commander in Europe
SD	Sicherheitsdienst
SDECE	Service de Documentation Extérieure et de Contre-Espionage
SHAEF	Supreme Headquarters, Allied Expeditionary Force
SHAPE	Supreme Headquarters, Allied Powers in Europe
SIGINT	signals intelligence, i.e. interception of broadcast transmissions
SOE	Special Operations Executive
UDR	Union des Démocrates pour la République
UNR	Union pour la Nouvelle République
USAF	United States Air Force
USAFSS	United States Air Force Security Service
USIA	United States Information Agency
WAAF	Women's Auxiliary Air Force

INTRODUCTION

President Roosevelt won domestic support for US involvement in the
European war by his intention to make neutral France a protectorate run
by an Allied Military Government of Occupied Territories (AMGOT) like
the eventually conquered enemy states of Germany, Italy and Japan. This
American-dominated government ... would have abolished all sovereignty,
including even the right to print money.

History Professor Annie Lacroix-Riz, quoted in *Le Monde diplomatique*,
May 2003

In the early evening of 9 November 1970 Charles de Gaulle was playing a game
of patience on a small card table a few paces away from the writing desk in his
modest home at Colombey-les-deux-Eglises in the Champagne region of France
where he had spent the day working on his memoirs. Falling to the floor with a
massive internal haemorrhage from the rupture of an aneurysm in the abdominal
aorta, he died instantly, two weeks short of his eightieth birthday.

The world awoke next morning to the loss of a great man and a great European.
French President Georges Pompidou's broadcast tribute expressed what most of
the nation was feeling, including those people who had voted against the man
known simply as *le général* on every possible occasion. 'General de Gaulle is dead,'
he said solemnly. 'France is a widow.'

In adversity Charles de Gaulle had been arrogant, demanding and infuriating
for his allies. Harold Macmillan called him 'the almost impossible ally'. In power,
he could be gracious, but also autocratic and inflexible, earning the undying hostility of US President Franklin D. Roosevelt and FDR's five successors. Few had
loved him, but millions had respected his integrity, as witness the flood of tributes
from all over the world, including many who had been his ardent critics in France
and abroad. The consensus was that he had saved his country's honour in 1940;
in 1945 he had restored the country's independence, despite Roosevelt's plan to
impose a military occupation on neutral France, as though it were a defeated
enemy belligerent; and in 1958 he had saved the nation from civil war for a second
time. The one jarring note in the media – a mocking article in a French satirical

weekly – was the object of public outrage so widespread that the magazine *Hara Kiri* fittingly committed suicide and ceased publication.

To President Pompidou, US President Richard Nixon wrote, 'I was profoundly upset and saddened by the death of General de Gaulle. My country considered General de Gaulle as a faithful ally in time of war and a true friend in time of peace … Greatness knows no national frontiers, and consequently the loss which France has undergone is a loss for all humanity.'[1]

Charles de Gaulle's wartime partner Winston Churchill died in January 1966 and the heartbeat of the British nation stopped for a moment. Few think of him now, for that is the fate of the great who rise to their destiny for one particular task, and are later an embarrassment in their decline. Franklin D. Roosevelt, too, is history's dust, except in the US, where his record in combating poverty and social unrest after the Depression keeps his memory on a level with that of Presidents Washington, Jefferson and Lincoln. Josef V. Djugashvili, aka Stalin, has almost been written out of the history taught in the schools of the many subject peoples his armies and political police terrorised for decades. But de Gaulle lives on in France, for without him it is very possible that Britain's nearest neighbour in the new Europe would have been inadvertently destroyed by Roosevelt in 1945. In the French presidential elections of May 2007, the victorious candidate Nicolas Sarkozy evoked Charles de Gaulle's name in the early stages of his campaign to gain votes, as his predecessor Jacques Chirac did many times – in each case by implying that he was in some way the political heir of the man they call simply *le général*.

What was so special about this man?

Notes
1. The broadcast tribute the morning after de Gaulle's death

PART 1

FIGHTING FOR A FOOTHOLD

1

A VERY SPECIAL RELATIONSHIP

During the Cold War, American uniforms were an everyday sight on the streets of Western Europe. Apart from the far left, who saw the world through glasses tinted in Moscow, most people believed what they were told by their governments: that the US presence east of the Atlantic was like having a big brother standing between our democratic way of life and the Russian bear, whose appetite had been whetted by carving out a European empire stretching from Karelia in the far north to include half of Germany, all of Central Europe and the Balkans, and which, given half a chance, would swallow up all the rest of us, too. Relatively few people knew that behind the comforting image of this protective 'big brother' was really Orwell's Big Brother, snooping on us and riding roughshod over our customs and laws.

American warships regularly participated in simulated NATO confrontations with the forces of the Warsaw Pact. American aircraft carrying nuclear bomb-loads constantly patrolled European airspace. US pilots initiated the dangerous game of 'straying' into Soviet territory to test the enemy's radar systems and time the reaction by armed fighter aircraft. America's nuclear-powered submarines, dedicated to delivering intercontinental ballistic missiles on targets deep within the Soviet Union, left moorings in a Scottish loch to 'play chicken' with similarly lethal Soviet subs in European waters. Beneath the grass of East Anglia and the peat of remote Scottish moors, launch silos euphemistically described as 'storage areas' in the British press, muzzled by the D notice censorship, held multiple-warhead ICBMs, the roar of whose motors would have been the last trump signalling Armageddon.

In 1984 *New Statesman* reporter Duncan Campbell wrote a book entitled *The Unsinkable Aircraft Carrier*. Subtitled *American Military Power in Britain*,[1] it set out the reality behind the 'special relationship' between London and Washington during the Cold War period. Even for British citizens who, like the author – a former Russian Linguist serving in the Royal Air Force in beleaguered Berlin – had played a part in the NATO defence system and learned through their work about many of the risks that were taken daily, Campbell's book contained revelations that made one's hair stand on end. Its wider readership was stunned to learn the reality of the 'special relationship', which successive British governments had portrayed as a great asset for the nation and the people.

During the research, Campbell and his collaborators exposed lie after lie that had been used by official spokesmen in and out of Parliament to mislead MPs and the media and sedate the public. Especially targeted by the deception operation were the several million people who lived in the densely populated areas of the country that had become prime targets in the event of nuclear war breaking out, due to the location of American bomber and missile-launching bases there and also to espionage activities carried out from British territory, sometimes by aircraft misleadingly painted with RAF insignia.

For example, when Labour MP Bob Cryer asked in Parliament for a complete list of US facilities in Britain, he had to repeat the question three times. At first, he was told by the Ministry of Defence that there were twelve bases. Then, the number was upped to fifty-one, and finally to fifty-four. Yet, working from published American sources, Campbell drew up and published a list of 103 US facilities in Britain. Digging further, he found that the Ministry of Defence had admitted in a parliamentary answer three years previously in 1977 that there were 'more than 100 ... defence facilities' as well as other facilities used by US forces in the United Kingdom.[2]

The numbers of American personnel at these 'facilities' fluctuated. At one time, a fifth of the US Air Force outside the States was stationed in Britain. In 1952 there were 45,000 servicemen and 3,500 American civilian contractors present in Britain, plus 28,000 dependents spread over forty-three airbases. After that, it seems that no one in Britain had any right to know how many US personnel were using these bases or what they were all doing here. Few British citizens were aware that, under the 1952 Visiting Forces Act, *US personnel were not subject to the laws of the United Kingdom*, but lived in a virtual American state created on British soil by that Act.

Campbell's title derives from declassified documents revealing that Britain was regarded by the Strategic Air Command (SAC) as an unsinkable aircraft carrier and ballistic missile launch pad. Unsinkable it was, but large tracts of the country were destined by Britain's US-designated role to be turned into a nuclear wasteland by Soviet retaliation if the Cold War went beyond a certain political temperature. SAC's best-case scenario gave large areas of Britain a habitable duration of perhaps six months; the worst case envisaged as little as thirty days in a hot war! But that did not matter to SAC because its UK command centre would have become airborne twenty-four hours a day in EC-135 flying command centres operating out of Mildenhall airbase in Suffolk under Operation Silk Purse long before then.[3] This was the opposite of the image purveyed by successive British governments, which inferred that the nation was safely sheltering under an American umbrella.

In the immediate post-war administration, Prime Minister Clement Attlee innocently went to Washington to clarify with President Truman how a dual US-British control of the recently developed strategic weapons based in Britain would operate. He was devastated to be informed that it was illegal for the US president to diminish his authority as supreme commander of United States armed forces by ceding any such joint control authority to any other person or agency.

Nearly four decades of the 'special relationship' later, Defence Secretary Robert McNamara admitted in 1983 that Britain had only a right to 'consultation (about the use of nuclear weapons based in the United Kingdom) ... with the party having the authority – in this case the US – making the final decision'.[4] In case there was any doubt what that meant, his assistant Paul Warnke made it crystal clear: 'If you mean that at a time of crisis you could be quite confident that American nuclear weapons could not be launched from your territory without your agreement ... then I think you would be deluding yourself.' He added, 'No piece of paper, no matter how well intentioned, is going to make any real difference at a time of crisis. The ... country that physically controls the weapon is going to make the decision.'[5] And that country was the United States. Nor was US control limited to US weaponry and personnel. The targets for British V-bombers at RAF Marham, for example, were allocated by Senior American Commander in Europe (SACEUR), not the British Ministry of Defence.

So much for what British Government spokesmen called the 'British veto' on US nuclear initiatives launched from the United Kingdom. If one can judge by her public pronouncements, even Iron Lady Margaret Thatcher, who was British prime minister 1975–90 and a great supporter of NATO, was deluded into thinking, or chose to pretend, that Britain had control over US nuclear weaponry on NATO bases here. Other NATO bases occupied by US forces in Britain also served as gigantic warehouses stocked with everything needed to conduct a major conventional war – from high-explosive blockbuster bombs and ammunition of all calibres to transportation, rations, clothing and contraceptives – all stored here for issue to US troops airlifted or shipped 'light' across the Atlantic. Effectively, this concession by the British Government meant that major ports like Liverpool, Southampton, Hull, Grimsby and Harwich, through which the incoming and outgoing troops would pass, became priority targets for Soviet nuclear retaliation, together with the millions of civilians living there.[6]

It might be argued that in a hot war those targets would have been nuked anyway, but Britain's population was in danger also during peacetime. The British

Government was aware that bombed-up American aircraft regularly overflew its cities on practice bombing runs, but was never told when or how many aircraft were involved, either before or after the fact. On every such flight there was a risk of systems failure, a crash landing, a mid-air collision or an H-bomb being jettisoned unintentionally – the last event happened on a number of occasions. Even today, the total of such incidents is hard to ascertain, but it ran well into four figures. After one crash of a nuclear bomber in America, it was found that six of the seven safeguards to prevent accidental detonation of an H-bomb's fissile core had failed.

Most of the NATO European allies were far more cautious than Britain in granting facilities for US forces on their territory. Greece, for example, never exempted US servicemen there from liability under Greek law and did keep a veto on the use to which bases there could be put under the bilateral agreement of 15 July 1983. Athens also levied a price for its cooperation, as did Ankara, Madrid and Lisbon, which shared a total of around $1.5 billion a year for their limited compliance.[7] Seven out of the fifteen NATO countries refused to have nuclear weapons on their US bases.

One of these was Spain. Yet, although the bilateral US–Spain treaty was far more restrictive on visiting forces than its British counterpart in that it granted no storage facilities for nuclear devices on Spanish soil, on 17 January 1966 a B-52 bomber of Strategic Air Command that had taken off from Seymour Johnson airbase in North Carolina had a mid-air collision with a KC-135 tanker based in Spain while refuelling over Palomares. On board the B-52 were not one but four B-28 H-bombs, with a total power that was not revealed, but could have been as high as 4.4 megatons, depending on their particular modifications. They would have been sufficient to annihilate the populations of four major cities and render them uninhabitable for a long period.

The four-man crew of the KC-135 were killed, as were three of the seven crewmen of the B-52, the others parachuting to safety. Immediately after the crash, a search operation was initiated. Its code name 'Broken Arrow' designated a top-level nuclear risk. 'Less serious' nuclear accidents were coded 'Bent Spear', with 'Blunt Sword' as the lowest category. Within hours of the Palomares crash, three of the H-bombs were traced on land or in shallow water, but the fourth bomb was missing for eighty days, despite all the state-of-the-art technical facilities of the US military deployed in the search. Although much was made of the fact that no nuclear explosion occurred as a result of the mid-air collision, the high-explosive triggers in two of the bombs had detonated on impact with the ground, spreading radioactive plutonium dust over a considerable tract of land and sea, and would have caused enormous loss of life in a built-up area. Another bombed-up B-52 that crashed near Thule in Greenland similarly released quantities of plutonium dust, after which it was estimated that several hundred people involved in the clean-up operation had suffered radiation sickness, a high percentage of them developing various cancers.

A number of accidents involving nuclear hazards on the ground occurred in Britain. Censorship kept details for the public extremely vague. After one such event, it was announced in the media that a 'fire had occurred in a storage area' on an RAF base in East Anglia. As two friends of the author, who were serving as rocketry guidance system technicians in the RAF at the time, said, 'Storage area! If only people knew what was being stored there.' The fire had been in a ballistic missile silo. Other areas designated 'Special Ammunition Stores' stocked not only the nuclear stockpile, but also extremely potent nerve gases. These areas, even on British bases, were guarded by American military police and many were out of bounds to British personnel.

On 26 July 1956 a B-47 bomber was taking off on a training flight from the US base at Lakenheath in Suffolk – one of SAC's four principal bases worldwide, although situated in close proximity to Cambridge, Norwich and Bury St Edmunds and thus placing these towns firmly on Soviet retaliation maps. The B-47 crashed into a storage igloo, inside which were stored three H-bombs. Aviation fuel from the aircraft's ruptured wing tanks spread in an immediate inferno over the bomber, the surrounding area and the igloo. Although the fissile cores had been removed, inside each bomb were several hundred pounds of high explosive as the triggering element. The fire crew correctly did not try to save the men inside the burning B-47, who were left to die, but concentrated on directing their foam hoses onto the igloo in a desperate attempt to stop the temperature inside mounting to the point where a large part of the base would be destroyed and a cloud of radioactive particles driven skyward even if no nuclear explosion occurred.

Concern that the base emergency teams could not contain the raging fire led to a panic request to the civilian divisional fire officer at Bury St Edmunds to send all his available fire-fighting units to the base, to be held there on standby. En route to Lakenheath – a journey of less than 20 miles – the British firemen were alarmed to encounter, heading at speed in the opposite direction, a long 'convoy of American cars full up with women and children. They were obviously panicking, simply trying to get away. It was a pretty amazing sight.' At least one US serviceman was recorded as running out of the main gates and leaping into a waiting taxi, telling the driver, 'Go anywhere. Just get away from here.' The neighbouring US base at Mildenhall was also evacuated, but the village of Brandon, much closer to the fire and the hazard of radioactive pollution, was not warned. After the emergency was over, the lies began, with the gullible British public being fed an improbable story that the hazard on the base had been limited to the 'cooking off' of the .50 calibre ammunition on board the crashed B-47.[8]

There was no obligation on American base commanders to inform either the local civil defence organisations or the British Ministry of Defence when incidents like this occurred. For twenty-three years, the public was not told the truth about the accident at Lakenheath, which only emerged in November 1979 in an unauthorised interview given by former SAC personnel to a North American local newspaper, in which they admitted that a large part of East Anglia could have 'become a desert' on 26 July 1956.[9]

With the introduction of intercontinental ballistic missiles in the sixties, SAC withdrew from Britain in 1965, leaving the United States Third Air Force – the most powerful air force in Europe – still based in the United Kingdom. Much was made of the dual-key launch systems for the ICBMs in Britain, but US technicians laughed at the idea that a British keyholder could have prevented a launch by refusing to turn his key. Conversely, the idea that the British Ministry of Defence could have ordered the launch of a dual-key missile without American say-so, was equally laughable.

In the air, on the ground and in the sea – the risks were everywhere. In 1978 abnormally high levels of cobalt-60 were discovered in the waters of Holy Loch, where the former Royal Navy submarine base, less than 30 miles from the centre of Glasgow, was used by the US Navy from 1960–92, most famously for refitting Polaris submarines. From what leakage the cobalt-60 came was never made clear. Three years later, a near-nuclear accident occurred at the base when a Poseidon missile containing ten nuclear warheads was being winched into the submarine USS *Holland* at the Holy Loch base. A malfunction of the hoist dropped the missile 17ft onto the USS *Los Angeles*.

How often did such things happen? In 1996 the Ministry of Defence admitted that seven accidents had taken place, but its Chief Scientific Adviser put the figure at twenty since 1960, while admitting that he had no idea whether his information was complete. A University of Bradford research paper estimated that only one in five of these near-nuclear accidents ever became public knowledge. What did Britain gain from all these risks? Certainly, British nuclear research was speeded up and successive British H-bombs bore close resemblance to US models, but that was because the Pentagon saved some money from its Cold War budgets by allowing Britain to produce some weapons following American designs.

As far as intelligence gathering went, the UK–USA agreement signed in 1947 envisaged two-way feeds between British and US agencies, as did subsequent agreements between the US and Commonwealth countries like Australia. In the event, a very low-profile US National Security Agency (NSA) unit in the US Embassy in Grosvenor Square monitored, and probably still monitors, British Government, military and civilian telecommunications. This agency, founded in 1952, has always been so high security that its initials were long said to stand for 'No Such Agency' or 'Not Saying Anything'. *All* British telephone, telex and data transmissions were accessible to the world's largest SIGINT facility at Menwith Hill in Yorkshire via a special landline installed between that base and Hunter's

Stones GPO microwave relay tower.[10] From there, they were fed back to multiple Cray super-computers at NSA headquarters in Fort Meade, Maryland. In 1955 and again in 1976, the British Government confirmed that the US had security of tenure at Menwith Hill, sometimes referred to as 'Field Station 83', for a period of twenty-one years.

The US Air Force Security Service (USAFSS) base at Chicksands – which was a prime nuclear warfare target between London and Bedford – monitored not only Warsaw Pact military and diplomatic transmissions, but also both civil and military transmissions of its NATO allies, including Britain. There is some evidence that the snooping at Chicksands also covered civilian communications of UK-based companies up against US competitors. Although the base had an RAF 'commanding officer', his role was purely for liaison duties and smoothing out problems with the local population, and no British personnel were allowed in the operational areas. Strange but true – as borne out when a Congressional Appropriations Committee queried why the NATO allies should not contribute part of a further $6.5 million required for an extension of the facilities at Chicksands. In the double-speak of the time, the reply was that, 'This facility supports a USAF operational requirement and the information gathered is not shared with NATO allies.'

This is Big Brother talking.

Across the Channel, France was among the NATO allies snooped on. There was nothing the French could do to stop it. But at least the French population was not exposed to the potentially far more lethal consequences of the alliance with Washington – largely thanks to one man.

When the hazard of geography aligned European governments on both sides of the Iron Curtain for or against the USSR or the USA irrespective of any ideology, a few brave statesmen rejected the role imposed on their countries by Moscow or Washington. Forgotten today outside Hungary, Premier Imre Nagy paid with his life in 1956 for daring to be a Hungarian and not a Soviet puppet. In what was called the 'Prague Spring' of 1968, Alexander Dubcek had the courage to reject Moscow's ruthless rule in Czechoslovakia. For this, he was expelled from the Party and demoted to the position of a forestry inspector in the eastern part of the country.

West of the Iron Curtain, French President Charles de Gaulle openly criticised the American domination of the North Atlantic Treaty Organization, in whose command theoretically all the partners had a say. Refusing the Pentagon's role for France as 'an unsinkable American aircraft carrier' exposed to possible nuclear retaliation for missiles launched against Soviet targets from bases in France, he expelled NATO forces from his country in 1966, while continuing to support the organisation in the event of unprovoked aggression.

The Axis warlords of the Second World War – Hitler, Mussolini and Japan's Emperor Hirohito – are to many young people studying this period almost as remote as Napoleon or George Washington. So, too, are the wartime Allied leaders – Britain's Prime Minister Winston Churchill, US President Franklin Roosevelt, the Soviet tyrant Josef Stalin and France's Charles de Gaulle.

Churchill came to power in May 1940 in a position of strength as the one man who could pull Britain out of defeat, albeit at the head of a coalition government. US President Franklin D. Roosevelt was elected for a third term in 1940 and went on to become the only president elected for a fourth term in the White House. After killing off or sending to the Gulag all his Party rivals and most of the Red Army's generals, the paranoid Soviet supremo Josef Stalin was the absolute ruler of what was called 'the Socialist sixth of the world', and chose to spend the first twenty-one months of the war as Hitler's ally. Any revisionist who doubts that should ask the Finns.

Of the wartime Big Four, only Charles de Gaulle began the Second World War as a substantive colonel backed by nothing except his integrity and an unswerving conviction that the inadequate military and political leaders of his country were cowardly traitors for seeking peace at any price. Rejecting the defeatism of French C-in-C General Maxime Weygand and Premier Philippe Pétain's pleas to Hitler for an armistice, in June 1940 de Gaulle flew to Britain in a cloak-and-dagger operation worthy of James Bond. With nothing to offer in return but an indomitable belief in his country, he placed his trust in the equally pugnacious new prime minister, Winston Churchill. When asked why he was doing this, he replied, 'To save the honour of France.'

In the twenty-first century few people talk about national honour, except politicians seeking to confuse the voters, but Charles de Gaulle was born in 1890, a child of the nineteenth century. Brought up in a fiercely patriotic Catholic home and educated by the Jesuits, for him words like 'honour' and 'duty' were the code by which a man should live, or die in the attempt. His concept of duty, however, did not mean slavishly obeying superiors who were wrong, because that conflicted with honour, which was the paramount virtue. Thrice wounded and taken prisoner in the First World War, he spent the inter-war years as an outspoken advocate of mechanised warfare, hectoring France's politicians and generals to drag the largest army in Europe into the modern era before it was too late.

He argued, lobbied and published books in the hope of convincing them to form armoured divisions with close air support and infantry backup – exactly the blitzkrieg tactics that won Hitler's victories in the Second World War. When the summer of 1940 saw General Heinz Guderian's panzer columns using these very ideas to rip through the weak points in the French line and drive the British Expeditionary Force into the sea at Dunkirk, acting Brigadier de Gaulle was one of the few Allied commanders who attempted to stem the tide by counterattacking with tanks that had inadequate armour, under-powered engines and obsolete cannon.

After his country was occupied and its leaders duped at every turn into believing that Hitler would offer them an honourable peace treaty – which never materialised – de Gaulle made the transition from soldier to politician, convincing other émigré officers and men from private soldiers to admirals and generals that he could, and would, lead them to victory. Imposing himself as the leader of a few thousand French servicemen in Britain – a movement he labelled *les Français libres* or Free French – he created a power base in the overseas territories of the French Empire. On occasion, this was done with British help, but he also had to combat deliberate obstruction by British officials at all levels.

The War Office despised his movement as the rump of those allies who 'had let Britain down in the Battle of France'. The Foreign Office repeatedly cut him out of the circuit, preferring to bribe and cajole the collaborationist regime of Marshal Pétain in Vichy from fear that it might otherwise hand the intact French navy over to Hitler. Time and again, only de Gaulle's unflinching courage and iron nerves saved him from being wiped off the military/political map. Such a man has few friends. Yet, the British and American press and public opinion continued to acclaim the one Frenchman who never gave up.

Although frequently infuriated by his intransigence, Winston Churchill stood by the man who had been his only ally in the dark days of the Battle of Britain and the Blitz, but was eventually forced, as the junior partner in the Atlantic Alliance, to submit to President Roosevelt's antipathy for de Gaulle. This was despite his undoubted status as head of *la France Combattante*, or Fighting France, in the French Empire and the only leader accepted by all the mutually hostile elements of the Resistance inside France.

Roosevelt's enmity began before he even met the tall, gawky Frenchman, because de Gaulle's reputation had preceded him. Secretary of State Cordell Hull had worked hard to implement Roosevelt's Good Neighbor Policy, a later modification of the Monroe Doctrine that sought to veil in double-speak the desire of the United States to dominate its Latin American neighbours. In the nineteenth century, this had been achieved by gunboat diplomacy on the European colonial model, which continued as late as 1927, when US ground forces with air support invaded Nicaragua, the Dominican Republic and Haiti.

As Roosevelt reportedly said of the corrupt Dominican dictator Trujillo, 'He may be a sonofabitch, but he's our sonofabitch.' De Gaulle was nobody's sonofabitch, but was, in Harold Macmillan's words, 'an almost impossible ally' because he never swerved from the path of patriotism as he saw it. When British influence conflicted with French interests, he went his own way. Nor had he any compunction in denouncing and thwarting American plans to impose a military government on his country after its liberation from German occupation.

None of the many enemies he made during the Second World War and his years in political office after the war was ever able to accuse de Gaulle of corruption or accommodating people or political parties of whom he disapproved. On the contrary, he gave the lie to those wartime allies who tried to diminish his achievements by allegations that he was driven by personal ambition to place himself on the throne of France. On 20 January 1946 he resigned from the hard-won position as first head of government of his liberated country, rather than be embroiled in the machinations of the squabbling, power-hungry politicians who had brought the Third Republic to its ultimate humiliation of defeat and enemy occupation in 1940.

On 1 June 1958, after twelve years openly criticising the defects of the Fourth Republic that earned France the formerly Ottoman epithet of 'the sick man of Europe', Charles de Gaulle was brought back to power as the only person capable of drafting a new constitution and persuading the French people to accept it. Elected first president of the Fifth Republic, he introduced policies so unpopular that around thirty serious attempts were made on his life during the presidency, mostly by renegade army officers who opposed the withdrawal from French North Africa, to which de Gaulle as both general and politician saw no alternative.

De Gaulle's foreign policies also earned him enemies. The memory of his opposition to Britain's half-hearted first attempt to join the European Community still festers in the corridors of Whitehall. The Pentagon never forgave his criticism of the American entanglement in Vietnam, where its generals made all the mistakes that the French had made when it was their colony – and went on to waste no one knows how many hundreds of thousand lives of US soldiery, their South

Front page of *Le Figaro*

Vietnamese allies, Viet Cong and North Vietnamese Army, without counting the *millions* of innocent civilians killed to eventually no purpose at all. When on Capitol Hill measures are taken to ban importation of French champagne or cheese there is always a hint of revenge on a great European who had the effrontery not to allow his country to become a buffer state in the game of American geopolitics.

The story of this man who had the courage to say 'No!' to the White House – not once but several times – begins on 30 September 1938. (See the front page of the mass-circulation French daily *Le Figaro* reproduced opposite.)

British Prime Minister Neville Chamberlain and French Premier Edouard Daladier might be fooling themselves and most of their fellow citizens that day with the fiction that they had bought off Hitler by abandoning the Czech people to his lust for *Lebensraum* at the meeting with him in Munich, but in London Winston Churchill, head of what they derisively called 'the war party', was not fooled. Across the Channel, at least one French professional soldier shared his certainty that war was coming, and was agonised that his superiors refused blindly to prepare for it. Twenty-two months later, with the German armies already in Paris, he wasted no time saying 'I told you so', but set out to do what he believed destiny had intended him for.

Notes

1. First hardback edition published in London by Michael Joseph
2. D. Campbell, *The Unsinkable Aircraft Carrier*, London, Collins/Paladin, 1986, p. 15
3. Ibid., p. 18
4. Ibid., p. 310
5. Ibid.
6. Ibid., pp. 81–2
7. Ibid., p. 322
8. Ibid., pp. 51–3
9. Omaha, Nebraska, *World Herald* of 5 November 1979
10. Campbell, *The Unsinkable Aircraft Carrier*, pp. 159, 168

2

THE MAN OF THE MOMENT

On Sunday 16 June 1940 the swastika flags had already been fluttering for two days in the summer breezes that stirred the leaves on the plane trees in Parisian parks. There was even a huge red-white-black banner lording it arrogantly over the Arc de Triomphe at the top of the Champs-Élysées. To civilians daring enough to stroll through the deserted French capital, in which the only traffic was the orderly progression of motorised and horse-drawn columns of men in field grey, it was clear that Hitler had claimed the City of Light for his own by branding it with the hooked cross chosen thirty years before by the otherwise unknown poet Guido von List as a symbol of anti-Semitism. On every abandoned government building hung the enormous Nazi banners that would stay there for the next four years, two months and nine days. Some French people were actually relieved that the Germans had arrived so quickly: two weeks earlier, US Ambassador William Bullitt had cabled the State department that the French prime minister and members of his Cabinet feared a communist uprising in the capital and other industrial centres as the Germans approached, leading to a bloodbath.[1]

The weather was hot and humid over most of France, but the political hot-spot was Bordeaux, the major city and port of the south-west to which France's government had fled for refuge from the invading German armies that had entered an undefended Paris on the preceding Friday. With the enemy spearheads advancing as much as 100km in one day, with 5 million bewildered refugees jamming the roads by day and spending their nights in barns, schoolrooms or in the open air, with casualty figures running into the hundreds of thousands and an entire French army surrounded in the north-east of the country, Prime Minister Paul Reynaud was told by his shrewd and manipulative mistress the Countess de Portes that he should resign and let someone else sort out the mess. When questioned why he had given way to her pressure on another matter, he once replied,

'After an exhausting day in politics, a man will say anything to get some peace at home.'

In fairness to Reynaud, it has to be said that he had accepted the premiership during the phoney war only three months earlier, by which time it was already too late to make the necessary preparations for what was bound to come, even had he had a workable majority. Fundamental differences of opinion within the Cabinet on whether to surrender or fight would probably have ended his administration earlier, had not the crossing of the French frontier by 2,000 German tanks on 10 May forced the squabbling factions to compromise at least temporarily.

After Reynaud handed his resignation to President Albert Lebrun in Bordeaux that Sunday evening, Lebrun called the leaders of the Senate and the Chamber of Deputies to a consultation. Although all three men were personally in favour of continuing the fight, Lebrun resisted the house leaders' urging to invite Reynaud to form another cabinet on the grounds that to do so would simply prolong France's agony.

Shortly after 9.30 p.m. an aircraft with RAF roundels landed at the joint military/civilian airport in Mérignac to the west of the city carrying Major General Sir Edwin Louis Spears, head of the British military mission to Reynaud's now defunct government. With him was his French opposite number, returning from a second fruitless mission to London that week, pleading for military assistance. A tall, awkward and aloof brigadier whom Reynaud had appointed undersecretary for defence only eleven days earlier, 49-year-old cavalryman Charles André Joseph Marie de Gaulle learned of the resignation from two of his staff on stepping out of the aircraft and was immediately driven by them into Bordeaux, to find out for himself what was going on.

In accordance with tradition, whereby outgoing prime ministers suggested likely successors, a few days earlier Reynaud had suggested that Lebrun should ask Marshal Philippe Pétain, the great hero of the First World War, to form a new government. Lebrun therefore summoned the 84-year-old marshal, who arrived in civilian clothes looking like a stern but benign grandfather. Accustomed during his eight-year term as president to lengthy negotiations in such situations, Lebrun was relieved when the marshal took out of his wallet a handwritten list of men he proposed including in his Cabinet. Because the marshal had a horror of new faces, all were politicians with whom he had worked in previous administrations. Knowing them all well, Lebrun heaved a sigh of relief that France had a new prime minister prepared to take over the reins of government in a country staring defeat in the face.

British Prime Minister Winston Churchill had heard Charles de Gaulle treating the outgoing premier with scant respect, on one occasion calling Reynaud '*un poisson gelé*', or frozen fish. De Gaulle also detested the Countess de Portes and mistrusted her influence over Reynaud, so details of the late-evening conversation between the outgoing prime minister and his ex-under-secretary of defence would make interesting reading, but are not available. All we know is that, after Reynaud had brought de Gaulle up to date, neither man deluded himself that Pétain would continue the fight. Assessing the situation as a professional soldier, the marshal had long since advised surrender, and 99 per cent of the population wanted nothing but an end to the fighting. To de Gaulle's mindset, this was a short-sighted attitude: he considered the marshal not only too old for the job, but a prisoner of his mid-nineteenth-century worldview. Pétain had been born a scant few weeks after the end of the Crimean War and saw the German invasion of 1940 as a rerun of the Franco-Prussian war of 1870. De Gaulle, on the other hand, had already decided that this present invasion was but the start of what would become a global war. His plan – had he been in Weygand's position – would have been to order the French armies, navy and air force to make a fighting withdrawal to French North Africa and there combine them with the enormous reserves of manpower and resources of the French Empire to resist the Germans until they were eventually defeated by the untapped military-industrial potential of the United States.

Having informed Reynaud that he would never surrender and therefore intended returning to Britain, the only country still resisting Hitler's victorious forces, de Gaulle accepted the sole help Reynaud could offer. From secret funds over which he still had control, he handed over 100,000 francs as start-up finance for a no-surrender operation in London. De Gaulle's next call was at the hotel where British Ambassador Sir Ronald Campbell was staying, to inform him and Spears of his decision. With Churchill's authority, Spears agreed that he might fly back in the RAF aircraft next morning.

At 6 a.m. French time Paul Reynaud was awoken to take a call from the White House. It was 11 p.m. in Washington. On the line was international lawyer René de Chambrun, whose father-in-law was prominent French politician Pierre Laval. Having spent several hours that day briefing President Franklin D. Roosevelt, de Chambrun was asking for the latest news. Protesting that he had resigned – which itself was news in the White House – Reynaud told de Chambrun to call Marshal Pétain. The line kept breaking up, and de Chambrun was afraid he would not get another connection, so he asked Reynaud to relay to his successor Roosevelt's advice to sue for an armistice on one condition: that the French fleet must not be handed over to the Germans.[2]

Roosevelt was one of the few Americans to have read Hitler's *Mein Kampf* and thought he understood European politics. On the return to France of Premier Edouard Daladier from the disastrous Munich conference in 1938, Roosevelt had warned him that, without the United States firmly on-side, the French–British alliance would be beaten, adding that the American people had no wish to become involved in the coming European conflict.[3] At the time, the United States had an army smaller than that of Romania, with only nine infantry divisions and not a single armoured division. Since 1935, when the signs of approaching war became obvious, successive legislation had made it more and more difficult for the country to become embroiled in another adventure like the First World War. However, before the end of that year Roosevelt approved the French purchase of advanced US warplanes. By 1940 France had contracted to buy $425 million worth, but only 10 per cent had been delivered by the time of the German invasion.[4]

It has to be said that it was with understandable relief that the mass of the French population learned after dawn on 17 June that Pétain's first act as head of government just after midnight had been to ask Hitler, 'as soldier to soldier',[5] for an armistice to put an end to the fighting and loss of life that marked the five weeks since German troops had crossed the frontiers of Belgium and Holland and wheeled left to rip through the allegedly impregnable French defences in many of the same places as their fathers and grandfathers had done in 1870 and 1914. With no formal channels of communication open between the fleeing French Government and Berlin, the request had to be relayed by the Spanish ambassador via his government in Madrid. Meanwhile, men in uniform at the front and civilians of both sexes and all ages on the crowded roads were dying – the latter most often as victims of low-flying Stukas, whose Maltese cross insignia and screaming sirens brought terror on each strafing attack.

De Gaulle, however, summed up the situation as follows:

> On 17 June, the last proper government of France died in Bordeaux. A team brought together by defeatism and treachery took power in an atmosphere of panic as a clique of shabby old politicians, businessmen devoid of honour, opportunist civil servants and bad generals rushed to take over in conditions of servitude. An old man of eighty-four, sad shadow of a past glory, was raised shoulder-high to endorse the capitulation and trick a stupefied nation.[6]

Whatever doubts de Gaulle may have had about the course that he should follow vanished at the news of Pétain's request for an armistice. However, since he was still a serving officer under military discipline, albeit no longer under-secretary for defence, he covered his tracks by ostentatiously making for that afternoon several appointments which he had no intention of keeping. He was seen sitting on the desk of General Laffont lecturing him calmly, as though it were obvious to anyone, 'The Germans will lose this war in the end. France must hold out.'[7]

The third passenger in Spears' car driving out to the airport that day was cavalry reservist Lieutenant Geoffroy Chodron de Courcel, a peacetime lawyer and diplomat who had been appointed aide-de-camp to de Gaulle only ten days previously. De Courcel was privy to his master's plan and had volunteered to be part of it. The tarmac at Mérignac airport was seething with people both in and out of uniform seeking an aircraft to take them away before the Germans arrived. France being a *pays d'accueil* with a tradition of welcoming political refugees from central and Eastern Europe that dated back to the Revolution, the civilians were mainly Jews and anti-fascists, both French and foreign, who knew all too well what lay in store for them if they were still on French soil after an armistice was agreed. A few French diehards of all ranks in uniform also demanded an aircraft in which to reach Britain or French North Africa, where they could continue the fight.

However, the ground crews were deaf to all entreaties. Since they had no way of escaping, they refused to ready or refuel the many civil and military aircraft on the base for people they regarded as runaways. Spears' plane was among the very few ready for take-off but, after de Gaulle's 'luggage' of several heavy boxes of confidential files had been discreetly removed from Spears' car and stowed behind the cabin seats, the pilot understandably refused to take off before they were lashed down, in case he had to take violent evading action on meeting Luftwaffe fighters during the long flight up the Atlantic coast to Britain.

De Gaulle despatched his equally tall and gangling aide-de-camp into the surrounding chaos to hunt for anything with which to tie down the cases, leaving him and Spears standing by the aircraft. In appearance a dour, pipe-smoking career soldier, Spears was also a linguist, a businessman, politician and author – most of whose many talents would be called upon in his role as Churchill's go-between with de Gaulle in the months to come.

Had the contents of the illicit files been suspected, both men could have been arrested on the spot and the course of the war and shape of post-war Europe changed – all for want of a ball of yarn. Increasingly tense as the minutes ticked by, Spears puffed at the pipe which seldom left his lips while de Gaulle dragged on a cigarette, both men pretending that they were saying their goodbyes, as would have been natural before Spears left and de Gaulle returned to take up whatever new duties might await him in Bordeaux.

General Spears later recalled:

> At last Courcel appeared, his stilt-like legs carrying him fast (through the crowd) although he appeared to be moving in slow motion. In his hand, a ball of string. I hope that never again will this commonplace article be so important to me. Our troubles were over. [The aircraft] had begun to move when, with hooked hands, I hoisted de Gaulle on board. Courcel, more nimble, was in in a trice. The door slammed. I had just time to see the gaping face of my chauffeur and one or two more beside him.[8]

Their flight path lay directly over the sinking French liner *Champlain*, going down with 2,000 evacuated British troops aboard after hitting a mine. Over La Rochelle and Rochefort, they flew through columns of smoke from French ships bombed in the harbours below them and from harbour installations, ammunition dumps and fuel reserves fired to prevent them falling into German hands. Over Brittany, huge tracts of forest were invisible below clouds of smoke from the demolitions. During a refuelling stop in Jersey, Spears went personally to find a cup of English coffee for his guest. Tasting the insipid liquid, de Gaulle thought it was tea, but the sour taste was as much in his mouth as in the brew. He had had plenty of time on the flight to reflect on the double irony of his defection. Not only was he breaking his officer's oath of loyalty and obedience, but the new head of government he was defying had been his protector during the inter-war years. Known to his brother officers as *le poulain préféré*, or 'favourite son', of the ageing marshal, for whom he had spent two years writing *Le Soldat à travers les Ages*, which was published under Pétain's name, de Gaulle had virtually no other friends in the army hierarchy.

In 1938, when he was about to publish under his own name a political document entitled *La France et son Armée*, Pétain wrote him a furious letter to the effect that the work had been written as part of his job. De Gaulle replied:

> Without going into the reason which led you to end my collaboration with you eleven years ago, it will not have escaped your notice that (in the interim) my circumstances have changed. I was thirty-seven. Now I am forty-eight. Those who have wounded me include yourself, monsieur le Maréchal. I have lost my illusions and renounced my ambitions. As to my ideas and the style with which I express them, I was then unknown, but have since begun to be known. In short, I am no longer so compliant and anonymous as to let other people claim what talent I have in the field of writing and history.

Ten days later, Colonel de Gaulle met the venerable marshal in Paris. Pétain ordered him to hand over the proofs of his new book. De Gaulle replied, 'Marshal, I am yours to command militarily – not in literary matters.'[9]

In another book, published in 1934,[10] his had been one of the few voices raised west of the Rhine during the 1930s to warn his political and military masters of the need to modernise the French army by ceasing to replay the First World War with a few tanks attached to each regiment and creating instead armoured divisions complete with their own motorised infantry, air and artillery support. An arrogant certainty that he was right and they were wrong had earned him the undying hostility of the generals who were going to lose the battle of France in 1940. He had also published a book enshrining his belief in the need for France to have a professional army, as against the reliance on largely conscripted armed forces traditional since Napoleon's time.

Among his readers east of the Rhine was General Heinz Guderian, whose own book *Achtung! Panzer!*, published three years later,[11] owed much to the writings of de Gaulle and British Major General J.F.C. Fuller. Whereas Hitler gave Guderian full rein to implement the creation of the fast-moving armoured panzer columns with close air support that wrought the defeat of Poland, Holland, Belgium and France, both de Gaulle's masters and Fuller's had turned deaf ears to their arguments for modernising outdated command structures and embracing new technology.

After the blitzkrieg invasion of Poland in September 1939, when all his ideas were exploited by the Wehrmacht and the Luftwaffe flying close-support missions, de Gaulle had sent to eighty of the top political and military leaders in France a memorandum in which he stated that, when the German attack came in the west, it would be led by armoured columns with close tactical air support. The only way, he said, for the French army to combat and contain such an assault was immediately to regroup all tanks in autonomous armoured divisions with air support on call. Unfortunately, nobody paid attention, except for those who sought to denigrate this pretentious colonel and his preposterous ideas. Undeterred, de Gaulle spoke his mind to a group of British Members of Parliament visiting the front during the phoney war, before the shooting started. 'Gentlemen,' he said, 'this war is already lost. We have to prepare to win a different one with machines.' The MPs departed similarly uncomprehending.[12]

Since crossing the French frontier on 10 May, the Wehrmacht and Waffen-SS tankers did not have it all their own way in smashing through the French defences. A few Allied commanders stalled them here and there by counter-attacking with inadequate forces and outdated equipment. When General Henri Georges Corap was sacked from command of Ninth Army after allowing the Germans to break the Meuse line, in the consequent reshuffle 49-year-old de Gaulle was given command of 4th Armoured Division with the rank of acting brigadier, which made him the youngest officer of general rank in the French armies. Despite the grand title, his division was a scratch assembly of very disparate qualities, not a tool that gave him the chance to put into practice what he had been preaching.

Tasked with delaying the enemy until two infantry divisions could take position in his rear at Laon in Picardy, he counter-attacked after dawn on 17 May with the aim of cutting Guderian's supply line. His command consisted of three battalions. One was equipped with B1 Mk 2 heavy tanks with a 75mm gun that had, however, only been test-fired and was untried in combat, plus a company of D2 medium tanks. The other two battalions were of lighter Renault R35 tanks with an obsolete 37mm cannon.[13] It was not much with which to take on battle-experienced German panzer troops in tanks whose armour his guns could not pierce, but the 30km drive north-east to the road junction at Montcornet was accomplished with several successful skirmishes en route.

At this point, de Gaulle's plan foundered on that German genius for battle-field improvisation which was to wrong-foot Allied commanders so many times during the war. Approaching Montcornet at 3.30 p.m., the French column was less than 2km from the command post of 1st Panzer Division in the village of Lislet. General Kirchner, the irascible, injured divisional commander, refused at first to believe that a French counter-attack had managed to advance so near at a moment when all his tanks were either undergoing maintenance or parked with their crews resting, so he evacuated the village and despatched a staff officer to Guderian's HQ 5km distant. Finding some tanks emerging from the mobile workshops, the officer ordered them immediately into action, while a battery of 88mm guns opened up on the French, reducing Lislet to ruins, in which a number of de Gaulle's tanks were left burning. After Stuka dive-bombers joined the fray, French losses by the time withdrawal was complete totalled twenty-three out of ninety tanks, as against German losses of no tanks at all. As a French officer remarked after observing the futile charge of the British Light Brigade at Balaklava, '*C'est magnifique, mais ce n'est pas la guerre.*'

Two days later, with reinforcements boosting his forces to a total of 150 tanks of various types, plus an artillery regiment in support, de Gaulle moved at dawn on 19 May against the line of Guderian's main thrust, whose spearheads were far in advance of their supporting infantry. Numbers are not everything: only thirty of these tanks were the updated B1 model with 75mm guns; forty or so were type D2 with 47mm guns; and the rest armed with the 37mm gun with a range of 600m at most.[14] At Crécy-sur-Cerre, 13km north of Laon, it was again the Germans' multi-purpose 88mm guns that stopped them. Despite de Gaulle making desperate pleas for air support to keep off the Stukas that were brewing up his tanks, no French aircraft appeared and he was forced to pull back once more – losing, in his own opinion, the only chance of halting the German advance by cutting off Guderian's spearheads before the supporting infantry arrived to consolidate their territorial gains.[15]

On the following day, with some reinforcements, he moved against the German bridgehead on the left bank of the Somme opposite Abbeville after a British armoured attack had failed to reduce it. With a force of more than 130 tanks, including thirty-three B1 Mk 2s, he pushed in the attack so relentlessly that the day's end saw only twenty-four tanks still combat-worthy. Despite the French capturing some 250 prisoners, the beachhead held firm, thanks largely to the German 88s. It was in this engagement that de Gaulle found one tank commander had withdrawn his unit from combat to avoid what he considered a pointless waste of his men's lives. The newly appointed brigadier yelled at him, 'That's what soldiers are for, to lay down their lives when ordered to.' He also promised that if the victim of his anger survived the imminent engagement with German armour, he would personally have him shot.

These examples from de Gaulle's brief command of 4th Armoured Division explain why no officer or man from the division ever volunteered to serve under him again. Pétain once observed that his style of command lacked any understanding of human nature. 'It was heartless,' he said. Nevertheless, the small success with which de Gaulle had used his limited resources to practise what he had preached between the wars emboldened him to telephone Premier Reynaud before reporting in Paris to French commander-in-chief General Maxime Weygand. Appointed on the same day as the Abbeville battle – when the battle of France was already lost[16] – General Weygand was furious that de Gaulle had short-circuited the normal hierarchy to approach the prime minister directly. It was he who would shortly sign de Gaulle's death sentence, but in the citation for de Gaulle's time with 4th Armoured Division he wrote: 'An admirable leader (who) attacked an enemy bridgehead ... penetrating more than five kilometres into the enemy lines and capturing several hundred prisoners and valuable materiel.'[17] It does not sound much of an achievement, but the other three hastily assembled armoured divisions had achieved nothing and been wiped out in the first week of combat.

Unfortunately for France, in the chaos of the German breakthrough not even officers as tenacious and aggressive as Acting Brigadier de Gaulle could achieve much at the front, so on 5 June 1940 Reynaud appointed him under-secretary of state for defence in a government that was numbed at being abandoned by its last ally after London withdrew the British Expeditionary Force from the harbour and beaches at Dunkirk. News of the appointment reached de Gaulle in a way that illustrates the depth of the chaos. Although a divisional commander in contact with the enemy, no channel existed for Reynaud to communicate his appointment directly to him. He was informed of it the following day by a general who happened to have heard of it in a radio broadcast.

On 9 June de Gaulle flew to London on the first of two missions to seek *any* help from the new coalition government headed by Winston Churchill, who had planned to send a second expeditionary corps to France with two squadrons of RAF fighters immediately after the Dunkirk evacuation.[18] It being Sunday, he was driven from the airport through streets filled with normal traffic and saw the parks filled with casually strolling people, the long queues outside the cinemas and the uniformed doormen outside clubs and hotels. Britain was a different world from the country in chaos he had left behind. By then the Germans had taken more than 100,000 prisoners at a cost of 60,000 casualties. Having lost thirty divisions in the campaign, Weygand could still just about muster forty-nine deployable divisions, plus the seventeen divisions locked up in the Maginot Line. Against him were deployed 130 German infantry divisions and ten divisions of tanks. After a brief breathing space, they began a new offensive on 5 June. Two days later, Major General Erwin Rommel had broken through towards Rouen and by 9 June German tanks had crossed the Seine and the Aisne rivers. When the panzers drove through the breach toward Châlons-sur-Marne and turned eastwards towards the Swiss frontier, all the forces defending the Maginot Line were swiftly surrounded.

De Gaulle returned to Paris empty-handed. Churchill's War Cabinet, having written off France as a lost cause, was not prepared to invest one more aircraft or one more tank in its defence. However, the British premier was so impressed by the undiminished morale and inflexible determination to fight on shown by Under-Secretary de Gaulle – who accepted that the British could not afford to lose any more aircraft in the defence of France, but must keep them in reserve for the attack on Britain which could not fail to come – that he afterwards told his inner circle of intimates that de Gaulle was the one man in France to watch.[19]

The final unhappy Franco-British summit meeting during the invasion took place at the Château du Muguet near Briare in central France on 12 June. Discussion of diplomat Jean Monnet's last-minute plan for a political and military union of the United Kingdom and France came to nothing despite support from both heads of government. At this conference, after two years of hostile silence, de Gaulle met Pétain again. Sporting the seven stars of a Marshal of France on his kepi, he had glanced at de Gaulle's two new stars denoting the rank of brigadier and cut dead the protégé he had formerly lauded as the most intelligent officer in the French army.

A Francophile who liked the company of soldiers, having himself served in uniform, Churchill had made it his business during the phoney war to meet most of the French top brass. He formed a poor impression of them. Generals Billotte and Blanchard he considered 'inexplicably incapable'. At Dunkirk, the negative attitude of Admiral Abrial had infuriated him. He rightly had a low opinion of General Vuillemin, head of the ill-equipped and under-trained French air force, and was appalled at the lack of strategic grasp and the pessimism of General Weygand,[20] whom de Gaulle shrewdly assessed as a good second-in-command – in which capacity Weygand had served Marshal Foch well in the First World War – but a hopelessly indecisive commander-in-chief.

The British prime minister was, however, impressed by de Gaulle's revolutionary suggestion to make the best of available resources by combining British light armour with the heavier French tanks. It showed both originality and positive thinking at a time when half the French Cabinet and military commanders seemed more interested in running away from the advancing Germans than in resisting them. Churchill later wrote, 'On leaving the meeting of 12 June, I saw General de Gaulle standing, stolid and expressionless, at the doorway. Greeting him, I said in French, "*L'homme du destin.*" He remained impassive.'[21]

The man of destiny remained impassive apparently because he did not hear the remark in the general hubbub of the meeting breaking up for the British party to fly back to the safety of their island fortress in a twin-engined DH95 Flamingo aircraft protected by a squadron of RAF fighters while the French participants took the road for Bordeaux in an assortment of official and private vehicles, as their predecessors had done during the German invasion of 1914. Had Reynaud's under-secretary for defence heard Churchill's salutation, it would have made no difference, for Charles de Gaulle was a man who had always listened to his inner voices and needed no telling that his hour of destiny was approaching. A product of Jesuit education and an intensely patriotic Catholic home, where grace at mealtimes was often followed by short extempore speeches in Latin, earnest discussions of political events and literary criticism, he believed that Providence had created France both for greatness and exemplary misfortune, to be tested as the Biblical Job had been. As a young man, if his soul was exalted by his country's great buildings like Notre Dame Cathedral, the palace of Versailles and Napoleon's tomb in Les Invalides, it was also profoundly disturbed by the social unrest he saw around him.[22] He also believed as fervently as Joan of Arc had done that it was his destiny to save his country in its hour of need.

The army was his life. In the entrance exam to the military academy of St Cyr, he had been placed only 119th out of 221 candidates, yet on graduating two years later in 1912, his reports described him as a highly gifted cadet of exceptional decision-making and natural authority – this despite his nickname of 'the big asparagus stalk'. By the end of 1915, he had been wounded twice, promoted to captain and decorated with the Croix de Guerre. Taken prisoner at Verdun, he attempted escape several times and in the interim improved his German. Between the wars, he married, bought a family home and irritated intellectually inferior officers of superior rank by arguing that the next war would be very different. Crucially, at the beginning of the war, de Gaulle was serving in Metz under General Henri Giraud, who was not impressed with this outspoken and disrespectful colonel on his staff.

On the afternoon of 15 June Under-Secretary de Gaulle boarded the French destroyer *Milan* at Brest, in company with a group of top scientists taking France's supply of heavy water to safety in Britain. This was probably the first time his path crossed that of Harold Macmillan, who had been sent by the Ministry of Supply to Plymouth to take charge of the heavy water, but had no idea what it was and was too embarrassed to ask anyone.[23] After landing at Plymouth, de Gaulle reached London early the next morning. One of his first acts was to radio orders for the French transport *Pasteur*, which was bringing one thousand 75mm guns, thousands of machine guns and a vast supply of ammunition from the United States, not to continue its course to a French port, but to divert to Britain, so that all this materiel should not fall into the hands of the enemy, but serve to replace some of the British weaponry and munitions left behind at Dunkirk. At lunch in the Carlton Club, he told Churchill that his acceptance during the meeting in Tours of the hopelessness of France's situation was being read by France's politicians as tacit permission from the British prime minister to seek an armistice. Hearing this, Churchill took aside his personal assistant Major Desmond Morton for a private conversation. Thirty minutes later, the British ambassador in Bordeaux scuttled back to Reynaud to reclaim a memorandum accepting the essential necessity for an armistice.

De Gaulle's other concern at the luncheon was to stress to his British hosts that François Darlan, the enigmatic admiral who had single-handedly built the French navy into the world's fourth largest between the wars against all the resistance of successive governments, would never hand his fleet over the Germans, no matter what the terms of an armistice.

After reporting back to Reynaud in Bordeaux on 16 June, empty-handed for the second time, de Gaulle was thus putting all his trust in Britain by deciding to return there with Spears. Their plane landed a little before noon on 17 June at Heston aerodrome – best known as the place where Prime Minister Neville Chamberlain waved the piece of white paper, supposedly signed by Hitler, and promised 'peace in our time' to the newsreel cameras and press photographers on returning from the 1938 Munich Conference. Knowing exactly what he wanted in the immediate future, de Gaulle was driven into London with Spears, feeling, as he said, 'like a swimmer setting out to cross a mighty ocean'. After a brief luncheon at the Royal Automobile Club, he was driven to his new home – a small apartment on the fourth floor at 8, Seymour Place,[24] which belonged to his principal private secretary at the defence ministry, who had lent him the keys.

From Seymour Place, Gen Spears took de Gaulle to Downing Street, where Churchill greeted his solitary ally with tears in his eyes. For a man who could be so ruthless, he wept easily and was often moist-eyed when recalling that meeting, for at the time de Gaulle was the only straw at which he could grasp. Had he come at the head of an army, what a propaganda coup that would have been! However, a staunch believer that some men were marked by destiny for greatness, Britain's prime minister was certain this awkward and reserved French officer was, like himself, one of that rare breed. They were at that moment kindred souls. Yet, when de Gaulle asked permission to broadcast to France, Churchill was uncertain what good could come of allowing a substantive colonel, whose name was unknown to the French public and who now held no official government post, to use the BBC airwaves for a speech that would almost certainly alienate France's new government. He therefore temporised by saying that permission would have to await definite confirmation of an armistice *and* the approval of the War Cabinet.

Confident nevertheless that he would shortly be making the broadcast, de Gaulle had de Courcel borrow an attractive young brunette whom he knew from the French economic mission in London to retype the intended speech from his manuscript drafts. The recruitment of 24-year-old Elisabeth de Méribel doubled the manpower under de Gaulle's command.

That evening, his quasi-religious sense of vocation was apparent on meeting the wife of Jean Monnet, head of the French mission, to coordinate industrial and particularly armament production in Britain and France. Monnet was also the man who had originated the idea of the political union of the two countries. To Madame Monnet's question, what was the current mission in Britain of ex-Premier Reynaud's former under-secretary for defence, de Gaulle replied stiffly, 'Madame, I am not *en mission*. I am here to save the honour of France.'[25]

Notes

1. O.H. Bullitt, *For the President, secret and personal*, Boston, Houghton Mifflin, 1972, p. 37
2. R. de Chambrun, *Ma Croisade pour l'Angleterre*, Paris, Perrin, 1992, pp. 120–1
3. P. Billotte, *Le Temps des Armes*, Paris, Plon, 1972, p. 232
4. A. Beevor & A. Cooper, *Paris after the Liberation*, London, Hamish Hamilton, 1994, pp. 11–12
5. Spoken in his broadcast to the nation
6. ed. M. Jullian, *de Gaulle – Traits d'esprit*, Paris, Cherche-Midi, 2000, p. 95
7. F. Kersaudy, *de Gaulle et Churchill*, Paris, Perrin Tempus, 2003, p. 77
8. Gen E. Spears, quoted in J. Owen & G. Walters (eds), *The Voice of War*, London, Penguin, 2005, p. 56 (abbreviated by the author)
9. Jullian, *Traits d'esprit*, pp. 89–90
10. C. de Gaulle, *Vers l'Armée de Métier*, Paris, Berger-Levrault, 1934
11. Published in English under the same title by Cassell, London, in 1937
12. J. Marin, *de Gaulle*, Paris, Hachette, 1973, p. 53
13. C. de Gaulle, *Mémoires de Guerre: L'Appel 1940–42*, Paris, Plon, 1954, p. 44
14. Ibid., p. 45
15. C. Williams, *The Last Great Frenchman*, London, Little Brown, 1994, pp. 89–91
16. De Gaulle, *L'Appel*, p. 54
17. W. Thornton, *The Liberation of Paris*, London, Rupert Hart-Davis, 1963, pp. 91–92
18. Kersaudy, *de Gaulle et Churchill*, p. 49
19. Williams, *The Last Great Frenchman*, pp. 89–91, 96–97
20. Kersaudy, *de Gaulle et Churchill*, p. 49
21. W.S. Churchill, *The Second World War Vol. 2: Their Finest Hour*, London, Penguin Classics, 2005, p. 162
22. De Gaulle, *L'Appel*, pp. 7–8
23. P. Mangold, *The Almost Impossible Ally – Harold Macmillan and Charles de Gaulle*, London, Tauris, 2006, p. 26
24. Now renamed Curzon Place
25. J. Monnet, *Memoirs*, London, Collins, 1978, p. 24

3

'THE FLAME MUST NOT GO OUT!'

The following day was the 125th anniversary of Napoleon's defeat at the Battle of Waterloo. Brought up by a father who had imbued him with a passionate sense of French history, de Gaulle could not have chosen a less auspicious date to announce that he had thrown in his lot with the English. Another complication of what seemed a simple speech was that he had no wish to appeal openly to soldiers in France to desert their posts so long as they were still fighting the enemy. Working with two fingers on an unfamiliar QWERTY-keyboard upright typewriter, Elisabeth de Méribel laboriously retyped one after another handwritten draft, rendered so difficult to decipher by all her new employer's alterations and deletions that de Courcel had to dictate most of the text to her.

What was de Gaulle's mood at this moment? 'He was calm,' Elisabeth recalled later. 'A tall man in a business suit, he was like a rock in the middle of a stormy sea.'[1] When at last he was satisfied with the speech, it was – although he later denied this – then submitted for approval to the War Cabinet by Minister for Information Alan Duff Cooper, who scored through two sentences regarded as too inflammatory. In the absence of Churchill, who might have bulldozed it through, Neville Chamberlain in the chair had it minuted that the idea of the text being broadcast was unacceptable because an appeal to the population of France by de Gaulle would offend the new French Government of Marshal Pétain, with which it was hoped diplomatic relations could continue, the armistice agreement still being unsigned.

Learning of the decision from Duff Cooper, Spears went post-haste to the House of Commons, caught Churchill emerging from the Chamber after speaking and pleaded de Gaulle's cause with the argument that the broadcast could be a clarion call resulting in hundreds of military aircraft sitting at Bordeaux and other French airports being flown to Britain for use by the RAF. Churchill, however, refused to go against the War Cabinet's decision. He was notorious for keeping his own hours, often working through the night and catnapping in the daytime, so there was nothing unusual in him being asleep when the pro- and anti-de Gaulle supporters arrived at Downing Street later that afternoon seeking a revision of his decision. Tired and irritated at being awoken shortly before he himself was to broadcast to the nation, he tore off his slumber mask and eventually agreed to de Gaulle's broadcast going ahead, provided that the War Cabinet rescinded its veto. After Spears' and Duff Cooper's energetic lobbying resulted in individual permissions from each member of the War Cabinet, de Courcel hailed an ordinary London taxi in Seymour Place about 6 p.m. and got in with de Gaulle and Elisabeth, whom they dropped off at her flat before continuing along Oxford Street to Broadcasting House in Langham Place.

Because the broadcast became the stuff of legend, many sub-legends grew up around it, usually based on accounts by BBC staff who claimed to have been present. The bald facts are that European News Talks Assistant Elizabeth Barker received a telephone call from the Ministry of Information, asking the BBC to give de Gaulle air time after the 10 p.m. news in the French Service. When told that the text of the speech had already been censored and passed for transmission, she thought it odd, because normally that was a BBC function and she was unaware that it had the majestic blessing of the War Cabinet.

Shortly afterwards, de Gaulle swept into the main reception area of Broadcasting House, headquarters of the most famous broadcasting organisation in the world at the time, with General Spears following and de Courcel in attendance to act as his interpreter. De Gaulle's father, who had been wounded in the Franco-Prussian War, had sent him as a child to stay with German families each summer holiday, with the result that he was fluent in German. English, however, he had only begun to study at the war college and, while he had a fair understanding of the spoken and written language, he was never at his ease speaking it.

Broadcasters become accustomed to dealing with people from all strata of society, but for Miss Barker de Gaulle's height and aloof bearing, his immaculate general's uniform with riding boots polished like glass, the kepi covered in gilt oak leaves and white dress gloves carried in the left hand must have been impressive. Leaving his companions in a room where they could hear the broadcast over a loudspeaker, she conducted the General to the fourth floor of the building. In studio 4C or 4D, which would be demolished by a German bomb shortly afterwards, a French service newsreader was seated at a baize-covered desk with a large microphone, reading the news. Seeing the kepi with its two general's stars placed upside-down on the table beside him and a large hand deposit two white gloves in the kepi, the studio manager looked up from his script – and silent tears ran down his face at the sight of a French officer beside him in central London at that moment.

Asked for a brief example of voice level by the engineers, de Gaulle said, '*Moi, Général de Gaulle.*' He then delivered the speech that had cost so many hours of redrafting. It was, on the face of it, a simple appeal from a patriotic soldier. Yet like most political speeches, it was replete with fine-sounding phrases and vague promises. Had they heard it, the Jesuit teachers of de Gaulle's childhood would have been proud. For the historian, the most notable aspect is the soldier-politician's prescient military forecast that the war would be decided, not by valour or force of arms, but by the industrial might of the United States. No other person had said as much then, nor would for some time to come:

A government has been formed by those who for many years have led the French armies. On the grounds that our armies are defeated, it has approached the enemy to put an end to the fighting. It is true that we have been, and are, overwhelmed by the enemy's strength on the ground and in the air. More than manpower, it is the tanks and planes and tactics of the Germans that have made us retreat. It is the tanks, the planes and the tactics of the Germans which have surprised our leaders and reduced them to the pass in which they find themselves today. But has the last word been uttered? Must all hope be abandoned? Is this the final defeat? No!

Believe me, I know what I am talking about when I tell you that nothing is lost for France. The same means that have defeated us can one day bring victory because France is not alone. She is not alone!

He repeated the phrase again for emphasis:

She is not alone because she has a vast empire behind her and can continue the struggle by uniting with the British Empire which rules the waves. Like England, she can use the unlimited industrial resources of the United States.

This war is not limited to our unhappy land. This war has not been decided by the Battle of France. This war is a world war. All the mistakes, all the delays and all the suffering cannot take away the fact that the world has means enough to crush our enemies one day. Brought low today by mechanical strength, we can win in the future by superior mechanical strength. The destiny of the world is at stake.

I, General de Gaulle, here in London, invite the French officers and soldiers with or without their weapons and who are, or may one day arrive, on British territory to contact me together with engineers and armament technicians who are in Britain or can get here. Whatever happens, the flame of French resistance must not and will not go out. Tomorrow, I shall speak to you as I have today over Radio London.[2]

The announcement that he would broadcast again the following day was news to the BBC staff, since no such arrangement had been sanctioned by Downing Street. De Gaulle then politely shook hands with everyone present and stalked loftily out of the building.

Few people in France actually heard the four-minute speech at 10.00 p.m BST.[3] Across the country, the whole front line was in chaos due to another broadcast. In his speech of 17 June, Pétain had said, '*Il faut cesser le combat.*' While he intended this ambiguous phrase to mean, 'We must find a way to stop the fighting', it could also mean, 'You must stop fighting.' Many army units took it as his permission for them to lay down their weapons.

One of the few who did hear de Gaulle was Lucien Neuwirth, a 16-year-old boy in the Haute Loire *département*. He caught the faint voice from London in the earphones of his crystal set tuned into the 31m band entirely by chance, became one of the first *résistants* and would become a Gaullist politician after the war. However, François Mauriac, later a supporter, was probably speaking for most French people when he remarked at the time: 'Purely symbolic, de Gaulle's obstinacy. Very fine, but ineffective.'[4] An abbreviated version of the speech distributed in clandestinely printed copies by a few enthusiasts caused bafflement to most readers, who reasoned that France's two most famous soldiers, Philippe Pétain and Maurice Weygand, still gallantly at their posts, must know the situation better than this unknown officer who had fled to London. There was also the worrying thought that, should the man who styled himself over the crackling airwaves '*moi, Général de Gaulle*' lose his solitary gamble – as seemed very possible at the time – he and his supporters could legally be executed for high treason by the French Government.

Going home to his borrowed apartment after the broadcast, de Gaulle knew that he had burned his bridges. Although he had stopped short of inciting armed rebellion in France or desertion by serving members of the armed forces, he was a soldier who had himself deserted his post while on active service. That alone merited the death sentence. There could be no going back now. On the very anniversary of France's humiliation by the English at the hands of the Duke of Wellington, he had, for better or worse, thrown in his lot with Winston Churchill and Britain.

In those days before tape-recording facilities, the BBC had only six channels of disc recorders. These were already committed, being partly reserved for Churchill's speech. Thus, no recording of this historic broadcast was made. De Gaulle had assumed it would be. Returning to Broadcasting House for his second broadcast, when he was received by Director General F.W. Ogilvie, de Gaulle learned that this was not the case, and gave broadcaster Leonard Miall, then a 26-year-old European News talks editor, a severe dressing-down for this omission, which Miall clearly remembered fifty years later. He was trying in his poor French to explain the shortage of facilities, but the General was not mollified.

Peace was restored only when the General agreed to repeat the substance of his first broadcast on 24 June in the third transmission. This was recorded, and has been replayed many times as the original speech.[5]

If de Gaulle was expecting a flood of volunteers in response to the call of 18 June, he must have been very disappointed by the trickle it produced from the several thousand French civilians who had come on business or in some official capacity to Britain and been trapped there by the sheer speed of the German breakthrough. Nor was it much more productive among the thousands of servicemen who had been evacuated at the time of Dunkirk or returned from the abortive Anglo-French-Polish combined operation in German-occupied Norway. Some Frenchmen already in Britain found it less than easy to track down de Gaulle's temporary HQ. After one officer was brusquely told to go away by embarrassed French embassy staff, who now took orders from Vichy, it was the doorman who whispered de Gaulle's address to him as he departed.

Volunteers making their way to Seymour Place that week were few indeed and included none of any political importance. The first to knock on the door on the morning after the broadcast was a French mechanic working on aero engines for Hispano-Suiza. De Courcel had acquired a visitors' book, in which the mechanic wrote his name and contact details, and was told, 'We'll let you know.' There were no uniforms, weapons or accommodation to offer the volunteers. The future author and diplomat Romain Gary had come to London to fly aircraft against the Luftwaffe. Learning that he was to be placed in the reserves, he flew into a temper and was called into de Gaulle's presence to be disciplined. Unrepentant, Gary announced that, if he was not to be allowed to fly for Free France, he would join the RAF. Unimpressed by verbal heroism, de Gaulle told him to go ahead, adding, 'And make sure you get yourself killed.' Gary saluted and was leaving the room, when the General called after him, 'Actually, nothing will happen to you. It is only the best ones who get themselves killed.'[6]

Czech, Polish, Dutch and Belgian refugees were among the foreign volunteers enlisting to serve in British uniform, together with a small number of Americans, Canadians and other Commonwealth citizens who happened to be in Britain, but it was no part of de Gaulle's plan for Frenchmen to serve in the British armed forces. His intention was far more ambitious: the constitution of an alternative French army, navy and air force – under Allied command, if need be, but officered by Frenchmen, with French as the language of command and himself as commanding general. However, most French servicemen in Britain had had enough of fighting and opted for repatriation. One week after the broadcast of 18 June the number of volunteers sleeping on camp beds in the vast exhibition hall at Olympia was in the low hundreds.

For de Gaulle personally, the only good news on the day immediately after the first broadcast came by telephone from Plymouth. En route to Brest on 15 June, to cross the Channel aboard a French destroyer, he had found time to say farewell to his dying mother in Paimpont and also instructed his wife Yvonne to bring their son and two daughters to Britain as soon as possible. The call from Plymouth was to announce their arrival in Britain. Yvonne's journey with 18-year-old Philippe, 16-year-old Elisabeth and 12-year-old Anne had nearly ended in disaster. Contacting the British consul in Brest as her husband had instructed, she was promised passage on a Polish freighter, but luckily the car in which she and the children were travelling broke down on the way to the port, delaying their arrival in Brest until after it had sailed. The Polish ship was attacked by German E-boats in mid-Channel and sank with no survivors. Hustled aboard a small British coaster in Brest harbour just before it cast off its moorings, Yvonne and the children arrived safely in Plymouth on 19 June and managed to get through by telephone to Geoffroy de Courcel, who ran with the news to de Gaulle. His reaction was a nod and, 'So, my wife and children have arrived, to reinforce us.'[7]

That morning, the staid headline in *The Times* in London was, 'France is not lost: General's message to the nation'. The *Los Angeles Times* went overboard with, 'French Leader sounds the call – asserts Franco-British union and American supplies can crush the foe!' With censorship still sporadic in France, many newspapers in regions not occupied by the Germans printed versions of the broadcast from London that had been taken down in shorthand, a prerequisite for journalists at the time.

Newspaper from 19 June 1940

Reading *Le Petit Marseillais* that morning, reservist infantry officer Second Lieutenant Pierre Messmer typified French soldiers in France who refused to accept the armistice. Technically a deserter, he was in civilian clothes in Marseille trying to find a boat to North Africa. Skipping over the headlines, 'The French armies continue combat' and 'Towns of over 20,000 inhabitants will not be defended', what caught his eyes was 'General de Gaulle issues a call for all-out war!' In London one month later, Messmer was promoted to full lieutenant in the Gaullist 13th Demi-Brigade Blindée of the Foreign Legion, with whom he would later see action in West and East Africa, Syria, the Western Desert and Tunisia.

On 19 June de Gaulle's niece Geneviève was a refugee in Locminé in Brittany, sharing a mattress with her grandmother in borrowed accommodation. Seeing the first German motorcyclists arrive with no French soldiers resisting them, their hearts sank until they heard a priest, who had listened to the broadcast from London the previous evening, trying to raise morale by telling the refugees about it. He could not recall the name of the speaker, but when he said that he had been under-secretary for defence, Geneviève's grandmother burst out proudly, 'That's my son, *Monsieur le Curé* – my son!'[8] She was to die of natural causes a few weeks later, but how right de Gaulle had been to tell his wife to leave France was proven when among those kin who paid a price for his intransigence was his brother Pierre, deported to Germany in 1943. His sister and her husband were also imprisoned and sent to Buchenwald, with Geneviève being deported to Ravensbrück in 1944 as a VIP hostage held in solitary confinement.

Spears noted on 20 June that the broadcast de Gaulle intended to make on 19 June was postponed[9] in case it disturbed the new French Government at a time when a British diplomatic mission in Bordeaux was encouraging leading French politicians to continue the fight after moving to French North Africa. They included Paul Reynaud, who did not leave, but who killed the Countess de Portes in a motoring accident a few days later under very questionable circumstances and then spent the war years in various German prisons. The Foreign Office plan came to naught. Of the twenty-six *députés* and one senator who did board the SS *Massilia* in the Gironde estuary during a gale on the night of 19 June and set off for Morocco next morning, many were Jewish, leaving more to avoid their inevitable fate if taken prisoner by the Germans than because they seriously contemplated fighting on from North Africa. On arrival in Morocco, they were imprisoned by Résident Général Noguès, loyal to Pétain, and returned to France, to face imprisonment and worse.

To function as de facto leader of militant French servicemen in Britain, de Gaulle needed office accommodation. Spears arranged for him to take over space on the third floor of St Stephen's House on the Thames embankment opposite the Houses of Parliament. As to accommodation for the family, Madame de

Gaulle and the two girls were settled in a nondescript house at Petts Wood in Kent, which obliged the head of the family to commute daily up to town.

Yvonne de Gaulle was rarely seen in London. Ten years her husband's junior, she was a pretty, religious and very shy woman, who was never a part of his political life. It was in those days not normal for public figures to expose their wives and children to the media, but in this case there was a special reason for wanting privacy because it was considered shameful to have a handicapped child, and 12-year-old Anne had been born with Down's syndrome. She was the one person to whom her father showed physical affection, reading to her each evening when at home and laboriously teaching her to play whist with him. When it had been suggested after the initial diagnosis that the proper place for her was in a specialised home, he had announced that it was the family's duty to make Anne's life as happy as it could be and not pass this obligation on to professional carers. His deep yearning for her to have a normal life comes out in the comment he made in 1948 at her funeral at the ancient church a few minutes' walk from the family home in the small village of Colombey-les-Deux-Eglises in Champagne-Ardennes. 'At last,' he murmured, taking Yvonne's hand as the coffin was lowered into the earth, 'she is like all the other children.' That evening, he wrote to his other daughter Elisabeth, '(Anne's) soul is now free. But the death of our poor suffering child who was without hope, has caused us immense pain.'[10]

Subject to depressions, like Churchill, de Gaulle must have been disappointed by the poor response to his broadcast, but showed no outward signs as most of his compatriots evacuated from Dunkirk ignored the call to arms and opted to go home, having had enough of war. Nor did his formal offer to Weygand, nominated Pétain's Minister of National Defence on 17 June, to continue serving as a useful a link with the British Government, elicit any more than a curt order to return to his duties in France. He then wrote a personal letter to Weygand, suggesting that his former commander-in-chief should consider setting himself up as the leader of national resistance and offering the assurance of his loyal obedience in such a case.

Sincere or not, the offer was never put to the test because the letter was eventually returned, marked, 'If Colonel de Gaulle (retired) wishes to communicate with General Weygand, he should use the proper channels.'[11] Before then, on 30 June de Gaulle received via the French Embassy in London the order to report for court martial at the St Michel prison in Toulouse on a charge of deserting his post in time of war. The court duly sat and, on Weygand's instructions, condemned him in his absence to the maximum penalty: death by firing squad.

De Gaulle's reaction was, 'I consider [the verdict] null and void. Vichy's men and I will explain our positions after the victory.'[12]

Notes

1. In her interview on French television channel A2 on 18 June 1990
2. Usually, this was abbreviated in handbills as follows:

France has lost a battle, but France has not lost the war. A makeshift government may have abandoned all honour and yielded to panic in capitulating and delivering our country into captivity, yet nothing is lost! Nothing is lost because this war is a world war. The immense forces of the free world have yet to come into play. One day, they will crush the enemy and France must be present at the victory on that day to regain her liberty and her greatness. Such is my sole aim. That is why I ask all French men and women, wherever they may be, to join me in action, in sacrifice and in hope. Our homeland is in mortal danger. Let us all fight to save her. *Vive la France!*

3. French clocks were one hour ahead of London at the time. De Gaulle says he broadcast after the 6 p.m. news, but that does not accord with the BBC 'Programme as Broadcast' form (source Pierre Lesève, former BBC Producer, French Service)
4. H. Guillemin, *Parcours*, Paris, Seuil, 1989, p. 400
5. The account of the evening of 18 June at Broadcasting House is taken from Leonard Miall's letter dated 28 June 1990 to the editor of *The Independent* magazine, which he wrote to correct some rather more glamorous accounts
6. ed. M. Jullian, *de Gaulle – Traits d'esprit*, Paris, Cherche-Midi, 2000, pp. 76, 95
7. Ibid., p. 102
8. Ibid.
9. Document FO 24349 in PRO at Kew
10. C. de Gaulle, *Lettres, Notes et Carnets*, Paris, Plon, 1986, Vol. 5, p. 247
11. J. Fenby, *The General*, London, Simon & Schuster, 2011, p. 138
12. Jullian, *Traits d'esprit*, p. 96

4

PERFIDIOUS ALBION

On 22 June the armistice agreement forced on Pétain's government by the collapse of the Allied armies was signed at Rethondes in the forest of Compiègne. Hitler insisted that the ceremony take place in the Compagnie Internationale des Wagon-Lits dining-car No. 2419. Serving as General Foch's mobile office during the First World War, it had been used when the defeated Germans signed the surrender that ended the First World War in November 1918. Arriving at Rethondes at 3.30 p.m. on that hot summer afternoon less than twenty-two years later, the French team under General Charles Huntziger asked for an immediate cessation of hostilities. Across the table, Hitler and Goering enjoyed the reversal of roles in silence. As German spokesman, General Wilhelm Keitel refused Huntziger's request because Hitler had laid down that no concession was to be made to the defeated French before they had signed. After they had signed, there would, of course, be no need to make concessions.

Huntzinger spent three hours in intermittent telephone communication with Bordeaux attempting to clarify the *Diktat* with which he was confronted, before signing it at 6.50 p.m. – forty minutes before Keitel's ultimatum ran out. With those few strokes of his fountain pen, France was divided in two.

To relieve the German forces of the burden of garrisoning the entire country, Pétain was to remain the legal ruler of the whole country after certain border adjustments. Most of the three *départements* making up the provinces of Alsace and Lorraine were to be annexed into the Reich under their ancient titles of Elsass and Lotharingen. West of them was a *Zone Réservée*. The *départements* of Nord and Pas-de-Calais were for strategic reasons to be governed by the German military administration of Belgium. South of this lay *la Zone Interdite*, or forbidden zone.

The northern and western three-fifths of the country, including its financial centres, most of its industry, oil and mineral reserves and the strategically vital

Channel and Atlantic littoral, would be occupied by German forces for the duration of the continuing war against Britain. There, the French Government would wield authority subject to the Wehrmacht and other German organisations. In the Free Zone, comprising the south-eastern two-fifths, it was to have sovereign powers. Fifty-two *départements* were thus occupied in whole or in part, with Vichy's theoretically unfettered writ to run in thirty-four *départements* and parts of seventeen others. No mention was made of Germany occupying the overseas territories of the French Empire, for fear of them declaring for the British.

However, in keeping with France's neutrality, the accord laid down specifically that the French navy – which was still intact because it had not been involved in

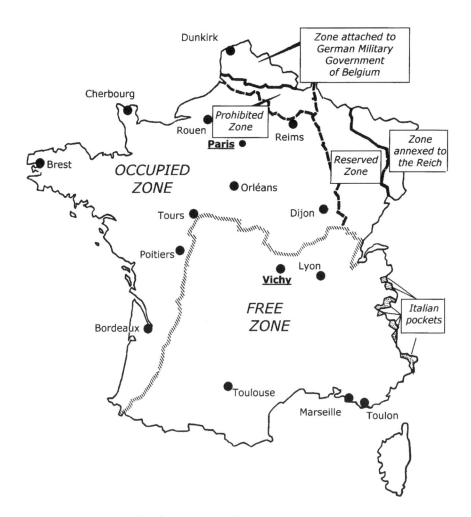

Map of France as divided by the armistice, 22 June 1940

the fighting – was not to be handed over for military use by Germany, but would be immediately demilitarised under German and Italian supervision. This had been foreseen by Adm Darlan when promising Churchill that his ships would under no circumstances be handed over to Hitler for possible use against Britain.

The same undertaking was reiterated to First Lord of the Admiralty A. V. Alexander and the First Sea Lord, Admiral of the Fleet Sir Dudley Pound, who had flown by seaplane to France on 18 June. Darlan informed them that he had signalled the fleet throughout the world on 28 May that no return to French or other German-controlled ports should be made by vessels at sea or on foreign station except if specifically ordered by himself. Similarly, all commanders of naval vessels in French ports were ordered to keep the sea cocks manned night and day, so that the ships could be scuttled at a few minutes' notice, should German or Italians troops try to take them over by force of arms.

As far as the other French armed services were concerned, the air force had virtually ceased to exist after the destruction of most of its outdated aircraft, whether in the air or on the ground. The armistice provided for army and air force units not already captured to withdraw to the Free Zone for disarming and demobilisation. However, all surrendered and captured troops were to be held as POWs. Thus, Huntzinger's signature consigned 1.6 million French soldiers to captivity in German camps until a peace treaty was signed. That, at least, was the understanding on the French side. Since no treaty was ever offered by Hitler, their captivity was to last up to five years, until they were liberated by the Allied advance in 1944–45.

Withdrawing its last diplomats in France, Britain had to face the fact that the Vichy state was now neutral, but neutral under German control. De Gaulle at that moment became 'our' Frenchman, with a nuisance value that won him permission to make a second broadcast at 10 p.m. BST that evening. No longer having to be careful not to embarrass his British hosts by upsetting Pétain's government, he said unambiguously:

> Any Frenchman who still has his weapons, has the absolute duty to continue resisting (the enemy). To lay down one's arms, to abandon a military position, to accept the surrender of any French territory to the enemy, would be crimes against the nation.[1]

His access to the BBC airwaves was still conditional. Gladwyn Jebb was on duty at the Foreign Office in the evening of 26 June when the text of the speech de Gaulle intended delivering that night arrived for vetting at 7 p.m. Making what he considered minimal alterations, he rushed with it to the Hotel Rubens, where de Gaulle was dining. Emerging a little after eight o'clock in patently bad humour, he eyed the Old Etonian diplomat up and down with a haughty, 'And who are you?'

Jebb explained his position and said that, although the late arrival of the script had left him without any superior to consult, he had made 'slight alterations'. 'Show me,' said de Gaulle. After a pregnant pause, he added, 'I find them ridiculous. Perfectly ri-dic-ulous!' Jebb explained that, if he did not accept them, he could not broadcast. 'Then,' said de Gaulle, 'I accept. It's ridiculous, but I accept.'[2]

It was a choice of that or no broadcast, but he had already decided that his political impotence meant fighting for every advantage in London. When lawyer and journalist Maurice Schumann reported to him for duty on 28 June after escaping from France by leaping aboard a Polish freighter leaving the harbour of St-Jean-de-Luz, the General placed him in charge of information services. His directive to the man who would make more than 1,000 broadcasts to France before the Liberation was, 'Remember that we are too weak to make any compromises.'[3]

De Gaulle was about to learn that Churchill's goodwill did not mean that the Foreign Office was his friend – far from it. And he certainly had no reason to think that the slight reputation he had gained in France by the appeal of 18 June was about to be undone by the very man in whom he had placed his trust. Frustrated that the British armed forces could not make any meaningful gesture on land, Churchill decided to use the Royal Navy to show the world how Britain would stop at nothing to win the war. Reasoning that *any* promise could be broken under *force majeure*, he intended to make sure that Darlan would be in no position to go back on his undertaking to keep the French fleet out of German hands.

On 24 June Sir Dudley North, the admiral commanding the North Atlantic station based in Gibraltar, paid a courtesy visit on HMS *Douglas* to the important French naval base at Mers el-Kebir in Algeria in the hope of persuading Admiral Marcel Gensoul to throw in his lot with the Royal Navy by bringing his ships over to the British side. Quite properly, Gensoul reminded North that he took his orders from Darlan and Pétain, and that he already had orders to scuttle if worse came to worst.

Also in the Mediterranean that day, the captain of the French submarine *Narval* defied orders to remain in the Tunisian port of Sousse and put to sea, destination Malta. Sighted on the surface of a heavy sea at 8 a.m. on 26 June, *Narval* was nearly sunk by HMS *Diamond*, a Royal Navy destroyer on patrol. At first taken for an Italian vessel, *Narval* was only saved by the quick reactions of an officer on *Diamond*'s bridge, who recognised a message being flashed by a signal lamp in an obsolete code. Challenged to identify his vessel by *Diamond*, the French captain signalled back: 'French submarine *Narval* making for Valletta to join the Royal Navy.' The only other French vessel not in a British port to rally to the British was another submarine, the *Rubis*, which was operating in Norwegian waters with the British North Sea Fleet. After the captain democratically let the crew of forty-four vote on the action to take, a majority of forty-two voted for Britain, the dissenters being repatriated after docking at Dundee.[4]

De Gaulle's enemies often accused him of naked ambition. Yet, on 24 or 25 June – accounts differ as to the exact date – he learned that General Noguès in Morocco had informed Weygand that 'the panic in Bordeaux' had prevented his superiors from 'objectively assessing the possibilities of resisting (the Germans) in North Africa.'[5] Noguès invited Weygand to 'reconsider the orders that he [Noguès] had been given to execute the [provisions of] the armistice agreement' that affected the army in North Africa and protested that, if they were not countermanded, he could 'not obey them without blushing'.

As de Gaulle wrote in his memoirs, had a general of Noguès' seniority raised the flag of resistance in the French overseas territories, the whole French Empire would have followed his lead.[6] He immediately cabled Noguès:

> I have taken the initiative of setting up a national committee to represent the ... resistance [to the German occupation]. The British Government has just declared officially that it would be prepared to recognise such a committee. It is of the utmost importance, general, that you accept command of this committee.[7]

Offering to serve under Noguès was hardly naked ambition. However, from Morocco there came no reply to his offer. Noguès had backed down on second thoughts and was obeying Weygand's orders, whether blushing with shame or not. In the rest of the empire, only General Catroux in Indochina and General Legentilhomme in Somalia stood firm against the armistice. Their reward was to be removed from their posts, while their many thousand subordinates, both French and colonial, meekly accepted the orders from the government of France which, driven out of its temporary refuge in Bordeaux by the arrival of German occupation forces in the south-west, decamped to temporary and very inconvenient quarters at Clermont-Ferrand in central France. There, politician Pierre Laval, who was serving as one of the two vice-presidents of the Council of Ministers or Cabinet, proposed the abolition of the Third Republic on the grounds that it was responsible for the defeat. On 30 June, the Cabinet debated his proposition, with some ministers arguing that a better way to put the country back on its feet was to give Pétain six months to govern, unfettered by parliamentary control. Laval wanted more. A very successful courtroom lawyer, he gradually wore down all resistance with his argument that only a strong France could negotiate on equal terms with Germany the peace treaty that would replace the armistice agreement and gain the release of her 1.6 million POWs. Ergo, the rotten Third Republic had to be terminated.

That could only be legally done by a National Assembly of both the Senate and the Chamber of Deputies, calling which required the assent of the president of the Republic. Laval leaped up from the conference table and drove to the nearby town of Royat, where President Lebrun was quartered. An hour later he returned with Lebrun's assent to the National Assembly. Overwhelmed by Laval's fait accompli, Pétain gave way.

There being no facilities in Clermont for holding such a meeting, Foreign Minister Paul Baudouin suggested moving the seat of government to Vichy - a prosperous and fashionable spa some 50km north-east of Clermont that had 15,000 hotel rooms, a modern telephone exchange and a direct railway link with Paris. Thus it was to Vichy that the ministers, senators and deputies made their way on the afternoon of 1 July, since when the name of the town has been synonymous with collaboration.[8] It was in Vichy also that US Ambassador William Bullitt caught up with the government, after staying in Paris because he could see no point in following the Reynaud administration on its flight from the capital. He it was who persuaded Secretary of State Cordell Hull and President Roosevelt that the armistice allowed Pétain to exercise a genuine sovereignty, that Pétain was not hostile to the Allies and that the old Marshal was 'the one factor that restrained Darlan and Laval from more active collaboration with the Nazis.'[9] Their unquestioning acceptance of Bullitt's purely personal opinions were to distort American policy towards France for many years after his return to the United States in July 1940.

On the night of 1 July, British weapons were trained upon French servicemen for the first time since Waterloo. On Churchill's own admission 'overwhelming force'[10] was used to neutralise 500 French marines and a battalion of infantry under the command of a French admiral in Portsmouth, as well as double that number in Plymouth and Falmouth. Royal Navy prize crews were put aboard forty or so French warships in Portsmouth, Plymouth, Falmouth and Cowes harbours. In Portsmouth harbour the world's largest submarine *Surcouf* was moored alongside the Royal Navy submarine HMS *Thames*, on board which the French captain and crew had been entertained. In the confusion of the midnight seizure by men they knew, three British seamen and one French sailor were killed. These measures were taken in anticipation of hostile French reaction to Churchill's plans for the following day.

At 3 p.m. on 2 July, he ordered the British Admiralty to signal Vice Admiral Sir James Somerville, commanding Force H in Gibraltar, to implement Operation *Catapult*. To stiffen his resolve, Churchill instructed the Admiralty to signal Somerville: 'You are charged with one of the most disagreeable and difficult tasks that a British admiral has ever been faced with, but we have complete confidence in you and rely on you to carry it out relentlessly.'[11] Before dawn on 3 July, Force H hove to in the mist off Mers el-Kebir, the French navy's most important base in North Africa. Ashore, demilitarisation was going ahead in compliance with the armistice agreement. Ships' boilers were cold and reservists had been demobilised. Naval aircraft were mostly disarmed and the coastal batteries' shells had been returned to stores, with breech-blocks removed and locked away.

At 6 a.m. the destroyer HMS *Foxhound* requested permission to enter the harbour. After some to-ing and fro-ing by bilingual officers from both sides, by 7.45 a.m. Gensoul was reading a signal from *Foxhound* which read:

> The Admiralty is sending Capt Holland to confer with you in the hope that his proposals will permit the gallant and glorious French navy to remain on our side. In this case, your vessels will remain under your control and you need have no care for the future. A British squadron is standing out to sea to bid you welcome.[12]

With the mist clearing, French lookouts discerned the silhouettes of eleven British destroyers, the cruiser *Hood*, the battleships *Resolution* and *Valiant* and the aircraft carrier *Ark Royal*, whose torpedo-carrying Swordfish aircraft were already in the air. From *Hood* came the flashing of an Aldis signal lamp: 'We hope that our proposals are acceptable and that you will be on our side.'[13]

The proposals from the War Cabinet in London gave Gensoul the choice between three unacceptable courses of action:

1. To sail with the British ships and fight until victory over the Germans and Italians.
2. To sail with skeleton crews to a British port, the crews to be repatriated as soon as possible.
3. If he believed himself obliged to stipulate that his vessels might not be used against the Germans and Italians because that would compromise France's neutrality, to sail under escort with skeleton crews to a French port in the Antilles such as Martinique where the ships could be demilitarised or handed over to the (then neutral) USA and the crews repatriated.

Should Gensoul reject all three courses of action, he must scuttle all the vessels under his command within six hours. Failing this, Admiral Somerville was charged 'to take all necessary measures to see that your ships do not fall into German or Italian hands.'[14]

Ordering all ships to make steam and prepare for action, Gensoul repeated the assurance given to Sir Dudley North nine days previously: in no circumstances would he allow his vessels to fall intact into the hands of the Germans or Italians. 'However,' he signalled, 'the first shot fired against us will result in the whole fleet turning against Great Britain – a result diametrically opposed to that sought by the British Admiralty.'[15]

Somerville ordered Swordfish from *Ark Royal* to mine the harbour entrance, which ruled out any chance of Gensoul complying with the ultimatum! He also signalled the Admiralty that he was ready to commence firing on the French. At 1.15 p.m. with still no shot fired by either side, Gensoul signalled the British that he was in communication with his government and was prepared to seek an honourable solution. 'Do not,' he said, 'take the irreparable step.'

At 3.15 p.m. the French vessels had steam up and gun turrets were pointing in the direction of Force H. Gensoul signified his willingness to consider disarming and sailing to the Antilles or the USA, but unescorted and with no Royal Navy personnel on board. Captain Holland relayed this apparent breakthrough to Somerville, who replied that it was unacceptable.

The French Admiralty now radioed Gensoul that *all* French warships in the Mediterranean were steaming to his rescue. With the signal intercepted and decoded in London, where the prime minister and former First Lord of the Admiralty was determined to do things his way, the result was an instruction to Somerville to end the business rapidly or find himself confronting French reinforcements. To fire on vessels of a neutral country with which Britain had been allied until shortly before, and with which she was not at war, was a breach of international law. Yet Somerville bit the bullet, signalling Gensoul, 'If none of the proposals is accepted by 17.30 BST – I repeat by 17.30 – I shall have to sink your ships.'[16]

Although the French warships now had steam up and could return fire until their limited stock of shells ran out, little manoeuvring was possible in the confines of the harbour, of which construction had never been finished. They were thus sitting ducks for the Royal Navy's bombardment which killed a total of 1,297 French sailors, with several hundred wounded. While giving first aid and shrouding the corpses, many rescue workers were killed when three flights of Swordfish from *Ark Royal* flew in at deck level with machine guns blasting everything and everyone in sight.[17]

As Gensoul had prophesied, the political result was the opposite of what Churchill may have hoped. François Mauriac summed it up: 'Mr Winston Churchill had united France against England – perhaps for many years.'[18] One ancient cruiser was sunk and the admiral's flagship put out of action for months, but after the British mines had been cleared the rest of the damaged fleet steamed at battle-readiness to Toulon, where they were nearer by far to the Germans. There, sixteen months later, on 27 November 1942, they were scuttled by their crews in compliance with Darlan's instructions after the Wehrmacht crossed the Demarcation Line and occupied the former Free Zone, following the Allied invasion of French North Africa.

Churchill had apparently no regrets then or later, considering the action strategically justified because the boarding of vessels in English ports 'showed how easily the Germans could have taken possession of any French warships lying in ports which they controlled.'[19] This spurious justification entirely overlooks his knowledge that Darlan's order to scuttle did not apply to the vessels lying in British ports, where the commanders and crews thought themselves among friends. Astute parliamentarian that he was, the British prime minister gave an account of the action at Mers el-Kebir to a stunned and silent House of Commons on 4 July, but took care to end his report with a gung-ho speech that roused all his listeners to stand up and cheer, as though they were endorsing Operation *Catapult* retroactively.

In Alexandria, a far better way of achieving the same result had been found by Admiral Andrew Cunningham, whose subtle persuasion effected the demilitarisation and immobilisation of a squadron of French naval vessels commanded by Admiral Jean-Paul Godefroy. It was Cunningham who remarked that Operation *Catapult* had been executed 'with perfect perfidiousness' and suggested that its inevitable effect on the French attitude to Britain would have made the title Operation *Boomerang* more appropriate.[20]

Marcel Gensoul retired two years later, refusing for the rest of his life to discuss the tragedy of Mers el-Kebir. After returning to Gibraltar, Captain Holland showed his disgust at the illegal action in which he had been obliged to take part by resigning his commission, to spend the rest of the war in the Home Guard. Inevitably, German and Vichy propaganda made the most of the horrific news by full photo reports in newspapers and posters everywhere asking, '*And these were your allies?*'

As far as many French people were concerned, Mers el-Kebir was the final straw that killed any sympathy for the British cause. It made the furious and grieving Admiral Darlan an implacable enemy for Britain and provided a heaven-sent opportunity for Nazi propaganda to claim that France's true enemy was perfidious Albion and not the Reich. Obliged to submit the text of his next speech for the BBC for prior approval by Downing Street, de Gaulle consented with the rider that, if asked to change a single word, he would never broadcast again.

The broadcast of 8 July was a masterpiece in which he managed, not to excuse what had happened at Mers el-Kebir, but to place it for his listeners in the context of a merciless world war, in which terrible decisions had to be taken:

> Let me say first of all that every Frenchman learned of the sinking of French vessels by our allies with pain and anger – pain and anger that come from deep within. There is no reason to hide this and, for my part, I am expressing it openly. I suggest to the English that they spare us and themselves any idea of calling this hateful tragedy a naval victory. ... And I ask my French listeners to consider this from the only point of view that is finally justified, which is victory and deliverance.
>
> By a dishonourable compact, the government that was in Bordeaux had agreed to place our ships in the hands of the enemy. There is not the slightest doubt that ... the enemy would one day have used them, whether against England or our own empire. Therefore, in plain language, it is better that they be destroyed. I prefer to know that even our beautiful, dear, powerful *Dunkerque*

has been sunk at Mers el-Kebir than to see her one day under a German flag shelling English ports or Algiers, Casablanca or Dakar.

By provoking this bombardment and then seeking to turn the reaction of the French people against our betrayed allies, the government that was in Bordeaux shows itself in its proper role of a compliant subordinate. In exploiting the event to pit the English people against the French, the enemy is in his role of conqueror. Although the event was both deplorable and detestable, let it not cause a rift between Englishman and Frenchman, but be seen for what it is by all clear-thinking men in their role as patriots.[21]

Churchill could have asked for no more; a sycophantic endorsement of the British action would have been counter-productive. Yet, behind his impassive public face, and despite the public speeches, de Gaulle admitted in private that the irregular trickle of volunteers to his banner dwindled to nothing after Mers el-Kebir – so much so that he contemplated taking his family to Canada and retiring there.

Churchill's gratitude, however, expressed itself in many ways. He ordered that everything possible should be done to make the Free French Bastille Day parade on 14 July an impressive occasion. To the Minister for Information, he wrote, 'It is important to continue General de Gaulle's broadcasts and to have our propaganda transmissions relayed by every means in Africa. I am told that the Belgians are prepared to help in the Congo.' And to the secretary of state for war:

It has become extremely important and urgent to complete the equipping of the three (Free French) battalions, the tank company and [de Gaulle's] HQ etc. It is apparent that arrangements have been made for this, but I should be grateful if you would this speed up by all means in your power.

On 5 August he told the War Cabinet that General de Gaulle and the Free French forces in Britain had the same objectives as the British Government and should be assisted in every possible way. On 18 August he instructed Hugh Dalton, Minister for Economic Warfare, to make sure de Gaulle was consulted about all future propaganda tracts to be dropped over France and the French colonies.[22]

Never before had the *entente cordiale* between Britain and France been so cordial; nor would it ever be again.

Notes

1. C. de Gaulle, *Discours et Messages*, Paris, Plon, 1970, Vol. 1, p. 5 (abbreviated by the author)
2. Lord Gladwyn, 'de Gaulle' in *The History Makers*, London, Sidgwick and Jackson, 1973, p. 364
3. ed. M. Jullian, *de Gaulle – Traits d'esprit*, Paris, Cherche-Midi, 2000, p. 101

4. C. Williams, *The Last Great Frenchman*, London, Little Brown, 1994, pp. 89–91, 117

5. C. de Gaulle, *Mémoires de Guerre: L'Appel 1940–42*, Paris, Plon, 1954, p. 91

6. Ibid., p. 91

7. C. Cogan, *Oldest Allies, Guarded friends: The United States and France since 1940*, Westport, Praeger, 1994, p. 29

8. For a fuller description of the abolition of the Third Republic and move to Vichy, see D. Boyd, *Voices from the Dark Years*, Thrupp, Sutton, 2007, pp. 47–63

9. Williams, *The Last Great Frenchman*, pp. 160–61

10. W.S. Churchill, *The Second World War Vol 2: Their Finest Hour*, London, Penguin Classics, 2005, p. 207

11. Ibid., p. 209

12. Boyd, *Voices from the Dark Years*, pp. 51–6

13. Ibid.

14. P. Masson in *1940 La Défaite*, Paris, Tallandier, 1978, pp. 461–70

15. Ibid., pp. 461–70

16. Boyd, *Voices from the Dark Years*, pp. 51–6

17. A full account of the engagement may be found in Boyd, *Dark Years*, pp. 51–6, 59, 89, 95, 178

18. Article in *Le Figaro*, 15 July 1940

19. Churchill, *Their Finest Hour*, p. 207

20. A. Vulliez in *1940 La Défaite*, p. 458

21. F. Kersaudy, *de Gaulle et Churchill*, Paris, Perrin Tempus, 2003, pp. 86–7 (abbreviated by the author)

22. Ibid., p. 89

5

GAINING STATUS

From the moment when de Gaulle's substantive rank of colonel was taken away by the court martial's verdict and sentence, his authority over other French officers and men in Britain depended entirely on them choosing to nail his colours to their masthead and thus share with him the status of traitors to their own government. Nor was he the champion of all French émigrés who refused to recognise Pétain's armistice. Statesman Jean Monnet was only one who considered that he was on an ego-trip and somewhat paranoid – as did diplomat Roland de Margerie, who had had the opportunity of observing de Gaulle closely on the first mission to London seeking renewed British help after Dunkirk.

However, the influential Breton businessman René Pleven, who had been European director of the Automatic Telephone Company before the war, was sick of politicians pussyfooting around and supported de Gaulle's up-and-at-'em stance. Another supporter from day one was Alfred Bellenger, the London director of the society jewellers Cartier, who gave de Gaulle the exclusive use of his Bentley, so that he could travel in appropriate style and not have to arrive at important functions in a taxi. Other great names of the future political creed that would be called *Gaullisme* who made their way to London included journalist Maurice Schumann, barrister René Cassin and Polish-born Gaston Palewski, who had been Reynaud's astute *chef de cabinet* until sacked in a political quid pro quo engineered by de Gaulle's bête noire the Countess of Portes during the phoney war.[1]

Outwardly de Gaulle was totally confident in continuing to title himself 'general', leaving it to his listeners to decide whether this meant brigadier general, major general, lieutenant general or full general in English military terminology. That could really only be determined by the ranks of those serving under him. It was therefore a stroke of luck that Vice Admiral Emile Muselier chose to rally to him in London. Appointed military commandant of the major city and busy commercial port of Marseille in 1938, Muselier had been promoted to vice admiral by Darlan in October 1939 and then sacked six weeks later after allegations that he had been taking bribes. Enforced retirement at the age of 57 did nothing to lessen Muselier's self-confidence. He was immediately offered high positions in commerce and entrusted with the priority destruction of war materiel to stop it falling into the hands of the Germans.

Whether from political conviction or to thumb his nose at Darlan for believing the accusations, nine days after the Germans entered Paris Admiral Muselier sailed out of Marseille harbour in a commandeered British coaler, the *Cydonia*, commanding a small army of volunteers he had rounded up to continue the fight. Persuading the captain to sail through minefields that he had himself ordered to be laid, and of which he had been careful to bring the charts, Muselier arrived safely in Gibraltar and finally reached Britain by seaplane on 30 June, leaving his volunteers following in the trawler *Président Houduce* and two other merchant vessels.

This admiral with a shady past burst like a Gallic fireball into the staid offices of the Free French. Every Englishman's idea of an extravert, gesticulating, charming Mediterranean Frenchman in his admiral's uniform, he was the antithesis of the aloof, reserved general who, on the following day, appointed him officer commanding Les Forces Navales Françaises Libres – the Free French naval forces, wherever they might be – and also, provisionally, of Les Forces Aériennes Françaises Libres, by which was meant any Free French air force units that might be created.

The appointment was to give de Gaulle several headaches later. Most people, on first meeting him, were somewhat in awe of his physical stature and grand manners. To Muselier, being unimpressed by fine uniforms and exalted rank, we owe the most graphic description of the man he accepted as his commander-in-chief in that summer of 1940. The admiral's first impression was physical height and ungainliness, accentuated by the comparatively small head on such a large body, with hips as broad as a woman's:

> His grey eyes did not look squarely into one's own, but always turned away when answering a direct question. The chin ... did not suggest a strong will. The nose was powerful, almost Bourbon. The ears, badly formed, stuck out widely.[2]

De Gaulle had no illusions about his physical appearance. He once said, 'We giants can never be completely at ease. Armchairs are always too small for us. Tables are too low. Beds are too short, and the people we are talking to, are too far away.'[3]

Never one to let grass grow under his feet, on the day of his appointment Muselier launched his own appeal to naval and air force personnel and established an alternative, albeit skeletal, French admiralty with his deputy, Captain Georges

Thierry d'Argenlieu – a lean, chain-smoking and passionately patriotic reservist who had been a barefoot Carmelite monk between the wars and would eventually return to the cloister after achieving admiral's rank himself. Two days later, Muselier invented for 'his' navy a new national ensign to distinguish its vessels from Vichy ships. The cross of Lorraine, which he chose in honour of his Lorrain father, thus became the emblem of all Gaullist forces, causing Churchill to grumble ungenerously when the relationship with de Gaulle had deteriorated that the greatest cross he had to bear during the war was the Cross of Lorraine. Like de Gaulle, Muselier was to be condemned to death – in his case by a naval court martial sitting at Toulon on 23 October 1940. All his personal property was also confiscated and on 2 February 1941 he was deprived of his French nationality by Vichy.

A less flamboyant early supporter was an ex-classmate of de Gaulle at St Cyr military academy. Lieutenant Colonel Raoul-Charles Magrin-Vernerey commanded the French force at Narvik and brought with him to London from that operation Foreign Legion Captain Marie-Pierre Koenig, plus 500 men of the Legion's 13th Demi-Brigade. 13 DBLE, as it was known, became legendary for its military exploits under the Free French flag during the war.

When Magrin-Vernerey and his men escaped from Brest shortly before the port was closed by the arrival of the German spearheads, 22-year-old British legionnaire John Yeowell was one of those who boarded the Southern Railway's Twickenham ferry for the crossing. Half a century later, he recalled disembarking at Plymouth to the music of a Royal Marine band on the quayside very appropriately playing *Marche Lorraine* to welcome them.[4]

However, most of Magrin-Vernerey's legionnaires who had been at Narvik chose to remain in France and make their way back with their officers to the Legion bases in North Africa. Thus, the Foreign Legion fragmented into a small minority fighting for de Gaulle and the majority content to sit out the war in their traditional bases south of the Mediterranean, in Syria/Lebanon and in Indochina before and during its occupation by the Japanese. Before the war was over, there would be several occasions in Syria and North Africa when the sacred creed that legionnaires never fired on legionnaires was broken, Magrin-Vernerey being one of the officers who refused to participate in such actions.

Although French military personnel in Britain were accommodated in a number of makeshift camps, it was to Trentham Park near Stoke-on-Trent that he brought 13 DBLE. Changing his rather too noticeable name to the *nom de guerre* Monclar in the hope of avoiding reprisals on his family in France, he found himself commanding the only organised formation there. At the time, the camp held 2,000-plus men in various uniforms who had chosen not to return home with the majority of French evacuees from Dunkirk. Sleeping in the open air on the first night and in tents thereafter, they were reduced to killing deer roaming in the park for food. Making up the shortage of rations by 'liberating' livestock and vegetables from their neighbours, as soldiers always do, did nothing to endear them to a local population that without any justification despised them for wearing the uniform of a country which had 'let Britain down' by surrendering to Hitler.

Many of the Spanish legionnaires had arrived in France as communist political refugees after Franco's victory in the Civil War and enlisted in the Legion to avoid being locked up in French internment camps. Because they still took orders from their Party commissars, sometimes in conflict with their officers, they had a poor record for discipline. So it was not too much of a surprise when, morale being at an all-time low, the Spaniards mutinied and were driven under escort to Stafford prison after a harangue from Monclar along the lines of: 'This is not the International Brigade, but 13 DBLE. And you are not worthy to call yourselves legionnaires.'[5] However, some of their officers regarded Legion discipline as an internal affair, and were enraged by this incarceration in British custody among common criminals.

It is a basic tenet of military life that officers must keep their men busy because idle hands swiftly become undisciplined, but what could they do with no weapons to drill with, no tasks allotted them and in many cases no kit or even proper uniforms? As discipline and morale plunged, most English-speaking legionnaires like John Yeowell simply walked out of the camp and joined the British armed forces – some of them to find when they next set foot in France many years later that they were still officially listed as deserters, liable to instant arrest.

A visit to Trentham Park by de Gaulle at the end of the month and his promotion of Monclar to full colonel did nothing to improve the unrest. A Montgomery or a Patton would have taken the opportunity to win over the men on that day by a rousing pep talk and personal contact, handing out cigarettes and asking, 'Where do you come from, soldier?' Unfortunately, de Gaulle lacked the popular touch and did not even deliver a speech. He seemed not to understand the loyalty that would accrue to him by reassuring them all that they had not made a ghastly mistake. Instead of that paternal concern for their welfare which legionnaires especially were accustomed to receiving from their officers, all the men at Trentham Park got was a brief glimpse of an ungainly man in general's uniform stalking past a guard of honour without speaking to anyone and climbing back into the Bentley.

The following day, de Gaulle asked permission of the local military authorities to visit camps at Aintree and Haydock near Liverpool, where several thousand French sailors had been assembled. Permission was refused. Significantly, on 1 July 1940, that day so full of evil omen, 636 out of 1,619 officers and men at Trentham Park exercised their right to repatriation by boarding trains for Bristol, where the SS *Meknès* was to transport them to French North Africa. The bitter division between those leaving and those staying resulted in the Legion guard of honour refusing to present arms for those departing, while the thirty-one officers who were going with them shook Monclar's hand, muttering embarrassed excuses about wives and families whom they would otherwise not see for the duration of the war. At Bristol, 300 of the Spanish mutineers lay down on the dockside, refusing to go aboard the *Meknès* in the fear that on arrival in French Morocco they might forcibly be driven across the border into Spanish territory, to end up before a firing squad.[6] Many stayed in Britain, eventually serving with the Pioneer Corps.

De Gaulle's view of their problems and his obligations to resolve them was somewhat Olympian because his sights were literally set on higher things. On 11 July he wrote to Jacques de Sieyès, an old classmate at St Cyr who now headed the US offices of the perfume company Patou, appointing him unofficial ambassador-cum-press officer in Washington and head of an ad hoc purchasing organisation to procure supplies of all kinds from the United States. Knowing de Sieyès' connections, he also asked him to spare no efforts in touching the vein of sympathy for France that existed in certain quarters of the capital. Unfortunately, several other Frenchmen in the US also thought they represented the Gaullist interests, which led to confusion, backbiting and the internecine squabbling that seems to characterise émigré organisations.

Apart from that one visit to Trentham Park, the General showed little interest in the men there until he needed them in August for a desperate bid to validate his claim of representing a proud and independent France. However, with the British people he was becoming more popular, thanks partly to an initiative by Churchill's personal assistant Major Desmond Morton in hiring PR consultant Richmond Temple to build a positive image both in Britain and abroad of the country's last remaining – and largely unknown – ally.

'Churchill wants to sell me like a bar of soap' was its subject's disparaging remark.[7] Yet, he was accosted everywhere by Britons who wanted to shake his hand and congratulate him during his public appearances in London, which included taking the salute at a brave little march-past by 200 men of various French services on 14 July – the anniversary of the storming of the Bastille in 1789 – and afterwards laying a wreath at the statue of First World War Allied commander-in-chief Marshal Ferdinand Foch near Victoria Station. Individuals also showed their sympathy after the newspapers carried the news that he had been sentenced to death with the confiscation of all his property by sending gifts of money and jewellery to eke out the slender finances of his fledgling movement.

It was a great relief to move out of the cramped, borrowed flat in Seymour Place and the offices in St Stephen's House in favour of more spacious accommodation at No. 4, Carlton Gardens. Set in a quiet cul-de-sac in London's ultra-chic St James's, the house had been the home of Foreign Secretary and Prime Minister Lord Palmerston, and was thus a fitting seat for a government-in-exile, as de Gaulle already considered his movement to be. As to where the money came from, it seems that Reynaud's cash in hand was soon spent and current outlay financed from what amounted to a bank robbery committed by British agents during the retreat in June 1940 when they 'discovered' a cache of French francs worth some £13 million in the courtyard of a bank, presumably about to be burned before the Germans arrived. Transported to Britain, the money was used to finance the Free French movement.[8] Such was the chaos of the French retreat before the German invasion that the story is not as far-fetched as it sounds. In June, officials of the Finance Ministry, panicking near Saumur with the Germans approaching, actually paid a street-cleaner to burn banknotes to the value of 25 million francs.[9]

Although living with his family in Kent and commuting daily to work in London, de Gaulle frequently spent the night at Carlton Gardens after being guest of honour at dinners hosted by Spears. The stodgy boarding-school food then generally served in gentlemen's clubs troubled him less than most Frenchmen; far from being a gastronome, he had only one recorded predilection – for bouillabaisse – other than which he ate canned vegetables, sausages or whatever was available with equal lack of interest. Another Gallic trait entirely lacking in him was unpunctuality: he liked to live by the clock, rising, taking his meals and going to bed at regular hours. On occasion he would forbid dinner guests being served the first course if they arrived late at table: they had to wait until the main course was served.

The heavily masculine ambiance of Gen Spears' entertaining was occasionally lightened by the presence of his wife, who devoted most of her time to running a hospital for French sick and wounded in Aldershot. Another society lady 'doing her bit' for France was Lady Peel, who turned her London home into a hostel for the Free French, while a group of lesser ladies opened and ran Le Petit Club Français in St James's Place. Charitable works by upper-class ladies susceptible to Gallic charm was one thing, but Spears was after tougher prey. His Francophobe dinner guests came from two important sectors that were not going to be won over by stories planted in the newspapers.

The Foreign Office diplomats and senior civil servants argued that the existence of de Gaulle's self-appointed alternative French administration in London achieved nothing positive and simply complicated relations with France's legal government in Vichy, while many senior soldiers wanted nothing more to do with the French armed services after the 'poor showing' they had put up in May and June. Considering French servicemen in Britain to be 'useless mouths', British liaison officers frequently advised undecided French military personnel that signing up with de Gaulle might prove a fatal error for themselves and their families and that they would do better to pack up and go home. Partly as a result of this, some 1,100 of the French naval officers and men prevented from reboarding their ships at British ports after Operation *Catapult* opted for repatriation by the *Meknès* on 24 July. When she was sunk in the Channel by a German E-boat, more than

400 men drowned. Coming so soon after Mers el-Kebir, many French people felt that it was the fault of the British for putting them in this unfortunate position.

The following day a key figure arrived in London. Infantry Captain Viscount Philippe-Marie de Hauteclocque chose the *nom de guerre* Leclerc and would become de Gaulle's heroic liberator of Paris in 1944. Wounded and taken prisoner in the defeat, Leclerc had escaped and made his way through Spain to London. His detractors in the army hierarchy considered him of mediocre intellect and his uncommunicative, preoccupied nature did little to dispel these calumnies. However de Gaulle cared little about such things and promoted him to colonel because his knowledge and experience of the colonies made him the ideal man for a plan he was hatching.

A gentleman's handshake was one thing, and the understanding between himself and Prime Minister Churchill was both warm and mutually respectful. There was no reason at the time to think that circumstances might compel a British prime minister to reject his first ally, but de Gaulle recognised the political importance of getting their relationship expressed on an official footing, because their personal relationship could one day be worth nothing, should Churchill be killed in an air raid or forced to resign. Therefore, his legal adviser Professor Cassin fought tooth and nail with the Foreign Office officials with whom he had to deal. General Spears commented that the negotiations regarding the text of the agreement eventually signed between the British Government and General de Gaulle were conducted with such exasperating tenacity by Professor Cassin that even the best disposed members of the Foreign Office ran out of patience with him. But Cassin was right to press for every advantage at this moment; there would never be another time more favourable to de Gaulle's formal recognition by Britain, and every point he could wring out of the Foreign Office was crucial.

Apart from any other consideration, de Gaulle's situation and that of the Free French was without precedent – a situation that always sends shivers up a diplomat's spine. He was behaving, and demanding to be recognised, as a head of state, but the legitimate head of state of neutral France was Marshal Pétain, with whose government in Vichy the Foreign Office was dancing a delicate diplomatic gavotte that infuriated de Gaulle. As far as he was concerned, Pétain was a traitor and one did not deal with traitors. The Foreign Office disagreed. Like the US State Department, it saw the continuance of negotiations with Vichy as necessary to keep Pétain and Darlan from handing over the French fleet to Hitler and encouraging them not to tie any tighter the knots that now bound France to her conquerors. Formal recognition of de Gaulle was out of the question because he was not a head of state and conferring any official status on his strategically insignificant forces might incite the openly collaborationist members of Pétain's government to force the Marshal's hand into declaring war on the German side. The US diplomats in post also had an undefined intelligence role, which seems to have achieved little apart from identifying the personalities and factions vying for power under Pétain.

De Gaulle's negotiations to formalise his relationship with the British Government broke down six times. Each time, a different protocol was drawn up, only to be rejected like its predecessors. Whatever the Foreign Office point of view, Churchill was determined to set the relationship with de Gaulle and the Free French on a formal footing, so the following exchange of letters in French took place – not on Foreign Office letterhead but datelined from No. 10. As Churchill once remarked, he was at this stage – with the Battle of Britain raging and preparations for a German invasion occupying many hours of the day – like a man on his deathbed who reflects that he has spent much time worrying about things that never happened. That he took the time to set out the understanding with de Gaulle at this juncture indicates how important he considered it, whatever the Foreign Office might argue to the contrary:

> 10, Downing Street,
> Whitehall,
> 7 August 1940
>
> My dear General,
>   In your capacity, recognised by His Majesty's Government of the United Kingdom, as the leader of all free Frenchmen, wherever they may be, you have kindly informed me of your ideas regarding the organisation, the employment and conditions of service of the force, currently being set up under your command, of French volunteers who rally to you to defend the Allied cause.
>   I am now sending you a memorandum which, if you accept it, will constitute an agreement between us relative to the organisation, use and conditions of service of your forces.
>   I take this opportunity to declare that His Majesty's government is resolved, after the victory of Allied arms, to guarantee complete restoration of the independence and greatness of France.
>   Yours sincerely,
>   Winston Churchill

The attached memorandum read as follows:

Agreement between His Majesty's government and General de Gaulle
I
1. General de Gaulle is setting up a French force consisting of volunteers. This force, which includes naval, land and air force units and technical and scientific elements, will be organised and employed against the common enemies.

2. This force will never have to bear arms against France.

II

1. This force will so far as possible keep the character of a French force, as to personnel and particularly discipline, language, promotion and postings.

2. As required by the state of its equipment, this force will have priority in claiming and using materiel (particularly weapons, aircraft, vehicles, munitions, machines and provisions) already brought by any French forces, or which will be brought by such forces, into territories under the authority of His Majesty's Government of Great Britain or where the British High Command has authority. In the case where the command of a French force shall have been delegated by General de Gaulle in agreement with the British High Command, no transfer, exchange or reattribution of the equipment, possessions or materiel of this force will be ordered by General de Gaulle without prior consultation and agreement with the British High Command.

3. His Majesty's government will supply to the French force – as soon as possible – the shortfall in materiel necessary to bring the equipment of its units up to the level of British units of the same type.

4. The ships of the French navy shall be allocated as follows:
   a) the French force will arm and put into commission all the ships for which it can furnish crews;
   b) the allocation of the ships armed and put into commission by the French force under Clause a) will be subject to an agreement between General de Gaulle and the British Admiralty, to be reviewed from time to time;
   c) the ships which shall not be allocated to the French force under Clause b) shall be made available for arming and commissioning as ordered by the British Admiralty;
   d) among the other ships mentioned under Clause c), some may be commissioned directly by the British Admiralty, while others may be commissioned by other Allied navies;
   e) the crews of ships serving under British control shall include, if possible, a proportion of French officers and ratings;
   f) all the ships of the French fleet remain French property.

5. Possible use of French merchant ships and their crews in connection with military operations of General de Gaulle's force shall be subject to agreement between the general and the interested British ministries. Regular liaison will be set up between the Shipping Ministry and General de Gaulle regarding the use of remaining merchant ships and crews.

6. General de Gaulle, as supreme commander of the French force, hereby declares that he accepts the general directives of the British Command. If need be, he will delegate the direct command of one or another part

of his force with the agreement of the British High Command to one or more British officers of appropriate rank without this affecting [Clause 2] of Article I.

III

The status of French volunteers shall be established as follows:

1. The volunteers shall enlist for the duration of the war, to fight the common enemies.

2. They shall be paid on a basis to be determined separately between General de Gaulle and the interested Ministries. The period for which the rates of pay are to apply shall be fixed by agreement between General de Gaulle and His Majesty's Government.

3. The volunteers and their dependents shall enjoy pensions and other benefits in the event of injury or death of the volunteers calculated on a basis to be agreed between General de Gaulle and the interested Ministries.

4. General de Gaulle will have the right to set up a civilian administration as necessary to organise his force. The numbers and salaries of members of this organisation shall be fixed in agreement with the British Treasury.

5. The general also has the right to recruit scientific and technical staff for military purposes. The numbers, methods of payment and employment of this staff shall be fixed in consultation with the interested Ministries of His Majesty's Government.

6. His Majesty's Government of the United Kingdom shall make every effort on the conclusion of peace to assist the French volunteers in regaining all the rights, including nationality, of which they may have been deprived as a result of joining the fight against the common enemy. His Majesty's Government is prepared to make special arrangements for these volunteers to acquire British nationality and shall take all necessary measures for this purpose.

IV

1. All expenses incurred in setting up and maintaining the French force in accordance with this Agreement shall provisionally be charged to the interested Ministries of His Majesty's Government of the United Kingdom, which shall have the right to institute controls and checks as necessary.

2. The amounts disbursed in this respect shall be considered as advances and accounted for separately. All questions of the final settlement of these advances and of any amounts credited in compensation by mutual agreement shall be the subject of a later agreement.

V

This Agreement takes effect as from 1 July 1940.

[signed]   General de Gaulle

[signed]   The Prime Minister of His Majesty's Government of the United
Kingdom

To this, de Gaulle replied as follows:

Carlton Gardens, No 4,
S.W. 1
7 August 1940

Dear Prime Minister,

   You have kindly sent me a memorandum relative to the organisation, the
employment and the conditions of service of the force of French volunteers
currently being set up under my command.

   In my capacity, recognised by His Majesty's Government of the United
Kingdom as leader of all the Free French who rally to me to defend the
Allied cause, wherever they may be, I have just informed you that I accept this
memorandum. It will be considered as constituting an agreement between us
relative to these questions.

   I am happy that the British Government has taken the opportunity to affirm
that it is resolved to guarantee the complete restoration of the independence
and greatness of France.

   For my part, I confirm to you that the French force being set up is intended
for joint operations against the common enemies (Germany, Italy or any other
hostile foreign power) including the defence of French territories and of British
territories, their lines of communication and territories under British mandate.
Yours very respectfully,
   General de Gaulle[10]

It is interesting that Churchill's letter has 'free Frenchmen,' played back to him
by de Gaulle as 'Free French', which would become the title of his force. The all-
important thing for him was that, in the exchange of letters which took place at
Chequers, Churchill had recognised him on behalf of the British Government as
the leader of all French servicemen outside France who wished to continue the
fight – and not just those in Britain. In the long term, de Gaulle's greatest gain
from this exchange was the express undertaking 'after the victory of Allied arms,
to guarantee complete restoration of the independence and greatness of France'.
It was a promise on which he was determined to collect.

Notes

1. Further details in D. Boyd, *Voices from the Dark Years*, Thrupp, Sutton, 2007, p. 5
2. E. Muselier, *de Gaulle contre le Gaullisme*, Paris, Editions du Chêne, 1946, p. 13
3. ed. M. Jullian, *de Gaulle – Traits d'esprit*, Paris, Cherche-Midi, 2000, p. 14
4. Personal communication to the author
5. Personal communication to the author
6. D. Boyd, *The French Foreign Legion*, Thrupp, Sutton, 2006, pp. 256–59
7. J. Lacouture, *de Gaulle*, Paris, Seuil, 1984, Vol. 1, p. 416
8. C. Williams, *The Last Great Frenchman*, London, Little Brown, 1994, p. 125
9. Boyd, *Dark Years*, op. cit., p. 16
10. The originals of these documents are in the archives of the Ministère des Affaires Etrangères in Paris under the reference *Guerre 1939–1945/Londres-Alger/35 (fol. 123–126)*

6

OPERATION MENACE

At the peak in June 1940 there had been some 30,000 French servicemen in Britain. Nearly 200 ships had brought 19,000 soldiers and sailors plus 2,500 civilians from France. Another 2,500 merchant seamen had arrived in the crews of 136 merchant vessels of all sizes and several hundred fishermen from northern France had sailed their own boats, mostly crammed to the gunwales with passengers, across the Channel.

Of all these, a small number of trained fighter pilots with French and other nationalities who had been fighting in France were immediately enlisted in the RAF, critically short of pilots for the Battle of Britain, which began on 10 July with Luftwaffe attacks on shipping in the Channel and bombing raids on the mainland at night. The Royal Navy managed to sign on 700 French sailors, but even that low level of recruitment is surprising after Mers el-Kebir. It also has to be admitted that the British civilian and military authorities showed little keenness, at a time when all priority was being given to preparations for a German invasion, to take on the additional burden of accommodating, feeding and equipping thousands of Frenchmen who had already rebelled against their own government and might turn their coats again. So, most went back to France.

By mid-August, de Gaulle's army, navy and air force was down to a hard core of less than 3,000 officers and men, of which one-third was composed of Monclar's foreign legionnaires who had been at Narvik. With the Germans now controlling the French coastline from Belgium to Spain, the only practicable route for further recruits to his cause lay across the Pyrenees and through Spain to Gibraltar or Portugal – a long journey so fraught with risks as to deter all but the most determined or desperate.

To gain further support and justify internationally his title as leader of 'all free Frenchmen, wherever they may be', de Gaulle had to prove his mettle by undertaking some positive military action against the enemy – and winning. Attacking mainland France was out of the question, although a first blow for Fighting France had been struck by French aircrew in RAF bombers taking part in a raid on the Ruhr on 21 June.[1] However, in the first broadcast on 18 June de Gaulle had mentioned two strategic keys to reversing the defeat. One lay in what he had called 'the unlimited industrial resources of the United States'. Churchill, being the son of an American mother, was already working to build his 'special relationship' with President Franklin D. Roosevelt that would make those resources increasingly available. There was little de Gaulle could do to help in that direction, although he had as yet no concrete reason to suspect the venomous hostility to which he would later be subjected by the incumbent in the White House. The other key highlighted on 18 June was the French Empire in Africa and Asia. 'France ... has a vast empire behind her,' he had said.[2] It was to these territories that he now turned his attention.

The attitude of European colonial administrators at the time is best described as patriarchal in the 'white dominions' and far more authoritarian in Africa and Asia. The vast majority of subjects of the British king-emperor George VI lived in India, but the Viceroy Lord Linlithgow did not consult *any* of the 390 million Indians over whom he ruled when echoing on their behalf the declaration of war from London on 3 September 1939. So secure did the British feel in their possession of the Raj that the commander-in-chief of the Indian Army did not even bother to cut short his fishing holiday in Kashmir on hearing the news. In the major British possession of the western hemisphere, John Buchan, then Governor General of Canada, was awoken by his secretary on the morning of 3 September 1939 with the news of Prime Minister Neville Chamberlain's broadcast from London at midday BST, in which he announced the expiration of the ultimatum and ended 'this country is now at war with Germany'. Buchan thereupon instructed his secretary to declare war on Germany in the name of the Dominion of Canada. When asked whether the declaration should not await the approval of the Canadian Parliament in Ottawa, he replied, 'It's nothing to do with the Parliament. I am the Governor General.'[3]

Had Britain been defeated in 1940, it is extremely unlikely that her 'white' dominions such as Canada, Australia and New Zealand would have considered themselves bound by any armistice conditions imposed by the Germans, but India would almost certainly have taken the opportunity of seizing the freedom from British rule that had been demanded with increasing vigour for several decades by Mahatma Ghandi and other leading Indian politicians, both Muslim and Hindu. As it was, the outbreak of the European war and Britain's defeat in continental Europe prompted Pandit Nehru's dominant Congress party to vote two words of advice to their rulers: 'Quit India!' Support from all shades of political opinion for the campaign so rapidly gathered strength that Winston Churchill

sent Sir Stafford Cripps to the sub-continent promising as a sop 'full independence within or outside the Commonwealth' after the war in return for loyal support and limitless supplies of cannon fodder for the duration of hostilities.[4]

The French Empire, however, had no 'white' countries in it. Quebec, although
an obstinately French-speaking province, had been part of the British Dominion
of Canada since 1763. Even in French North Africa, the 1 million European settlers were vastly outnumbered by the predominantly Arabic-speaking inhabitants
of the Maghreb – Tunisia, Algeria and Morocco. Elsewhere, France's empire was
peopled by Asians and Africans with some native puppet aristocracy and a thin
stratum of Europeans occupying posts of responsibility.

From his childhood steeped in the history of France, de Gaulle was well aware
of the danger of inciting the native inhabitants of the colonies to rebel against
their Vichy administrators. He foresaw exactly the problems that would be caused
when American OSS officers gave modern weapons and military training later
in the war to Ho Chi Minh's Viet Minh guerrillas resisting the Japanese occupation of Vietnam. This proved a key factor in their ability to launch the war of
independence that began after the return to French sovereignty in 1946. In his
broadcast of 30 July 1940, de Gaulle prophesied, 'One of the first consequences of
these abominable armistices [*sic*] will be the alienation and probably the revolt of
the native peoples of the Empire.'

When considering the map of the world on the wall of his office in Carlton
Gardens, he saw a large proportion of it coloured pink to denote the 'family of
nations' composing the British Empire and Commonwealth, with whom he was
now allied as the recognised head of the Free French. France's empire had virtually all been acquired after Napoleon's final defeat, marking the end of his obsession with building an empire that stretched from the Urals to the Atlantic. Her
European expansion blocked from then on, by 1940 France had extended her
dominion over 64 million people of many subject races, spread over a total area of
nearly 12 million square kilometres.

French North Africa comprised Algeria, which was technically a part of France,
and the two protectorates of Tunisia and Morocco. French West Africa was home
to more than 14 million indigenous inhabitants and a mere 17,631 European
administrators and *colons* in Cameroun, French Congo, Dahomey, French Guinea,
the Ivory Coast, Niger, Mauritania, Senegal, French Sudan and the mandated territories of Togo and Cameroun. French Equatorial Africa was made up of Gabon,
French Congo, Oubangui-Chari and Chad – a total of 3 million natives and
4,687 Europeans. On the other side of Africa lay Djibouti in French Somaliland
and the islands of Madagascar and Reunion. In the Middle East, Lebanon and
Syria were both French protectorates at the time.

France's other major possessions lay in Indochina, where Cambodia and
Vietnam, with its strategically important rubber-producing areas, together

covered 740,000 square kilometres, with a population of more than 21 million, including 41,600 Europeans. In the western hemisphere were the French Antilles and French Guiana, plus two islands off the coast of Canada, St-Pierre and Miquelon. There were also French concessions in China and India and a scatter of smaller possessions in the vastness of the Indian and Pacific oceans.

Looking at the map on the wall in Carlton Gardens, it was glaringly obvious to de Gaulle that logistically the easiest place to strike a blow against Vichy was in Morocco. Easy to access by sea from Britain, its main cities lying largely on, or near to, the Atlantic coast, it was also the most difficult of the Maghreb countries to reinforce from France, which is why the joint chiefs of staff would choose to prepare the invasion of German-occupied Europe by landings in Morocco in 1942. However, because parts of the country had never been completely subdued even by decades of punitive colonial warfare and very few of the native inhabitants wanted to prolong French rule a day longer than necessary, it was, like neighbouring Algeria and Tunisia, still heavily policed by the Foreign Legion, regular army units and locally raised regiments loyal to Vichy, despite these forces having been drained of much manpower by France's requirements for the European war.

In any event, persuasion there had already failed. In his broadcast from Britain on 22 June, de Gaulle had shown his hand by appealing obliquely, 'In the [French North] Africa of Clauzel, of Bugeaud, of Lyautey, of Noguès, all men of honour have the strict duty to refuse to execute enemy orders.' By classing Resident General Noguès of Morocco with three of France's heroic colonial generals, he had hoped to flatter him, but the flattery fell on deaf ears, not least because Noguès was a substantive lieutenant general and had no intention of being told what to do by an acting brigadier. Not only did he stay loyal to Vichy, but curtly told the British diplomatic mission, sent to persuade him to release the senior military and political figures arrested on his orders when they arrived at Casablanca after fleeing Bordeaux aboard the *Massilia*, to go home empty-handed on the grounds that what he did, or did not do, in Morocco was none of London's business.

Churchill's War Cabinet then considered Operation *Susan* – the landing of a joint British and Gaullist expeditionary force in Morocco to release them by force and claim the country for Britain. Happily, the chiefs of staff lost no time in aborting this fantasy, on the simple grounds that it would be madness to send out of the country on such a lunatic scheme *any* troops that might be needed to defend Britain against German invasion.

De Gaulle was therefore obliged to turn his eye southwards. Since the colonies in French Indochina were too far distant and anyway threatened by Japan's inevitable entry into the war and her urgent need of the rubber produced there, the solution had to lie in subverting the French administrators of the west coast and equatorial African colonies, who had ignored overtures from London and stayed loyal to Pétain because their salaries were paid from Vichy, which also controlled their pension funds. There were, however, relatively few military units stationed in them, which made them a softer target than the Maghreb. Their strategic value to the anti-German war effort was, he saw, considerable. The territories of French Equatorial Africa stretched all the way from the Atlantic coast to the borders of the Anglo-Egyptian Sudan. If he could capture or seduce this group of colonies away from Vichy, Allied aircraft would have a safe corridor right across Africa.

Ironically, although the essence of his programme was to win over the few civilian and military Europeans who ran these colonies, it was to the black governor of Chad that de Gaulle owed his first success. Born in French Guiana, Félix Eboué was a governor with a mind of his own, interested in the people he governed, their culture and languages. On hearing the call of 18 June, he had jointly with Colonel Marchand, who commanded all French troops in Chad, despatched to London a cable of support for de Gaulle's nascent movement. Chad was a landlocked colony lying more than 800km from the Atlantic coast at its nearest point. Although more than twice the size of France, it numbered only 1,053,006 inhabitants ruled by 378 Europeans under Governor Eboué, but its strategic importance lay in its position in the plumb centre of the northern half of Africa, sharing a common border with the Anglo-Egyptian Sudan. De Gaulle therefore despatched Pleven, Boislambert and Leclerc to West Africa with the aim of fostering dissent in three other French possessions lying between Chad and the Atlantic coast. With them went the enterprising Colonel Edgard de Larminat, who had attempted a Gaullist coup in French-occupied Syria at the time of the armistice, been arrested and then spirited out of the country and into British-occupied Palestine by a commando of foreign legionnaires from 6 Régiment Etranger d'Infanterie.[5]

With a force of some twenty men, Leclerc and de Larminat took the port of Douala and the whole of Cameroun came with it. De Larminat then crossed the Congo River to Brazzaville, ousted the vacillating Vichy administrators and declared the French Congo for de Gaulle. With the official proclamation of secession from Vichy made by Chad and Cameroun on 26 August, followed by French Congo two days later, de Gaulle had secured a total of 2 million square kilometres of Africa – more than four times the size of France. At very small cost in lives and material, he had a safe air corridor for Allied aircraft from the Atlantic coast of Africa to Sudan and Egypt.

As a slight smokescreen for Vichy's benefit, one thousand French-officered colonial infantry from the Ivory Coast were despatched from a camp in Britain where they had languished since the fall of France. Anticipating repatriation, they were landed instead in the British Gold Coast colony – now Ghana – where they provided a much needed boost to de Gaulle's skeleton forces.

Around the world, other French possessions followed Eboué's lead. On 26 June, New Caledonia declared for de Gaulle, followed by the New Hebrides

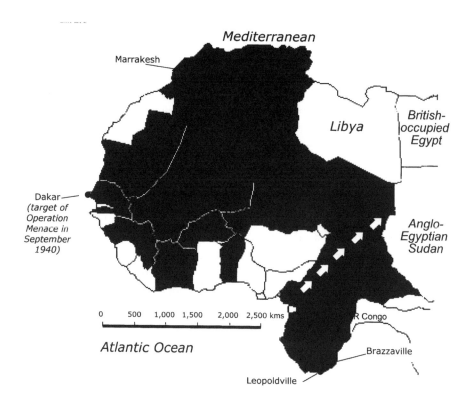

De Gaulle's safe air corridor from the Atlantic coast to Egypt and Sudan

on 20 July. The five French trading enclaves in India followed suit on 9 September after Churchill had issued them with an ultimatum to declare for de Gaulle or risk being blockaded for the duration of hostilities.

The next colonial 'target' on the wall map in Carlton Gardens was now Dakar, capital of Senegal. It lies at the westernmost point of the African continent and has one of the best natural harbours on the continent's Atlantic coast. Under Vichy control it would be the perfect base from which Grand Admiral Karl Doenitz's U-boats – which were at that time impossible for ships to detect when submerged – could, with the help of reconnaissance flights by the Glen-Martin bombers and Curtiss fighters stationed at Ouakam airfield in Senegal, hunt down Allied convoys steaming through the narrowest part of the Atlantic Ocean between Africa and South America. On the other hand, Dakar in Allied hands would provide both an important coaling station for merchant and Royal Navy ships and a safe haven for merchant shipping routed via the Cape of Good Hope while the Mediterranean–Suez Canal–Red Sea route was barred to them.

The Vichy regime being equally aware of Dakar's strategic importance, the port was defended by well-sited shore batteries, plus the guns of ships in harbour. However, on-the-ground intelligence from British and other agents was that 70 per cent of the European population of Senegal was anti-Pétain, largely because the armistice left them unable to export their ground nuts and palm oil to the customary European markets. Less prosaically, Churchill assumed that de Gaulle's initiative 'shone as a star in the pitch black night' for them.[6] Whether or not it had done so before Mers el-Kebir, the final nail in this coffin was the torpedo attack by Swordfish aircraft from HMS *Hermes* on the French battleship *Richelieu* in the harbour of Dakar on 8 July. Although immobilised, the *Richelieu* could still fire her 15in guns, to add to those onshore.

Misled by the faulty intelligence, de Gaulle devised a plan of campaign with General Spears and Maj Morton, not to attack Dakar frontally, but to win the civilian and military administration of Senegal over by persuasion, backed by a show of force. This was approved by Churchill on 3 August as Operation *Scipio* – until somebody decided that using the name of a Roman general whose honorific had been 'Africanus' was less than subtle, and it was changed to Operation *Menace*.

Still attempting to improve relations with Vichy France – which was legally a neutral country, although collaborationist to excess – the Foreign Office tried to veto this operation, which it considered might provoke Pétain to declare war against Great Britain. At this, Churchill waved a cable from the British Governor of Nigeria pointing out the danger in which the British colonies in West Africa would lie, should Germany install Luftwaffe and naval bases in the French West African colonies.[7] On 4 August it was calculated that *Menace* could be mounted to permit a landing by the end of the month. As originally planned, it was to be militarily a Gaullist operation, with transportation only provided by the Royal Navy, since this was thought less likely to antagonise the French in Senegal than the arrival of a mixed Franco-British invasion force.

However, it rapidly became apparent that de Gaulle's total strength was inadequate to make a show of force that would enable the Vichy authorities governing Senegal to capitulate without losing face. On the issue of strength, estimates vary wildly, most British sources quoting a figure of 2,500 officers and men, although de Gaulle claimed something under 7,000 by mid-August, perhaps because he counted every French serviceman still in Britain, including the wounded in hospital and colonial troops also.

Whatever the exact truth, in the early hours of 8 August Churchill instructed the chiefs of staff through General Hastings Ismay that 'De Gaulle should take Dakar at the earliest moment. If ... it can be taken peaceably, so much the better. [If not] an adequate Polish and British force should be provided and full naval support given. The operation, once begun, must be carried through.'[8]

For de Gaulle, the most important paragraph stated: 'It is not intended, after Dakar is taken, that we shall hold it with British forces. General de Gaulle's administration would be set up, and would have to maintain itself, British assistance being limited to supplies on a moderate scale.'[9]

Another reason for Churchill's personal interest in Dakar was that its acquisition would mean that 'the Poles and the Belgians (in London) would also recover their gold, which was removed before the armistice to Africa'. The gold reserves, held at Bamako 1,000km inland from Dakar, totalled £60–70 million – a considerable sum at the time – but Churchill's interest was not altruistic. At a stage when every purchase of war materiel from the United States had to be paid for in advance, and with the British reserves being swallowed up at an alarming rate, he intended to use the gold of his allies for Britain's immediate needs. De Gaulle dug in his heels, insisting that any recovered French gold should be used only for purchases needed by his forces. Spears warned him that his obstinacy could cause the British to call off Operation *Menace*, but he refused to give way.[10]

He won the point because Churchill was impatient that so much time had already been lost. To block any covert political resistance to the operation, his order to General Ismay included the words, 'The risk of [Operation *Menace* provoking] a French declaration of war and whether it should be courted is reserved for the Cabinet.'[11]

The immediate danger that worried him was leakage of the plan to the enemy, which would enable Vichy to reinforce the garrisons in Senegal before de Gaulle could get there. And security was poor. In his own words, 'The sealing of the [British] island[s] was not [then] to be compared with what we achieved later in the supreme operations of "Torch" and "Overlord".'[12] At this early stage of the war, security was everywhere lax. French officers, briefed on the plan and excited at the prospect of combat after the weeks of inaction and falling discipline among their troops, drank publicly to the toast of 'Dakar!' in a Liverpool restaurant. But the British were no better. Churchill criticised the way assault landing craft transported from Portsmouth to the ships being assembled at Liverpool were escorted by troops in tropical-issue uniforms.

As 'the few' gave their lives in the skies above south-east England, Operation *Menace* was delayed time and again. The end of August was replaced by 8 September as the target date but, by the time the Gaullist force of two Free French battalions with four Royal Marine battalions left the port of Liverpool on 31 August, it had been belatedly realised that the transports could not travel at the speed of warships, but only make eight or nine knots. The date was put back again – to 18 September. In the event, even that date proved impossible. De Gaulle was travelling aboard SS *Westernland*, a Dutch ship, with Monclar's 13 DBLE on her sister vessel SS *Pennland*. They rendezvoused in the Irish Sea with their Royal Navy escort, including the outdated battleships *Barham* and *Resolution* with their destroyer screens, and HMS *Ark Royal* – the flagship of Admiral Cunningham, which had done so much damage at Mers el-Kebir.

The course they took was a wide loop out into the Atlantic in the hope of evading Luftwaffe reconnaissance flights from airfields on the French Atlantic coast. At this stage, another element entered the equation. Alarmed by the rallying of Chad, Congo and Cameroun to de Gaulle, Admiral Darlan obtained German approval to despatch three of Vichy's most modern capital ships and three light cruisers from Toulon, destination Dakar. Designated Force Y, it left Toulon early on 9 September and headed at full speed for the Straits of Gibraltar. Six hours later, the British Consul-General in Tangiers cabled Admiral North, commanding North Atlantic Station in Gibraltar, with copy to the Foreign Office in London, that he had intelligence from a reliable agent of a Vichy squadron about to attempt the passage of the Straits within the following seventy-two hours. In London, the disruption caused by German bombing raids on the capital delayed the forwarding of his cable to the Admiralty by four days. Meantime, Admiral North was, in Churchill's words, '*not* in the Dakar circle, and took no special action'.[13]

At 6 p.m. on 10 September the British naval attaché in Madrid was informed officially by his Vichy opposite number that Force Y would pass through the Straits early on the following morning. He alerted the Admiralty and Admiral North on Gibraltar. The London copy was deciphered and passed to Director of Operations Division (Foreign), who was aware of *Menace*, but simply placed it with the First Sea Lord's telegrams for routine perusal. Before dawn on 11 September a British destroyer sighted Force Y making 25 knots 50 nautical miles east of Gibraltar. Admiral Somerville, commanding Force H in Gibraltar harbour, placed HMS *Renown* at one hour's readiness to sail, but took no other action. Arriving abeam of the Port War Signal Station, the Vichy vessels identified themselves as a neutral force and, in a normal exchange of courtesies, were wished, '*Bon voyage!*'

Panic stations in London! Belatedly receiving the order to despatch *Renown* in pursuit of the Vichy squadron, Somerville's only recorded reaction was to say to his flag lieutenant that their Lordships of the Admiralty 'must be mad'.[14] At the same time, Admiral Cunningham was ordered to detach from his force three cruisers and HMS *Ark Royal* with a destroyer screen to intercept the Vichy vessels north of Dakar. It was too late: they had already entered Dakar harbour. To what extent the attitude of Somerville and Sir Dudley North was influenced by their distaste for Operation *Catapult* is impossible to say. North carried the blame: he was dismissed from the Navy for his 'deplorable lack of initiative'[15] in allowing the French squadron to pass through the Straits and his name was not cleared until 1957.

At 2 p.m. on 16 September, the War Cabinet called off Operation *Menace*, considering that the reinforcement of Dakar's defences by the heavy guns of Force Y and the military personnel aboard those ships rendered the taking of Dakar now impossible of success. The signal from London to Lieutenant-General Noel Irwin, commanding the British military contingent with Cunningham, ended politely, 'unless General de Gaulle has any objections'. De Gaulle not only had objections, but also convinced General Irwin that there was still a chance of winning Dakar. This surprised the War Cabinet and delighted Churchill because, 'It was very rare at this stage in the war for commanders on the spot to press for audacious courses.'[16]

On 17 September when the *Menace* force ended its long loop across the Atlantic by reaching Freetown, some 800km south of Dakar, the Foreign Office was delighted to welcome to London another French general who, they hoped, would replace the troublesome de Gaulle, the equally troublesome Admiral Muselier having left the country on 4 September for Alexandria. Having been governor of Damascus in 1920, he seemed to de Gaulle the ideal man to promote a *coup d'état* in Syria and unseat the pro-Vichy High Commissioner General Fernand Dentz – in other words, to pull off the coup that had nearly cost de Larminat his life.

The new arrival in London, on whom the Foreign Office placed its hopes, was General Georges Catroux, who had been Governor General of French Indochina until sacked in July after violently disagreeing with orders from Vichy. He had then cabled his son in London to convey his support for de Gaulle, but the Foreign Office thought that, with a little massaging of his ego, Catroux's seniority of rank would make him want to replace de Gaulle as head of the Free French. It was not to be. A POW in Germany during the First World War, Catroux had been sent after three attempted escapes to the punishment camp at Fort IX in Ingolstadt, where thrice-wounded Captain de Gaulle, who had made five escape attempts, was a fellow prisoner. Arrived in London, Catroux disappointed the anti-de Gaulle faction in the Foreign Office by informing them that he had no intention of usurping the authority of his old comrade in adversity and was quite happy to serve under him.

Ever the British bulldog, Churchill changed tack on hearing that Irwin and de Gaulle wanted to push on with *Menace*. On 28 September he signalled, 'We give you full authority to go ahead and do what you think is best to give effect to the original purpose of the expedition.'[17] On 19 September, the First Sea Lord informed the War Cabinet that four ships from Force Y had left Dakar, carrying reinforcements for the garrisons in the colony of Gabon, to stop it falling into de Gaulle's hands. The following day, the Vichy ships heading south met Cunningham's force heading north. Intercepted, the captain of the cruiser *Primaguet* consented to retire to Casablanca under escort by two Royal Navy ships, while the other three Vichy vessels under Admiral Bourragué turned tail and increased speed to thirty-one knots, losing their Royal Navy pursuers until the cruiser *Gloire* developed engine trouble and was escorted by the British back to Casablanca. Bourragué's two other ships made it back to Dakar, after which the admiral was immediately sacked by a furious Darlan, who confirmed his standing orders that British ships sighted within 20 nautical miles of French territory were to be fired on immediately.[18]

After this skirmish with no shots fired, de Gaulle's optimism grew, but was about to take a severe knock. Cunningham's force arrived off Dakar in thick fog early on 23 September. At dawn, two Luciole light aircraft in French colours but carrying no armament took off from the flight deck of *Ark Royal* and landed at Ouakam airfield. The pilots, wearing French uniform, were immediately arrested. British and French aircraft from *Ark Royal* dropping leaflets were fired upon by the anti-aircraft batteries ashore. The next contact was made by d'Argenlieu, who entered the harbour with a small force in two ships' motorboats, to be driven off with machine-gun fire, sustaining wounds that cost him six weeks' hospitalisation. A radioed message from de Gaulle to Pierre Boisson, the Vichy Governor General of French West Africa, was answered by fire from shore batteries aimed at the British ships hardly visible in the fog, provoking the rather plaintive signal from Cunningham to shore after *Cumberland* had been hit about 11 a.m. 'I am not firing at you. Why are you firing at me?' The reply was: 'Withdraw to twenty nautical miles offshore.'[19] That afternoon, a landing by Gaullist marines along the coast at Rufisque in the hope of rallying the local population was driven off by strafing attacks by the Curtiss fighters from Ouakam and Cunningham's force was obliged by accurate fire from the port to withdraw seaward.

A report of the inconclusive engagement evoked Churchill's signal: 'Having begun, we must go on to the end. Stop at nothing.'[20] This prompted a midnight radio warning from Cunningham to Boisson that an all-out attack by the British vessels could be expected at 6 a.m. unless Boisson indicated willingness to hand the port over to de Gaulle. The spurious justification given was that the port would otherwise be handed over to the Germans, who were nowhere near. Boisson's reply was that he would defend Dakar to the last round. In the exchange of fire next morning, a total of 400 15in shells were fired by the Royal Navy to no effect, the port being hidden from view by a protective smoke screen, while the Vichy shore batteries and 15in guns aboard *Richelieu* managed to damage HMS *Barham* despite the protection of the fog.

De Gaulle faced up to the failure of the operation with outward calm: persuasion had failed miserably and it was obvious that the use of force was serving only to further alienate his countrymen ashore. Irwin and Cunningham, however, determined to show whose ball the game was being played with and continued the duel at longer range on the third morning – with the only significant hit scored by either side being four of *Ark Royal*'s aircraft shot down and serious damage to HMS *Resolution* during a torpedo attack by a Vichy submarine that put her out of action for several months. Cunningham thereupon disengaged 'in view of the condition of the *Resolution*, the continued danger from submarines and the great accuracy and determination of the shore defences'.[21]

It was scant consolation to de Gaulle that Churchill vaunted his courage in the House of Commons on 28 September, reaffirming his confidence in the Free French movement. The prime minister could also congratulate himself that the Foreign Office fears of provoking Pétain to declare war on Britain had been proven groundless. Both Churchill and de Gaulle later argued that Operation *Menace* had been successful, not in its original aim, but because Cunningham's presence in the right place at the right time had prevented Admiral Bourragué's force from stiffening the will and reinforcing the numbers in the Vichy garrisons south of Senegal, thus leaving the field in that direction wide open to the Gaullist invitation to change sides. While that was true, in the immediate aftermath as Cunningham's force sailed south to land the Free French at Douala in Cameroun, their commander-in-chief kept to his cabin in a deep depression, humiliated at what he knew the world would consider the resounding failure of his first major gamble.

From cables shown to him by Spears, it was swiftly obvious that the chiefs of staff and the Foreign Office were blaming allegedly poor security within the Free French forces for triggering the despatch of Force Y from Toulon. Although this was both unproven and wrong, de Gaulle's enemies in the Foreign Office and the chiefs of staff used it as the justification to exclude the Free French from future strategic planning. Across the Atlantic, too, Force Y's reinforcement of Dakar was wrongly attributed to security leaks within the Free French. Looking ahead to the eventual entry of the United States into the war – which he had prophesied as the beginning of an Allied victory – de Gaulle foresaw that when the time came for US forces to invade Vichy territory there would be many in the corridors of power in Washington who would use the alleged breach of security in Operation *Menace* to exclude Free French participation.[22] And so it was to prove when the US invaded Morocco in 1942. Even as late as D-Day in June 1944, when he had 400,000 men fighting for the Allies, he was not to be told the date until the day before – and all because of the alleged poor security in the planning of Operation *Menace*.

Churchill had been right in refusing to be panicked by the threat of Vichy declaring for Germany. On the contrary, Pétain's Foreign Minister Paul Baudouin now approached Sir Samuel Hoare, British ambassador in Madrid, to open a new phase of negotiations with the Foreign Office. If the British Government did not wish to throw the Vichy administration completely into the German camp, he argued, it must permit food shipments from the colonies to the Free, or unoccupied, Zone. If this was done, Vichy would ensure that neither the food thus received, nor its equivalent, was passed on to the Germans. As a guarantee of this, he added that, in the event that the Germans interfered with this arrangement, the Vichy Government would transfer its seat to North Africa and revive the union with Britain!

The Foreign Office reply indicated that British support for de Gaulle in the colonies that had rallied to him was unshakeable but that a relaxation of the blockade between pro-Vichy colonies and France could be possible, providing that the government of which Baudouin was a member proved it could act independently of the German and Italian occupation forces and if it were to show a new spirit of cooperation.[23]

Advised by Churchill of these negotiations, de Gaulle replied on 3 October, not without irony, that this was the first time a member of Pétain's government had officially envisaged continuing to fight in alliance with Great Britain. However, he warned, Baudouin's initiative was due more to desperation engendered by internal chaos in France than to a genuine change of foreign policy. Lastly, he pointed out that strengthening the links between Pétain's government and the pro-Vichy colonies would make it all the more difficult to win the latter over to the Allied cause.[24]

Notes

1. C. de Gaulle, *Mémoires de Guerre: L'Appel 1940–42*, Paris, Plon, 1954, p. 99
2. Broadcast of 18 June
3. John Buchan, *Memory Hold the Door*, London, Hodder & Stoughton, 1940
4. D. Judd *The Lion and the Tiger*, Oxford, OUP, 2004, pp. 151–9
5. A. Geraghty, *March or Die*, London, Fontana, 1987, p. 222
6. W.S. Churchill, *The Second World War Vol. 2: Their Finest Hour*, London, Penguin Classics, 2005, p. 419
7. Ibid., p. 421
8. Ibid.
9. Ibid.
10. De Gaulle, *L'Appel*, p. 126
11. All quotations are from Churchill's memorandum to General Ismay dated 8.viii.40 quoted in Churchill, *Their Finest Hour*, pp. 420–31
12. Churchill, *Their Finest Hour*, p. 423, words in brackets added by author
13. Ibid., p. 425
14. C. Williams, *The Last Great Frenchman*, London, Little Brown, 1994, pp. 128–9
15. Ibid., p. 129
16. For Churchill's account of Operation *Menace*, see *Their Finest Hour*, pp. 420–37
17. F. Kersaudy, *de Gaulle et Churchill*, Paris, Perrin Tempus, 2003, p. 108
18. Williams, *The Last Great Frenchman*, pp. 126–32
19. De Gaulle, *L'Appel*, p. 133
20. Ibid.
21. Churchill, *Their Finest Hour*, p. 434
22. De Gaulle, *L'Appel*, p. 139
23. Kersaudy, *de Gaulle et Churchill*, pp. 107–8
24. Ibid., pp. 108–9

7

FIRST BLOOD

De Gaulle arrived in Douala on 8 October, still smarting from the humiliation of his rejection at Dakar. With Cunningham's ships gone, he and his men found themselves greeted everywhere by the inhabitants of Cameroun as conquering heroes, not supplicants of Britain. General Spears, whose unhappy lot it had been as head of the liaison mission to mediate between de Gaulle and the equally obstinate Ismay and Cunningham, noted sourly that the main object of all this adulation gradually regained the arrogance that so often made him deaf to reason.

Chad, Cameroun and French Congo already having declared for him, de Gaulle now planned the reduction of the Vichy regime in the neighbouring colony of Gabon. The decision to invade was not taken lightly, however. It was one thing for the Royal Navy to kill Vichy troops by shelling Dakar, but the invasion of Gabon would mean for the first time that French soldiers loyal to de Gaulle would be killing comrades loyal to Pétain. Monclar was only one of the officers and men of 13 DBLE to weep openly at the grim prospect ahead of them.[1]

The invasion was planned as a classic three-pronged attack, with de Larminat leading one column overland from Cameroun to meet up with another column coming overland from French Congo, while Leclerc took ship and landed on the coast with a third small force. From the first victories at Mitzic on 27 October and Lambaréné on 5 November to the capital of Gabon, Libreville, on 9 November, there was resistance by the Vichy garrisons and casualties on both sides. Gaullist Lysanders added to the carnage by flying missions out of Douala to bomb Libreville airport. D'Argenlieu's minuscule navy also made its mark by setting the Vichy cruiser *Bougainvillea* ablaze. As Monclar had foreseen, this was the stuff of bloody civil war. And then, suddenly, with the taking of Port-Gentil, it was all over, bar the shouting of '*Vive la France libre!*' One of the last casualties was Governor Masson, who had declared for de Gaulle, changed his mind twice more and spent his last hours persuading the senior Vichy soldier General of the Air Force Têtu and the garrison of Port-Gentil to surrender and save needless casualties. Masson committed suicide by hanging himself in his cabin during the return voyage to Douala. That might sound tragic-comic but epitomises the dilemma of colonial administrators and military commanders far from France: their sworn loyalty was to the far-distant but legitimate government in Vichy, which many of them despised.

De Gaulle had meanwhile departed to meet Eboué and Marchand in Chad. And that was nearly the end of the Free French adventure, for engine trouble forced his Potez 540 aircraft to crash-land in a swamp. Safely arrived nevertheless in Fort Lamy, he met General Catroux, who had just flown in from Cairo. It could have been an awkward meeting but when de Gaulle raised his glass to toast Catroux the tone of the senior general's reply indicated to all present that, so far as he was concerned, de Gaulle had achieved a political status that placed him above rank and seniority.[2] Catroux recounted how the British in Egypt wanted him to lend his name to a joint operation against the Vichy occupation of Syria and Lebanon, which had been French protectorates since the dissolution of the Ottoman Empire at the end of the First World War. As events were to prove, both Frenchmen were right to be suspicious of British intentions in the Levant after General Dentz's Vichy forces had been overcome.

German disinformation to the effect that Vichy was going to turn at least a part of its fleet in Toulon over to Hitler caused Churchill to write on 20 October to President Roosevelt, requesting him to warn Pétain that the US would take a most grave view of any such step. That same evening at Chequers, just as his staff and close associates were preparing for bed, he was seized with the idea of appealing directly to the French people and spent the next hours dictating a speech to be translated for him to broadcast the following day. In the evening of 21 October, in the middle of an air raid, he delivered the speech in his inimitable drawling voice and with characteristic accent: '*Français! Pendant plus de trente ans …*'

Making the point that for more than thirty years in peace and war he had sided with France and was still marching along the same road, he repeated the prayer inscribed around the *louis d'or* coin: *Dieu protège la France*. London was being bombed at that very moment, he admitted, but 'we shall never stop, we shall never weary, we shall never give in'. He warned that when good people had the misfortune to be 'attacked and heavily smitten by the vile and wicked' they must be careful not to fall out with one another and thus strengthen their common enemy. The war was not over, he said, because both Britain and France had powerful friends across the Atlantic. He asked of his French listeners that, if they could not directly help Britain at that time, at least they should not hinder the British war effort.

He warned also against believing German propaganda that the British intended grabbing French ships and French colonies, saying that Britain's sole aim was to beat the life and soul out of Hitler and win from other countries only their respect. He hinted that some Frenchmen were already working against the Germans, but could not go into details because 'hostile ears are listening'. And he ended with the classic, '*Vive la France!*'[3] It was an extraordinary tour de force. How many people actually heard the speech is unknown, but the news that the indomitable British prime minister had taken the trouble to make such a speech in French for Pétain's suffering subjects to hear in their own homes made a great impact.

On the diplomatic front, Roosevelt's warning to Pétain and Darlan about any plans to hand over the fleet in Toulon was accompanied by the oblique threat that such an act would result in the US failing to support France in reclaiming her overseas possessions after the war. The wheels of diplomacy ground slowly on despite everything. It was no help to Churchill that the millionaire US ambassador to the Court of St James was Joseph P. Kennedy, a strong supporter of the Democratic Party and personal friend of Roosevelt. Later best known as father of the assassinated President John F. Kennedy, Joseph P. was not only hostile to Britain but regularly cabled Secretary of State Cordell Hull his defeatist views that Britain could not hold out and would eventually submit to Hitler, as had her European allies. His resignation in November 1940 came after the Battle of Britain had been won, a German invasion staved off indefinitely and the worst of the Blitz over, by which time his views had been proven wrong, but had left their imprint in Hull's mind at least.

On 22 October economics professor Louis Rougier arrived in London from Vichy to negotiate a modus vivendi with the British Government. Churchill kept him waiting two days for an appointment, at which no conclusions were reached, although Rougier was told that the colonies which had rallied to de Gaulle were outside the scope of any talks. Four days later, rumours that Pétain had signed a peace treaty with Hitler made Churchill so furious when his talks with Rougier resumed that he threatened to send the RAF to bomb Vichy and to harry Pétain's government wherever it went. The unflappable professor of economics pointed out that the rumours of a peace treaty were just German disinformation to drive a wedge between Vichy and London.

The result of his visit was a curious document balancing threats and promises, some added in the margin in Churchill's own hand. If London and Washington were playing a diplomatic game with Vichy, the balls were being returned with skill, Pétain and Darlan managing to keep both the British Foreign Office and the Department of State in Washington guessing as to exactly what they had agreed with the Germans. Churchill was frankly baffled to the point of telling Foreign Minister Lord Halifax that it would be better if Pétain had gone all the way down the path of humiliation, in which case either there would have been a national uprising against him or Britain could have treated France as an enemy power. As it was, Vichy's waiting game and the hopes it engendered in Washington enabled Cordell Hull to kill stone dead any US support for de Gaulle.

It was at this point that de Gaulle created an autonomous administration for his swiftly acquired empire, to make the point that its links to Vichy were severed. Entitled the Le Conseil de Défense de l'Empire – the Empire Defence Council – its members were General Catroux, Vice Admiral Muselier, General de Larminat, governors Eboué and Sautot, Surgeon General Sicé, Professor Cassin, Captain d'Argenlieu and Colonel Leclerc. His manifesto proclaimed over the radio from Brazzaville, capital of the French Congo, on 27 October was tantamount to a declaration of war against Vichy France. He concluded the speech loftily:

> I shall exercise my powers in the name of France and solely in order to defend her. I solemnly undertake to render an account of my actions to the representatives of the French people as soon as it is possible for them to be freely designated.[4]

That time was obviously a long way off, and meantime de Gaulle had only to answer to the Council.

The Foreign Office had intended the Rougier negotiations to be kept secret from de Gaulle but, one way and another, he was *au courant*. As president of the Empire Defence Council, he wrote to Churchill on 2 November that any negotiations with Vichy personalities should only be undertaken in conjunction with the Free French. He also wrote direct to Roosevelt, assuring him that the Free French had sufficient men and means to take over the French possessions in the western hemisphere, and asking for US agreement to this. This direct approach and the manifesto so infuriated the Foreign Office – which considered that it should have been consulted first – that the initiative lost de Gaulle any friends he may still have had there. Yet Churchill understood his attitude, both as to his refusal to have any truck with Vichy and his independent stance, by which he hoped to prove to all his compatriots that he was not simply a pawn in Britain's game. To try and smooth things out, he cabled de Gaulle on 10 November with an update of the negotiations with Vichy and asked him politely to return to London for an urgently needed meeting to smooth things out before they got any worse.

In Brazzaville, de Gaulle was playing his own diplomatic games by crossing the mighty river that divided it from Belgian Congo to pay a courtesy visit on Governor General Ryckmans in Léopoldville and receive Ryckmans' thanks for the protection the Free French presence in West and Equatorial Africa afforded the Belgian colony. A message of support also reached him from the most important person in the French colonial service: Inspector General of the Colonies Cazaux conveyed the support of the European population of Indochina, while regretting that there was nothing concrete they could do to aid his movement at this time.

De Gaulle also discussed with Leclerc the best use to which they could put the enormous spread of acquired territories of French Equatorial Africa; from Brazzaville north to the border of Italian-occupied Libya was almost 3,000km, all of which territory was under his control. It made the ideal jumping-off point, from which to attack Italian forces in Libya threatening British-occupied Egypt and also provided a safe aerial corridor across Africa for Allied aircraft, as Churchill was quick to recognise. On 6 May 1940, before Italy had declared war on France, motorised columns of Mussolini's troops had entered French Saharan territory, to the fury of many colonial army officers. Among them, Major Colonna d'Ornano immediately declared for de Gaulle on hearing the appeal of 18 June.

A handsome 45-year-old professional soldier who habitually went about wearing Tuareg robes, d'Ornano had been one of Marchand's supporters in bringing Chad over to de Gaulle. Inspired perhaps by a battalion of French marines in Cyprus declaring for de Gaulle and seeing action with British Eighth Army at Sidi Barrani, this experienced desert soldier was promoted by Leclerc to lieutenant colonel and ordered to mount a surprise attack on the Italian base at the oasis of Murzuq 300km into south-west Libya. After crossing several times that distance of desert to get there, the attack on 11 January 1941 was a success, although costing D'Ornano's life. He died with the distinction of being the first Free French hero.

On 15 November de Gaulle visited the Vichy prisoners taken in Gabon, hoping to win them over, but once again, as at Trentham Park, he failed and they were interned with General Tétu at Brazzaville. He could have done with the reinforcements because it was now decided to split his small army in three parts. The smallest was to stay on garrison duty in the equatorial colonies. The others were to demonstrate that Free France was also *fighting France*, making a positive contribution to the Allied war effort.

Inspired by d'Ornano's success at Murzuq, Leclerc set off with a column of 400 men on the most ambitious Gaullist action so far after being promoted to lieutenant colonel by de Gaulle on 25 November. It was nothing less than an odyssey of 4,000km across some of the harshest and most hostile terrain in the world to link up with the British Eighth Army on the coast of Libya after attacking and reducing whatever Axis strongpoints they found along the way. At the same time 13 DBLE re-embarked for the long voyage around the Cape of Good Hope and up the east coast of Africa to play their part in evicting the Italian occupation forces from Eritrea, which threatened the British in Egypt as well as communications with India.

On 17 November de Gaulle left Africa feeling no longer Churchill's poor relation, having gained an immense spread of territory at very little cost in lives and materiel and with his forces already in action against the enemy. He had even written again to his former commander General Weygand, who had been appointed Vichy commander-in-chief in French North Africa, suggesting that

Weygand bring the large forces under his command there over to the Allied side. There was no reply.

The Britain to which de Gaulle now returned was greatly relieved by having won the Battle of Britain. The Blitz continued, but any threat of imminent invasion had been staved off. However, on 27 September the Tripartite Pact had been signed, making Japan a partner of Germany and Italy. Under it, Berlin and Rome gave Tokyo a free hand against British, French and Dutch possessions in south-east Asia. At this time when tempers were short all round on the British side, Churchill's long-term worry was how to balance the books. Britain had entered the war with reserves of about $4,500 million. By November 1940, even after requisitioning $335 million from private investors, only $2,000 million remained, and the greater part of this was in investments not easily encashable.[5] With national bankruptcy not far off, given the rate of spending on war materiel and vitally needed supplies for the civilian population, Churchill was reduced to writing what he considered his most important communication of the whole war in order to keep flowing across the Atlantic to Britain the supplies without which her army and air force could not fight and her people would end up close to starvation.

It was a closely argued letter of nineteen long paragraphs to President Roosevelt, ending,

> If, as I believe, you are convinced, Mr President, that the defeat of the Nazi and Fascist tyranny is a matter of high consequence to the people of the United States and the Western Hemisphere, you will regard this letter not as an appeal for aid, but as a statement of the minimum action necessary to achieve our common aim.[6]

The drafting took him and Lord Lothian, the British ambassador recalled from Washington for the purpose, most of November. Finally despatched on 8 December, the carefully crafted begging letter reached Roosevelt on a Caribbean cruise aboard the warship *Tuscaloosa*. Presidential adviser Harry Hopkins afterwards told Churchill that FDR sat on deck in his wheelchair rereading and pondering it for several hours. Apart from his own inclinations, he must doubtless have been thinking of the reaction, when Churchill's text became known, of the 800,000 members of the America First Committee[7] – an influential pressure group that resented even the current level of aid to Britain and would oppose any increase from fear that this would lead to direct American military involvement in the European conflict. The first article of the Monroe doctrine elaborated by President Monroe on 2 December 1823 was that the United States 'would not interfere in the internal affairs of, or the wars between, European states'. Although FDR's predecessor Woodrow Wilson had chipped away at this cornerstone of

US foreign policy by declaring war on the Central Powers in 1917, there was still a strong body of opinion which held that America's prosperity depended on staying out of Old World quarrels.

Roosevelt was a consummate politician and had enacted in what were called 'the first hundred days' of his first administration in 1932 the 'New Deal' economic policy aimed at revitalising those sectors of the country's economy devastated by the Great Depression. So detested had he been by the right wing for this social engineering that businessmen had been known to drink to the prospect of his assassination. Having realised the error of the US *selling* its help in the First World War, he now appreciated Churchill's argument about the inadvisability of extending credit that could never be repaid. Persuading Congress of this, however, would require all his negotiating skills and the dangling of incentives before interest groups.

His subsequent persuasion of the Congress to pass the Lend-Lease Act began with a homespun simile used at his press conference on 16 December. Likening Britain's plight to that of a neighbour whose house is on fire, but may be saved by lending him a garden hose, he affirmed that no one would ask for payment for use of the hose, only that it be returned after use. In the same way, war materiel needed by Britain – whether ships, aircraft, guns or whatever – should be lent for the duration of hostilities. In Churchill's words, it was 'the most unsordid act in the history of any nation'.[8]

Roosevelt, it seemed, had decided that the long-term defence interests of the United States, and not cash in the bank, should determine what help be given to Britain and her eventual allies in the struggle against the European dictators. The less idealistic reality was that, from then on, independent Britain had become a client state of Washington, for she could not exist without American supplies on a vast scale, yet had not the reserves to pay for them. Since this help did not have to be paid for, it was in the nature of things that the donors could impose whatever conditions they wished on its use.

On returning to London from building his power base in Africa, de Gaulle had to put his house in order. Unfortunately, Muselier was a meddler, poking his nose into everyone's business and alienating many people thereby. The Free French in Britain represented just about all shades of French politics and were united only by dislike of Pétain's policies, so it was not surprising to anyone except de Gaulle, who assumed that subordinates would automatically be loyal to him, that various factions had predictably been conspiring with, and against, each other. A breakaway group under former socialist *député* André Labarthe, who now used the *nom de guerre* Major Fontaine, exemplified what de Gaulle called the French talent for divisiveness, having gone so far as to found a French-language magazine that was both anti-de Gaulle and anti-German!

Captain André Dewavrin, a mild-looking, prematurely bald graduate of the elite Ecole Polytechnique who had been a lecturer at St Cyr military academy, was interviewed by the General on his arrival in London and asked three questions: 'Are you a womaniser?' 'Do you know about criminals?' 'Have you been in combat?' To each question, the reply was negative. 'Perfect,' said de Gaulle. 'I'll put you in charge of my Intelligence Service.'[9]

Dewavrin, promoted to major, thus became the head of what would eventually be called Le Bureau Central de Renseignements et d'Action (BCRA), running all the Gaullist agents and networks in France. For his slender budget, supplies and training, he was dependent on SOE, through whom he obtained RAF aircraft to drop agents and supplies into France. Although Churchill on several occasions accorded priority to the provision of aircraft for this purpose, often the RAF and SOE impeded the work of BCRA.

During one of de Gaulle's absences, Dewavrin decided to tighten up internal security and introduced procedures such as checking waste-paper bins and examining blotting paper in mirrors, to see who was and who was not reliable. The cloak-and-dagger atmosphere was enhanced by the liberal use of code names. Dewavrin became 'Colonel Passy' and appointed a Major Howard and Warrant Officer Collin to look after internal security.

After de Gaulle's return, Admiral Muselier reported all this to him and gained his consent to sacking the intrusive major and his assistant. The mistake was to let them work out their notice, during which time Howard passed to friends in MI5 four letters apparently incriminating Muselier, against whom he had a paranoid fixation. The New Year 1941 thus began unfortunately for the future of British-Gaullist relations. In the absence of de Gaulle, spending the holiday with his family in Shropshire, the over-stressed Churchill simply ordered the arrest of just about everybody connected with the letters. Muselier was celebrating the New Year with his men in Portsmouth. On returning to his London home on 2 January, he was arrested by two detectives from Scotland Yard. He insisted on changing into civilian clothes to avoid the dishonour to his uniform by being seen wearing it while under arrest by British policemen, but was locked up first in Pentonville and then in Brixton prison without being questioned, charged or shown the 'evidence' against him. Others arrested in the early morning raids included several Free French officers and their lady friends in various stages of undress.

The news was broken to de Gaulle on 2 January by Churchill's new Foreign Secretary Anthony Eden. According to the letters on notepaper bearing the heading of the Vichy-loyal French Embassy in London, Muselier had apparently divulged the plans of the Dakar operation to General Rozoy, the recently repatriated air attaché; he had obstructed recruitment of sailors into the Gaullist navy; and he had been prepared to deliver the submarine *Surcouf* to Vichy for £2,000. De Gaulle immediately saw through the intrigue and declared the letters to be forgeries.

Summoning General Spears, he ordered him to communicate to the British Government the ultimatum that it had twenty-four hours to release Muselier and apologise or risk Free France severing all connection with it. Liaison officers of any rank are always suspected by their charges of being spies for their employers and by their employers as being overly sympathetic to the people they are supposed to be watching, and this placed Spears in an uncomfortable position. However, he did as told, with the result that Muselier was released and exonerated, with the British Attorney General personally assuring de Gaulle that everyone responsible for this lamentable affair would be punished.

De Gaulle was furious, considering that, even had the papers been genuine, any accusations against his subordinates should be handled by his own security organisation under Colonel Passy. Suspecting that MI5 had planted Howard and Collin in his organisation and organised or at least encouraged the fabrication of the forgeries, he sacked all the British staff in Carlton Gardens and was only persuaded with difficulty to reinstate them. The whole business nevertheless left a bad taste in his mouth. Much later, he would write, 'This lamentable incident, which threw into sharp relief the precariousness of our situation with our allies could not fail to influence my attitude to the relationship with Britain.'[10]

Confronted, Howard and Collin confessed to the forgeries. De Gaulle accepted the apologies of Churchill and Eden and used their understandable embarrassment as a lever to negotiate an agreement on 15 January which stated that all Free French personnel in Britain were henceforth under Gaullist jurisdiction. He was also accorded the privilege of a personal interview with King George VI.[11] However, paranoia is infectious; Muselier now perversely suspected that de Gaulle had planned the whole unhappy business, and started a whispering campaign against him after moving his naval/air force HQ to its own offices in Westminster House. In Carlton Gardens and Colonel Passy's HQ in Duke Street what de Gaulle termed a glacial silence signalled 'a sort of vacuum created all around the Free French. No meetings, no correspondence, no visits, nor lunches either. Nothing could be resolved. We were ignored, as though the alliance was ended.'[12]

In Africa, at least, progress was more straightforward. Leclerc's reconnaissance patrol reached the Italian-occupied oasis of Koufra in Libya on 7 February 1941. Observing the enemy in this base that sat astride an important communications and supply route from the coast to the Italian forces in Ethiopia, it reported that a Gaullist bombing mission by twelve Lysanders – each could only carry twelve anti-personnel bombs – and six lumbering Blenheims had, not surprisingly, had little effect in softening-up the target. Eleven days later Leclerc's main force arrived and laid siege to the Italian positions, frightening the defenders by hauling their single 75mm mountain gun from place to place as rapidly as possible between bombardments to convince the men inside the perimeter that they were surrounded by a much larger force.

After ten days of this war of nerves, but few casualties, the Italians asked to parley under a white flag and accepted Leclerc's promise that all prisoners would be correctly treated. The siege over, news of this first Gaullist success and of the first enemy prisoners taken by Free French troops reached London, where the BBC reported it as a significant Allied victory. On the following day, having fully justified de Gaulle's confidence in him, Leclerc swore an oath in front of his men 'to lay down my arms only after our colours, our fine colours, float once again over the cathedral of Strasbourg'.[13] The moment is still commemorated in Paris by the Square of the Oath of Koufra, just off the Porte d'Orléans.

Slowly, in London the ice thawed. Telephones began ringing again. Letters were delivered. Old contacts dropped in. On 9 March de Gaulle was spending the weekend at Chequers as Churchill's guest, when his host woke him up, literally dancing for joy, with the news that Congress had passed the Lend-Lease Bill.[14] In Roosevelt's famous phrase, the United States had consented to become 'the arsenal of the democracies', with Congress granting to FDR the authority to aid any nation whose defence he believed vital to that of the United States and to accept repayment 'in kind or property, or any other direct or indirect benefit which the President deems satisfactory'.[15]

Lend-Lease was, on the face of it, an extraordinarily generous gesture of support and assistance, as well as being a giant step towards direct participation in the European war, but the immediate price was that Churchill was now Roosevelt's man, his future freedom of action being limited to alternatives that would not jeopardise the vital support of Washington, where de Gaulle was *persona non grata*. More than ever determined to keep dealing with Pétain, Roosevelt upgraded the post of *chargé d'affaires* in Vichy to the rank of ambassador and asked General William Pershing to accept the post because he and the Marshal were friends from the time when Pershing commanded the American Expeditionary Force in France during the First World War. Old and ill, Pershing declined. Advised by Cordell Hull, Roosevelt therefore offered the ambassadorship to another personal friend, Admiral William Daniel Leahy. On Leahy's retirement in 1939, he had been told by the president, 'Bill, if there's a war, you're going to be right back here, helping me lead it.' Leahy's appointment was a curious one. He neither knew France, nor could speak or understand its language. His brief on taking up the post in January 1941 was to keep the French Fleet neutral by alternately cajoling and bribing Pétain's hard-pressed government with supplies of food and other non-strategic materials. As far as Leahy was concerned, the existence of de Gaulle's movement was an irritant that only complicated his job. It was an attitude shared by both Hull and Roosevelt.

On 19 March the financial, economic and monetary agreement between the Free French and the British Treasury that had been envisaged in the protocol of 7 August 1940 was at last signed. By then de Gaulle was already heading for the Middle East – in his own words, 'flying with simple ideas towards the complicated Orient'.[16] He landed in Cairo on 1 April, his arrival preceded by a cable from

Churchill to commander-in-chief Middle East General Archibald Wavell telling him not to worry about upsetting Vichy administrations in the Middle East, which was London's concern, but to give 'full weight to the views of General de Gaulle, to whom His Majesty's Government have given solemn engagements, and who has their full backing as leader of the Free French movement'.[17] In addition, on 4 April de Gaulle received a warm cable from Churchill, somewhat watered down by the Foreign Office, confirming that His Majesty's government had complete confidence in the Gaullist movement, which represented the hopes of all French people for the restoration of France and the French Empire.[18]

Notes

1. S. Travers, *Tomorrow to be Brave*, London, Corgi, 2001, p. 78
2. C. de Gaulle, *Mémoires de Guerre: L'Appel 1940–42*, Paris, Plon, 1954, p. 143
3. W.S. Churchill, *The Second World War, Vol. 2: Their Finest Hour*, London, Penguin Classics, 2005, pp. 451–5
4. C. de Gaulle, *Discours et Messages*, Paris, Plon, 1970, Vol. 1, p. 39
5. Churchill, *Their Finest Hour*, pp. 491, 493
6. Ibid., pp. 494–501
7. The Committee eventually dissolved itself after the Japanese attack on Pearl Harbor and urged its members to support the war effort.
8. Churchill, *Their Finest Hour*, p. 503
9. ed. M. Jullian, *de Gaulle – Traits d'esprit*, Paris, Cherche-Midi, 2000, p. 223
10. De Gaulle, *L'Appel*, p. 159
11. C. Williams, *The Last Great Frenchman*, London, Little Brown, 1994, pp. 140–2
12. De Gaulle, *L'Appel*, p. 176 (abridged by the author)
13. Plaque in Place du Serment de Koufra, Paris
14. De Gaulle, *L'Appel*, p. 177. In fact, the Lend-Lease Bill was not formally passed until 11 March. Either de Gaulle's diary was at fault, or Churchill was telling him that the Bill was *about* to become law.
15. Ibid.
16. De Gaulle, *L'Appel*, p. 181
17. W.S. Churchill *The Second World War, Vol. 3: The Grand Alliance*, London, Penguin Classics, 2005, pp. 77–8
18. F. Kersaudy, *de Gaulle et Churchill*, Paris, Perrin Tempus, 2003, p. 134

8

A QUESTION OF PRIORITIES

Churchill's support and instructions to Wavell had little effect on his subordinates. To them 'the frogs' in Free French uniform were still 'the cowards who let the British army down in France'. When 13 DBLE under Colonel Monclar reached Port Sudan, British ambulance driver Susan Travers found it hard to account for her compatriots' mistrust of the legionnaires who had refused to surrender and were now defying the French Government to fight alongside them.

Reinforced by a column of Black Chadian soldiers that had come all the way overland, 13 DBLE was trucked into Eritrea, to fight at Kub-Kub and Keren before moving on to Massawa, the strategic port and capital of Italian Eritrea. After a ferocious bombardment, on 8 April 1941 a mixed British/Gaullist force captured the town, Monclar's arrival being greeted with fascist salutes by the local population, who believed this to be a polite form of European greeting.

While Leclerc was reducing the garrison at Koufra, General Dentz had received orders from Vichy to collaborate with two German Intelligence operatives, sent to survey Syrian airfields with a view to them being used as staging posts for Luftwaffe aircraft in support of Iraqi Prime Minister Rashid Ali's planned uprising to drive the British out of his country. Catroux reported to de Gaulle that Dentz disliked the idea but would nevertheless obey orders. However, Catroux thought that many of the 30,000 French and colonial troops in Syria/Lebanon – including the Foreign Legion's Syrian regiment 6 REI – would be prepared to change sides providing the Free French arrived in such force that they could reasonably lay down their arms.

Unfortunately, de Gaulle could muster in this theatre only about 6,000 men with ten tanks, eight field guns and a couple of dozen aircraft. General Wavell was not prepared to help at a time when he was already over-committed in Libya and Greece and expecting an imminent German attack on Egypt. His refusal to lend troops, the cosy relationship between Dentz and the British Consul General in Beirut, and the fact that the Royal Navy blockade did not even stop Vichy ships taking Gaullist sympathisers from Syria/Lebanon back to incarceration in France, prompted Spears to protest on de Gaulle's behalf to Foreign Minister Eden. Back came the reply from the chiefs of staff in London: 'Any Free French coup against the Syrian administration must be ruled out absolutely.'[1]

Caught in the machinations, de Gaulle declared on 20 April in *Le Journal d'Egypte*:

> I am a free Frenchman. I believe in God and the future of my country. I am nobody's man. I have a mission, and one only: to pursue the struggle to liberate my country. I solemnly declare that I have no connection to any political party or politician of either the Right or the Left. I have only one aim. It is to save France.

Frustrated, he flew back to Brazzaville and ordered Catroux to leave Cairo as an indication of his disapproval of the British attitude to the French Levant.[2] Over Radio Brazzaville on 22 April 1941, he broadcast his manifesto to listeners in French North Africa and France. It included these words: 'Rise up and rid yourselves of these bad leaders as our fathers have done many times in history. Come and join our advance guard fighting for the liberation.'

Back in the Middle East, events were moving fast, however. After Rashid Ali sent troops to besiege the RAF airbase at Habbaniya at the beginning of May, Luftwaffe aircraft began landing at Syrian airfields and airlifting substantial amounts of weapons and munitions to the Iraqi insurgents.[3] With British access to Iraqi oil at risk and the overland route to India threatened, de Gaulle found his idea of invading Vichy-occupied Syria and Lebanon was now the flavour of the month in London. On 8 May Churchill instructed the chiefs of staff through General Ismay:

> A supreme effort must be made to prevent the Germans getting a foothold in Syria as a jumping-off ground for the air invasion of Iraq and Persia. It is no use General Wavell being vexed at this disturbance on his eastern flanks.[4]

Next day, Churchill cabled de Gaulle, asking him to return to Cairo. For the first and only time, de Gaulle replied in English: '1. Thank you. 2. Catroux remains in Palestine. 3. I shall go to Cairo soon. 4. You will win the war.'[5] On 14 May Eden in London and Spears in Cairo were still urging de Gaulle to return to Cairo. He reached there on 25 May after taking time to despatch René Pleven to Washington as his 'ambassador', charged with setting up some kind of contact with the State Department, representing the interests of the liberated colonies, purchasing military materiel if possible, boosting information and propaganda and widening the basis of support for the Gaullist cause in the United States. It was a shopping list impossible to fulfil.

Back in Cairo, de Gaulle found Wavell resigned to a joint Franco-British operation in the Levant after the crushing German victories in mainland Greece and the Greek islands had reduced his commitment on the ground in that theatre at least. The next blooding of Free French troops was to be crucial. The prospect of fighting and killing fellow legionnaires of 6 REI so distressed Monclar that he was relieved of command of 13 DBLE, which passed to Marie-Pierre Koenig, now promoted colonel. Against the combined invasion force of British, Indian, French and Australian troops under the British General Sir Henry 'Jumbo' Maitland Wilson were ranged General Dentz's thirty battalions – a mishmash of 35,000 colonial infantry, aircraft and tanks – and 6 REI. Forgetting the lesson of Dakar, de Gaulle seems to have believed once again that Dentz's troops were only awaiting the arrival of the Free French force in Syria, accompanied by a symbolic show of Allied force, to change sides. That he was wrong again was shown when air drops of French-language safe-conducts by Free French flyers were replied to by thousands of leaflets from their Vichy counterparts, inviting the Free French to desert de Gaulle and obey their legal government.

The political situation changed radically when Hitler tore up the German-Soviet Non-Aggression Pact on 22 June. With the mighty, if ill-prepared, USSR now allied to Britain by force of circumstance, de Gaulle saw clearly that, while Churchill would become increasingly Roosevelt's client, the mere despatching of however many convoys of US materiel to Murmansk would never persuade Stalin to do anything he did not want to do.

The opening of Operation *Barbarossa* required all available Luftwaffe units to be transferred to the new eastern front. The Syrian airlift was called off, but it was too late for the British to withdraw. With Dentz's forces making a reasonable resistance, on 19 June de Gaulle met in Cairo with the autocratic British Ambassador Sir Miles Lampson in the presence of both Wavell and Catroux. They agreed – and the Foreign Office was accordingly advised – that the Free French would take over the administration of the protectorate after Dentz had surrendered, on two conditions: first, that independence would eventually be granted to Syria and Lebanon; and second, that no person or unit of the Vichy forces in Syria–Lebanon would be prosecuted or punished for their actions in the recent fighting. In addition, all captured or surrendered materiel must be handed over to the Allies. The Free French would be given every facility to encourage their surrendering comrades to change sides, with those refusing to do so being freely repatriated. De Gaulle's representative would be present at the armistice negotiations.[6]

De Gaulle then returned to Brazzaville, the 'capital of his empire', where he was horrified to discover that, although Dentz asked for an armistice via the US consul in Beirut on 18 June, combat continued for three further weeks without

Wilson sending any ultimatum to Beirut. Not until 14 July was an armistice signed at St-Jean-d'Acre in British-occupied Palestine (now Akko) with no representative of the Free French present. On the following day, de Gaulle discovered that the text of the armistice agreement contained none of the clauses he had agreed on 19 June because General Wilson had concluded a secret agreement with Dentz's representative, modifying the terms of the armistice.

Its wording was bitterly inappropriate for the anniversary of the storming of the Bastille, for the document held no mention of Free France and ignored completely Churchill's phrase in the letter of 7 August 1940: *His Majesty's Government is resolved, after the victory of Allied arms, to guarantee complete restoration of the independence and greatness of France*. After the armistice, not only were Free French officials denied access to the Syrian and Lebanese governments, de Gaulle's officers were not allowed to have contact with either the surrendered Vichy troops or the Lebanese and Syrian colonial units in French uniform. The ultimate lunacy in de Gaulle's eyes was that the Royal Navy was to permit transports sent by Admiral Darlan to conduct back to France or North Africa, *together with their personal weapons*, the thousands of trained soldiers in Syria/Lebanon whom the Allies might very well find themselves fighting a second time sooner or later. Additionally, the substantial stocks of materiel that had to be left behind were to be absorbed into British stores and not made available to the Free French, as he considered they should be under Article II of the protocol of 7 August 1940. Even General Spears, long weary of his go-between role, had to agree that this was absurd.

From Brazzaville, on behalf of the Empire Defence Council, de Gaulle denounced the armistice agreement on 16 July and flew back to Cairo, taking the opportunity to harangue every British diplomat at each stopover about the treachery of the Middle East Command. Churchill's personal representative in Cairo was Minister of State Resident Oliver Lyttelton, a smart moustached veteran of the First World War who had spent the intervening years in business until standing for Parliament in 1940. Lyttelton's only weapon to counter de Gaulle's severe displeasure was to argue that he had placed himself and his forces under British command. The immediate riposte was, 'Yes, for the purpose of fighting the common enemy, but when we eventually land in French territory, do you intend to use that clause to justify governing France?'[7] Lyttelton hedged. De Gaulle persisted: what authority had the British to promise national independence to territories of the Levant mandated to France by the League of Nations? The legal position was clear: independence could only be granted by an elected French government after the country was liberated. In the meantime, he was France – not an elected representative, perhaps, but the only Frenchman in authority free to make his own decisions, so long as Pétain's government was controlled by the Germans.

Like so many others in face-to-face argument with de Gaulle, Lyttelton dodged the bullets, replying that that he would pass on to London the points made. However, the armistice had been signed and must now be implemented. De Gaulle rightly riposted that neither he nor his representative had ratified it and Free France was therefore not bound by its terms. Furthermore, if in three days the armistice had not been revised, all Free French forces would cease to take orders from the British High Command and he would immediately order Catroux to take command of Syria and Lebanon using whatever force was necessary *against whatever forces sought to oppose him*. In addition, Free French units would be ordered to pursue contact with surrendered Vichy forces with a view to recruitment and taking over all their arms and equipment before it could be further sabotaged.

London's reply a few hours later was conciliatory: Lyttelton was empowered to write a letter there and then to the effect that Britain had no intention of usurping France's authority in the Levant. Mollified but not pacified, de Gaulle stood his ground until Lyttleton was authorised by London to write for him an 'interpretation' of the armistice agreement, confirming that Britain had no intention of interfering with French control of Syria/Lebanon under the League of Nations protectorate. To this, de Gaulle added a reiteration of the agreement reached with Sir Miles Lampson and Wavell.

On paper, an awkward situation had been resolved. However, on the ground British officers continued to obstruct their Free French allies, allowing Dentz to concentrate the majority of his surrendered forces at the port of Tripoli, ready for embarkation with their personal arms in transport ships sent by Darlan. While doing nothing to stop the Vichy forces destroying or sabotaging heavier weapons, stores and equipment, the British did prevent the Free French contacting their compatriots, with a view to recruiting those who did not wish to return to occupied France. The British attitude is all the more inexplicable after Dentz's bona fides were blown when it was discovered that fifty-five British officers taken prisoner in Syria had been despatched to France just a few hours before he demanded the ceasefire.[8] With Catroux installed in Beirut as High Commissioner for Syria/ Lebanon, Gaullist officials took over again the administration of the Levant against more or less continual obstruction by British troops. On one occasion Catroux was barred from entering his own HQ by an armed and over-zealous Australian sentry. The British brigade occupying the Jebel Druze region actively assumed command of the local troops until Monclar arrived on the scene and ordered his men to fire if fired upon, whereupon the British withdrew.[9] The anti-Gaullist attitude seems to have been a mix of the prevailing pro-Arab sentiments of many British officers compounded by the dislike of the War Office and Foreign Office of everything de Gaulle stood for. When he arrived in Beirut on 27 July, he was immediately aware that General Wilson's troops were ignoring completely his agreement with the British Government in the person of Lyttelton. This, they continued to do until 7 August and later, tearing down French flags on public buildings and resisting at gun point on occasion the reasonable efforts of the Free French to assume administrative responsibilities and avoid a vacuum after the departure of Vichy officials, although many of those remaining in the protectorate were reinstated for the simple reason that there was no one to replace them.

On 17 August de Gaulle informed Spears that the situation in Syria/Lebanon required reinforcements in the shape of the Free French parachute company still in Britain. Should the Air Ministry refuse to supply transport for them, the Admiralty could hardly fail to find accommodation to ship them out, given the enormous tonnage of French vessels requisitioned for Britain's use. It was a risky form of 'diplomacy' between allies, but he was pushed to it by the flagrant disregard of Free French authority throughout the invasion and occupation of Syria/Lebanon. However, if he expected Churchill's support in this, he was to be disappointed. Even for someone who crowded so much work into every twenty-four hours, squabbles in the Levant had a low priority compared with the prime minister's latest move to align the US ever more firmly against Germany.

Notes

1. A. Eden, *The Reckoning*, London, Cassell, 1965, p. 245
2. F. Kersaudy, *de Gaulle et Churchill*, Paris, Perrin Tempus, 2003, p. 130
3. Ibid., p. 129
4. W.S. Churchill, *The Second World War, Vol. 3: The Grand Alliance*, London, Penguin Classics, 2005, p. 289
5. Kersaudy, *de Gaulle et Churchill*, p. 136
6. C. de Gaulle, *Mémoires de Guerre: L'Appel 1940–42*, Paris, Plon, 1954, pp. 200–1
7. Ibid., p. 207
8. Kersaudy, *de Gaulle et Churchill*, p. 147
9. Ibid., p. 148

9

'LUNCH, OR A BATTLE – YOU CHOOSE!'

At a five-day conference with Roosevelt on board HMS *Prince of Wales* off the coast of Newfoundland, Churchill was obliged to put his signature to a joint declaration of intent on 14 August 1941. Known as the Atlantic Charter, it stated that neither Britain nor the United States sought any territorial expansion out of the war, nor would they impose any political changes without the free assent of the peoples concerned because every nation had the right to choose its own form of government. Sovereign rights and self-government would be restored to those who had been forcibly deprived of them and the seas would be made free for all. In addition, worldwide collaboration would improve labour standards, benefiting economic progress and social security. After the destruction of Nazi tyranny, the signatories would establish a peace under which all nations could live safely within their boundaries, without fear or want; pending a general renunciation of force, potential aggressors would be disarmed.

If that all sounded highly commendable, the sting came in the clause that the Atlantic partnership would promote equal access for all states to trade and to raw materials after the war. Whilst this too might seem an admirable aim, its implication was that the days of the British, French, Portuguese, Belgian and Dutch empires were numbered, not because it was immoral to hold colonial peoples in subjection, but because the European colonial powers maintained systems of imperial preference between the mother countries and their overseas colonies and dominions, which disadvantaged US manufacturing industries by imposing tariffs unfavourable to American products.

On his return to London, Churchill tried to pretend that the Atlantic Charter was 'primarily intended to apply to Europe',[1] but nowhere was this stated, and the Monroe Doctrine – still the basis of American foreign policy – only stated that the United States recognised and would not interfere with existing colonies and dependencies *in the western hemisphere.* There was therefore no precedent in US foreign policy inhibiting American interference in the eastern-hemisphere empires of the European countries with the aim of opening up vast new post-war markets for American manufactured goods.

Because of all these other concerns preoccupying Churchill, when de Gaulle's political secretary Maurice Dejean formally complained to Anthony Eden and Major Morton in London about the treatment meted out to the Free French in Syria/Lebanon, Eden and Morton confessed that the Cabinet had not been kept informed by Middle East Command. Although an internal Cabinet paper criticised Wavell for being over-generous to Dentz's negotiators, there were many in high places who considered that de Gaulle's lack of respect for Oliver Lyttelton and the office he held was intolerable, no matter the slights and hostility he had suffered. Lyttelton had written at length to Churchill his version of the confrontation, including Spears' and his own view that a complete rupture with the Free French forces was very much on the cards unless de Gaulle could be replaced as their leader. He ended, 'If this is diplomacy, I'm glad I chose another profession.'[2]

Despite everything, de Gaulle eventually claimed that 127 Vichy officers and 14,000 of their men changed sides, plus 290 officers and 14,000 men of the colonial troops, who had not been offered repatriation while 25,000 officers and men were repatriated under the protection of the White Ensign.[3] With this expanded manpower and the equipment that had been taken over, he had every justification in visiting Wavell's replacement in Cairo and assuring the new Commander-in-Chief Middle East General Claude Auchinleck that as soon as their training and regrouping was complete, he would again place his forces in the Middle East under British command *for the purpose of fighting the common enemy.* Auchinleck, still getting his feet under the desk, defused an awkward political situation by murmuring, 'Rommel will certainly provide the opportunity for that.'[4]

Returning to Brazzaville, de Gaulle decided once again to enlist public opinion on his side and gave an interview at the end of August to George Weller, a correspondent for the influential American newspaper *Chicago Daily News,* in which he announced that he had proposed to the USA that it should take over and use the ports of liberated French African territories, much as the British had swapped bases for obsolescent destroyers. The difference was that he asked for nothing in return except that the bases be used to block any German or Vichy French expansion in Africa. To Weller's question why the British Government had still not broken off relations with Vichy and recognised the Free French movement as the only true representatives of France, de Gaulle threw the cat among the pigeons by replying baldly that it was too scared of the French Fleet being placed under German control and would go to any lengths to avoid that possibility.

And yet, fourteen months after deserting his post in Bordeaux on 17 June 1940, the wall map in his office in Carlton Gardens told its own tale. He could congratulate himself on being the master of a vast empire and commander-in-chief of many thousands of men in Free French uniform fighting the Axis alongside soldiers from Britain and her Commonwealth and Empire. He had come a long way since the lonely flight from Bordeaux with Spears on that torrid day in June the previous year, but one thing had not changed: he was determined that his allies must accept him as the sole representative of France, never mind that both the State Department and the Foreign Office continued to deal with Pétain's government who, in his eyes, were just a bunch of traitors and opportunists.

On the downside, he had alienated most of the British officers and officials who had to work with him by his refusal to accept a subordinate role in the early days when his followers were just a few bewildered refugees. As he must have known, the substance of Weller's interview proved the final straw when it reached London, with its implication that Britain was somehow using Vichy as an intermediary for a deal with the Germans over the French Fleet. Churchill was furious when he read it, declaring that de Gaulle must be off his head, and it was time to replace him with a more malleable leader for the Free French.

Specific instructions were issued from Downing Street that the press should not even mention his return to Britain. All government departments were instructed to break off contact with the Gaullists. Nevertheless, individuals on both sides sought to alleviate the situation. Banned from using the BBC, the General retaliated by forbidding *any* Free French participation in its broadcasts. In Carlton Gardens and on his strolls in the neighbourhood, the source of all this dissension seemed blithely untroubled: he knew Churchill's volatile temperament rarely let his bad moods last for long. When Major Morton called at Carlton Gardens on 2 September, de Gaulle admitted that the prime minister had always treated him with great generosity; however, the same could not be said for his underlings. Generals Spears and Wilson were mentioned by name. When Morton referred to the famous cable summoning the paras to Syria, de Gaulle smiled disarmingly and excused himself by saying that he had been extremely angry at the time because of the way he and his movement – and by implication, France – were being treated by General Maitland Wilson's staff.

The thaw continued, Churchill agreeing to receive de Gaulle on 12 September. Shortly before the due time, he warned his personal private secretary Sir John Colville that he would rise to acknowledge de Gaulle's entrance into the Cabinet Room, but not shake his hand. Normally he could not be restrained from speaking his idiosyncratic French, but on this occasion to mark his displeasure, he would speak English and Colville would have to interpret. De Gaulle arrived promptly, as usual. Churchill waved his visitor to a seat on the other side of the conference table. De Gaulle sat, but said nothing, leaving his host to initiate the conversation:

Churchill:	'General de Gaulle, I asked you to come here this afternoon …'
Colville:	'Mon Général, je vous ai invité à venir cet après-midi …'
Churchill:	'I didn't say, mon Général. And I didn't say that I invited him.'

Colville sweated his way through multiple objections of the sort until it was de Gaulle's turn to speak. He, in turn, objected to Colville's translations, at which Churchill said that, if he could not do better, he should find someone else who could. Embarrassed, Colville left the Cabinet Room and summoned a Foreign Office colleague with perfect French. Meanwhile, neither Churchill nor de Gaulle uttered a word. The Foreign Office man fared no better, emerging from the Cabinet Room after only a few minutes as embarrassed as Colville had been, having been told by both men that he was a rotten interpreter and they would continue the discussion without him.

Churchill now laid into his guest for expressing anti-British sentiments in public and de Gaulle replied with his reasons for objecting to British policy in Syria/Lebanon, recounting many of the acts of hostility directed at himself and his men. To avoid future embarrassment, Churchill advised him to form an executive council that might restrain him from further undiplomatic utterances of the kind that had so upset everybody. After an hour, Colville grew worried and tried to listen to what was going on, but the doors of the Cabinet Room were made for privacy, and he could hear nothing through them. Eventually summoned, he entered the room to find the prime minister and his guest seated side by side, Churchill holding forth in French with gusto and de Gaulle making a fair show of enjoying one of his host's famous cigars.[5]

Whether he would have taken the advice to form an executive council is anyone's guess, but leaked details of the long discussion at No. 10 encouraged Admiral Muselier to plan a palace revolution. On 18 September he delivered to Carlton Gardens a demand that the movement be henceforth directed by a committee whose prior approval would be necessary before de Gaulle made any decisions or public announcements. In a private dining room at the Savoy Hotel next day, he assembled his closest followers together with a few British observers, including Major Morton, one of whom remarked afterwards that he had never known it took so much brandy to foment a revolution.

The plan hatched over the table in the Savoy was predictable: Muselier would become president of the committee packed with his supporters, reducing de Gaulle to a figurehead or honorary president without executive power. However, when Muselier and Labarthe visited him on 21 September in Carlton Gardens, he ignored their plan entirely. Announcing that the president of the new committee would be himself, he informed them coldly that they might sit on the committee but there would be no question of their appointees displacing officers loyal to himself, as they had planned.

They departed in a huff, learning next morning from Maurice Dejean that the names of the new council were about to be published and included none of Muselier's cabal. To this, Muselier retorted that 'his' Free French navy would have no more to do with de Gaulle, but work directly with the British Admiralty. De Gaulle's reaction was calm but firm: Muselier was informed that he had twenty-four hours to come to his senses, failing which he would be relieved of his command.

The same afternoon, de Gaulle informed Churchill of the composition of the new committee and also that Muselier's excessive personal ambition made him unacceptable as a member of it. Churchill requested that the announcement of the council members be delayed for twenty-four hours while various mediators scuttled back and forth between Downing Street, Muselier's HQ and Carlton Gardens. Finally, Muselier was back in the council, but without supporters. De Gaulle was satisfied so long as Muselier confined himself to commanding 'his' navy and refrained from plotting against him.

Slowly things settled down to an appearance of normalcy. To avoid a repeat of the Brazzaville incidents, Churchill had issued orders that de Gaulle should be denied facilities to leave the country but, since the General had no reason to do so, he may have been unaware of this. In particular, two small dots on the wall map nagged at him. Off the coast of Newfoundland are two tiny islands that are French territory. St Pierre and Miquelon had a combined population of 5,000 people with no love for their Vichy administrators. The islands also had a powerful radio transmitter that beamed anti-Gaullist propaganda into North America and could be used to transmit coded messages to U-boats enabling them to intercept Allied convoys, which made the British Admiralty favour de Gaulle's plan to liberate the islands and replace the Vichy administrators. Foreign Minister Anthony Eden nevertheless insisted that this could only be done with the prior approval of the governments of Canada and the US. From Ottawa came a swift go-ahead; from Washington, silence.

Once again, de Gaulle's overtures to Washington were blocked by the 70-year-old Secretary of State, Cordell Hull, who persisted in treating Vichy as the legitimate French Government. Also, Roosevelt had little respect for Europeans, never mind a French substantive colonel who had repeatedly bitten the hand that subsidised his movement. Having been assistant secretary for the navy, Roosevelt prided himself on his knowledge of geography, but neither he nor Hull had much understanding of European politics – as would become apparent when the war ended with Stalin having manoeuvred the White House into handing him on a plate a position of power in eastern and south-eastern Europe that he could never have won by force. Roosevelt's prejudices as far as France was concerned were doubly complicated by his having spent several holidays there as a boy, learning to speak reasonable French. He had chosen to spend part of his honeymoon there and confessed to liking the country, much as a tourist today might like Thailand or India without having any understanding or sympathy for the aspirations of their inhabitants.

And yet, one important threshold was crossed on 11 November when Washington announced that Free France was henceforth entitled to Lend-Lease facilities without using Britain as an intermediary – which may have been due to news from Vichy of Pétain's progressive knuckling down under the German yoke. The 100,000th French volunteer worker was just departing to work in the Reich, enticed by promises of higher pay and better food, and the Marshal was greeted by Goering at their meeting in St. Florentin with a shouted, 'Tell me, Marshal. Who won this war? You or us?' Visibly shaken by this gross discourtesy, Pétain replied with a quiet sarcasm that escaped Fat Hermann, 'I had not previously been quite so aware how badly we had been beaten.'[6]

History has a way of imposing itself – in this case, in the shape of the crippling aerial attack on the US Pacific Fleet at Pearl Harbor on 7 December 1941. The White House's consequent declaration of war on Japan and her Axis partners was what Churchill had been hoping for. De Gaulle had all along prophesied that this moment would be the beginning of Germany's defeat. At the same time, he remarked to his aide-de-camp Major Pierre Billotte that *active* US participation in the European war would place Britain in the position of a very junior partner, with Churchill's choices limited in future to the options approved by Washington.[7] Discussing the event with Colonel Passy, he looked even further into the future and foresaw the defeat of Germany as likely to be followed by armed confrontation between the US and the USSR – a war which, he thought, America might lose.[8] De Gaulle must have thought that the US declaration of war made him Roosevelt's ally. He was all the more angered when the US Navy requisitioned fourteen French vessels lying in American ports one week later. However, with the White House preoccupied elsewhere, for once he had both the Admiralty and the Foreign Office backing his plan to liberate St Pierre and Miquelon. Churchill even punned that it was time to remove Muselier's muzzle and let him get on with the job. Muselier was already in Halifax, Nova Scotia, ostensibly to inspect *Surcouf* and other French vessels on Atlantic convoy escort duty. He assembled three corvettes for the liberation of the islands but then got cold feet. A leak from the Foreign Office that the Canadian and US governments were about to land personnel on the islands to take over the radio transmitters came with the news that Washington, although at war with Germany and Italy, had no intention of breaking off relations with Vichy France and had in fact agreed with Pétain's High Commissioner for the French Antilles and Guyana to maintain the status quo in *all* French possessions in the western hemisphere. Muselier was ordered to go ahead.

Churchill arrived in Washington on 22 December for a strategic appreciation of the war in both hemispheres. Both Roosevelt and Cordell Hull greeted him warmly: their alliance was to be enshrined in the Declaration of the United Nations – by which term was meant the twenty-seven nations united against the Axis powers, but not including Free France. Christmas Eve was spent in the White House with Canadian Premier Mackenzie King, but on Christmas morning the mood changed with the arrival of a copied cable from Muselier to the Admiralty in London:

> I have the honour to inform you that, in compliance with the recent order from General de Gaulle and at the request of the inhabitants, I arrived this evening on the island of St. Pierre and have liberated the islands for Free France and the Allied cause. Enthusiastic reception.[9]

Roosevelt was furious that the man he regarded as an upstart general at best should have the effrontery to interfere in his backyard, i.e. the western hemisphere. Cordell Hull issued a broadside, referring insultingly to Muselier's force as the 'so-called Free French vessels'[10] and demanded what measures Mackenzie King's government intended to take to restore the status quo ante in the islands. Since they were neither US nor Canadian territory, but indubitably French possessions, the question was very interesting, in that it implied Washington had already decided that France would *not* have a Gaullist government after the war. A more proper stance would have been wait and see. King replied that Canadian public opinion was overwhelmingly pro de Gaulle and that there was nothing he could do about it.

Unfortunately for Hull, *New York Times* journalist Ira Wolfert had been with the invasion force and her despatches aroused an enormous wave of sympathy in the public for the plucky small force of Free French sailors who had carried out the operation.[11] Largely for this reason, both north and south of the forty-ninth parallel public opinion supported de Gaulle's initiative, as demonstrated when the State Department mail room was 'spammed' with thousands of letters addressed to the 'so-called State Department' or 'so-called Secretary of State Cordell Hull'.

Churchill's return journey was by way of Ottawa, where he delivered to the Canadian Parliament on 30 December a paean vaunting the courage of the Free French who had chosen the path of honour rather than prostrate themselves beneath the jackboot; he foresaw a post-war France taking again her rightful place among the great nations. Privately he warned de Gaulle that the action on St Pierre and Miquelon had earned him the bitter enmity of Roosevelt and Cordell Hull, who had threatened to resign. To soothe his wounded feelings, Roosevelt debated with Churchill whether the battleship *Arkansas* might be sent to force the Free French off the islands – or to blockade them and starve the Free French out. That this would have constituted a flagrant breach of French sovereignty seemed to occur to neither man: in their eyes anything happening in the Americas required the approval of Washington.

Churchill undertook to bring de Gaulle back into line, cabling Foreign Secretary Anthony Eden on 13 January that he must, by whatever means, persuade de Gaulle to back off in deference to the White House and Department of State. Poor Eden used his best endeavours, but to no avail. In de Gaulle's eyes, neither Roosevelt nor Hull had ever shown him the slightest courtesy in reply to his offers of port facilities in the Gaullist territories in Africa and in the Pacific and Indian oceans – of increasing strategic importance in the war against Japan – let alone the substantial deposits of nickel in New Caledonia that could be exploited by the US armament industries. When Eden warned him that Washington was on the point of despatching a cruiser and two destroyers to eject Muselier's small force from the islands, the General replied calmly that the US Navy vessels would have to stop at the limit of territorial waters 20 nautical miles offshore, after which Muselier would be delighted to entertain the American admiral to an excellent lunch.

'And if the cruiser does not stop at the limit?' Eden asked.

'Our people will give the customary warnings.'

'And if the Americans continue?'

'It would be most unfortunate, because then our people would have to open fire!'[12]

Eden threw up his hands in horror, at which point, as so often when he held a winning hand, de Gaulle became amenable; it was adversity that made him impossible to deal with. The compromise reached was that Muselier and his force would evacuate the islands *on paper and for official consumption only*. The secret clauses of Eden's deal were that the ships would leave, but the admiral and the Free French marines would stay on the islands to participate in their administration and guarantee their security. Churchill was furious that de Gaulle had not given way 100 per cent to Roosevelt and Hull, and continued to press him for this after his return to Britain. It was an extraordinary performance in the middle of the greatest war the world had known: the prime minister of Great Britain humiliating himself by reneging on his own agreement of 7 August 1940 over French sovereignty and relentlessly bullying de Gaulle – essentially in order to save face for the American secretary of state, since there was no other issue at stake.

At the end of February, Muselier returned to Britain and a triumphant welcome from the Free French, which made him more difficult than before. When he resigned from the Committee, de Gaulle ignored his threat to take 'his' fleet with him. The War Cabinet then wasted forty-five minutes discussing this before charging Eden with forcing de Gaulle to reinstate his admiral. De Gaulle replied blandly that Muselier was a drug-addicted meddler, to whom he was giving thirty days' sick leave on condition that he avoided any contact with the Free French navy. Muselier did not comply, and was given thirty days' house arrest. When the Admiralty took his side in the dispute despite the British Government having specifically agreed that French discipline was an internal matter, de Gaulle broke off relations entirely, withdrawing to the country. Told by an aide that his hosts considered him impossible to deal with, he replied sniffily, 'If I wasn't, I'd be serving on Pétain's staff at this very moment.'[13] Thanks largely to Eden's mediation, reason prevailed at last. On 23 March the War Cabinet backed de Gaulle against his recalcitrant admiral and Muselier disappeared into the limbo reserved for those who gamble for the highest stakes and lose everything.

What had de Gaulle gained by the affair of St Pierre and Miquelon?

By deliberately going against the wishes of the US Government, which considered the entire western hemisphere its own sphere of influence, he had shown the world – as pointedly as Churchill had at Mers el-Kebir, but without bloodshed in this case – that he would stop at nothing to gain his avowed end of seeing every inch of French territory liberated from control by Vichy.

Notes

1. D. Judd, *The Lion and the Tiger*, Oxford, OUP, 2004, p. 159
2. F. Kersaudy, *de Gaulle et Churchill*, Paris, Perrin Tempus, 2003, pp. 149–51
3. C. de Gaulle, *Mémoires de Guerre: L'Appel 1940–42*, Paris, Plon, 1954, p. 217
4. Ibid., pp. 199–224
5. Kersaudy, *de Gaulle et Churchill*, pp. 159–65
6. D. Boyd, *Voices from the Dark Years*, Thrupp, Sutton, 2007, p. 139
7. P. Billotte, *Le Temps des Armes*, Paris, Plon, 1972, p. 187
8. Kersaudy, *de Gaulle et Churchill*, p. 174
9. Ibid., p. 177
10. C. Williams, *The Last Great Frenchman*, London, Little Brown, 1994, p. 168
11. Ibid., p. 169
12. De Gaulle, *L'Appel*, pp. 238–32. A fuller account is to be found in Kersaudy, *de Gaulle et Churchill*, pp. 181–82
13. ed. M. Jullian, *de Gaulle – Traits d'esprit*, Paris, Cherche-Midi, 2000, p. 91

PART 2

FIGHTING FOR FRANCE

10

ASSASSINATION AND OUTRAGE

The spring of 1942 saw the Wehrmacht and Himmler's parallel army the Waffen SS on the offensive everywhere from Libya to the USSR. In the east, new Axis partner Japan had captured two proud bastions of the British Empire: December saw the fall of Hong Kong and in January the Malay Peninsula was overrun, with Fortress Singapore surrendering humiliatingly. Australia was pleading for US troops to stave off a probable invasion of her sparsely populated northern coastline. While few Asians were taken in by the propaganda from Tokyo about the vaunted 'Co-Prosperity Sphere', in which they were all going to share out the wealth of the European colonial exploiters, it was obvious that the sands of time were running out for the white races as masters of the Asian continent. Even the long-entrenched British in the mighty Raj awoke to the unthinkable threat on her eastern flanks as the Japanese headed into Burma.

In Libya the Free French were making their biggest contribution so far to the Allied efforts to keep Rommel out of Egypt. Assigned on 4 February to the 'box' of Bir Hakeim in Libya, 13 DBLE under Brigadier Koenig held out against vastly superior odds for four months in night-time temperatures below freezing and daytime temperatures around 50°C, with rations running short after the box was encircled. Even water had to be air-dropped in whenever there was a let-up between raids by the Italian and German air forces. It was, as someone remarked at the time, not a job one would wish on one's best friend, but at Bir Hakeim, and the following battle of El Himeimat, Auchinleck seems to have regarded his French officers and men as expendable.[1]

Maurice Schumann recalled the evening of the break-out from Bir Hakeim. He was walking through the blackout along a London street with the General when they were accosted by two French prostitutes. One of them produced a photo of de Gaulle from her handbag, which, for once, he agreed to autograph. Schumann recalled him writing on it, *To Madame X, working for the Entente Cordiale.*[2]

Denied any consultation over the Western Desert campaign or any other theatre of operations and not allowed by Churchill to leave Britain after the affair of St Pierre and Miquelon in case he irritated Washington again, de Gaulle continued working on his long-term aim of detaching from Vichy all the French overseas territories. The world's largest island, Madagascar had been recognised by Britain as a French protectorate since 1890 and was thinly occupied by forces loyal to Vichy. In February and again in April 1942 he submitted detailed plans for the invasion of the island by Free French forces transported and supported by the Royal Navy. Before the final split with Muselier, he had intended the meddling admiral to command the liberation of the island and then be awarded its governorship to keep him out of the way.

Given the lightning advance of the Japanese in Asia and the strategic usefulness for both German and Japanese submarines and armed raiders disguised as merchant vessels of the ports on this huge island, separated from the coast of southeast Africa by the 250-mile-wide Mozambique Channel, one might have thought that reclaiming Madagascar from its Vichy administration under Gouverneur Général Annet would have had a high priority at least from her lordships of the Admiralty as protectors of merchant shipping. Unfortunately, both there and at the War Office a whisper of 'Dakar' or 'Levant' was enough to kill any prospect of another Franco-British combined operation.

De Gaulle's plans were consigned to filing cabinets, but his strategic point had been taken, with the result that some effort was put into planning a British takeover of the island. Churchill apparently thought it would be a pushover – some said, because his wife Clementine had once met Annet on a train and thought him a charming man!

Thus was under-resourced Operation *Ironclad* launched on 5 May, securing the naval base of Diego Suarez[3] on the northern tip of the island two days later. The Admiralty could be happy at having so easily attained its primary objective but apparently no one had given much thought to occupying even the main towns of this island with its 2,480 miles of coastline and a span of nearly 1,000 miles north to south by 350 miles east to west. Querying his further instructions, Admiral Syfret commanding the operation was ordered to work out a modus vivendi with Annet's officials, whereby they could continue to run the rest of the island, leaving him in control of its principal naval port.

De Gaulle learned of *Ironclad* when a press agency called him at 3 a.m. on 5 May to ascertain his reaction. That is not hard to imagine, nor is the language in which he couched it. This time, it was he who refused to speak to his British contacts. Finally persuaded to see Foreign Secretary Eden on 11 May, he tried to turn the insult into an opportunity by offering Free French help in persuading Annet to change sides and bring the manpower of the island into the war on the Allied side. For linguistic reasons alone, that seemed a good idea. When it was rejected, de Gaulle announced that he intended to return to Free French Africa since he was wasting his time in Britain, but Churchill refused to hear of it, since *Ironclad* had given his troublesome guest more reason than ever to suspect Britain's motives in the French colonies. Eden's diplomatic way of conveying what amounted to a form of house arrest was to pretend that a critical stage in the war required de Gaulle to be available for consultation in London. Apparently mollified, de Gaulle agreed to defer his departure by six weeks, but meantime learned that a joint Anglo-American operation against Dakar and French Niger was being planned – with the exclusion of Free French forces. Oil was not exactly poured on the troubled waters between Carlton Gardens and Downing Street when the US Government invited Vichy's military attachés in Washington to the 30 May Memorial Day ceremony at Arlington National Cemetery in Virginia, while ignoring the Free French representatives who wore the same uniform as the heroes fighting for their lives in the Allied cause at Bir Hakeim.

On 10 June, only hours after Koenig had extricated most of his men, including the wounded, from the encircled box and through the minefields to safety by night, de Gaulle was invited to Downing Street to be congratulated on the magnificent feat of arms his men had just achieved. Churchill excused the taking of Diego Suarez without consultation as being due to American insistence that the French not be involved but promised that Britain had no long-term designs on Madagascar. That, de Gaulle retorted, overlooked entirely that his plans were to secure the whole island and use its vast reserves of manpower for the common good, whereas British and American policy of accommodating Vichy both in France and overseas was severely damaging the Allied image in the eyes of uncommitted French people.

Churchill attempted to excuse the American policy by saying that Hull and Roosevelt hoped it would one day pay off by encouraging Pétain to re-declare war on Germany. This was a nonsense that de Gaulle refused to take seriously. Even Admiral Leahy, Roosevelt's obsessively pro-Pétain ambassador in Vichy, ought to have realised that the marshal would have been mad even to consider re-entering the conflict while the better part of 2 million of his soldiers were locked up in German POW camps. It would, in any event, have been logistically impossible for him to declare war against the occupation forces whose heavy hand lay over three-fifths of his country, including most of its mineral resources and heavy industry, while the Axis controlled the Mediterranean and the Vichy navy was immobilised in ports under enemy surveillance. As to the vast reserves of manpower sitting out the war in French North Africa, Weygand and the other commanders had several times rejected invitations to bring their forces over to the Allies. Conversely, when British and American fears of Vichy handing the fleet over to the Germans were voiced, de Gaulle pointed out that the risk was illusory because combat with Dentz's forces in the Levant had lasted nearly seven weeks, during which Pétain could have declared war on the invaders of Syria/Lebanon or handed Darlan's fleet over to Hitler in protest, yet he had done neither.

Churchill had to admit that his visitor was kept up to date by his sources in mainland France, which gave de Gaulle an opening to protest at the indifferent British support for Gaullist resistance operations in France. His appeal of 18 June had said that the flame of French resistance – with a small 'r' – must not go out, but even he had to admit that the flame flickered faintly in the gloom for the first months of the Occupation. Yet, even those obstinately courageous individuals who were actively gathering intelligence received little help from London, while most of the information they garnered at risk of their lives and liberty about German dispositions, fortifications and movements of troops and vessels including submarines was filed away after reaching Britain marked *Unreliable* because SOE believed that it was too good to be true and must be bait fed by the Germans in some devious double game.

Paranoia is the occupational disease of intelligence officers, but the lack of action taken on all this hard-won intelligence was extremely demoralising for the men and women in France fighting the German occupiers.

Dewavrin now used the *nom de guerre* 'Colonel Passy'. His intelligence service, which ran the many small RF (République Française) networks in France, was dependent on the British supplying the aircraft for dropping arms, supplies and agents into France and collecting agents for consultation in London, as well as the small boats for dropping agents on the Brittany coast and supplies of French currency, transmitters, arms and ammunition. Each time relations between the British Government and the Free French cooled, Passy's men saw urgently needed aircraft inexplicably grounded, boats allegedly undergoing repair, crews unavailable and supplies drying up overnight. Their colleagues in Colonel Maurice Buckmaster's Section F of Special Operations Executive suspected that the RF networks in France were riddled with double agents and therefore mistrusted everything emanating from them. On occasion, they also subverted Passy's agents for their own ends.

There were in France three sets of resistance networks, each with its own agenda, a situation that led to internecine conflict and betrayals. Those run by Passy were working for an eventual liberation and restoration of French independence. Those run by Buckmaster were gathering intelligence for British strategic warfare. The communists, having been driven underground during the phoney war after being banned for their defeatist activities, were the best-organised clandestine group because they had already formed into cells that limited damage in the event of capture. They had, however, been pro-German from the start of the war until 22 June 1941 when Hitler invaded the Soviet Union after tearing up the Molotov-Ribbentrop Non-Aggression Pact. Since then they took their orders from Moscow and pursued a policy of assassinations of German personnel and sabotage that had nothing to do with the liberation of France and everything to do with keeping on garrison duty there entire divisions of the Wehrmacht that Hitler might otherwise have posted to the Eastern Front.

At the beginning of 1942 de Gaulle had looked ahead to the eventual invasion of France and determined to bring together as many as possible of the different groups to form a cohesive 'army of the interior' that could be a real factor in the difficult task of wresting a bridgehead from troops who would have had several years to prepare their defences and tactics by the time the Allied build-up made a successful invasion of Normandy possible. Hitler's Atlantic Wall – a chain of bunkers, minefields and anti-landing devices covering all possible landing sites – was gradually stretching westwards from the Belgian frontier along the Channel and from there down the Atlantic coast to Spain. Softening that up would be a job for the bombers and heavy naval guns of the invasion forces, but preventing reinforcements from arriving at the bridgeheads after the first landings was a job for the Resistance, using sabotage and effective intelligence gathering to identify strategic bombing targets such as petrol and ammunition dumps, communications centres and armoured units vulnerable to air attack while being transported to the front.

The secondary purpose of the 'home army' was to counter-balance the communists in the power vacuum when Vichy's infrastructure crumbled after the invasion, but it could only do this if all the other movements were united. De Gaulle therefore despatched into France on the night of 1 January 1942 an able negotiator tasked with welding the disparate Resistance groups into a clandestine army, using persuasion and bribery in the form of money and deliveries of the arms, ammunition and explosives without which they could not function. Jean Moulin had been the youngest prefect in France. Under his alias as 'Max', an art dealer with a legitimate gallery in Nice, he was to prove the right man for the job, his undoubted competence being marred only by a fatal over-confidence that would lead to his arrest, torture and death.

When the Free French sources in Washington later learned of American intentions to impose on liberated France, Belgium and Holland an American-dominated Allied Military Government of Occupied Territories (or AMGOT in the jargon of the day) a unified command of the non-communist Resistance movements became even more important to de Gaulle, who saw AMGOT as an error of thinking which was likely to drive many people into the communists' arms for a second war of liberation, this time against the Allied occupiers.

Catroux and others had indicated to British contacts that ignoring de Gaulle was a way of insulting an ally, whether intentionally or not. On the other hand, they said, the General's wounded vanity would respond favourably to any massaging of his ego. Charles Peake, Churchill's replacement of General Spears as liaison officer with the Gaullist National Committee, also argued that there were good reasons for listening to the opinions of the one senior French officer who had never been wrong in this war. Unfortunately, the Anglo-Saxons – as de Gaulle called them – have never been good at French psychology and the advice had passed unheeded until now. It seems to have been Eden who not only used the idea of consultation in London as a cover-up for Churchill's refusal to let de Gaulle out of the country but also brought pressure on the chiefs of staff to at least go through the motions of consulting de Gaulle. Overnight the carping and criticism of his hosts ceased so that by the end of July de Gaulle was informed that there was no reason to prevent him returning to Africa.

He was still there in September, by which time the planning of Operation *Torch*, a largely American invasion of French North Africa, had reached a critical stage. Aware that no one would be able to control his outspoken reaction to the exclusion of Free French troops if he was still in West Africa when the attack went in, Churchill invited de Gaulle to return to Britain, intending to acquaint him with the plans for *Torch* shortly before the date of the invasion. Forbidden to do this by Roosevelt, he devised a sop in the shape of Madagascar. Thus on 6 November Eden called on de Gaulle and informed him that it had been decided to hand the island over to the Free French. De Gaulle was neither stupid nor as ill-informed as Washington would have liked but Madagascar was a prize worth having.

On 8 November 1942 Anglo-American forces under the command of Lieutenant General Dwight D. Eisenhower landed at eight places on the coasts of Morocco and Algeria. Nine thousand men and sixty-five tanks went ashore at Mehdia to secure the airbase at Port Lyautey. To take Casablanca from north and south, 19,000 men and another sixty-five tanks disembarked at Fedala and 6,500 men with 108 tanks at Safi. Air cover was given by 172 aircraft flying off the carriers. Roosevelt had wanted to keep this an exclusively American enterprise but, since his troops were unblooded and fresh from training camps, he had been persuaded to accept the participation of battle-experienced British personnel, though not of Fighting French officers and men who were both experienced in combat and knew the country well. The depth of ignorance in Washington of the situation in North Africa was such that even US diplomat Robert Murphy, stationed in Algeria, was moved to note that Eisenhower's staff seemed to think they were invading 'a primitive country of mud huts deep in the jungle'[4] and not a developed and complex society where 300,000 trained soldiers with modern weapons awaited them.

Awoken at 6 a.m. by Colonel Billotte with the news of the landings in Morocco, de Gaulle arrived at Downing Street six hours later to be greeted by an apologetic Churchill, who was surprised at his guest's positive attitude and even more surprised at the text of the speech the General made over the BBC that evening, exhorting every French citizen in North Africa to aid the Allies who had landed there as a first step to the liberation of France.

Once again General Noguès remained loyal to Pétain and gave orders to reduce the Allied bridgeheads. At Casablanca the fighting continued for three days and US General George Patton was only restrained from ordering the bombardment of the city itself by the last-minute surrender of Noguès' troops there. The battleship *Jean Bart*, however, continued firing until silenced by American air strikes. The architect of *Torch* was Roosevelt's man Robert Murphy, who, in various diplomatic posts and latterly as 'consul' in Oran, had attempted to enlist Weygand and several other generals to bring the Vichy forces over to the Allies at the moment of the invasion. None had actually agreed, although General Henri Giraud had been smuggled out of the Free Zone aboard the submarine HMS *Seraph* and transported to Gibraltar under the impression that he was to be commander-in-chief of the invasion forces both in North Africa and in France. Giraud's ambition was to be frustrated: told that the invasion would be commanded by General Dwight D. Eisenhower, he was offered instead command of all French forces in North Africa *after* the invasion, which he refused.

All the plans changed at the last moment, due to the presence in Oran of Admiral Darlan, whose son was in hospital there, suffering from poliomyelitis, at the time of the invasion.[5] Murphy therefore concluded a deal with him for Darlan to take command of all Vichy forces in North Africa on condition that he ordered an immediate ceasefire. On the morning of 10 November, the deal was done. Twenty-four hours later, the German forces in France crossed the Demarcation Line and occupied what had been the Free Zone, to secure the now vulnerable French Mediterranean littoral. On 13 November, Darlan's appointment as High Commissioner for North Africa, acting 'in the Marshal's name', was recognised by Noguès, with Giraud appointed commander-in-chief of the armed forces. In London, the news of Darlan's appointment was greeted with disgust and incredulity by de Gaulle and all the émigré governments in exile. The British and American press openly disapproved of the Roosevelt administration giving power to the man who had been Pétain's prime minister until ousted by Laval, calling him 'America's first Quisling' and 'one of the greatest living traitors'. Even the staid *The Times* in London evoked the admiral's undeniable record of collaboration. Winston Churchill said publicly that he ought to be shot.

Whether the fact that Darlan's son had contracted polio gave him some special status in the eyes of Roosevelt, who had been crippled by the disease in 1921, is impossible to ascertain. It was hardly a question de Gaulle could raise in a long letter to Roosevelt, pleading for a revision in his attitude to Fighting France. The White House made only an oblique response: at the presidential press conference on 1 December, Roosevelt, who was trying to repair his public image by placing responsibility for the deal with Darlan firmly on Cordell Hull's shoulders, said that he had not invited de Gaulle to come to Washington but, if he did come of his own accord, he would agree to see him, 'preferably after 8 January'. It was hardly the tone to adopt after the three most important Resistance organisations in the southern zone had written to London a letter signed jointly with four political parties and three trade unions confirming that as 'General de Gaulle is the uncontested head of the Resistance … we demand that the destiny of French North Africa be immediately entrusted to him'.[6] The BBC refused to transmit the text of the message.

Whatever the reasons for Roosevelt's endorsement of Admiral Darlan, Washington's embarrassment was to be ended with Shakespearean drama shrouded with mystery. While others expressed their dissatisfaction with Roosevelt's protégé verbally, a group of young men who had been working under General d'Astier de la Vigerie in the North African Resistance decided to form the Corps Franc d'Afrique and take action in protest against the Americans keeping in place the same generals who had handed Tunisia over to the Germans without a shot being fired. On Christmas Eve, d'Astier de la Vigerie flew off to London for consultations and landed to hear the news that Darlan had just been assassinated by 20-year-old Fernand Bonnier de la Chapelle, who had literally picked the short straw when a group of the Corps Franc d'Afrique planned the attack.

The fairness of his court martial was seriously prejudiced by the fact that his coffin was ordered before the evidence was heard. Giraud refused to allow any appeal against its verdict: guilty. Darlan's unfortunate assassin was shot immediately afterwards before it could be established who had ordered the assassination. Although the Gaullists were blamed for organising the killing, so too were the royalists in Oran who supported the Count of Paris as pretender to the throne of France. To complicate things further, since Bonnier had been among the young men given weapons training by Murphy's contacts in the OSS, some people wondered whether the real motive for the killing was to remove Darlan from the board after he had served his purpose as interim governor of North Africa and thus enable Hull and Roosevelt to live down the embarrassment of having backed so ardent a Pétainist.

General Giraud now moved up with the blessing of the Americans to take over Darlan's post, while still keeping command of all French forces in North Africa. As far as the inhabitants of the territories were concerned, nothing had changed since before the invasion. Vichy's men were still in office. The Marshal's photographs were everywhere displayed in public buildings and even officers' messes. The paramilitary Pétainist Service d'Ordre Légionnaire openly patrolled the main towns 'to keep public order'. The media were openly anti-Gaullist and anti-Allied. Pétain's legislation dispossessing Jews and communists remained in force and was even extended, Jews being forbidden to serve as officers in the armed forces so that they could not later use their military citations, decorations or wounds to justify restitution of French citizenship.[7] Young résistants who had acted as guides for the Allied troops and those who had taken part in the uprising that seized Algiers on 8 November were thrown into prison as traitors and Giraud approved the award of the Croix de Guerre for soldiers who had killed some of the volunteer guides in combat.[8]

Twenty-seven key figures in the North African Resistance were despatched to a punishment camp in the Sahara under atrocious conditions. Estimates vary as to the exact number of patriots held in prison and internment camps, but there were somewhere between 8,000 and 25,000 held under Vichy laws for 'crimes' such as having been Freemasons, or being Jewish or simply being pro-de Gaulle. A furious de Gaulle confided in Charles Peake that he intended disbanding Fighting France if something were not done about this scandalous state of affairs. There was even talk of moving his headquarters to Moscow and transporting his forces to the eastern front. Having served under Giraud in Metz at the start of the war, de Gaulle knew him to be a competent soldier who was totally lacking in political sense. To resolve the appalling situation in Algeria, on 25 December he sent a cable offering to place all his forces under Giraud's command and suggesting a meeting in North Africa or Chad. With no reply from Giraud, his request for a plane in which to leave Britain was blocked because of 'bad weather' – in fact because Churchill refused to be party to any move against Washington's intention to govern French North Africa through Giraud and the former Vichy administration.

De Gaulle was immobilised but not muzzled. His broadcast of 28 December made public the way in which Fighting France was being kept at arm's length while Eisenhower's staff continued to deal with a *second* commander in North Africa who made no secret that he regarded himself as Pétain's representative there. In the names of the National Committee and the Committee for the Defence of the Empire, de Gaulle called upon Giraud to meet him without delay to examine how to integrate their forces in keeping with the democratic traditions of the Republic and how they could work together until France once again had an elected government. The final straw was Giraud's cold rejection of his offer: a cable arrived on 29 December stating that the moment was not propitious for a meeting because of the 'profound emotion in both military and civilian circles due to the assassination (of Darlan)'.[9]

De Gaulle therefore issued a communiqué on 2 January 1943, stating openly that Fighting France was being deliberately kept out of the liberated French territories of North Africa. Churchill tried to stop publication, but the best Sir Alexander Cadogan at the Foreign Office could achieve was to have several phrases toned down. The cat was out of the bag with a vengeance. After questions were asked in the House, the press on both sides of the Atlantic seized on the communiqué, provoking a deluge of critical mail addressed to the State Department and White House, which made the reaction to Hull's gaffe over St Pierre and Miquelon seem nothing by comparison.

At this juncture Foreign Secretary Anthony Eden found himself in open conflict with his American opposite number who accused the British Government of encouraging de Gaulle's anti-American propaganda. Mainly to have a voice in Eisenhower's councils at Allied Forces HQ, Churchill detached Harold Macmillan from the Ministry of Supply and sent him to Algiers as Minister Resident. It was also understood that Macmillan would attempt to reduce friction between de Gaulle and Giraud. To avoid being treated as an interfering Brit by the Americans, Macmillan spent the first months in what he termed masterly inactivity, pretending to regard the posting as a sinecure while making it his business to get to know the key players on a friendly basis.

For London and Washington, this was at the turning point in the war. In the Pacific, the Japanese had suffered their first major defeat at Guadalcanal. In Russia, Field Marshal von Paulus had surrendered at Stalingrad, where Axis losses included 800,000 dead. In North Africa, the British had taken Tripoli and were advancing westwards, while the Anglo-American forces in Algeria were pressing eastwards towards Tunis and Bizerta, squeezing the Axis forces between them. Yet, de Gaulle's war – to liberate France – seemed no nearer victory. He did not consider French North Africa liberated, either. In his eyes, it was under occupation by American troops and administered by officials still loyal to Vichy, both elements equally hostile to Fighting France. In the USA the job of his several representatives had been complicated since December 1942 by the presence of a separate diplomatic mission sent by Giraud, still the candidate of choice in the White House, despite everyone who had to deal with him agreeing that he had not the slightest talent for administration and was politically a dead loss.[10] To de Gaulle, it was small consolation that a Free French administration took office in Madagascar on 8 January.

Churchill, however, considered that this sop to de Gaulle obliged him to come to heel and that the top secret summit conference planned to take place at Casablanca would be the ideal context in which to bring together the two French generals, under conditions where they could not refuse to get along with each other. He arrived in the high-security zone in the Casablanca suburb of Anfa on 13 January, one day before Roosevelt, who landed in a strange mood. It was the first time he had flown since taking office and the clandestine departure from Washington made him feel that he was on holiday, having escaped the heavy burdens of running a country at war and being the chief executive of the armed forces. Murphy was not alone at the conference in noting the president's almost schoolboyish refusal to take seriously some of the important issues to be discussed.

Eisenhower also noted that his president talked as though he could arbitrarily impose his will on the French and other inhabitants of an occupied enemy country, whereas local policy was to encourage cooperation with the existing infrastructure of French North Africa and avoid situations that would divert a part of the Anglo-American expeditionary force being used to maintain civil order. Roosevelt's attitude was due less to confusion than to his obsession with decolonisation. It was a strange priority at this crucial stage of a world war, when every ally was precious and de Gaulle's political star was in the ascendant both inside France and abroad. The president's son Elliot was the confidant that evening to whom he expanded on the same theme – in this case holding that the millions of inhabitants of India should be allowed to choose whether to remain within the British Empire or achieve complete independence.[11]

Criticism in the American press of FDR's and Hull's policy in North Africa inclined him to agree with Churchill that it was important to unify the mutually hostile French factions outside France. The difference was that Churchill knew this would be a delicate task, whereas Roosevelt regarded it with a frivolity that boded ill for the outcome. They were, he said, marriage brokers bringing together Giraud the groom and de Gaulle the bride. All Murphy had to do was to bring Giraud from Algiers while Churchill told de Gaulle to come from London, after which the US president would unite them in marital harmony. However difficult 'the bride' might have been in the past, how could she quibble when the world's most powerful man told her to accept the match that had been arranged? And once the 'marriage' had been concluded, all the irritating critics would have to change their tune.

On 16 June, Churchill cabled de Gaulle to join him in Morocco for a meeting with Giraud and to bring General Catroux with him. Giraud's first meeting with Roosevelt on the following day was superficially a great success, with the president expressing his intention for Giraud to continue as head of the French armed forces in North Africa, with de Gaulle and his second-in-command and a third, political, Frenchman acting as civil governor of French North Africa. Giraud asked for arms and materiel to equip 300,000 men and thought this had been agreed.

After the meeting, however, Roosevelt shrewdly summed up the man he had just met as a poor administrator and no political leader – in short, a 'rotten plank', on which Murphy had chosen to take his stand.[12] Poor Murphy came in for quite a lot of stick. He was accused by Roosevelt of causing serious embarrassment by putting in writing that the US would restore the French Empire after the war. His loyalty perhaps affected by this unjust criticism, he noted that the president no longer had the triumphant smile familiar to all the world from his photocalls, but was:

> a very sick man in a wheelchair with grey and ravaged face and trembling hands. From time to time, with visible effort ... he could produce his famous smile but a minute later his face fell like a curtain'.[13]

De Gaulle, having just received from Giraud a second rejection of his offer to meet, was summoned on 17 January to the Foreign Office, where Eden and Cadogan showed him the cable from Churchill in Anfa. De Gaulle read it in silence. Meeting Giraud as Frenchman to Frenchman was one thing. Being sent for like a lackey to meet him in the context of an Anglo-American summit conference where his hands would be tied and his options restricted was altogether different. Eden tried to smooth things over by saying that the prime minister had gone to great lengths to arrange the meeting, to which de Gaulle riposted that there were only two French authorities: Vichy and himself. Giraud, he said, represented no one and nothing. It was a discreet way of reminding his listeners that, if he were now to break off relations with the British Government, a large part of their intelligence operation in occupied France would cease working overnight.

In any case, de Gaulle said, he would need to consult the National Committee before replying to Churchill's summons. He returned at 5 p.m. – without consulting the committee – to hand Eden a politely worded refusal to go to Morocco, based largely on the argument that Giraud had rejected his overtures but in fact to make the point that he was no one's dog to come running when called. In Anfa, Churchill was mortified by the refusal of the man Roosevelt regarded as his client. Roosevelt's jocular reaction was to cable Eden, 'I've brought the groom. Where's the bride?' Cordell Hull also received a cable in these terms, referring to the General as 'Lady de Gaulle', as though he were a capricious young girl refusing to marry her wise father's choice of partner.[14] Observing these reactions at close hand, Murphy detected his president's scarcely veiled amusement at Churchill's discomfiture.

The prime minister was caught between two fires but adroitly set the bait he felt sure would bring de Gaulle to heel by cabling Eden to inform him that decisions were being taken which would affect the future of French North Africa. Since they would not be changed later, he would find himself regretting his rejection of the invitation to participate in them. Eden received the cable on the morning of 19 January and read it that afternoon to a Cabinet meeting, whose consensus was that parliamentary and public opinion would not react favourably to any pressure *forcing* de Gaulle to go to Anfa. Yet, if he did not go, the prime minister's wrath would fall on them all. It was decided to pass the essence of Churchill's message on to de Gaulle, but in a more diplomatic wording.

This time the General did inform the Committee, explaining that he had no intention of going where he would be unable to talk privately with Giraud, but would be under pressure from the British and American leaders. However, Catroux, Pleven and others disagreed so strongly that the eventual consensus was for acceptance of the invitation. The reply handed to Eden on the evening of 20 January was a grudging acceptance, making the point that its recipient was coming to a meeting of whose agenda he had not been informed after being expressly ignored on all matters relating to French North Africa until then.

He was coming therefore in the interests of France and the French Empire and because the course of the war demanded it. When Churchill arrived later that evening with this news at Roosevelt's villa, the president's cold silence was followed by a murmur of congratulations as he headed for his bedroom.[15]

De Gaulle arrived with his entourage at Anfa in a foul mood because there had been no guard of honour to salute him at Casablanca airport, guarded by American soldiers with not a single French uniform in sight. He had been driven in an American car whose windows were covered in mud as a security precaution to a requisitioned villa within the high-security zone, which his hosts pretended was the property of a Scandinavian expat after he had been furious at the idea that French citizens should have their property requisitioned by foreigners. Invited to dinner at Giraud's neighbouring villa, he refused to eat until the American sentries there were replaced by French ones. In the high-security zone, he felt himself Roosevelt's prisoner, and had no doubt that this was his host's intention. It was, he wrote later, an outrage to behave towards him in this way on French soil.[16]

Notes

1. For a more detailed account of Bir Hakeim and El Himeimat, see D. Boyd, *The French Foreign Legion*, Thrupp, Sutton, 2006, pp. 268–77
2. ed. M. Jullian, *de Gaulle – Traits d'esprit*, Paris, Cherche-Midi, 2000, p. 81
3. Now Antsiranana
4. R. Murphy, *Diplomat among Warriors*, London, Collins, 1964, p. 135
5. A. Beevor & A. Cooper, *Paris after the Liberation*, London, Hamish Hamilton, 1994, p. 20
6. F. Kersaudy, *de Gaulle et Roosevelt – Le Duel au Sommet*, Paris, Perrin, 2006, p. 187
7. General Giraud's 'Note de service' No12/1 of 15 November 1942 and 'Note de service' No. 40 C.MAGP/CAB. of 30 January 1943 signed by General Prioux
8. H. Macmillan, *War Diaries*, London, Papermac, 1985, p. 24
9. F. Kersaudy, *de Gaulle et Churchill*, Paris, Perrin Tempus, 2003, pp. 240–1
10. D. D. Eisenhower, *Crusade in Europe*, London, Heinemann, 1948, p. 143
11. E. Roosevelt, *As He Saw It*, New York, Drell, Sloan and Pearce, 1946, pp. 74–5
12. Ibid., p. 91
13. A. Beaufre, *La Revanche de 1945*, Paris, Plon, 1966, p. 195
14. Quotes found in C. Williams, *The Last Great Frenchman*, London, Little Brown, 1994, p. 210
15. Roosevelt, *As He Saw It*, pp. 107–8
16. de Gaulle, *L'Unité*, Paris, Plon Pocket, 1956, pp. 93–4

11

ANGST AT ANFA

The two generals' dinner, which began politely enough with an exchange of courtesies, deteriorated from the point when Giraud said openly that his desire to fight the Germans did not mean that he rejected the authority of Pétain's puppet government. Nor had he any intention of replacing generals Noguès and Boisson, or any other of the greater and lesser fry that had served Vichy in North Africa before the Allied invasion and were still in office. To de Gaulle, this was anathema. The low point was probably reached when Giraud called him, 'Gaulle', omitting the 'de'. He retorted by saying that it formed part of his name, the family belonging to the lesser aristocracy of Champagne. Giraud then regaled everyone at the table with the story of his heroic escape from a POW camp in Germany and his clandestine journey through Alsace and the Occupied Zone.

De Gaulle asked how he had been captured in the first place. It was an unkind cut, coming from an officer who had himself been taken prisoner in the First World War, but by then it was clear to de Gaulle that Giraud's five stars and 300,000 men made it impossible for him to consider a two-star brigadier with 50,000 men currently under his command as anything other than subordinate.

Host and guest parted without making any arrangement for another meeting. The following morning, de Gaulle kept to his villa in the high-security zone until requested by Macmillan to pay a visit on Churchill. This went little better than the dinner with Giraud, after de Gaulle opened by saying that he would have refused to come to Anfa had he known he would be surrounded by American bayonets in a Morocco they were treating as an occupied country, not a liberated French possession. Churchill could take it no longer and exploded in turn, accusing de Gaulle of gross ingratitude to the man without whom Fighting France would not exist.

Macmillan had assessed both Giraud and de Gaulle and come rapidly to the conclusion that Giraud had no political sense at all and would simply be an unwitting tool of the Americans.[1] After the shouting was over, Churchill sat down with de Gaulle and informed him that he was backing to the hilt Roosevelt's solution to the leadership of liberated French overseas territories and the French forces outside France. Under this, Giraud and de Gaulle were to be named joint presidents of an executive committee, with Giraud continuing as commander-in-chief of all armed forces, largely because Roosevelt had promised to him personally the vital arms and other equipment necessary to put them into the field alongside their allies. As to Noguès and the others, all would stay in place, whatever their past; Washington had no wish to divert troops from the front in Tunisia to keep public order in Algeria or Morocco and regarded this as the best path to follow. De Gaulle replied that, while he had immense respect for Churchill and Roosevelt personally, neither leader had any understanding of the issues, nor any right to make decisions affecting French sovereignty. Churchill tried to calm him down by pretending that the coalition government he had been called upon to head in May 1940 had been no easier to control than the proposed executive committee – a comparison that de Gaulle rightly brushed aside.

As a parliamentarian of many years' standing, Churchill was accustomed to ending apparently violent arguments without any personal animosity to his opponents. Watching the General stalk back to his own villa through the gardens of the Little America in which they were staying, Churchill turned to his trusted physician Lord Moran with a smile:

> His country capitulated. He's a refugee. If we cease to support him, he is lost. Yet, to look at him, you would think he was Stalin, with 200 divisions at his back. I didn't spare him. I told him that if he does not cooperate we shall drop him. But he pays no attention. My overtures and threats alike have no effect on him whatever.[2]

Dinner that evening for the prime minister, who probably held the all-time statesman's record for daily consumption of brandy and champagne, was his least favourite meal, being alcohol free in deference to Roosevelt's guest of honour, King Mohammed V of Morocco. Feeling decidedly too dry afterwards to mediate at de Gaulle's planned after-dinner meeting with the president, Churchill endeavoured to have it postponed until the following morning, but presidential adviser Harry Hopkins was against this. De Gaulle arrived looking as stiff and awkward as usual to be subjected to Roosevelt's well-mustered charm assault, hidden behind which was a clear if subtly couched echo of Churchill's warning that he could either go along with American plans for the liberation of his country or be dropped into the limbo reserved for those with political ambitions who have sailed against the winds of state and run aground on a hostile shore, never to be refloated.

The company dismissed, apart from the inner circle including Hopkins, Roosevelt got down to brass tacks. The atmosphere was deliberately casual with no secretary in the room, although an aide was taking notes behind a half-open door. Also hidden behind doors and the curtains were a posse of armed secret service men. There had been no such precautions when Giraud met the president. To set the scene, Roosevelt led with the extraordinary announcement that none of the French leaders outside France had any right to represent the French people as a whole. Therefore, the Allies fighting to liberate France had arrogated to themselves the right to treat her population as irresponsible children, for whom the major political decisions had to be taken by others. Until France was liberated and democratic elections could be held, the contenders for political power must all pull together for the common good in a team captained by himself as president of the senior partner in the alliance.

If that was the gist of it, the listener with pen and shorthand pad strained to hear de Gaulle's rejoinders. He was speaking very quietly in an effort to contain his anger that yet another foreigner should tell him what was good for France. Agreeing that elections should be held to elect a representative government as soon as practicable after the Liberation, he stressed that the majority of his fellow-citizens who were anti-collaboration had already opted for him either as leader of the Resistance or commander-in-chief of Fighting France. To Roosevelt's point that he had not been *elected* and therefore could not speak for France, the reply was that Joan of Arc had not been elected either when she took up arms against the invader. Her authority, which had enabled her to lead troops in the field, came from her own integrity and her actions, as did his. After half an hour's conversation, de Gaulle left the presidential villa, remarking to a companion that he had just met a great statesman and that he and Roosevelt had both understood each other. Such was the president's gift that few people meeting him face to face failed to fall under his spell.

In Anfa, the bride and groom of this forced marriage met the following morning. After Giraud stated his acceptance of Roosevelt's formula, de Gaulle accused his rival of compromising himself by his loyalty to Pétain and continuing to do so daily. Now was his chance to redeem himself by declaring for Fighting France and becoming a modern-day Foch to de Gaulle's Clemenceau. He was wasting his breath. Incapable of understanding what was wrong with his political position, Giraud retorted that he had a far greater number of men under arms. Therefore, de Gaulle should rally to his banner and place himself under Giraud's command, as he had been at the start of the war.

There was simply no common ground, but Roosevelt required the appearance of compromise to defuse the criticism of his policies at home. He had already spent a large part of the night dictating, with the help of Churchill and Murphy, a carefully worded press release stating that the two generals accepted the principles

1 In May–June 1940 Adolf Hitler's Panzers swept the French and British forces aside to conquer France in a six-week blitzkrieg. *(Author's collection)*

2 French head of state Pierre Pétain (left, in uniform) capitulated. Lawyer/politician Pierre Laval (with him, right) became prime minister and made Pétain Dictator of France. *(Author's collection)*

3 Acting Brigadier Charles de Gaulle said that France had lost a battle, but not the war. He flew to Britain to found the Free French fighting forces. At first they numbered just two: him and his aide-de-camp. *(Author's collection)*

4 Winston Churchill was Britain's new prime minister. With no other allies still fighting Hitler, he believed in de Gaulle, and called him 'the man of destiny'. *(Author's collection)*

5 Condemned to death by a French court martial, de Gaulle broadcast on the BBC French service, telling his compatriots not to lose heart. *(Author's collection)*

6 & 7 Volunteers to join his crusade were few in number. Some did not even know how to button their British battledress uniforms. *(Author's collection)*

8 & 9 The flow of volunteers dried up completely after the Royal Navy shelled disarmed French warships in harbour at Mers el-Kebir (below). The battleship *Bretagne* was sunk (left) and 1,297 French sailors killed, with thousands more wounded. *(Author's collection)*

10, 11 & 12 In August 1941 the Atlantic Charter was agreed between Churchill (above, left) and US President Franklin Roosevelt (above, right). *(Author's collection)*

13 & 14 Roosevelt feared de Gaulle's integrity and did everything to split Churchill and de Gaulle at the 1944 Marrakesh conference (above). He picked General Giraud (with him below at the conference) as leader of Free France because he could be easily manipulated. *(Author's collection)*

15, 16 & 17 The two generals fought. De Gaulle won, to command 400,000 men. Roosevelt ordered Supreme Allied Commander General Dwight D. Eisenhower (above, right) not to even tell him the date of D-Day. De Gaulle finally got to France eight days later in his own ship, a deeply unhappy man (left). *(Author's collection)*

18 Touring the Allied bridgehead in Normandy, de Gaulle was welcomed by British Commander-in-Chief Field Marshal Bernard Montgomery (left). *(Author's collection)*

19 While welcoming the arrival of American forces, many French civilians displayed banners reading *Vive de Gaulle!* *(Author's collection)*

20 & 21 De Gaulle defied stay-behind snipers to lead thousands of supporters down the Champs-Élysées (above). The Americans then made a show of force, doing the same (below). *(Author's collection)*

22 & 23 After escorting his old friend Churchill in liberated Paris (left), de Gaulle changed his uniform for a suit, becoming the civilian head of France's first post-war government (below). *(Author's collection)*

24 & 25 Disgusted by the professional politicians who had caused France's defeat in 1940, de Gaulle resigned, retiring to his modest family home in Champagne (below) and there writing his memoirs in the sunlit study (left). *(Author's collection)*

26 & 27 His great joy was spending time with his wife and daughter, Anne, afflicted with Down's syndrome (below). But he kept his finger on the political pulse of the country and mistrusted the massive NATO base in Paris (above). *(Author's collection)*

28 & 29 Elected president of France in 1958 (left, seated alone in the National Assembly), he made a million enemies in French Algeria (above). After he gave the country independence, they made thirty attempts to assassinate him. *(Author's collection)*

30 American General Lauris Norstad refused to divulge the siting of NATO's nuclear armoury in France, so de Gaulle kicked NATO forces out of his country. *(Author's collection)*

31 Five US presidents refused to help de Gaulle's independent defence policies until Richard Nixon (at microphone) finally accepted France as an independent ally. *(Author's collection)*

32 & 33 After resigning as president, de Gaulle took a holiday in Ireland with his wife (above), in order not to complicate the election of his successor. The respect that most French people hold for him is symbolised by the immense Cross of Lorraine that now looms over the little village where he is buried. *(Author's collection)*

of the United Nations – a grouping of allies that excluded Fighting France – and intended to form a joint committee to govern the liberated countries of the French Empire, with themselves as joint co-presidents. Confronted with the text, Giraud accepted it without thinking. It was, in any case, his habit to sign papers placed before him by an aide-de-camp without reading them.

By then, whatever inclination de Gaulle may have had the previous evening to march to Roosevelt's drum was dissipated by the news that the president had told King Mohammed during the dinner that the days of French rule in Morocco were numbered, now that America was in charge, and that Mohammed ought to entrust the modernisation of his country to American Big Business.[3] Churchill, too, was in de Gaulle's black books for having jumped the gun and tricked Giraud into fixing the rate of exchange for the pound sterling at 250 francs instead of the true value, which was 176 francs to the pound. For security reasons, no one had told de Gaulle that the conference was to end that afternoon. When he learned this, the realisation that he was not to be consulted or even informed about the Allies' future planning put him in no mind to sign the press release brought for his perusal by Robert Murphy and Harold Macmillan. He refused to put his name to it, saying that the implication of him handing over control of the empire to a new committee was unacceptable, as it was to the four members of the National Committee who had accompanied him to Anfa.

Churchill was furious to the point of incoherence that his protégé, who had first refused to come to Anfa and had eventually been persuaded to come at the last moment, was now refusing to knuckle down for the president and agree to Giraud's terms. The final straw was his refusal to add his signature to a press release. Their meeting that morning was so bitter that Churchill omitted it from his memoirs and de Gaulle called it the worst argument they had in all the war. Churchill accused him of deliberately sabotaging the compromise plan with Giraud, and promised that on return to Britain he would turn the press, public opinion and the House of Commons against the arrogant Frenchman who had insufferably embarrassed him in front of Roosevelt, should he now persist in refusing to sign the communiqué. In turn, the leader of Fighting France accused the prime minister of betraying the long-term interests not only France, *but of Britain and Europe too*, in order to appease Roosevelt at all costs.

Between the villas the scurrying of go-betweens continued, de Gaulle's unco-operative stand being toned down for Roosevelt's benefit by Macmillan and Harry Hopkins. When Macmillan reported that de Gaulle's analogy had been to suggest Giraud should be Foch to his Clemenceau, Roosevelt laughed, 'Yesterday he wanted to be Joan of Arc. Now he thinks he's Clemenceau!'[4] The similes became further distorted when the president cabled Hull that de Gaulle thought he was Joan of Arc and Clemenceau. Even Churchill got into the circuit by muttering that all they needed was some bishops to burn Joan of Arc. At least the sour

joke discharged enough of Roosevelt's ire at being crossed by a substantive colonel for him to listen to Hopkins' pleading that de Gaulle should be humoured
into some kind of acceptance of the communiqué, just for the sake of appearances
on the other side of the Atlantic. Afterwards, since he was Churchill's protégé, it
was for the British prime minister to take him to task, if necessary by turning off
the supply of finance and resources that kept Fighting France together.

The rest of that day at Anfa was a confusion of comings and goings. At
11.30 a.m. Giraud attempted to get the president's confirmation of the arms delivery he had been promised, but was fobbed off on Eisenhower. After his departure,
de Gaulle and his advisers were shown into Roosevelt's villa, where he calmly
informed the president that he was not going to sign any communiqué until it
was agreed that Giraud was to be his subordinate. Roosevelt pulled out all the
stops of his considerable battery of tricks, from outright bullying to pleading a
great sense of shame that the two generals could not put their differences behind
them in the cause of liberating their occupied homeland. He went on to explain
that he needed for home consumption a dramatic announcement of some progress between de Gaulle and Giraud at the summit. At this, de Gaulle promised to
agree to some formula for the press, but not the communiqué as it stood.

By this juncture it was nearly noon, the time scheduled for the closing press
conference, of which de Gaulle had no foreknowledge. Hopkins, the arch-fixer,
now contrived to manoeuvre both Churchill and Giraud into the room. With
them, perhaps as a smokescreen, came what de Gaulle described as a crowd of
aides and officers in uniform, in front of whom Churchill reiterated his attack on
de Gaulle's uncooperative attitude for Roosevelt's benefit. Pointing the finger at
the object of his anger, he inveighed against him while everybody else diplomatically pretended not to notice that way his ill-fixed dentures kept clacking in his
mouth. The famous phrase he had used earlier in their private meeting, '*Si vous
m'obstaclerez, je vous liquiderai,*' was modified to the more reasonable, '*Il ne faut pas
obstacler la guerre!*'

Hopkins won the day. To palliate Churchill's outpouring, Roosevelt instinc-
tively reverted to charm and pleading: would not de Gaulle at least assent to
being photographed with the prime minister and himself and General Giraud?
De Gaulle said that he would, adding that he respected Giraud as a great soldier.
Roosevelt's instinct told him to risk another turn of the cards, 'And will you
shake General Giraud's hand in front of the cameras?' Everyone held their breath,
to hear de Gaulle say in English, 'I shall do that for you.'[5]

With the president lifted from his chair and carried outside, de Gaulle emerged
into the garden to find himself confronted with a horde of press cameras and
reporters, shorthand pads in hand and pencils poised. Film cameras whirred, flash-
bulbs popped, capturing the false truce with the US president, the British prime
minister and two French generals sitting on the terrace of a requisitioned villa

in the Moroccan sunshine. Delighted at the success of his latest ploy, Roosevelt called on de Gaulle to stand and shake Giraud's hand. The two men stood and shook hands rather awkwardly. Relieved it was all over, de Gaulle stood back, only to be asked by the president for a retake as some of the photographers had missed the shot.

The generals departed, leaving a temporarily mollified Roosevelt satisfied that the 'marriage' he had brokered had just been celebrated before the media, albeit not consummated. In the homely manner he had evolved in his 'fireside chats' over the radio, he and Churchill sat in the rattan chairs answering the reporters' questions about the conference and the course of the war. It was during this session with the press that Roosevelt apparently used for the first time the phrase 'unconditional surrender', announcing that there would be no question of doing a deal with the German leaders because the war would be continued until they were beaten and Germany was on its knees. Given that Allen Dulles at the OSS base in Berne and other American officials in Europe had already had received feelers from important German civilian and military personalities seeking a way out of the war, if Hitler could be got rid of, this was hardly just another 'aside', but a major statement of policy that came ill from the man who had ordered his military and diplomatic representatives to overlook the collaboration of most of the officials and many of the officers in French North Africa, with whom they were working and would continue to work for months to come. Nobody seems to have commented on it at the time but a number of journalists in Morocco for the Anfa conference had managed to visit some of Giraud's punishment camps and there found political detainees locked up with common law prisoners under atrocious conditions. On return to the United States and Britain, their stories provoked outrage in their readers.

It was only ten weeks since Churchill had warned the British public not to regard the victory at the second battle of El Alamein as the beginning of the end but rather the end of the beginning. Since then, General Montgomery had pushed Rommel back on the defensive in Libya, the Japanese drive in the Pacific had petered out and Hitler had lost 250,000 men at Stalingrad, where von Paulus' surrender could be only a matter of days. Yet de Gaulle's understandable desire to be part of the planning and execution of the Allied war effort was to be frustrated for a long time to come. At his own press conference in London on 9 February he paid diplomatic lip-service to Roosevelt's qualities of statesmanship before going on to deplore publicly the way that the leadership of Fighting France was excluded from the councils of war. Foreign Secretary Anthony Eden's Principal Private Secretary Oliver Harvey noted that Churchill was so angered by his loss of face vis-à-vis Roosevelt at the Anfa conference that he considered breaking off all contact with its cause. Eden, however, had a more European outlook and a longer-term view of the continental balance of power that made him appreciate de Gaulle as the man to rebuild a strong France after the war, without which

Britain would have to ally itself with either the US or the USSR.[6] It fell to him to talk Churchill, who was understandably locked into the immediate future, out of any irreparable break and also to restrain some of the prime minister's whims to interfere in French domestic matters through Macmillan in North Africa.

From an unexpected quarter another voice counselled caution: King George VI warned Churchill that the British people had a deep distaste for Roosevelt's American-politician way of dealing with officials and generals who had collaborated with the Germans. Breaking with de Gaulle, however infuriating he could be at times, would be to put the government on the wrong side of that groundswell.[7]

The unwitting subject of their lunchtime discussion had been saying ever since the defeat of 1940 that his country would be liberated largely by American wealth and industrial resources. Whatever hopes he had entertained at Anfa, it was now plain that together or separately the men of Fighting France and Giraud's troops in North Africa would be a part of that campaign under American and possibly British command, but the lion's share of the credit would be claimed internationally – and for the history books – by Washington and London. Because there was nothing he could do about that for the moment, it was important to boost his support inside France. To this end, Jean Moulin was called back to London to be briefed for his next mission in occupied France.

In November 1942 he had drawn the three main movements of the southern zone – Combat, Libération-Sud and FTP – into a loose federation titled 'Les Mouvements Unis de la Résistance' (MUR). The 'united' of the title did not mean any sharing of command, since each refused to take orders from the others, but it was a first step. Moulin drove his troika with a loose rein, doling out subsidies from funds parachuted with arms drops – and then withdrawing support when someone became difficult. The next step for him was to bring all the Resistance organisations in both zones under the banner of Fighting France. Given the multiplicity of agendas, it would take all his negotiating skills – and much bribery. In the first five months of 1943 his subsidies totalled 71 million francs.[8] It was a small price to pay, to ensure that there would be two French armies involved in the liberation of their country – the men in uniform coming ashore from Allied ships and all the men and women in France unprotected by uniforms, who had the courage to fight the Germans and sabotage communications before and during the invasion. In the longer term, after the Liberation the command structure of such an organisation, however tenuous its grip on the communist elements, would be vital to prevent a demoralised and divided nation from plunging into civil war. Only thus could the Republic be re-established and the rest of the French Empire reclaimed in defiance of the American desire to see a weakened Europe forced to divest itself of its international primacy.

Moulin did not return to France until 21 March, his long stay in London being due to 'unavailability' of an RAF aircraft to fly him back. He was not the only one denied transport by Churchill's disenchantment with the Gaullist movement. Its leader also requested air transportation so that he could return to Africa but Churchill now dealt with him only through the National Committee, whose spokesman René Massigli was informed that there were no aircraft available for him either. A sceptical de Gaulle summoned Charles Peake on 2 March and gave him twenty-four hours to find a plane, failing which he would consider himself a prisoner of the British Government and act accordingly. The reply came in Peake's letter to Massigli: the government did not consider this a suitable moment for de Gaulle's trip and therefore 'regretted' that transport would not be made available.

Announcing that this made him effectively Churchill's prisoner, de Gaulle withdrew to yet another of the temporary homes his family had inhabited since coming to Britain, this time in Hampstead. In an understandable fit of pique, he cabled Eisenhower that he had been intending to come and see him but was prevented from leaving Britain by His Majesty's Government. Worse was to come. Irritated by hostile press reaction and mail and constantly embarrassed at the number of sailors deserting Vichy ships in US ports to enlist in Fighting France, Secretary of State Hull wrote to Eden that his president considered the British Government should take steps to silence the Gaullist propaganda machine. Eden's temperate reply was that the government could not shut down Carlton Gardens because doing so would unleash a furore of pro-de Gaulle feeling in Parliament, never mind the press.

He came under the same pressure during a visit to Washington the following month, when Roosevelt revealed why he so disliked de Gaulle in the course of describing his view of the post-war world. Only four seriously equipped armed forces would be allowed. The wartime Big Four – the US, Britain, China and Russia – would then be able to police the 'lesser countries' and force them to settle their differences without resort to arms. Those 'lesser countries' could have armies, but only weapons such as to enable them to keep public order, so that they were incapable of aggression. Without even raising the question of how the neutral countries could be deprived of their armed forces, since they were not involved in the war and thus were not going to be 'liberated' and then occupied, Eden commented that Belgium and Holland were bound to want to put their own houses in order after liberation. As to Germany, he learned, the president's plan was to divide the country permanently after a long occupation and separate it from France by an artificial buffer state called Wallonia, composed of part of Belgium, Luxemburg, Alsace and a stretch of northern France.[9]

From his days as under-secretary for the navy, and in some slight compensation for the difficulties of travel for a man in a wheelchair, Roosevelt had a passion for maps. Had he looked at a recent one of France, he would have seen that his plan matched almost exactly what the Germans had done by annexing Alsace and Lorraine into the Reich, creating the Forbidden Zone and a Reserved

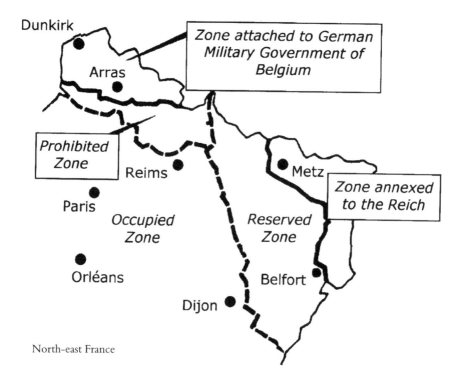

North-east France

Zone and placing the departments of Nord and Pas de Calais under the Military Government of Belgium.

There, in a nutshell, was the reason why de Gaulle had to be sidelined. With a political innocent like Giraud heading the provisional administration and *refusing* to get involved in any political question, the White House had every chance of pushing through its plan. Should de Gaulle be given or seize that power, there was no way he would consent to his country becoming a vassal state. Whatever his personal feelings of the moment about the general in self-imposed exile at Hampstead, Churchill was so alarmed at the American plan that he wrote to Eden in Washington on 30 March, 'This plan of putting France behind China even for European questions, and of submitting a disarmed Europe to the domination of the four powers could not fail to provoke violent controversy.'[10] He was preaching to the converted: Eden had been unable to make Roosevelt realise the dangers of his obsession with destroying the European empires, and likened the president to a conjuror juggling sticks of dynamite, unaware that they might explode at any minute.[11]

Unaware of Roosevelt's plans, de Gaulle was still hoping for an invitation to visit Washington, to build on the relationship which the president's charm offensive had caused him to think had been achieved in Morocco. The sub-text was that Churchill could hardly prevent him accepting such an invitation, and once outside Britain he would have freedom of movement again. Meanwhile, he had Catroux negotiating with Giraud in Algiers and winning some concessions, including relaxation of Vichy's anti-Semitic and anti-communist legislation. On the principle of his seniority to de Gaulle, however, Giraud would not budge. On 26 March he received from his bête noire, still confined in Britain, a list of the preconditions that must be satisfied before their forces could be placed under joint command. Top of the list was that the armistice agreement must be declared null and void. Second, Republican liberties must be restored in French North Africa. The more extremist Vichy civil servants were to be dismissed. Implied in this memorandum was the establishment of a body that could become a provisional government and political representation in French North Africa for the Resistance inside France.

Four days later, with no reply from Algiers, de Gaulle demanded an aircraft again and was told that a Liberator was available, only to be informed subsequently that it was having mechanical problems. Massigli was using Charles Peake as his channel to No. 10 and pouring on the flattery: yes, de Gaulle could be an infuriating man to deal with, as his own subordinates knew better than anyone, but he did have an immense personal respect for the prime minister and, if only Churchill consented to one friendly meeting with him before he left Britain, Massigli was sure he would not cause any trouble for the country that had protected him for so long.

To everyone's surprise, Churchill agreed, but then learned de Gaulle had not actually requested a meeting. Protocol decreed that it was therefore out of the question for them to meet. Informed of this by Massigli, de Gaulle sulked. If Churchill would not invite him to Downing Street, he was certainly not going to ask – and so on. History books often ignore the go-betweens but, without them to lubricate the machinery of diplomacy, it would grind to a halt. Between them, Peake and Massigli massaged the truth until it appeared de Gaulle had requested an interview.

On 2 April the General was received by Churchill, in the presence of Cadogan and Massigli. After a somewhat frigid reception – it was the first time they had met since the Anfa conference – de Gaulle declared that Churchill had made him a prisoner. Was his next move to send the leader of Fighting France to the internment camps on the Isle of Man? In decent French for once, Churchill chuckled, '*Non, mon general, pour vous, très distingué, toujours la* Tower of London' (for a distinguished prisoner like you, general, it will be the Tower of London).

The tension relaxed after Churchill told de Gaulle that he could leave the country whenever he liked. However, he wondered, would it not be better to await Eden's return from Washington first? And should not Catroux return to

London and brief the General on his progress in Algiers before de Gaulle headed for North Africa? As to what he did when he got there, Churchill was unequivocal: all the General's problems since the Anfa conference stemmed from his refusal to come when first invited and then to play his part in the American plans. With the battles going on to drive the Germans out of North Africa it was Roosevelt's priority to ensure that there was no civil unrest in Eisenhower's rear, and should de Gaulle foment unrest in Algeria among Giraud's supporters, there would be nothing His Majesty's Government could do to protect him. It would be forced to drop Fighting France like a stone.

De Gaulle replied that he had absolutely no intention of causing unrest, because to do so was against the interests of France. He added disingenuously that Murphy had estimated his supporters at only 10 per cent of the French in Algeria, so they could hardly cause much trouble, given that Giraud controlled all the French armed forces there *and* the forces of law and order! In any event, he held no animosity for Giraud personally and wanted only to find a way of working together with him, however much he detested some of the people behind him. Churchill leaped to the defence of Noguès, Boisson and the others, mentioning how helpful they had been to the Allies in the three months since the landings, at which de Gaulle said that what concerned him was how they had served France.

They parted civilly enough, but a deeper game was being played. On the same day the US Supreme Court ordered the release from American prisons 300 French sailors who had deserted from the Vichy battleship *Richelieu* in order to join Fighting France. OSS reports from North Africa to Washington made no secret about de Gaulle's overwhelming popularity, but Roosevelt remained deaf to this portent, as he was to most of the advice received from his administration. Among many top civil servants who criticised their president's refusal to listen, Secretary for War Henry Stimson actually asked him by telephone one day what was the point of having a Cabinet, whose members were always ignored.[12]

Two days later, after de Gaulle's reconciliation with Churchill, the Foreign Office passed to Carlton Gardens the text of a cable said to be from Eisenhower, expressing his appreciation of de Gaulle and deferring any visit to North Africa during the fighting in Tunisia, lest it should provoke a political crisis. Attached was a commentary in which the prime minister endorsed Eisenhower's view that the proposed visit was premature at a time when both he and Giraud must concentrate all their efforts on defeating the German forces in North Africa. Learning that the cable had not come from Eisenhower but had been concocted by the Foreign Office, de Gaulle flew into one of his legendary rages. He was trapped in a wilderness of mirrors.

Giraud's eventual reply to the memorandum came on 9 April. Disregarding all de Gaulle's argument, he proposed forming a council to govern the overseas territories, but with no other political power, while he would remain as commander-in-chief of all French forces outside France – answerable not to the committee, but to the Allied High Command. Giraud's lack of political sense was his undoing. While he continued formulating impossible conditions, the French civilian population of Algeria had taken to the streets in ever-increasing numbers, demonstrating in favour of de Gaulle. On 26 April Peyrouton demanded permission from Giraud to resign and return to his military duties as soon as de Gaulle could arrive. Command of Giraud's army was also proving a problem as entire units deserted to join the nearest Fighting French unit. Faced with all this and aware of his rival's near-total support in the Resistance, Giraud revised his conditions, proposing they should meet in Algeria, but well away from the main centres, with their danger of Gaullist demonstrations. Four days later, at Eden's suggestion, it was Churchill who proposed de Gaulle should leave for Algiers to put an end to the uncertainty there, since it was impossible to ignore the level of support for him in North Africa. Even Murphy, who had denigrated Gaullist support as being around 10 per cent of the civilian population, now claimed that it was nearer 90 per cent.

Yet de Gaulle was still biding his time in London when Churchill left for Washington at the beginning of May, there to be subjected to the arguments of Roosevelt and Hull: the behaviour of the Allied leader they wittily referred to as 'the bride' was intolerable; de Gaulle's propaganda services were creating dissension between the various races in Algeria; he considered himself a Messiah and *imagined* that the French people were solidly behind him. Roosevelt and his Secretary of State proposed no less than an enforced reorganisation of the National Committee, excluding de Gaulle's supporters and further diluting his influence by including both neutrals like Monnet and a number of Giraud's supporters in the overseas territories. Or perhaps an entirely new committee should be formed, with no pretensions of becoming a provisional government? That would be even better. Giraud would, of course, be both president of the committee and head of the armed forces. As to de Gaulle, why not do what the British had done with their embarrassingly pro-German ex-king, Edward Windsor, and make this troublesome Frenchman governor of Madagascar?[13] The give-away phrase in a memorandum to Churchill from the White House on 8 May was, 'It seems to me that when we enter France ... it must be as a military occupation, organised by English and American generals.'[14]

Although forced to listen to Hull and the president, and himself likening de Gaulle to a dog raised by a loving master that was now barking too much as well as biting the hand that fed him, Churchill refused to go along with the sidelining of his first ally. Yet, after a while it seems that Washington's desire to reshape the world was infectious: at a lunch on 22 May in honour of Canadian premier Mackenzie King, Vice-President Henry Wallace heard the British prime minister propose a post-war world controlled by a supreme international organisation dominated by the US, the British Empire and the USSR, with three subordinate regional organisations. The British Empire would, for geographical reasons, belong to all three. The US would dominate that for the western hemisphere and Pacific and it could also be a member of the organisation for Europe. In Europe, the old dream of a Danube Confederation was to be revived, with Prussia as a separate entity. France would be restored to her former eminence, although undeserving of it, for the sake of continental stability.[15]

Meanwhile, in the real world, Moulin's success in combining all the major Resistance movements in both zones under Le Conseil National de la Résistance (CNR) was radioed to London direct from Paris on 15 May. This was what de Gaulle had been waiting for. The news was immediately transmitted to Algiers, where its announcement over the radio finally pushed Giraud into lowering his sights. On 17 May he invited de Gaulle to join him in setting up an executive committee to be headed alternately by the two generals and with four other members, two from each side. The British Cabinet was immensely relieved that the dissension was ended after seven months of wheeling and dealing since the November landings. And then, as though a jinx were on the whole thing, on 23 May not one, but three cables code-named *Pencil 166, 167* and *181* arrived in London from Churchill in Washington proposing a complete break with de Gaulle and his movement.

On the face of it, the prime minister had finally given in to American pressure, especially the repeated argument that the money with which he funded de Gaulle came originally, like everything else in Britain by that stage, from the pockets of American taxpayers. But the timing is fascinating. Hull and the White House could not fail to have been informed by Murphy of the rapprochement between Giraud and de Gaulle, so the latest pressure on the British Government can only be construed as a last desperate attempt to block de Gaulle – not because of dissension between him and Giraud, but because they were getting together and this was the only way to undermine what promised at long last to become a unified French command fighting with the Allies.

Calling an emergency session of the War Cabinet, Deputy Prime Minister Clement Attlee and Foreign Secretary Eden replied in the voice of sanity. How, at the very moment when Giraud had proposed terms that de Gaulle could not refuse, could relations with Fighting France be broken off? What would be the point? At this juncture, just after the Germans had been driven from North Africa and Eisenhower was planning the crucial invasion of Sicily, it was important to remember that de Gaulle currently had 80,000 men under arms and loyal to him in the central and equatorial African colonies, in the Levant, and with the various Allied armies. In addition, the First Lord of the Admiralty counted forty-seven French naval officers with 6,000 ratings in four submarines, fifteen destroyers, plus corvettes flying the Cross of Lorraine – all of whom de Gaulle might take with him if expelled from the Allied war effort.

A rupture at this moment, the War Cabinet concluded, would be taken by Parliament and public as proof that the British Government was completely dominated by Washington. The replies from London to the *Pencil* cables were coded *Alcove 370, 371* and *372*. While worded diplomatically and expressing sympathy with Hull's and Roosevelt's feelings, the War Cabinet's mind was clear: this was not the time to drop de Gaulle. Eden noted in his diary that everyone present had the courage to speak up against the idea *in the absence of the prime minister.*[16]

De Gaulle's acceptance of Giraud's invitation was a polite reply on 25 May saying that he would arrive in Algiers at the end of the week and looked forward to working with him in the service of France. His preparations for this trip smacked of finality, including a letter to King George VI thanking him for the welcome that the King, his government and his subjects had extended in the tragic days of June 1940. Taking his leave of Eden in Churchill's absence, he was asked by the foreign secretary, 'What, after all this, do you think of us?' De Gaulle replied that the British people were second to none, but he could not say the same about the government's policy. A very civilised European by comparison with most British politicians, Eden took the liberty of saying that de Gaulle had caused the government more problems than all the other European allies put together, at which de Gaulle smiled, 'Of course. France is a great power.'[17]

Notes

1. P. Mangold, *The Almost Impossible Ally – Harold Macmillan and Charles de Gaulle*, London, Tauris, 2006, p. 40
2. Lord Moran, *Struggle for Survival*, London, Constable, 1966, p. 81 (abridged by the author)
3. E. Roosevelt, *As He Saw It*, New York, Drell, Sloan and Pearce, 1946, pp. 111–12
4. C. Williams, *The Last Great Frenchman*, London, Little Brown, 1994, p. 211
5. Ibid., p. 216
6. A. Beevor & A. Cooper, *Paris after the Liberation*, London, Hamish Hamilton, 1994, p. 18
7. J. W. Wheeler-Bennett, *King George VI*, London, Macmillan, 1958, p. 560
8. H. Amouroux, *La Vie des Français sous l'Occupation*, Paris, Fayard, 1961, Vol. 2, p. 58
9. A. Eden, *The Reckoning*, London, Cassell, 1965, p. 367
10. Ibid., pp. 372–73
11. Ibid.
12. R. Sherwood, *The White House Papers*, London, Eyre and Spottiswoode, 1949, Vol. 2, p. 719
13. F. Kersaudy, *de Gaulle et Churchill*, Paris, Perrin Tempus, 2003, pp. 280–83
14. F. Kersaudy, *de Gaulle et Roosevelt – Le Duel au Sommet*, Paris, Perrin Tempus, 2006, p. 289
15. J. M. Blum, *Diary of H. Wallace*, Boston, Houghton Mifflin, 1973, p. 202
16. Eden, *The Reckoning*, p. 386
17. de Gaulle, *L'Unité*, Paris, Plon Pocket, 1956, pp. 121–23

12

ONE STEP FORWARD AND ONE STEP BACK

Marking the end of his dependence on the British Government for permission to leave the country, it was a Fighting French aircraft that flew de Gaulle to North Africa on 30 May. Algiers' main airport was ironically called Maison Blanche – the White House – but Giraud refused to let the aircraft land there in case too many of de Gaulle's supporters drove out from the city and the demonstrations got out of hand.

The flight was diverted to Boufarik airport, 20km away, where the reception could not have been more different from the arrival at Casablanca in February. A French guard of honour presented arms, a French military band played *La Marseillaise* and the American and British representatives stood behind the French welcoming party led by General Giraud. Accompanied by Massigli, André Philip, Billote and Palewski, de Gaulle was then driven in a *French* car into Algiers for a luncheon at the Palais d'Eté through streets lined with supporters chanting 'Vive de Gaulle!' At the luncheon, de Gaulle could not resist a sarcastic, '*Tiens! Je croyais qu'il n'y avait pas de gaullistes en Algerie!*'[1] (I thought there were no Gaullists in Algeria.)

In the afternoon, the demonstrations and chanting continued. At ten o'clock on the morning of 3 June the two generals got down to business at the Lycée Fromentin. On one side of the table sat de Gaulle with Massigli, Philip and General Catroux. On the other, Giraud was supported by Jean Monnet and General Joseph Georges, an old protégé of Churchill, in whom he had great faith as a moderating influence on de Gaulle and whom he had had spirited out of France to act as a voice of reason in the negotiations.

The meeting swiftly reached deadlock when de Gaulle stated his conditions, namely that command of all French armed forces must be subordinated to the committee and secondly, that Noguès, Boisson, Peyrouton and a number of other ardently pro-Vichy functionaries must immediately be sacked. He did not go so far as to say that he wished them also to be punished for the sake of example. Over the next two days, he was balancing on a knife edge. On the one hand, the civilian population was on his side, as was evident every time he appeared in public. Getting nervous, Giraud accused him of seeking to install a totalitarian regime. Yet paradoxically it was he who had encircled Algiers with armoured units and placed military guards on all the key buildings – a precaution usually only taken if a putsch is imminent. Taking a personal pleasure in arresting as many Fighting French soldiers as strayed into his purlieu was the new chief of police for Algiers whom Giraud had just appointed – the resilient Admiral Muselier.

Also in Algiers during this uneasy series of meetings was Winston Churchill. If his principal reason for coming was to make a tour of inspection of the British troops being readied for Operation *Husky* – the invasion of Sicily – he was also urging Eisenhower that the landings on the island should be swiftly followed by invasion of the Italian mainland. A third reason for his presence was surreptitiously to keep an eye on de Gaulle's manoeuvring. The account Murphy sent to Washington of his conversation with the prime minister stated that Giraud was not the only one to fear his rival mounting a *coup d'état*. Churchill also thought him capable of doing that – although with what forces, it is hard to say, given that Giraud commanded the vast majority of French and colonial army units in Morocco and Algeria. It would have been a stupid thing to do in any case, since it would have forced Eisenhower to intervene at a time when he had more important things on his mind and better uses for his troops than keeping public order in the liberated areas.

De Gaulle stood his ground until the meeting constituted itself the Comité Français de Libération Nationale (CFLN), one of whose first acts was to approve the sacking of Noguès, Boisson and Peyrouton. The CFLN consisted of Monnet and General Georges, balanced by Massigli, Philip and Catroux from the Gaullist camp, with the two generals as joint presidents. Its function was defined as 'to exercise French sovereignty and to direct the French (war) effort in all its forms and wherever it may be'.[2]

Seven months of wheeling and dealing were apparently resolved. Churchill, who had been trying for two years to persuade de Gaulle to work in the framework of a committee that could temper his excesses, bestowed his blessing on the CFLN at a lunch hosted for its seven members, afterwards writing to Roosevelt that it seemed the ideal settlement of the de Gaulle/Giraud rivalry. With wishful thinking, he added that de Gaulle would now have to behave or be outvoted – which is odd, considering that he had three supporters on the committee and Giraud only two. So far as Churchill was concerned, it was a great relief that the exchange of letters between him and de Gaulle dated 7 August 1940, which had so embarrassed him once Roosevelt started pressuring him to drop his original sole ally, had been overtaken by events. Effectively, the British Government's relationship with Fighting France enshrined in those letters was now transferred to the committee in Algiers. That was not, however, the same as formally 'recognising' the committee as a body representing anyone or anything.

Churchill's initial stamp of approval hid internal dissension from the start. De Gaulle insisted that there should be a commissioner for defence sitting on the committee in addition to a commander-in-chief of the armed forces. Giraud insisted that both functions were his, in addition to the co-presidency, to which de Gaulle protested that the constitution of the Third Republic, which they were fighting to restore, required the military to be subordinated to the civil power. In any case, Giraud was only commander-in-chief of the forces in North Africa and was not recognised by the Fighting French troops in the other overseas territories, who still remained loyal to de Gaulle. For two acrimonious weeks the dispute dragged on, with him threatening to resign from the committee and Giraud asking Murphy for support. In distant London and Washington, Churchill and Roosevelt nagged respectively their representatives Macmillan and Murphy to get things sorted out, while the British and American press asked what exactly was going on in Algiers.

What was going on in Algiers was that, by a decree of the CFLN dated 7 June, seven supplementary members had been coopted – a majority of whom were Gaullists – thus reducing Giraud's political importance. Murphy explained to Washington that Giraud had appended his signature to the decree, apparently not understanding its import. Macmillan was unjustly lambasted by Churchill for allowing this manoeuvre by de Gaulle. This, in turn, upset Eden, who rightly resented the prime minister's interference in foreign affairs and knew there was no credible alternative to de Gaulle. On 12 June a confidential directive from No. 10 landed on the desks of British newspaper editors, directing them to be less sympathetic to de Gaulle. An unsigned article in the *Observer* of Sunday 13 June stated Churchill's position and prejudices to a nicety, which is hardly surprising, since he was the anonymous author,[3] having been a reporter in earlier life.

Roosevelt had still not taken the measure of his man. In Algiers, de Gaulle was consolidating his position, step by patient step. Boisson was about to be removed from his post despite the fulminations of Roosevelt that he was on-side in the vital port of Dakar; in fact, he had not surrendered it to the Americans, but handed it over to pro-Vichy Darlan as his direct superior. Marcel Peyrouton had been despatched to North Africa by the Americans and his dismissal was taken as a personal affront by the man in the White House, who now ordered Murphy to prevent the committee from sitting, so that it could take no further decisions. Cables from Washington to Eisenhower, who was in the middle of planning the invasion of Sicily, included a warning that the US Government would probably break off all relations with de Gaulle in the very near future. To justify this internally, a campaign of black PR aimed at de Gaulle was launched in the United

States, spanning the gamut of invective from allegations that de Gaulle was a fascist – presumably Pétain was not? – to a mysterious 'rumour' that he was a communist secretly financed by Stalin.

Not for the last time, the heavy hand of the White House and the State Department achieved the opposite of the desired result. Pointing out that he was exclusively concerned in planning Operation *Husky* and wanted no unrest in the rear areas, Eisenhower instructed the committee on 19 June that his president required Giraud to remain in post. This was tinder in a powder barrel. Reasonably enough, the members of the committee considered it an unwarranted intrusion in French internal matters. A military sub-committee was formed as an umbrella organisation covering both Giraud's troops in North Africa and de Gaulle's Fighting French, ostensibly to get around the nonsense of having a divided high command, and Giraud was summoned to accept its authority or resign.

Macmillan was obliged to attempt to persuade members of the committee to bow to Roosevelt's authority, notwithstanding his convictions that the president was behaving 'scandalously'.[4] Fortunately, Eisenhower agreed with him and attempted to moderate the White House's instructions on the ground. Tempers were frayed in London, too. Throughout the rest of June and early July Foreign Secretary Eden, backed by Sir Alexander Cadogan and Oliver Harvey in London with Macmillan in Algiers, argued that Churchill's duration-of-hostilities mindset, which made it imperative to align himself on every matter with Roosevelt's dictates, would cost Britain dearly after the war. What was important now, they said, was to look ahead to the peace. It was important for the stability of Europe that France should have a strong post-war government, which meant one headed by de Gaulle, because there was no other serious contender. Things had come a long way from the Foreign Office's antipathy to de Gaulle in 1940–41. Churchill's bizarre twenty-four-hour timetable was to lose Eden much sleep in arguments at No. 10 that dragged on into the small hours, gradually forcing Churchill to recognise that Parliament, Ambassador Halifax in Washington and even Eisenhower in North Africa wanted the CFLN to be formally recognised in everybody's long-term interest.

On 19 July, Churchill drafted a long cable for Roosevelt. Approved by Eden, it set out the British attitude to recognition of the committee. In his memoirs, he quotes it with the exception of the embarrassing last paragraph, in which he said that he had always thought it necessary for de Gaulle to be constrained by an executive committee that could prevent him from 'strutting about, playing at Joan of Arc and Clemenceau'. The embarrassment for Churchill lay in the final sentence, where he begged to be informed of Roosevelt's intentions, so that he could act in concert because he tried 'above all to model my behaviour on yours'.

This subservient pleading tone reveals to what extent Churchill had placed himself in the debt of the American administration and the duty of obedience which this exacted. Roosevelt's reply is equally revealing:

I think that ... we should not use the word 'recognise' because the meaning could
be taken to imply that we shall recognise the Committee as the government of
France after our landing on French soil. Perhaps the word 'approval' would ...
more accurately express my thoughts. But we must reserve the right to continue
dealing with the French authorities on the spot in each colony whenever that
would serve the Allied cause. Martinique is a good example.[5]

Divide and rule, it is called.

Roosevelt's ruling, and Churchill's reluctance to go against it, put Eden in
the awkward position of having to defend a position with which he disagreed.
On 14 June a question was addressed to him in the House of Commons: When
would His Majesty's Government recognise the French Committee of National
Liberation? With no reply, another MP asked the same question the following
week, when Eden was obliged to hedge, saying that the government was discussing this with 'other Allied governments'.[6] To Churchill, he maintained that recognising the Committee was the best way to strengthen it and therefore enable
the other members to control de Gaulle, but the prime minister was still awaiting
the green light from Washington.

On 10 July predominantly American Allied forces invaded Sicily. To reduce the
scale of losses in the vulnerable landing and bridgehead stage, the American OSS
had done a deal through members of the US Mafia with the bosses of the Sicilian
Mafia. Essentially, these men put the word around among the Italian troops defending the island that, if they chose to desert, they would be given civilian clothes
and hidden; if they chose to fight, not only did they put their lives at risk from
American shells and bullets, but their families would also be at risk from Mafia retribution. As a result, the Allied forces sustained only 22,800 casualties, against the
defenders' 165,000, of whom 30,000 were German – a reversal of the usual cost in
blood for a seaborne invasion against a defended coast. While it made good sense
in Washington to reduce casualties in this way, the story was understandably played
down afterwards. The second half of the same story is, however, history.

Among the concerns of the joint chiefs of staff planners was the perennial concern of the military for controlling extensive liberated areas whose infrastructure
has been damaged or whose administration is politically or otherwise compromised. Since the invasion of Italy was expressedly to rid the island of its Fascist
rulers, they would have to be replaced. Initially, when this stage of the war was
first discussed between the British and Americans, the transatlantic view was that
service officers should take over the civil administration. This had the disadvan-
tage that large numbers of officers and men would have to be withdrawn from
combat and support duties to take up these political posts. The British, however,
with their lengthy experience of governing colonies, won the day by arguing that
it would be better, as well as more economical in manpower, to use the existing

machinery of administration after deposing functionaries with a compromisingly fascist or otherwise questionable past.

One of the decisions taken at the Casablanca Conference in January 1943 had set up the Allied Military Government of Occupied Territories for Italy. A memorandum of 1 May 1943 defined the functions of this AMGOT as: to guarantee the safety of armed forces in the liberated areas and protect their lines of communication; to re-establish law and order so that normal civilian life could be resumed; to make available to the occupying forces the economic resources of the occupied territory; and to promote the political and military objectives of the Allied Forces through an efficient administration of the occupied territory. Most of the officers posted to AMGOT were given two months' training in local laws and customs at Yale or Charlottesville in Virginia, and were therefore known as 'sixty-day wonders'.

In Sicily, AMGOT was initially headed by Chief Civil Affairs Officer Major General Lord Rennell of Rodd, assisted by Brigadier General Frank McSherry as deputy chief civil affairs officer; under his orders were Royal Navy Commodore C. Benson for the eastern part of the island and, for the western half of Sicily a former lieutenant governor of New York, Italian-American Lieutenant Colonel Charles or Carlo Poletti, who had previously been making anti-fascist broadcasts to Italy from London.

Among the edicts of AMGOT in Sicily was an obligation for the inhabitants to accept Allied currency at an imposed dollars-to-lire exchange rate very favourable to the troops. AMGOT also controlled all the banks in Sicily and printed its own 'Amlire' notes in values from one to 1,000 lire. As the assembled prefects of Sicily learned from Poletti at the beginning of 1944, once the fighting moved north up the Italian peninsula, AMGOT was to be superseded by an Allied Control Commission. This remained in Italy long after the fighting was over and in fact supervised the first post-war elections in 1946.

When Poletti was promoted to succeed Lord Rennell in October 1943, he was effectively the ruler of the civilian population of Sicily, empowered to hire and fire every civil servant from regional prefects to road-sweepers. This was a man of whom Lucky Luciano said, 'He was one of our good friends.'[7] Poletti's policy of appointing *mafiosi* or people susceptible to Mafia pressure in replacement of deposed fascist officials and also many honest and politically uncompromised officials can only be construed as the payback for the help given during the invasion. Its effect was to retard and pervert the economic development of the island for half a century – until the *mani pulite* initiative that cost the lives of so many judges and police officials launched in 1992 could break the stranglehold of the Mafia in this and other parts of Italy.

On 2 July 1943, as the battles for control of Sicily were raging, to strengthen Giraud's political position, Roosevelt invited him to the White House, but had misread both French susceptibilities and the reaction of his own media, both of which condemned his statement during the visit that France had ceased to exist and his blatant failure to refer the invitation to the committee, whose servant Giraud was. Giraud could not have been more helpful to the Gaullist cause, making ill-advised comments at press conferences that, when quoted, seemed to imply he was pro-German. Despite the embarrassment this caused, Roosevelt did not withdraw his backing and the VIP treatment in Washington and Ottawa rather went to Giraud's head. His shortcomings as a leader became all too obvious to Murphy and others on his return to Algiers, where the usual 14 July celebrations turned into an immense demonstration in favour of de Gaulle, who replied to Murphy's congratulations on the turnout with, 'So these are the 10 per cent of the population who, you say, support me?' On another occasion, he summed up Murphy, a notorious socialiser, as a man who thought that 'France consisted of the people with whom he went to dinner'.[8]

That same month also saw the rallying to de Gaulle of the French Antilles and Admiral Godefroy's fleet still in the harbour at Alexandria. Yet, in London MPs were still asking in the House of Commons when His Majesty's Government would recognise the committee in Algiers. On 21 July and again on 4 August the question was tabled. Despite his own running battle with Churchill, Eden was obliged to answer coyly that he was unable to say when, or even if, the British Government would recognise the committee. The matter was still not resolved when he and Churchill arrived during the second week of August in Quebec for the Quadrant summit conference. The conquest of Sicily was by then a foregone conclusion; by 16 August Field Marshal Albert Kesselring, the German commander-in-chief Italy, would have withdrawn all but a rearguard of the German and Italian troops still fighting on the island. At the conference, the main topic was logistical and military preparation for the invasion of France eventually called Operation *Overlord*.

There was also a hidden agenda for the few cleared to know of it. Britain's work on developing nuclear weapons under the code name Tube Alloys was being subsumed into the American Manhattan Project based at Los Alamos in the desert of New Mexico, but the flow of information back to Britain had ceased when the US army took this over in June 1942. The Quebec Agreement signed on 19 August 1943 ostensibly restored mutual confidence in return for Britain handing over to the Americans all research and supplies, including the French heavy water sneaked out of Brest in June 1940. The president and prime minister agreed that their countries would never use the research or weapons against each other, or against third parties without joint agreement – nor would any information be shared with third parties, except by mutual agreement.

With all these pressing and weighty matters to be discussed, the British prime minister still found time to worry about the continued non-recognition of the committee in Algiers. Canadian premier Mackenzie King noted in his diary Churchill's request for his help in persuading Roosevelt to recognise the committee, so that London could do the same! At another level, Eden was locked in argument with Secretary of State Cordell Hull, to whom he made the obvious point that Britain lay only 20 miles from France and would need to be on good terms with its post-war government. Pointedly delaying recognition of the only body likely to form this government was, therefore, a far more serious matter for Britain than for the United States. Still imbued with hatred for the man who had liberated St Pierre and Miquelon without his permission, Hull would not listen, clinging obstinately to his fantasy that the committee would shortly auto-destruct and thus resolve Britain's problem.

In this stalemate, it seemed to Eden that things must end with the British Government 'recognising' the committee while Washington issued a statement 'approving' it *faute de mieux*, but not formally recognising it. Churchill's subsequent meeting with Roosevelt led him to the same conclusion, despite his desire to toe the White House line. However, in diplomatic terms this would indicate a rift in the hitherto undivided leadership of the Grand Alliance. On 24 August the conference ended with Hull noting in his diary:

> The President declared that he refuses to provide the means for de Gaulle to make a triumphal return to France and take power there. As for me, I am prepared to deal with the Committee for the territories which it controls, but no more. ... After the conference, the President told me that he would have been able to get much more out of Churchill, had Mr Eden not been present.[9]

Thus it was that on 27 August Britain recognised the committee's authority in the French overseas territories and as successor to the former French National Committee for the Levant, also considering it the body qualified to control the French war effort in cooperation with the Allies. While more reserved, the American declaration did include recognition of 'the authority of the Committee of National Liberation to administer the French overseas territories that recognise its authority'. It ended, 'This declaration in no way constitutes recognition of a government of France or the French Empire by the government of the United States.'[10] In Algiers the British declaration was read as a de facto transference of the relationship with de Gaulle set out in Churchill's letter of 7 August 1940, and the American declaration was regarded as being about as favourable as could be expected. Meanwhile, the clandestine hunt for another alternative to de Gaulle led American agents to contact Edouard Herriot, anti-German former president of the Chamber of Deputies, and former president of the Republic Albert Lebrun. Both men were under house arrest in France but neither was prepared to lend himself to Washington's plans to spirit them to North Africa, there to usurp de Gaulle's authority. The White House was thus compelled to stake all on its 'rotten plank', whose position in the committee had actually been weakened by his visit to Washington, and was further jeopardised each time he felt threatened and sought American support.

Giraud's lack of political sense now gave de Gaulle another weapon to use against him. After the conquest of Sicily, Mussolini had been deposed and replaced by a government under Marshal Pietro Badoglio, who negotiated an armistice with the Allied High Command and declared war on Nazi Germany. De Gaulle had been given to understand that the committee's representative could attend the signing of the Italian armistice because France was an interested party, seven pockets of territory in her south-eastern *départements* having been occupied by Italian troops. Learning the date only four days *after* the signature ceremony, de Gaulle was told by Eisenhower's headquarters that Giraud had been kept informed and it had been left to him to inform the committee. He had not done so, and had also failed to keep the committee fully informed of his plans to liberate Corsica from Italian and later German occupation after de Gaulle's emissary on the 'isle of beauty' committed suicide while being tortured by Mussolini's secret police there. Using the submarine *Casabianca*, Giraud supplied quantities of arms and explosives as well as substantial secret funds to the communist Maquis organisations on the island and conducted the liberation of the island as his personal war.

Within the Resistance, the main problem was the difficulty of keeping in line the communist elements, who were preparing their own agenda for the moment when Pétain's tottering regime fell, as the Italian Communist Party had done when Mussolini fell. It was with this in mind that de Gaulle attached great importance to General Leclerc's division being included in the troops going ashore in the first wave of Allied landings when it was France's turn to be invaded. On 9 September 1943 the CFLN therefore sent to Washington and London a draft protocol covering relations between the military and the provisional government of France after the invasion. The Foreign Office saw no objection to this. Who else could form a provisional government from scratch on D-Day? However, the War Office in London did not agree and opted for the American model of an AMGOT governing France for at least six months after Liberation.

One particular provision in the CFLN's draft protocol was for the attachment to each major military unit of specially trained officers of the Mission Militaire Française de Liaison Administrative commanded by Lieutenant Colonel Hettier de Boislambert. The duties of the MMFLA were to be twofold: to liase between the non-French Allied units and the local population after the invasion and to take responsibility for the thousand and one administrative problems from accommodation of the homeless to food supplies, sewage disposal and getting the hospitals working again in the liberated areas, ravaged by heavy fighting on the ground and relentless bombardment from aircraft and ships at sea. Seeing the MMFLA as a competitor to the totally controllable AMGOT solution to the same problems, neither Washington nor London gave any reply to Algiers. Not being privy to the planning of Operation *Overlord* – he would be kept in the dark until a few hours before the first waves landed in France – but realising that the absence of a reply meant the chiefs of staff intended to impose an AMGOT in liberated France, de Gaulle had had his worst fears confirmed by the actions of Poletti's civil affairs administration in Sicily.

With this in mind, on 17 September the CFLN took the next step towards an embryo democratic government by approving the establishment of a consultative assembly whose members could question and assert pressure on members of the CFLN. The Assembly was to be composed of representatives of the principal Resistance movements in France and all French political parties except the Pétainists. The idea was not new, but had been proposed as far back as 26 February 1943 in a memorandum to Giraud from Carlton Gardens. To be as democratic as possible in the circumstances, it was to be composed of forty representatives of the Resistance in France, twelve representatives of the Resistance outside France, twenty representatives of the parliamentary parties of the Third Republic, twelve representatives of the overseas colonies and twelve from the three North African countries.

Paradoxically, de Gaulle was about to make his worst decision of the entire war. The episode that enabled his critics in London, Washington and nearer home to say 'I told you so' while his supporters in the Foreign Office and elsewhere despaired occurred when British HQ Middle East finally pressured the Fighting French administration in Syria/Lebanon into allowing free elections between 29 August and 5 September 1943. After a predictable landslide vote that put the anti-French parties in power, the French administration accused the British of interfering and distorting the results; the British accused the French administration of everything short of falsifying the results. The impossibility of untangling the Levantine game of favours is illustrated by the case of a notorious drug dealer named Mokkadem, who was arrested during the run-up to the elections by the British Military Police while trying to smuggle a consignment of Lebanese hashish into Egypt. Handed over to the French for trial, he was acquitted by a court martial, although known to be guilty, because he was a pro-French candidate in the elections! When the British not unnaturally protested, de Gaulle's Delegate General Jean Helleu declared that if Mokkadem were sent to jail he would have to arrest also anti-French Camille Chamoun, to restore the balance. The Levantine logic is difficult to untangle.

Once the results were announced, Helleu was required by the new Lebanese president to transform his delegation into a diplomatic embassy and assume the duties of an ambassador, after handing over the reins of state to the duly constituted Lebanese authorities. In the absence of a treaty setting out the new relationship,

Helleu refused and returned to Algiers for consultations. Back in Beirut, he ordered French security forces to storm the presidential palace on 11 November and then arrested leading politicians before suspending the new Lebanese constitution. Eleven days of rioting and looting were echoed on the diplomatic level with protests from General Spears for Britain, from Washington and Moscow, as well as all the Arab countries. Churchill called the affair a flagrant violation of the Atlantic Charter – ignoring the fact that neither France nor de Gaulle was a signatory. On 13 November the CFLN despatched Catroux to release the imprisoned politicians and get the country running again in a blizzard of accusations and counter-accusations flying between the various authorities in the Levant.

The heavy-handed, nineteenth-century repression was no worse than subsequent British and American repression of local uprisings but enabled Churchill to prophesy darkly that the Lebanese debacle showed exactly what one could expect of de Gaulle should he ever achieve power in France. It was an error of judgement that was to cost the Gaullist cause dearly seven months later when the Allies invaded France. Across the Atlantic, it strengthened Roosevelt's prejudices. At the conference aboard USS *Iowa* with his chiefs of staff in preparation for the coming Teheran summit with Stalin, he was told by Admiral Leahy that France was likely to be rent by civil war after the Liberation. Agreeing, Roosevelt envisaged retaining several US divisions in the country 'to preserve order' and opined that France would not regain her pre-war status for at least the next twenty-five years. On being informed of FDR's plan to carve France up into zones of occupation and annexation, Leahy remarked that the Germans had already done that!

Notes

1. F. Kersaudy, *de Gaulle et Roosevelt – Duel au Sommet*, Paris, Perrin Tempus, 2006, p. 300
2. F. Kersaudy, *de Gaulle et Churchill*, Paris, Perrin Tempus, 2003, pp. 294–95
3. Ibid., p. 298
4. H. Macmillan, *War Diaries*, London, Papermac, 1985, p. 133
5. Kersaudy, *de Gaulle et Churchill*, p. 303
6. C. Williams, *The Last Great Frenchman*, London, Little Brown, 1994, pp. 290–1
7. www.americanmafia.com/Feature_Article_388.html
8. ed. M. Jullian, *de Gaulle – Traits d'esprit*, Paris, Cherche-Midi, 2000, p. 165
9. C. Hull, *Memoirs*, London, Hodder & Stoughton, 1948, Vol. 2, p. 124
10. Quoted in Kersaudy, *de Gaulle et Churchill*, footnote to p. 309

13

A GRUDGING APPROVAL

Among the papers placed on his desk by an aide-de-camp which he signed without reading them in October was Giraud's own resignation from the CFLN. His departure from the political scene caused few regrets; among those delighted to see him divested of all civil power were all the *résistants* he had jailed and refused to release – and Algerian Jews, the restitution of whose French nationality he had blocked until then. De Gaulle was now uncontrovertibly the committee's sole president. Inside twelve months, by a combination of persistence, persuasion and sheer nerve, he had transformed himself from the leader of 80,000 men to the political head of a French empire that stretched from the Caribbean by way of western and equatorial Africa to the Levant – and was also the now undisputed leader of the million French citizens in North Africa and an army of nearly 400,000 men, partially re-equipped by the Americans. Not that he had any intention of resting on his laurels ...

In the Consultative Assembly debate on foreign affairs at the end of the month, every speaker demanded that the Allies should recognise the Assembly as the provisional government of the Republic, since it was the only body inside or outside France that represented all shades of political opinion with the exception of the collaborators in Vichy. With the committee as its effective Cabinet, the Assembly also denounced the Clark-Darlan agreement of November 1942 on the incontestable legal grounds that Darlan had no authority to sign it in the first place. The agreement was therefore declared null and void, as were all laws enacted by the Vichy Government, which was regarded as a hiatus in the Third Republic.[1]

On the domestic front, pressure in the Assembly from CNR representatives brought about the arrest of Boisson, Peyrouton and Flandin – a move that scandalised Churchill, convalescing from pneumonia in Tunisia. Roosevelt cabled Eisenhower to intervene, but fortunately Eden's voice of reason instructed Macmillan to contact Eisenhower's chief of staff, General Walter Bedell Smith, and block any direct intervention. As he pointed out, the committee would reject any ultimatum, which could only be effective if backed by force, and that was unthinkable. At the very least, such outside intervention would align the neutral members of the committee with the extremists in Algiers and, since the arrests had been demanded by the CNR members, it would also alienate the Resistance inside France at this crucial time leading up to the Normandy invasion.

At the pre-summit meeting between Churchill and Roosevelt in Cairo during November 1943 Churchill argued for further Mediterranean initiatives but the US president was playing a different game. For him, Cairo was just the run-up to the Teheran summit conference – the first Big Three meeting with Stalin, which opened on 28 November. Both western leaders arrived at the Iranian capital tired and in ill health; Stalin arrived fit, boasting of the recent victories of the Red Army and enjoying the advantage conferred by making the other two statesmen travel so far for his convenience. Fully aware that Britain was much the minor partner in the western alliance, he held secret talks with Roosevelt, from which Churchill was excluded and in which Roosevelt's undoubted skill as a negotiator in American politics led him to underestimate disastrously the duplicity of, and overestimate his influence on, the Soviet leader. It was, in fact, Stalin who outsmarted the president and persuaded him to ignore Churchill's plans for the areas of south-eastern Europe, which he intended should be governed after the war by puppet regimes controlled from Moscow.

An unusual witness to all this was the British prime minister's bodyguard, Inspector Walter Thompson, who noted in his dairy how Roosevelt was accommodated inside the Russian compound, where Stalin could dominate him completely in conversations from which Churchill was excluded. When the British prime minister invited Roosevelt to lunch at his quarters in the British legation to catch up on these, he was openly snubbed. Thompson also commented on how the American president looked up to Stalin both literally from his wheelchair and figuratively, with evident admiration – and how he curried favour with Stalin by making jokes at Churchill's expense, which left Thompson's master 'very distressed'. A shrewd, although usually silent observer of the world leaders in whose company he spent so much time, Thompson wrote:

> [Roosevelt's] view of Stalin was emphasised on the occasion he remarked to Mr Bullitt, the American ambassador in Moscow (who had been ambassador in Paris in 1940): 'Stalin doesn't want anything but security for his country, and I think that if I give him everything I possibly can and ask for nothing in return, *noblesse oblige*, he won't try to annex anything and will work for a world of democracy and peace.'[2]

As Thompson commented, 'What a tragedy!'

One of the subjects on which Roosevelt acquiesced completely with the Soviet dictator was the future of France, agreeing that no Frenchman aged 40 or over who had participated in the provisional government should be eligible for office after the Liberation and fundamentally rejecting Churchill's belief that a strong France was important for a stable post-war Europe – which Stalin did not want. Roosevelt further declared that it would be necessary, not just to sort out the ruling classes in France as Stalin wanted, but 'to make all levels of French society honest'.[3] Apart from his physical handicap, Roosevelt was a very sick man with not long to live and tired easily. Stalin made the most of this weakness by frequently leading the conversation to the president's favourite hobby-horse of decolonisation, covering both French Indochina and British India – which Roosevelt agreed should be reformed 'on the Soviet model'![4]

It was astonishing behaviour for a US president whose chiefs of staff were already warning him that the US would almost certainly find itself in confrontation with Soviet forces at the end of the war with Germany.

Aged 69, Churchill too was exhausted and in failing health, exacerbated by the travel and stress. When pneumonia struck him on the way home, his doctor Lord Moran advised a long stay in the warmer climate of North Africa before returning to foggy, damp November Britain. Spending Christmas in Marrakesh, Churchill invited de Gaulle to visit him. The first two invitations evoked only the explanation that the General was too busy. He was also unwell, the stress of the past two and a half years aggravated by a recurrence of the malaria from which he had long suffered and by kidney problems. However, after Macmillan's persistent diplomacy gained an acceptance of the third invitation, all looked set for an end-of-year rapprochement until, on the day agreed for the luncheon, news arrived in Marrakesh about the executions in Italy of Ciano and the other Fascist leaders, which put the prime minister, already touchy about the two refusals of his invitation, in one of the dark moods that he called his 'black dog'.

Tempted to send an aide to the airport to call off the luncheon when de Gaulle landed, he was reasoned out of this by his wife Clementine. So that their prickly guest could not take offence, de Gaulle's arrival and reception were rehearsed in detail, but everything went wrong when an aide showed him into the villa by the wrong doorway. Instead of taking offence, the General put everyone at their ease by charming Clementine in English, which he continued to speak for the rest of the meal. Determined not to be outdone, Churchill responded by speaking French and the atmosphere is summed up by his joke that, now de Gaulle spoke such good English, he could at last understand the prime minister's highly idiosyncratic French!

Accounts of the after-lunch conversation differ, but for once de Gaulle did not take umbrage at Churchill's fatherly counselling not to annoy the Americans unnecessarily. Knowing how much the prime minister adored all kinds of military ceremony that gave him the opportunity of wearing his large assortment of military uniforms, at the end of the meal the General invited his host to take the salute at a march-past of French troops. This was arranged for the next day, Duff Cooper's despatch to the Foreign Office afterwards describing how the two leaders stood side by side on the saluting platform as contingent after contingent of smartly turned-out French, Moroccan, Senegalese and Algerian troops paraded past them. From the crowd attracted by the spectacle came almost as many shouts of '*Vive Churchill!*' as of '*Vive de Gaulle!*'

On his return to Algiers, de Gaulle told General d'Astier de la Vigerie, now Commissioner for the Interior, that the prime minister was looking his age and very tired. It was not concern for an old man's feelings that had held him in check, nor gratitude for past favours, but the hope of obtaining increased arms drops to the predominantly urban Resistance inside France and the Maquis units scattered over the countryside, both increasingly hard pressed by the SS and Gestapo, aided by Pétain's paramilitary Milice. The contact proved more fruitful than de Gaulle had expected: in February 1944 the RAF was to air-drop weapons enough to arm 16,000 men and March saw this figure doubled. Also in March, the build-up in Britain to Operation *Overlord* in the shape of several hundred thousand American troops and all the supplies they would need – with 1,200 warships, 800 transports and more than 4,000 landing craft – was so obvious that it was impossible for the Germans not to become aware of it through neutral diplomats. Since the scale and imminence of *Overlord* could not be hidden, a decision was taken to create a deception HQ headed by General George S. Patton, whose welter of spurious radio traffic to and from 'ghost' outstations in south-east England persuaded Hitler that the invasion would be launched at or near Calais.

On 2 December 1943 de Gaulle learned that James C. Dunn, Director of the Office of European Affairs in the State Department, had referred to an *irrevocable* decision to provide the invasion troops with AMGOT currency that the French would be obliged to accept as legal tender.[5] Since then, Jean Monnet had been trying to persuade the Treasury Department and the War Department that such a measure would effectively place France in the position of an occupied former enemy territory, like Italy, and not a liberated, friendly one.

It was finally agreed that these AMGOT notes would be redesigned and carry no identification of the issuing authority, but the words 'République Française' and '*émis en France*' (issued in France) with '*Liberté, Egalité, Fraternité*' on the reverse. With the departments of state, war and navy all agreed, Roosevelt intervened. He wanted '*République Française*' replaced by '*La France*' and no mention of '*émis en France*'. 'Since the notes will be issued by the Allied military command,' he wrote to Secretary Morgenthau at the Treasury Department on 6 January 1944, 'I shall put in the centre a French flag in colour, framed by an American flag and a British flag.'[6] When Morgenthau protested at the removal of '*République Française*' at a meeting with the president on 8 January, his objection was brushed aside with a sarcastic statement that nobody could know the form of the French Government after the war – and told that he sounded exactly like the Foreign Office, which was hardly a compliment in FDR's vocabulary. Morgenthau noted in his diary that Roosevelt's argument was based on de Gaulle being 'on the way out'. Nothing could have been further from the truth, except in Roosevelt's mind. The confusion in his thinking was made clearer that afternoon when Morgenthau relayed the gist of the White House meeting to his assistant Harry White, to the effect that the president had said it was Stalin's idea that the future French Government should include no member of the previous government.[7]

Told of the president's stance, Monnet was disappointed, but assumed his habitual persistent negotiation could change Roosevelt's mind. He was swimming against the tide in Washington, as indicated by the US refusal for Fighting France to have any say in the military occupation of Italy and the number of sixty-day wonders being trained in Charlottesville for duties in liberated areas of France.

Meanwhile in Algiers, Harold Macmillan was relinquishing his post to the man who would be Britain's first post-war ambassador to France, Alfred Duff Cooper. At their last meeting, Macmillan felt relaxed enough to ask the General what he really felt about the British. De Gaulle took his time before replying, 'You British are so annoying, the Americans so tiring, the Russians so disquieting. I prefer to be annoyed, rather than fatigued or disquieted.'[8]

The CFLN was still awaiting replies to its draft protocol, submitted six months earlier. On these being leaked to the British press, the *Manchester Guardian*, *Observer* and *Daily Herald* wanted to know why they had not been accepted. *The Times* and *Daily Mirror* joined forces with them. The problem was that London could not reply before Washington gave clearance and this was not forthcoming because Roosevelt persisted in clinging to Admiral Leahy's fantasy that the only person to whom the French population would rally during the Liberation was not Charles de Gaulle but Leahy's friend Marshal Pétain, who must therefore continue as head of state.

With only a small, and diminishing, percentage of the French population still remaining loyal to Pétain, this was pure cloud cuckoo land. Journalist Jean Galtier-Boissière reckoned that immediately after the armistice 95 per cent of French people were for Pétain; 50 per cent remained so until the occupation of the southern zone by the Germans in November 1942; 30 per cent remained loyal right up to the Normandy landings, but this number dwindled rapidly once the Allied bridgeheads were secure. In any case, if either Leahy or his president seriously thought for a minute that the retreating Germans would be stupid enough to fail to take the Marshal and other important political figures hostage in Germany after the Allied invasion, he must have been out of his mind.

The official mandate from the joint chiefs of staff to Eisenhower as Supreme Commander of the invasion forces was that he 'could consult the CFLN'[9] when

appointing civilian administrators of the liberated areas. Eden saw this as a potential source of confusion, as well as a constant burden of decision on Eisenhower,
who had many more pressing matters to think about. He therefore sought to have
the directive modified to the less ambiguous '*shall* consult the CFLN'.[10] As late as
17 April 1944, Roosevelt was still refusing to accept this, while de Gaulle was still
wishfully thinking that he would be invited to Washington for consultation and
receive the president's personal blessing as the only feasible leader of a provisional
government for France until national elections could be held after the whole
country had been liberated.

Except for Maurice Thorez, leader of the Parti Communiste Français (PCF),
who had spent the war years sitting safely in Moscow planning the party's takeover in the power vacuum after the invasion, there was no other candidate who
could call on *any* substantial support in the population. However, Roosevelt
ignored the advice of Stimson, Morgenthau, the Office of War Information and
even the despatches from Allen Dulles at the Berne OSS station in February
1944 to the effect that the Resistance numbered 200,000 armed men, whose
leaders accepted de Gaulle's authority. This last intelligence confirmed repeated
pleas from London for de Gaulle to be invited to Washington in recognition of
the important role the Resistance was to play in diverting German reaction to
the Normandy invasion and communicating to the Allies coordinates of strategic targets such as arms and fuel dumps and armoured units in transport. Even
Eisenhower found time to advise Washington that interrogations and reports of
escaped prisoners confirmed that public opinion in France was divided into a
minority who still supported Pétain and the majority who recognised de Gaulle,
with no third candidate in sight.

On the domestic political scene, Roosevelt was battling with a national railway
strike and a threatened one in the steel industries, added to which he was losing
support in Congress for his policies and was worried by the decision of General
Douglas MacArthur to run for president in the November 1944 presidential elections. But that was not the reason why he clung to his opinion that de Gaulle was
a man of straw, whom the winds of politics would soon blow away.

His long-term health problems complicated by bronchitis brought on by the
trip to Teheran, Roosevelt had been admitted to Bethesda Naval Hospital on his
return and there diagnosed as suffering from being overweight, dilation of the
aorta, heart trouble and high blood pressure – none of which was helped by a
regime of overwork, sustained by smoking thirty cigarettes a day and consuming
rather too many 'old fashioned' cocktails.[11] Unfortunately, the gravity of his condition was concealed by his personal physician. US Navy Admiral Ross McIntyre
was an ear-nose-and-throat specialist by training, who used his rank to quell dissent from colleagues on the president's medical team who knew how ill their
patient was. The cardiologist's report of life-threatening cardiovascular disease was

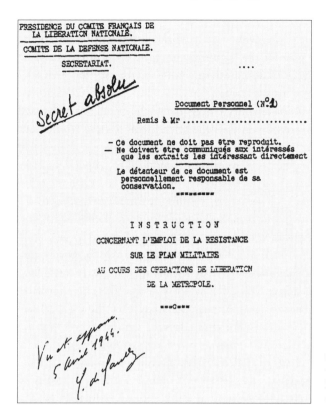

PRESIDENCE DU COMITE FRANÇAIS DE
LA LIBERATION NATIONALE.

COMITE DE LA DEFENSE NATIONALE.

SECRETARIAT.   ....

Secret absolu

Document Personnel (N°.1)

Remis à Mr ....

— Ce document ne doit pas être reproduit.
— Ne doivent être communiqués aux intéressés
  que les extraits les intéressant directement

Le détenteur de ce document est
personnellement responsable de sa
conservation.
=========

I N S T R U C T I O N

CONCERNANT L'EMPLOI DE LA RESISTANCE

SUR LE PLAN MILITAIRE

AU COURS DES OPERATIONS DE LIBERATION

DE LA METROPOLE.

===0===

*Vu et approuvé.
5 avril 1944.
C. de Gaulle*

Instructions to FFI. Cover sheet of instructions for use of Resistance during Liberation, signed by de Gaulle

suppressed. Other records went missing. President Roosevelt's malignant hypertension progressed without proper treatment or even regular monitoring.[12] As his mind clouded and his bodily systems failed one by one, he was too ill to be in unquestioned charge of anything more complicated than a wheelchair. Revising his opinion of de Gaulle or anything or anyone else was a physical impossibility.

From his own sources, de Gaulle was perfectly aware of the build-up in invasion forces in Britain. On 5 April he issued the *Secret Absolu* instructions to the key figures in the Forces Françaises de l'Intérieur, as the Résistance was now termed, in the hope of giving captured *résistants* some protection. Its military commander was General Koenig, the hero of Bir Hakeim, but Washington would not clear him for any details of the invasion date, nor even say where it would take place.

On 17 April, a total security clampdown forbade the sending of *any* coded messages from the United Kingdom, including diplomatic traffic, which meant that Koenig could not even communicate with de Gaulle in Algiers. At Teheran, Roosevelt had given in to Stalin's pressure for an early date for the invasion and promised that D-Day would be in May, but that was not possible. Exasperated at the long wait for a reply to the draft protocol, on 26 May the CFLN took matters into its own hands; by 2 June all official documents were headed *Le Gouvernement Provisoire de la République Française*. Roosevelt was hoist with his own petard: the long delay and the arrogance it demonstrated had brought the GPRF into being – in competition with his plan for the eventually liberated areas of France to be governed, as in Italy, by AMGOT administrators using as currency the AMGOT money, printed and ready for use on D-Day.

Apart from Morgenthau at the Treasury Department, who could not have failed to appreciate the situation, nobody on the Allied side seems to have worked out the effect of distributing in France several million francs in currency notes that had no official backing. The effect on an economy reduced to 20 per cent of its pre-war efficiency would have been a catastrophic inflation, to add to all the other problems of liberated France. One has to ask, was this the American intention?

The invitation from Churchill to come to London 'for consultations' with special permission to communicate with Algiers in code was handed to de Gaulle by Duff Cooper. The chiefs of staff had done everything possible to prevent this, not wishing him to be in Britain before D-Day itself at the earliest. It was Eden's influence on the prime minister that once again won the day. The cherry on the cake was Churchill's offer to send his personal aircraft for the General and another aircraft for his companions. For three days, de Gaulle stalled, arguing that unless participants at the 'consultations' included a representative of the State Department or American chiefs of staff, there was no point in going to Britain. After two very lively meetings of the GPRF that included threats to resign by Massigli and others, de Gaulle agreed to go, but it was only when he took his seat in one of the two RAF York aircraft at 3 p.m. on 3 June that Duff Cooper's staff was able to cable London that he was definitely coming.

Churchill's plan was to keep de Gaulle in Britain and bring him and his companions into the picture on D-Day+plus 3 or +4, deflecting any conflict over the administration of liberated territory by pretending that the Allies held only devastated beaches. On D-Day+8 or +9, he would then divert his awkward guest by arranging the long awaited visit to Washington for consultations including an interview with the president, which would keep the General out of the way even longer.

Arriving in Britain in the morning of 4 June, de Gaulle was welcomed at the airport by a military band playing *La Marseillaise* and handed a warm letter from the prime minister, inviting him with a few companions to arrive for lunch at about 1.30 p.m. aboard the train Churchill was using as his temporary headquarters near Portsmouth, after which they would together visit Eisenhower's HQ concealed in a nearby wood for a comprehensive briefing on the deployment of the thousands of aircraft and ships and the 2 million men eventually to be involved in *Overlord*.

The railway-mobile offices were spartan, to put it mildly, with a single telephone and one bathroom compartment – which Churchill monopolised for hours each day, to the discomfort of his staff. Eden arrived in time to escort de Gaulle along the tracks to the train, from which the prime minister alighted to greet him with open arms. At a green baize table in the main compartment, de Gaulle sat on one side with his ambassador Viénot and General Béthouart; opposite them, the prime minister sat between Eden and Duff Cooper. To Churchill's rather rambling opening, de Gaulle politely replied that the imminence of the invasion was obvious to anyone listening to the plethora of coded personal messages in the French service of the BBC standing by different Resistance units all over France. Churchill agreed that the messages were a give-away, but necessary, adding that some were deception, to complement the radio disinformation campaign generated by Patton's ghost army. After the first landings on the beaches of Normandy, the plan was for Eisenhower to broadcast a message to the French people, as would Queen Wilhelmina of Holland and King Haakon, the exiled king of Norway. When asked to record a speech to be broadcast to France early on D-Day de Gaulle agreed and said that he assumed he would be free to return to Algiers afterwards.

The meeting passed off amicably, as did the lunch aboard the train until Churchill raised the idea of de Gaulle going to Washington to discuss the administration of the liberated areas, and also the use of AMGOT francs in France. De Gaulle refused to be drawn, saying that this was all politics and that the only important thing at that moment was the coming battle, for which it was better to be in Europe than on the wrong side of the Atlantic. Socialist MP Ernest Bevin, who was present as a member of the War Cabinet, interrupted to say that the Labour Party would be offended if de Gaulle did not take up the offer to go to Washington.

De Gaulle reminded his hosts that he had sent proposals for the administration of the liberated areas nine months earlier and had no reply from the Foreign Office or the State Department; in any case, what business was it of British socialists whether he went to Washington or not? Roosevelt had never wanted to meet him before, and he had no intention of asking anyone's permission to be the leader of the provisional government, because he already was. So, let battle be joined and afterwards he would broadcast a speech. The tone degenerated further after he learned that the French population was to be ordered to accept the unauthorised AMGOT francs. To his mind, the only thing missing would be to hear that Eisenhower was about to proclaim himself ruler of France. So let them all go off to war with their fake banknotes. The politics could be sorted out afterwards.

Churchill intervened to warn him that in any open disagreement between the CFLN in Algiers and the American Government, London would side with Washington. De Gaulle said frigidly that he had noted this for future reference. Churchill added that the House of Commons would back him but Eden looked doubtful about that and Bevin said openly that the prime minister was speaking for himself, not the Cabinet. So the luncheon meeting ended sourly, despite Churchill's toast, 'To de Gaulle, who never accepted defeat.' The General lifted his glass and responded coolly: '*A l'Angleterre, à la victoire, à l'Europe!*'[13]

In Eisenhower's tactical HQ the Supreme Commander and General Bedell Smith gave de Gaulle a thorough briefing on the invasion, explaining how the first waves had been scheduled to leave Britain within hours and land at dawn the following day, 5 June, until the meteorologists revealed that there would be storms in the Channel that night, making a successful crossing by the invasion fleet impossible. A born diplomat despite the heavy burden of responsibility on his shoulders, Eisenhower asked for, and showed interest in, de Gaulle's observations, agreeing with him that the invasion should be launched as soon as the weather permitted, since the next favourable conjunction of tides would not occur for a month, after which autumn storms might make it impossible until the following spring.

The mood changed again as the visitors were about to leave and Eisenhower used the word 'proclamation' for the speech he was to make over the radio. De Gaulle brusquely asked by what right he would proclaim anything to the people of France and what he intended to say. Handed a duplicated copy of the speech, de Gaulle observed that Eisenhower was addressing the Norwegian, Dutch, Belgian and Luxemburg peoples as the commander of the Allied operation. But when he came to the French, it was to order them to carry out his orders and decree that 'the civil administration would stay in place until further orders' and 'after the liberation the French people will choose for themselves their representatives and their government.'[14] Not once was there a mention of de Gaulle, Fighting France or the GPRF.

Such was the tension at this moment that each participant afterwards recalled the argument differently. De Gaulle wrote that Eisenhower excused the text as a draft which he would modify on the basis of their conversation; Eden spoke of a 'misunderstanding'; General Béthouart's version was that Eisenhower said nothing could be changed because it had all been approved in Washington.[15]

Refusing to stay to dinner and return to London in the prime minister's train, de Gaulle collected his escort and departed by car, deeply insulted. Next morning, he sent to Eisenhower an amended draft of the proclamation speech but was told this was too late because hundreds of thousands of copies had been printed days before and were already at airfields ready to be dropped over France. That day, British political adviser to Eisenhower's HQ Charles Peake informed de Gaulle what was expected of him on D-Day, now scheduled for 6 June. At dawn radio messages were to be broadcast from King Haakon, Queen Wilhelmina, the grand duchess of Luxemburg and the Belgian prime minister. De Gaulle, however, refused to have his speech transmitted after Eisenhower's as this would imply his endorsement of what had just been said.

At the Cabinet meeting that evening, Churchill learned that 200 MMFLA liaison officers, who had been attached to Allied units in the first waves, were being unilaterally withdrawn by de Gaulle because no agreement had been reached with the Allied command on their duties and functions, once ashore. In the event only seventy-seven French marines, who were embedded in other units, did land on D-Day – a fact commemorated in 1984 when President François Mitterrand unveiled a monument at Ouistreham in their honour.[16]

At 9 p.m. Churchill was informed that de Gaulle had not refused to speak over the BBC, but simply to have his speech follow that of Eisenhower. Ambassador Viénot was to spend most of the night shuttling between Carlton Gardens and Downing Street, abused in both places as he sought as diplomatically as possible to heal the rift. Eden too had a sleepless night endeavouring to slow the escalation of tempers. At one point, well after the first parachutists and glider troops had landed in Normandy, Churchill dictated a deportation order for the General and ordered Desmond Morton to instruct Bedell Smith to find an aircraft in which to fly him back to North Africa, in chains if necessary, so that he would never again set foot in France.

Notes

1. de Gaulle, *L'Unité*, Paris, Plon Pocket, 1956, p. 253
2. T. Hickman, *Churchill's Bodyguard*, London, Headline, 2005
3. F. Kersaudy, *de Gaulle et Roosevelt – Duel au Sommet*, Paris, Perrin Tempus, pp. 352–3, quoting FRUS, 1943 Teheran Conference USGPO Wash 1961, pp. 484–5, 11/28/43
4. Ibid., quoting FRUS, 1943 Teheran Conference USGPO Wash, 1961, p. 486, 11/28/43
5. Kersaudy, *de Gaulle et Roosevelt*, p. 360
6. J.M. Blum, *The Morgenthau Diaries 1941–1945*, Boston, Houghton Mifflin, 1967, p. 167
7. Ibid., p. 168
8. Quoted in P. Mangold, *The Almost Impossible Ally – Harold Macmillan and Charles de Gaulle*, London, Tauris, 2006, p. 68
9. C. Williams, *The Last Great Frenchman*, London, Little Brown, 1994, p. 245
10. Ibid.
11. T. Morgan, *FDR*, London, Guild, 1986, pp. 710–11
12. M. Cooke, *Lords of Creation*, London, Robson, 2002, pp. 244–5
13. Kersaudy, *de Gaulle et Roosevelt*, p. 346
14. Williams, *The Last Great Frenchman*, p. 253
15. F. Kersaudy, *de Gaulle et Churchill*, Paris, Perrin Tempus, 2003, p. 357–61
16. *Memory and Power in Post-War Europe*, Cambridge, CUP, 2002, ed. J.W. Müller, p. 64

14

D-DAY

The morning of 6 June brought cautious confirmation of the landings: by dusk some 155,000 men would be ashore, although none of the first-day targets had been reached. With the pre-recorded speeches having gone out over the airwaves, Eden considered it imperative that de Gaulle should add his voice to those addressing the French people at this critical moment. De Gaulle agreed, but Viénot did not dare to ask him to submit the text for British approval. The Foreign Office fearing with good reason that his speech would be a denunciation of the Allies in general and Britain's prime minister in particular, at 11.15 a.m. Sir Alexander Cadogan instructed Duff Cooper to vet the text of de Gaulle's speech, but this was not forthcoming. The diplomats had to content themselves with authorising the BBC to record the General's speech, which could afterwards be suppressed, if too inflammatory.

By noon it was being recorded. De Gaulle opened with:

> The supreme battle has begun. It is, of course, the battle of France and the battle for France. The sons of France, whoever and wherever they may be, have the simple and sacred duty to fight the enemy by whatever means they can. ... The instructions of the French government and the French leaders which it has appointed must be followed exactly. Behind the heavy cloud of our tears and blood, the sun of France's true might is dawning.[1]

Reading the transcription of the speech very shortly afterwards, Cadogan noted the wording. De Gaulle had said 'the French government', not even the 'provisional government'. After brief reflection, Cadogan passed the speech for transmission, ruefully admitting to his staff that the prime minister would give him hell for it afterwards. His own minister meanwhile found himself allied with Bevin and Attlee in the War Cabinet, Eden speaking out firmly against any kind of 'punishment' for de Gaulle failing to dance to the American tune. Paradoxically, their argument was in essence the same one the Foreign Office had used for months *against* de Gaulle in 1940 and 1941: it was vital to be on good terms with France's new government, which could now only be one led by de Gaulle.

On 11 June – or 'D+5 Day', as the London *Observer* termed it – that respected journal had a curiously worded main headline: *France Revolting as Allies Advance.* Below it, the leading article was a paean of praise for General Koenig's FFI units, who were attacking German troops and conducting sabotage all over France to cut communications and slow the arrival of Hitler's reinforcements at the battle front. Behind the scenes was a hidden story of American reluctance to admit as late as 31 May that the Resistance came under French control; not until 2 June did SHAEF accept de Gaulle's nomination of Koenig for this role.[2] Elsewhere in the *Observer* a pool reporter gave a vivid description of 'the greatest sea terminus the world has ever seen', in the bay of the Seine, where supplies shipped across the Channel were disembarked, stored and despatched to the troops inland. From Helsinki came a despatch about the Soviet invasion of Karelia. Switzerland was calling up more troops for defence, and the first 2,000 German POWs had arrived in Britain from Normandy. British servicewomen were staffing tank parks behind the lines and WAAFs were helping to run the first RAF airfield established in France. On the home front, the Ministry of Food warned that some people were not following instructions regarding the new issue of ration books.

Every page was very upbeat. 'Our military correspondent' reported from 'somewhere in Italy' that the Eighth Army had taken Orsogna, with the Fifth Army 'speeding on'. The Polish Government exiled in London had issued instructions over the BBC to Poles serving in German uniform not to shoot at the Allied soldiers. Another correspondent 'with British Forces beyond Bayeux' reported the destruction of a heavy formation of Mk VI Tiger tanks that had threatened to split British and American forces. A single radio call for artillery support resulted in a truly Allied response, with a Royal Marines battery and American self-propelled guns zeroing in, together with naval guns from 'a British cruiser many miles away' at sea, while American Thunderbolt fighters were vectored in to strafe the German tanks.

The *Observer*'s political correspondent was also in the Bayeux area, filling a quarter-page with his report on 'the rebirth of France' and describing how the local population was 'Gaullist' in the true spirit of June 1940. Defying the American policy of treating liberated areas as occupied enemy territory, the correspondent argued strongly for:

the incorporation of France again into the framework of European civilisation, cleansed from Nazi mud and blood. In a Europe true to its own traditions of progress and humanity, France can be neither a Cinderella, nor a hanger-on. Europe without France would be shortened by a head at least.

In lamenting the suffering of France during 'almost 1,500 days of her servitude', the correspondent reminded readers that this suffering still continued:

> [France] has to pay still more for her liberation by the destructions of her towns and villages. No doubt, the mass of Frenchmen will accept this added price with sense and courage. But it would be unforgivable if, in addition to this price … new billions of francs, issued by a foreign power, were to be pumped into circulation to speed on the inflation of French currency.

The article ended, 'The future historian must have no trace of an excuse to say that the Allies liberated France, but failed to restore her self-respect.'

The paper's diplomatic correspondent contributed a two-column article on 'the outstanding problem of Allied diplomacy', by which was meant the American refusal to recognise the GPRF. In setting out the pros and cons concisely and not pretending that all French people supported the General or liked his authoritarian approach, the article pointed out that there was 'not the most shadowy suggestion of an alternative to the de Gaulle government', but there was 'a growing feeling in London that the British and American governments must now either recognise or repudiate General de Gaulle'.

If de Gaulle's demand to go to France were:

> refused or unduly delayed in acceptance, the implication will inevitably be drawn that his authority is feared and mistrusted by the Allies. Meanwhile, Washington and London are getting the worst of both worlds: the American policy is regarded by some journalists and many Frenchmen and friends of France as representing the stubbornness of Mr Roosevelt, while Mr Churchill is said to be clinging to the President's coat-tails. So long as the true facts remain unstated, the President's stand will continue to be interpreted as sheer caprice.

On this day, still less than a week after the invasion, with so many things happening, roughly a quarter of the straight news pages of the *Observer* were devoted to the unexplained hostility of Roosevelt to the only Frenchman with any appreciable civilian following, Pétain's supporters having dwindled to a tiny percentage of the population since the landings. If that were not enough, de Gaulle also had an army in Allied uniform and uncounted thousands in the FFI risking their lives in support of the landings. With thousands dying daily in Normandy, the diplomatic correspondent thought it important to point out the problems that continuing non-recognition of the GPRF and its leader would cause for Franco-British relations and indeed the future of Europe. More aware of the true issues than his president, the most important American in Europe, Supreme Commander General Dwight Eisenhower, deemed it politic to echo the acknowledgement of the magnificent contribution to weakening the German response given by de Gaulle's underground army commanded by General Koenig.

Churchill paid a lightning visit to the Normandy beachheads on 12 June, when the US VII Corps had still not reached the line planned for the first day of the invasion and stiff German opposition was containing the beachheads. On his return to Britain, he found the press release about his visit overwhelmed by an outburst of protest in the newspapers over the discourtesy of not including de Gaulle in the party visiting France. On 14 June, during Question Time in the House, several MPs again questioned the servility of the British Government in refusing to recognise the GPRF because of pressure from Washington. When the prime minister hedged, he was reminded that MPs had been awaiting replies to the same questions for months.

At that moment, a haggard-looking de Gaulle was in France, his face betraying all the stress he was under at what should have been a moment of triumph. Disembarking from the Fighting French destroyer *La Combattante* near Courseulles, he first visited the HQ of General Montgomery, who was concerned at the plight of his Seventh Armoured Division, being pushed southwards by German armour until the pressure was relieved by the US First Division. However, after a greeting that was courteous on both sides between Monty, dressed in baggy trousers and sweater devoid of insignia and his tall, immaculately uniformed visitor, de Gaulle headed into Bayeux to install François Coulet as his first Commissaire de la République in the liberated areas. Coulet had been his *chef de cabinet* in 1941 and 1942, so de Gaulle knew him well enough to have complete confidence in the way he would handle the Allied civil affairs officers in liberated Normandy, once installed.

One of Coulet's first acts was to disabuse the regional civil affairs chief Brigadier Lewis, who assumed Coulet was, in some way, his subordinate. Refusing to call on Lewis, in order to establish from the outset the proper protocol, Coulet sent a message to inform the brigadier that he would be delighted to receive him in his office. The reaction of other civil affairs officers in Normandy to Coulet and his small staff ranged from incomprehension to hostility. When Lewis came to call, he informed Coulet that he would tolerate his presence in Normandy until receipt of orders from his government clarifying the situation. Coulet spoke English well and had often served as de Gaulle's interpreter. He retorted with some force that he was there by order of the GPRF to uphold French sovereignty and needed no permission from Lewis or anyone else. Furthermore, he was not so stupid as to hinder in any way the military operations in the region; his job was to restart normal life for the civilian population that had suffered so much in the fighting.

Lewis' manner changed immediately to protestations of sympathy and willingness to collaborate.[3]

So much for AMGOT's sixty-day wonders! As for the AMGOT banknotes, Coulet informed General Koenig at the end of the month that civilians who had been paid with them for requisitioned goods or property or damage to property or goods supplied to the invasion forces found it hard to get anyone else to accept what they called the 'forged notes'. They therefore used them to pay their taxes, thus passing on to the authorities the problem of converting them into real money! Coulet instructed banks in the liberated areas to accept the AMGOT notes but not put them back into circulation. In this way, by the end of August scarcely any were still in use.

Rather more useful were the AMGOT postage stamps printed in the United States, which the GPRF agreed to use in order to replace the former stamps bearing Pétain's portrait. Now collectors' items bearing the image of the Arc de Triomphe and the words *France Postes*, they went on sale as early as 11 September in Normandy and later in Paris. Although the denominations printed on them did not correspond to the postal tariffs, an impressive 60 million were printed and sold. A second printing launched on 12 February 1945 brought another 99 million AMGOT stamps into France, this time with the correct values over-printed in black ink. Strangely, the perforation was done in two operations, horizontally and then vertically, which meant that the corners were uneven and made these issues particularly valued by collectors – and more so because the tariffs changed on 1 March, after which the GPRF was able to issue its own stamps. De Gaulle regarded the stamp business as yet another Allied interference, having requested the British Government soon after his arrival in London in June 1940 to have printed issues of stamps for use at the Liberation.[4]

His itinerary during the visit on 14 June took him Bayeux for a walkabout through the ruined streets of the heavily bombed and shelled town and thence to Isigny-sur-Mer, where he shook hands with the inhabitants who had survived the pre-invasion bombardments that were conservatively estimated by the US Government after the war to have caused 12,000 civilian deaths.[5] He also made many brief and well-received speeches. If his face was unknown to the French public due to a rigorous censorship of any photographs of him by the Vichy authorities, his voice was well known all over France from all the broadcasts from London. As his car was driving slowly along, a woman who had cut some flowers from her garden rushed up and threw the impromptu bouquet into his lap. Overcome with emotion, she called out, '*Vive le Maréchal!*' De Gaulle took this in his stride, remarking to his aide-de-camp, 'Yet another person who does not read the newspapers. Ah well, such is the force of habit. I'm sure she was a good Frenchwoman, all the same.' A parish priest rode up on his horse and rebuked the General for not shaking his hand earlier. De Gaulle got out to make amends, replying, 'I do not shake your hand, Monsieur le Curé. I embrace you.'[6]

On the voyage home, he boasted to Viénot and Béthouart on the bridge of *La Combattante* how the Allies with their AMGOT plans had been caught napping by the speed with which he had installed the first of the GPRF's civil administrators. To their voiced concern that the Allies would replace them with the sixty-day wonders, he replied confidently, 'You'll see. They will say nothing.'[7]

There were many reports by Allied observers of the warmth and size of the population's enthusiastic reaction to this brief visit and only one claiming any hostility to him at all. Between 8 and 20 June, the governments-in-exile of Czechoslovakia, Poland, Belgium, Luxemburg, Norway and Yugoslavia all defied Washington by recognising the GPRF. On 16 June, with bitter fighting continuing in Normandy and the invasion forces still a long way short of their objectives, de Gaulle left Carlton Gardens after Anthony Eden's first courtesy visit. The Foreign Secretary was received with great pomp and de Gaulle was generous in his praise of the British nation for the support it had given him. His farewell letter to Churchill was eloquent in its praise of the gallant British forces fighting for the liberation of France, but the reply was a frigid expression of regret at the failure to reach an understanding with Washington.

That 'misunderstanding' continued. Allied radio stations in North Africa were forbidden to refer to the provisional government, but the BBC did – an anomaly pointed out to the State Department by the British Embassy in Washington. As to the AMGOT currency, three days after the invasion, Churchill had cabled Roosevelt that de Gaulle was prepared to broadcast a declaration that this was legal tender, but would almost certainly refer to the provisional government or 'la République Française'. The US Treasury Department indicated that, since nobody had yet guaranteed the issue, de Gaulle could even denounce the notes as forgeries, in which case the Treasury would have to back them officially – to the tune of $400 million! Since Roosevelt's design did not look worthy of confidence and would have been easy to forge, the AMGOT notes were swiftly phased out.

A new wave of support for de Gaulle in the American press and radio had some effect on Roosevelt, whose half-hearted offer to receive the General if he came to Washington had been replaced by a direct invitation, thanks to Churchill's pleading. Yet, as late as 14 June, Henry Stimson noted in his diary, 'FDR thinks that de Gaulle will soon collapse ... He thinks that other parties will appear as the liberation progresses [and] said that he knew already of some of those parties.'[8] Since there were no 'other parties', it is impossible to see this as anything other than the delusion of a man desperately trying to prove himself right on an issue over which he had been wrong all along. As historian François Kersaudy remarked, in preparing his campaign for election to an unprecedented fourth term in the White House, Roosevelt must have been aware that he had made two fundamental errors of foreign policy regarding France: he had backed *all* the losers and he had not only failed to back the winner, but gone out of his way to obstruct and insult him as well. Privately calling his unwanted visitor 'a nut',[9] FDR was still clinging to the hope – presumably fuelled by Leahy's misinformation – that the first undeniable acclamation of the leader of the GPRF in the liberated areas was illusory and that support for de Gaulle would dwindle as the Liberation progressed and other contenders for power emerged.

The reply from Carlton Gardens to Washington's invitation was coolly diplomatic, saying that de Gaulle hoped circumstances would permit him to come. After discussing this with the GPRF in Algiers, the General decided that it was in France's interest for him to go – and so, on 26 June, the invitation was accepted, and Roosevelt's acknowledgement duly received. To the White House protocol department's 'hope' that de Gaulle would conduct himself discreetly and not embarrass the administration by going to New York, where his supporters were likely to demonstrate their enthusiasm for his cause in large numbers, he replied that it would be ridiculous to visit America without going to New York and that he could hardly hide from the public there.

De Gaulle, accompanied by Palewski and General Béthouart, landed in Washington on the torrid afternoon of Thursday 6 July, to be greeted by a salute of seventeen guns – not the twenty-one guns reserved to honour heads of state. If the US military was well represented by Generals Marshall and Arnold and Admiral King, the State Department was notably absent, as a way of communicating that the official invitation had not changed the visitor's status, so far as it was concerned. Curiously, Roosevelt, already visibly a very sick man, had invited Admiral Leahy to attend the reception at the White House, along with Cordell Hull, Sumner Wells and other luminaries of the administration. Once again, Roosevelt welcomed his guest in French: '*Je suis si content de vous voir.*'

On the following day Roosevelt poured on the famous charm at a formal luncheon. After toasting France, he turned to the General:

> A year ago, in last January, I met General de Gaulle for the first time and am happy that this is the second and that there will be a third and more. There are no great problems between the French and American people, nor between General de Gaulle and myself … [We] have discussed world affairs this morning and are in complete agreement on the future of the world and on German disarmament so that what has happened during these past five years may not be repeated for another fifty years. I propose a toast to General de Gaulle, our friend.[10]

The biggest present ever made to the American people was the Statute of Liberty. Paid for by a collection among the French people and unveiled on Liberty Island on 28 October 1886, it was entitled 'Liberty illuminating the world' by its sculptors and positioned so that the figure of Liberty gazed out across the Atlantic to France. The United States had concluded an 'entangling alliance' with France in 1778 and ended it in 1801. George Washington in his farewell address warned his fellow countrymen not to get entrapped in such alliances. Unbeknown to de Gaulle, the president's briefing by the State Department before their meeting summarised France as:

> a country which is sitting back, waiting for something to happen ... a country with such an inferiority complex that frank discussion is difficult, if not impossible ... a country convinced that the United States and Russia will have to fight it out in a war in the near future.

It was recommended that de Gaulle should be sent back to France with a small diplomatic victory of some kind, provided that he agreed that a 'sizeable American armed force should be kept in France to protect our lines of communication and supply to our occupying force in Germany'.[11] And there we have the sole reason for Roosevelt's invitation: it was an insurance against what was almost certainly going to be the future French government impeding the supply lines to the American army of occupation in Germany. De Gaulle probably worked that out for himself. It must, in any event have been alarming for the leader of Fighting France to hear the most powerful man in the world describing to him a future in which the United States was to be the global policeman, acting in concert with the USSR, China and Great Britain, and with an appearance of democracy conferred by the United Nations organisation,[12] which the four great powers would control. To enable rapid response to any threat to world peace, there were to be American bases worldwide, including in France. The GPRF still excluded from the UN, de Gaulle avoided an argument about sovereignty that would lead nowhere by confining himself to a remark that it would be important for the world to have a strong Europe, and for Europe to have a strong France.[13]

Despite the superficial civility, due to what de Gaulle characterised as the patrician manners of FDR, the president's true feelings came out in a curiously domestic setting when he later gave a present from his visitor – a 1.5m-long exquisitely engineered working scale model of a submarine made in the naval yard at Bizerta – to one of his grandchildren. The president's wife Eleanor protested that this was no way to treat a present from a head of state, but was overruled by her husband on the grounds that de Gaulle was no head of state, but 'only the head of a committee'.[14]

The reception in New York arranged by FDR's enemy Mayor Fiorello La Guardia was compensatingly tumultuous, as was the subsequent reception in Canada. Back in Algiers by 13 July, de Gaulle learned that holding his tongue in Washington had paid off: to gain the support for Roosevelt's presidential campaign of the strong pro-

Gaullist movement in the US, the State Department had just recognised the GPRF as the de facto civil administration of France during the Liberation. Although hardly generous, the announcement wrong-footed Churchill and the British Government, who ought to have been consulted beforehand. Eden was bitter. Failing to persuade the prime minister to ask Roosevelt to go the small step further and recognise GPRF as the provisional government, he argued that it was time for Britain to have its own foreign policy and not slavishly follow Washington.

Churchill would not do this, having already lost his confrontation with the combined chiefs of staff, who had – in keeping with Roosevelt's promise to Stalin at Teheran – allocated to Operation *Anvil*, the invasion of the south of France, the forces Churchill wanted deployed in south-eastern Europe. Fearing another rejection from an American administration obsessed with domestic issues in the run-up to the presidential election, he swallowed his own humiliation. On 2 August – which was D+59 – the Allies were still well short of the line they should have reached on D+19. In the Commons, the prime minister made no secret of his problems with de Gaulle, but added that he would never forget how the General had been Britain's first and only ally in 1940. He also declared that France must be represented in any Allied discussions about post-war Germany.

By 9 August, with British and Canadian forces launching a new offensive south of Caen, it seemed briefly that Roosevelt's hope of 'other contenders for power' appearing in France was about to be realised. With Pétain placed under house arrest by the SD after refusing any longer to exercise his functions as head of state, Prime Minister Pierre Laval reached Paris in the evening stitching together a last-ditch plan to fabricate a new government out of thin air. Edouard Herriot, 72-year-old former president of the Chamber of Deputies, was confined by the Germans as a hostage in a nursing home, due to poor health. Laval negotiated his release on 12 August and asked him to head a new government, but Herriot asserted that, under the Constitution of the Third Republic, only Jules Jeanneney, former president of the Senate, could reconvene the National Assembly – which on 10 July 1940 had endowed Marshal Pétain with dictatorial powers and voted itself into oblivion. Jeanneney, however, was in Grenoble.

To avoid Herriot being re-arrested by the Gestapo, Laval tried to persuade him they should flee together to Switzerland, but received the reply, 'Switzerland is too expensive, and I have no money!' Had it not been tragic, it would have been comic. Herriot was then driven off to a secure sanatorium near Potsdam by the Gestapo. As a final desperate move to save his neck, Laval – who, among his several offices, was also mayor of the Paris suburb of Aubervilliers – summoned the eighty other mayors of Greater Paris and persuaded them all to sign a pledge of support for him as president of their collective and as head of the government.[15]

From Algiers, de Gaulle regarded this desperate manoeuvring with contempt, but was far more wary of another simultaneous attempt to seize power in Paris.

The communist faction in Paris under the self-styled 'Colonel' Henri Rol was fomenting industrial unrest and also attempting to mount an armed uprising against the substantial German garrison forces occupying the capital. Since it was estimated that only 300 *résistants* in Paris had firearms and the training to use them, this would have resulted in a bloodbath. It was also militarily pointless, since General Von Choltitz commanding the German garrison in the capital had no intention of destroying the city on Hitler's orders and fighting to the last man as he had been ordered to do.

On 15 August – anniversary of the official birthday of Napoleon – a fleet of 396 Dakotas took off from Italian airfields to drop 5,000 US paratroops on southern France. In the second stage of Operation *Anvil* – now code-named *Dragoon* – and after a violent naval and air bombardment of the German defences, 25,000 French, French colonial and US soldiers landed between Toulon and Cannes from an invasion fleet of 2,000 transports and landing craft escorted by some 300 warships. On the same day, the formerly collaborationist Police Nationale went on strike to ingratiate themselves with the increasingly active FFI and a series of other strikes brought Paris to a standstill.

Notes

1. Charles de Gaulle's broadcast of 6 June
2. '*Des Prefets de Vichy aux Commissaires de le République*', ed. P. Masselin in *Espoir*, Paris, Institut Charles de Gaulle, 2004, 2e trim, p. 94
3. M. Hella, *L'Histoire du premier timbre de la Libération*, in *L'Echo de la Timbrologie*, September 2005, pp. 38–41
4. A. Beevor & A. Cooper, *Paris after the Liberation*, London, Hamish Hamilton, 1994, p. 29
5. Ibid., p. 33
6. E. Béthouart, *Cinq Années d'Espérance*, Paris, Plon, 1968, p. 251
7. F. Kersaudy, *de Gaulle et Roosevelt – Le Duel au Sommet*, Paris, Perrin, 2006 *met*, p. 412
8. W.D. Hassett, *Off the Record with FDR 1942–1945*, New Brunswick, Rutgers University Press, 1958, p. 257
9. S.I. Rosenman, *Public Papers and Addresses of F.D. Roosevelt*, New York, Random House, 1950, Vol. 13, pp. 1914–16
10. Beevor & Cooper, *Paris after the Liberation*, p. 252
11. The organisation was officially founded on 25 October 1945
12. F. Kersaudy, *de Gaulle et Churchill*, Paris, Perrin Tempus, 2003, p. 377
13. T. Morgan, *FDR*, London, Guild, 1986, p. 723
14. D. Boyd, *Voices from the Dark Years*, Thrupp, Sutton, 2007, pp. 241, 245–6
15. Ibid.

15

A STROLL DOWN THE CHAMPS-ÉLYSÉES

On 3 July 1944 Hitler sacked Field Marshal Gerd von Rundstedt for failing to throw the Allies back into the sea. Six weeks later, on 17 August, he sacked his successor Field Marshal Günther von Kluge after the Allies' breakout from the beachheads and subsequent advance eastwards towards Paris and the Reich. Fearing that he would be inculpated in the 22 July bomb plot to kill the Führer, von Kluge blew out his brains near Metz in Alsace, rather than be hauled before a People's Court and slowly strangled, hanging on a butcher's hook with the conspirators. In his farewell letter to Hitler, von Kluge wrote:

> I do not know whether Field Marshal Model will be able to restore the position. I hope so with all my heart. But if not, and if your new weapons, in which such burning faith is placed, do not bring success, then, *Mein Führer*, take the decision to end the war.[1]

The primitive V-1 rocket bombs had started landing on London in June but, 'new weapons' apart, no one could realistically hope for a German victory at this stage, with the Red Army advancing in the east and the twin invasions of France heading towards a meeting point somewhere east of Paris like two claws to pinch off the German armies in the west of the country if they did not retreat very rapidly. To hasten the link-up, Eisenhower's strategic intention was to bypass Paris to north and south. However, in the eyes of de Gaulle, the first priority lay in the complete liberation of his own country. He was totally against Eisenhower's plan not to push into Paris as soon as possible, both to liberate the millions of civilians cooped up there and for its symbolic value as the capital of France.

On 18 August de Gaulle left Algiers, flying via Casablanca and Gibraltar to Maupertuis in liberated Normandy, landing there on 20 August to be advised by

Koenig that a communist-led uprising had begun in Paris. Both Pétain and Laval had by then been compelled by the SS to leave France and were on the other side of the Rhine. On 22 August, while visiting Eisenhower's HQ in Granville, de Gaulle expressed dismay that the Allied plan was to cross the River Seine at Melun, Mantes and Rouen, but not at Paris. This was partly to avoid Allied supply lines having to feed 4 million or more civilians or having to restore the damaged infrastructure of greater Paris to working order, which would mean diverting precious reserves of fuel and manpower.

Conceding that Eisenhower was in overall strategic control, de Gaulle nevertheless stressed the political mistake it would be to leave Paris in enemy hands for a day longer than necessary. There were also military reasons why it was better to secure sooner rather than later the communications hub of the country. Eisenhower was embarrassed – the more so when de Gaulle insisted that the first troops to enter the capital *must* be French, i.e. Leclerc's 2nd Armoured Brigade, which had been completely re-equipped in Britain. Eisenhower's achievement in coordinating troops from so many countries, each with its own political agenda, and smoothing out the personality differences of generals under his command as difficult as Montgomery and Patton, is well known. Once again, despite all the conflicting pressures on him as commander-in-chief, he rose to the occasion and acceded to de Gaulle's request that the capital should be liberated as soon as possible to abort the communist uprising and that the first troops to enter it should be the French Second Armoured Division, supported by the US Fourth Division. The scale of the casualties an unplanned and unsupported uprising would have produced can only be guessed at; as it is, the archives of the Ville de Paris record 2,873 persons killed in August 1944.[2]

On 23 August the BBC announced somewhat prematurely that Paris had been liberated by the FFI, provoking scenes of jubilation in London and other British cities. The following day, American tanks and trucks pulled aside in the suburbs to let Leclerc's tankers spearhead the advance into the city centre, with Captain Raymond Dronne commanding a column of Sherman tanks and half-tracks of 501 tank regiment.

The end came with apparent ease. Datelined 'Paris 25 August 1030 hours', General Billotte addressed to von Choltitz a one-page ultimatum to the effect that further resistance was useless and gave him half an hour to accept the terms. Von Choltitz's reply was even shorter and more to the point. On a sheet of unheaded notepaper (see overleaf), he ordered, in both German and French, all German troops in his command to cease combat.

With his staff, the last German commandant of Paris was taken prisoner and the formal surrender document signed – twice. On the first occasion in a draughty office in Montparnasse railway station, 'Colonel' Rol objected that Leclerc's signature did not cover the FFI insurgents, whose commander he was. To avoid the

```
                    B E F E H L

Der Wiederstnd in dem Stuetzpunktbereich und Stuetzpunkten
ist sofort einzustellen.
```

```
                    v. Choltitz, Gen. d. Infanterie


ORDRE              Paris 25.8.44
Toute résistance dans les points d'appuis et leurs forces
doit cesser irrémédiablement.
           signé.  von CHOLTITZ
                 Général d'Infanterie
```

Paris Surrender. The bilingual scrap of paper that was von Choltitz's order for the German garrison of Paris to cease fire

danger of them refusing to cease fire, Leclerc had another copy of the document produced, which Rol insisted on signing first, with Leclerc's signature added below his name.[3]

Since the German communications networks were largely out of action, to halt the fighting Leclerc's officers toured the streets in loudspeaker vans with Wehrmacht officers beside them, making bilingual announcements near outposts still unaware that, for them, the war was over. Yet Parisians were still hearing gunfire twenty-four hours later during de Gaulle's triumphal march down the Champs-Élysées on 26 August. To avoid embarrassment, he had the firing attributed to stay-behind Germans. A rumour had it that the gunmen on the rooftops were *miliciens* who had nothing to lose by a last-ditch stand, but the synchronisation of the bursts of firing that cleared city centre streets at the time of the walkabout suggests that Rol's communist followers were discouraging people from demonstrating their acclaim of de Gaulle. Undeterred, he ordered generals Leclerc, Juin, Koenig and the heads of all the Resistance factions to remain one respectful pace behind him, and then strode ahead, standing head and shoulders above the crowds lining the great avenue. Relaxing briefly at the end of the day in the office in the War Ministry that he had left as a substantive colonel in June 1940, he turned to Maurice Schumann and said, 'No one could get me to do that again.'

His apparently improvised speech that day at the Hôtel de Ville was ill received by the Allied commanders whose forces had done most of the fighting since 6 June. De Gaulle's simplified view of the political situation was that the vote of 10 July 1940, by which the *députés* had given total power to Pétain, was devoid of legal validity. To the dismay of the Conseil National de la Résistance, he also considered it and its president Georges Bidault, who had succeeded Jean Moulin, to have no part in the government. When Bidault demanded that the General proclaim the restoration of the Republic, the reply was:

> The Republic has never ceased to exist. Free France, Fighting France, the Committee of National Liberation have all been a part of it. Vichy was always, and will remain, null and void. So, as head of the Republic's government, why should I proclaim it?

He was on thin ice, for both the GPRF and the consultative committee were composed not of elected representatives of the people, but men appointed by him.

The shape of his future policy was clear in the speech at the Hôtel de Ville: 'Paris has liberated herself. She has been liberated by her people, with the help of the whole of France, of Fighting France, of the only France, of the true France, of the eternal France.' He made no mention of the thousands of Allied casualties during the Liberation for two reasons: he wanted to build French pride and not tarnish the moment by mentioning gratitude to foreigners for liberating France from the German yoke; and secondly, he resented many of the improprieties committed by those foreigners during the Liberation.

Among many examples, General Leslie Groves, head of the Manhattan Project for developing the atomic bomb, had set up three missions based in Britain and code-named ALSOS to scoop up European nuclear know-how. ALSOS I was active in Italy; ALSOS II in France; and ALSOS III was reserved for Germany. A team from ALSOS II made it to Paris closely behind the first US troops and interrogated, among other French scientists, Frédéric Joliot-Curie. They paid no attention to his insistence that pooling of resources with Britain and the gift of the French heavy water in June 1940 gave France the right to share British nuclear technology under an agreement made with London by his agent *after* the 1940 collapse. Churchill had not mentioned this conflicting obligation when signing the Tube Alloys agreement. On another occasion, an ALSOS team discovered thirty tons of uranium ore near Toulouse, which was hastily shipped back to the United States without anyone bothering to ask or inform the French authorities.[4] Things got so bad that in February 1945 Joliot-Curie threatened his American contacts that if France was not allowed to join the UK–USA consortium, it would turn to the USSR and share information with them. Like so many threats, this achieved the reverse of its intended aim: Groves took the warning to heart and ruled that nothing of interest to the Russians should ever be allowed to fall into French hands.[5]

In the euphoria of the Liberation, few French people were aware that their liberators intended exacting a price for ridding France of the Germans:

Almost immediately after the humiliation of the Occupation and surrounded by the dilapidation and poverty of 1945, Paris rapidly managed to project its sense of cultural superiority. In St Germain de Prés, people may have been hungry, but the ferment of ideas after the repression generated an extraordinary excitement. This was the period about which every foreign student still dreams, when wandering from the Café Flore to the Deux Magots across the Quartier Latin – trying to conjure up (the sight of) existentialists arguing in cafés and Juliette Greco (singing) in a smoke-filled cellar club.[6]

Yet, while the general population breathed freely again, all the frictions of the Occupation still fermented between the political activists of all hues. The PCF reinvented itself as *le parti des fusillés* and claimed 75,000 martyrs shot by German firing squads, causing Jean Galtier-Boissière to remark scathingly, 'Of 29,000 French victims, we now learn that 75,000 were apparently PCF members!' Another PCF ploy was to label American MPs patrolling Paris in jeeps 'the new occupying power', but the need for military police was apparent, with the sub-prefect at Le Havre recording rape, theft and violence by US troops that had put 300 women in hospital since June. Popular humour renamed SHAEF (the Supreme Headquarters, Allied Expeditionary Force) as 'La Société Hotelière des Americains en France' because of all the luxury hotels and private houses it requisitioned.[7] And doctors and hospitals recorded an epidemic of sexually transmitted diseases.

On 31 August the GPRF moved house from London and Algiers to Paris, holding its first Cabinet meeting there on 2 September, from which moment it had all the appearance of a legitimate government, although not an elected one. There was certainly no other contender for the title. On 9 September de Gaulle enlarged and reshuffled his government and began on 14 September an exhausting series of visits to towns and cities all over the liberated areas. Like a medieval monarch showing himself to his people, he also dismissed functionaries and even Résistance heroes who displeased him and kept in post men he considered irreplaceable for the moment, including many like Maurice Papon, who had been instrumental in sending the Jews of Bordeaux to their death during the Occupation. A number of communists were among those whose day of glory ended after a few minutes' conversation with the General, also those in authority who had been too zealous in purging alleged collaborators. The priority, in de Gaulle's mind, was to re-establish order and weld the divided nation into one people.

This meant an end to the freedom of action which many Resistance and Maquis groups had enjoyed. As early as 23 September most of the young men in the FFI found themselves conscripted after the General made it clear that the war with Germany was not over and that their service to France would continue in uniform and under military discipline until it ended. The strongest resistance to this policy came understandably from the *milices populaires*. Founded by the PCF initially as *milices ouvrières*, or workers' militia, their numbers prompted Churchill to voice his fears in Quebec that September that communist antipathy to de Gaulle would provoke civil war in France.[8] Roosevelt wrote to Cordell Hull on 19 September in justification of the continued non-recognition of the GPRF, now firmly established in Paris, 'because it held no mandate from the people'.[9] Did he really believe that normal elections could have been held in a country where total war was still being fought over large tracts of the north-eastern *départements*, where tens of thousands of civilians were trapped in the pockets of resistance around the major Atlantic coast ports of Lorient, St Nazaire, La Rochelle and Bordeaux under regular Allied bombardment for eleven months after D-Day, and of whose adult citizens almost 2 million were in German hands as POWs and forced workers?

To still the protests from rank-and-file communists, on 30 October de Gaulle gave two posts in the provisional government to PCF members. He also pardoned and allowed to return to France the party's secretary general Maurice Thorez, who had spent the last five years in Moscow after deserting the army during the phoney war. His deputy Jacques Duclos was anyway under strict instructions from Moscow not to cause problems for de Gaulle, so long as his armed forces were fighting Germany and thus taking some pressure off the eastern front. When Thorez returned to France in January 1945, he made a point of telling his followers not to rock the boat. 'We need,' he said, 'one state, one police force, one army.' To striking miners, he ordered, 'Roll up your sleeves and get on with the reconstruction of the nation.' All was, on the surface, harmony at this stage. When de Gaulle disarmed the *milices patriotiques*, which were largely communist-led, he pooh-poohed the fears of his supporters that the PCF would mount a *coup d'état*.

'The Communists are no danger,' he said. 'No more so than reeds painted to resemble iron bars. In any case, to make a revolution, you need revolutionaries – and I am the only revolutionary in France.'[10]

The programme of the GPRF included the establishment of special courts to try and sentence to death major collaborators and public figures of the Vichy regime. Energy resources including the coal mines were nationalised, as was the giant Renault motor company, the Gnome et Rhône aero engine factories and the largest French airline, Air France. This was not socialism per se; as early as 18 June 1942 de Gaulle had announced in a speech at the Royal Albert Hall that the propertied minority in France who had betrayed the nation and were profiting from the Occupation would be divested of their wealth after the war, and promised that the masses who bore the brunt of the Occupation should be rewarded after the eventual victory with a fairer share of the nation's wealth. All this was a masterly show of authority by a leader who had yet to receive a single vote in a democratic election.

Adding continuing insult to previous injury, on 28 September Churchill had informed the House of Commons that His Majesty's Government was about to recognise the government of Italy, formerly an enemy country – but not that of France, which even at the nadir of collaboration with Hitler had never declared war against the Allies and now had a provisional government representing all shades of opinion that had fought the Germans, both inside France and abroad. Again, MPs rose to protest that it was time for Britain to decide its relationship with its closest neighbour, and not wait any longer for Washington to dictate what could, and what could not, be done or said in Westminster. The lobby correspondents hastened from the debate to fuel editorials in the major newspapers criticising a new meaning of the word *attentiste*.

If the British press was hostile towards its own government's attitude, public opinion and newspapers south of the Channel also interpreted as hostile London's refusal to recognise the body now governing France. Duff Cooper, who was at last ambassador in an embassy in the capital of the country to which he was accredited, was still not allowed to call the GPRF a government. He wrote to his friend the MP Harold Nicolson, 'What would we [British] say if de Gaulle dared to declare in a major speech that it was high time *we* held a general election?' This was a reference to the unwillingness of Churchill to hold elections until the war in Europe was over. Duff Cooper also reminded Nicolson that the longer Britain delayed its recognition of the GPRF, the more ridiculous it looked to the world and the less goodwill it would gain in France when the long-delayed recognition was eventually conceded.[11] Without any animosity toward Duff Cooper, another MP asked in the Commons on 8 October whether it was not ridiculous for him to have the rank and status of an ambassador to a government that his own did not recognise.

Accustomed as they were to covering up for their political masters, the suave diplomats in the Foreign Office had by now had enough. On 20 October Cadogan wrote to Eden suggesting that Roosevelt be advised the British Government intended to recognise the GPRF in a week's time – this in order to ascertain his reaction. As both men were aware, it was the right moment to do this, just before the elections in which Roosevelt would not want to lose the votes of the many supporters of de Gaulle in the USA.

Did Roosevelt, eager to seize every potential vote, forget all about his obedient ally in Downing Street and His Majesty's Government in Westminster? Or was his next action a deliberate gesture of contempt? Whichever, on 21 October Cadogan was awoken by the Foreign Office duty clerk with the news that US Ambassador Jefferson Caffery in Paris had been instructed by Washington to announce that the State Department was prepared to grant recognition. The following day US Ambassador John Winant in London informed the Foreign Office that the Paris Embassy had been instructed to go ahead and formally recognise the GPRF at midday. Cadogan immediately cabled Duff Cooper to do the same.

Churchill was for once dumbstruck at this political betrayal by the man he had thought his friend in the White House. Again, he swallowed his pride, writing to the president that he had been 'somewhat surprised by the sudden *volte-face* by the State Department' and hoped that the Russians, who had also agreed to synchronise their recognition with Washington, would not be offended. Roosevelt's communications with the prime minister suffered from an obvious preoccupation in the White House with domestic matters: when Churchill passed on to the Foreign Office the president's suggestion that it would be necessary to wait two or three days before concluding the recognition, Cadogan contacted Winant, who tried to find out what was going on. At the same time Cadogan advised the prime minister that Duff Cooper could hardly be instructed to delay recognition when his American opposite number already had his instructions to go ahead.

And so in a flurry of cables and embarrassment London, Moscow and Washington recognised the GPRF and the Assembly as the provisional government of France. As Duff Cooper had foreseen, it was done so late and so clumsily that what should have been grounds for friendship between nations achieved nothing of the sort, de Gaulle declaring coldly that 'the government is satisfied that they want to call it by its proper title'. He was more concerned at what seemed a deliberate American policy of restricting France's role in the advance towards Berlin, so that her claim to participate in talks on the future of Germany, which had invaded her territory three times in seventy years, could be ignored. He told Allied journalists in Paris that his plan to put ten further French divisions into the field by the spring of 1945 was on hold because, although the resuscitated French army had rifles and other personal weapons a-plenty, since D-Day it had not received sufficient armour or heavy weapons to equip a single formation. When he added that this was to some extent because of the damage to port installations complicating deliveries, a journalist asked, 'You said, "to some extent," general?' De Gaulle nodded. 'That's what I said.'[12]

Was it true that the US was withholding arms and equipment from French divisions at this juncture? Apparently so, and the key seems to lie in Cordell Hull's memoirs: '[Roosevelt] wanted a Four-Power organisation to be the world policeman, using the forces of the United States, Great Britain, Russia and China. All the other nations *including France* were to be disarmed (under this plan).'[13]

Such was the scale of French losses in the First World War that the anniversary of the armistice in 1918 is still celebrated in every town and village in France. Churchill's love of military ceremony was partly the reason he wanted to visit liberated Paris for the ceremonies on 11 November 1944, but de Gaulle saw no reason to bend over backwards to share this national event with the man who had told him to his face that he would always side with Washington against Paris. Fortunately, the diplomats on both sides of the Channel were intent on healing rifts, not rubbing salt in wounds. Duff Cooper talked to René Massigli; Massigli talked to Georges Bidault, now French Foreign Minister, and Bidault set to work on de Gaulle. He said that Churchill might come any other day but 11 November. Bidault persisted, arguing that Armistice Day was the right time to honour a warrior like him in his old age and that neither ingratitude nor anger are political attitudes.[14]

Unaware of the diplomatic moves, Churchill had been intending to come to France without an invitation, in order to visit Eisenhower. Duff Cooper warned that this would be the last straw for his relationship with de Gaulle. Fortunately, the reception of the formal invitation from Paris changed this but the diplomats' work was not yet done. The official British reply said frigidly that the prime minister would *not* be accompanied by his wife. The French proposed to accommodate the prime minister in the Foreign Ministry building on the Quai d'Orsay. The British preferred him to stay in the embassy on the rue de Rivoli. Then the Foreign Office advised Paris that political discussions might be held during the visit and Bidault warned Eden that this might damage even further the fragile relationship between Churchill and de Gaulle.

When everything seemed to have been more or less arranged, the British security services came up with an alarming rumour that German stay-behinds might assassinate the prime minister. As late as 9 November, no one was certain that the visit would take place and the uncertainty seems to have stirred up all the animosity in the two main protagonists. It must have been an extraordinary relief for everyone making the arrangements when Churchill climbed the steps into his personal aircraft on 10 November and took off for Paris – accompanied not just by his wife but also his daughter Mary. De Gaulle, Bidault and other ministers welcomed the prime minister's party at Orly airport and drove with them to the Quai d'Orsay, where the entire first floor had been lavishly prepared for the guests. Churchill's obsession with long hot baths was catered for by a gold-plated bath that had been reserved for Hermann Göring; the prime minister was delighted that Eden only had a silver-plated one in his suite.

The procession next morning saw Churchill in the uniform of a Marshal of the Royal Air Force and cap festooned with golden oak leaves sitting beside de Gaulle in an open car escorted by several hundred mounted riders of the Garde Républicaine with drawn swords and burnished breastplates and helmets gleaming in the bright sunshine. Behind the troops lining every metre of the route, vast crowds cheered their passage, while at each window people leaned out, waved tricolour flags and Union Jacks, shouting themselves hoarse. Each time Churchill raised a hand in his trademark V-sign, the cries of '*Vive Churchill!*' rivalled those of '*Vive de Gaulle!*' After laying wreaths on the tomb of the Unknown Soldier from the First World War beneath the Arc de Triomphe, the two leaders led a cortège down the Champs-Élysées side by side to take the salute at a march-past of French and British troops.

For the crowds, it looked as though the two wartime leaders were the best of peacetime friends.

Certainly, de Gaulle put aside any animosity that day to give Churchill the lion's share of the limelight. His speech at the state luncheon in the War Ministry, serving as presidential residence, was eloquent and generous in its praise for the man and the country who had stood by France in 1914 and 1940. After admitting that they had had their disagreements, he included Foreign Minister Eden, who had worked so long for recognition of the GPRF, in the toast concluding, 'We lift our glasses ... in honour of England, our ally of yesterday, today and tomorrow.'[15]

Churchill's equally moving response was delivered with tears in his eyes – in English. He switched to his own brand of French afterwards at a two-hour conference upstairs with Bidault and Massigli supporting de Gaulle and Eden and Cadogan on Churchill's side. Churchill omits from his memoirs any mention of these important discussions, which continued the following day at the Foreign Ministry where all the outstanding differences between the two countries were discussed without voices being raised even when de Gaulle, who had served in Syria/Lebanon between the wars, raised the prickly matter of General Spears' repeated interference in French affairs there. When he asked for Britain's help to procure equipment for *eight* new divisions he had raised, but which lacked the vital communications equipment, armour, artillery and transport necessary for the advance into Germany, Churchill agreed to try and persuade the Americans to release supplies. As to the French desire to have a zone of occupation in Germany after the victory – as France had had after the First World War – he replied that the last Big Three conference had divided the Reich in two, with the eastern Länder to be occupied by the Soviets and the west by the British in the north and the Americans in the south. Britain was happy to further divide her zone to give the French a zone of occupation of their own. As to its size and geographical extent, well, that was something to be decided between friends, wasn't it?

It was de Gaulle who raised the question of post-war American bases in territory controlled by Britain, France and Holland. Dakar was one base mentioned, Singapore another. To Churchill's suggestion that the bases could be ceded to the United Nations, the French reply was an emphatic 'No!' A right of use was acceptable, but cession definitely not. To de Gaulle's question what the British could do to help restore French sovereignty in Indochina, the reply was that he should talk to the Americans about that.

The suggestion led to de Gaulle's reflection that Washington's intention to dismantle the European empires and end their systems of imperial preference should be tempered by a warning from America's friends of the dangers in destroying political systems which had grown up over centuries in order to replace them with policies that were no more than pie-in-the-sky – untried ideals that might sound workable in a democracy like the United States, but would produce chaos in the very different societies of Africa and Asia. Churchill was already aware that Britain, although ending the war on the winning side, had been bankrupted by the war and would find herself unable to hold on to her own Asian colonies. He confined himself to commenting that overseas possessions formerly necessary for strategic reasons would become more and more costly and were possibly unnecessary in the age of modern transportation and communication.

Finally, he admitted that many unnamed people in London and Washington had been uneasy about the possibility of armed strife between the Gaullists and the communists during and after the Liberation – and even of his visit being interrupted by civil disorder. As he had seen on his motorcade that day through the city where tens of thousands of communist voters lived, there was clearly no risk of this, and he congratulated de Gaulle on having avoided a civil war.[16]

The new *Entente Cordiale* was to last another twenty-four hours. After dinner in the British Embassy, de Gaulle welcomed his guest aboard the sumptuously equipped presidential train that was to take them to Besançon for a tour of inspection of General De Lattre's First Army, about to launch a massive attack in northeast France. Defying the worsening weather, the day of 13 November was spent in a series of inspections of France's reborn army, with the intention of ending at a vantage point in the mountains, from which to witness the battle on the following day. However, extreme cold and deep snow prevented the train from reaching its destination, to the great relief of Churchill's daughter Mary, who was worried that spending ten hours outdoors in foul weather inspecting troops and military installations that day was about to bring on a recurrence of her father's pneumonia.

Churchill was none the less well pleased with his visit and particularly noted the respect amounting almost to fear shown to his host by the half-dozen senior generals they met.[17] It is saddening, therefore, to read his report of the visit to President Roosevelt dated 15 November, in which he attempted to deny reports of the discussions in Paris that had appeared in French newspapers by pretending that nothing of import was mentioned. He did, however, fulfil his promise to de Gaulle by pointing out how the French had been excluded from the councils of war and denied equipment, without which their divisions could not participate in the drive into the Reich, pointing out that 'before five years are out, a French army must be made to take on the main task of holding down Germany'. Referring to Stalin as 'U.J' – Roosevelt called the Soviet leader Uncle Joe – Churchill mentioned that he would be cabling him in Moscow to say that no agreements had been made, or undertakings given, while in Paris. After suggesting that the next summit conference, with or without Stalin, should include de Gaulle, he betrayed his insecurity by hastening to reassure the president that he was 'not putting on French clothes'.[18]

There is no mention in Churchill's war memoirs of his resuscitation in private conversation with de Gaulle of Monnet's 1940 proposal for a treaty of unity between France and Britain, to which de Gaulle replied, according to his own war memoirs:

> If you wish it, I am ready. Our two countries will follow our lead. America and Russia, embroiled in their rivalry, will not be able to ignore it. Moreover, we shall have the support of many states and world opinion which instinctively fears the great powers. It would enable England and France to make peace together, just as we have, twice in thirty years, confronted a war together.[19]

An opinion poll that month found only 33 per cent of French people approving US policy towards France.[20] If de Gaulle's diary is a true account of the private conversation between the two leaders at some point in the train journey to Besançon, it would be the first overt reference to the forty-year-long Cold War confrontation of the USSR and USA, and reflects his awareness that the idea of allying France with the Soviet Union that had seemed attractive in the desperate days of 1941 and 1942 when he was so ungenerously treated by 'the Anglo-Saxons', had been replaced in his mind by a more sober appreciation of the postwar balance of power, making it preferable to regard those same 'Anglo-Saxons' as the best defence against Soviet designs in Europe.

One immediate casualty of Churchill's visit to Paris was General Spears in Beirut, who received a cable from Downing Street shortly after Churchill's return inviting him to resign on 15 December. This was not purely a gesture to de Gaulle, for Eden, Cadogan and Duff Cooper had all been urging this for some time, to put an end to his deliberate undermining of French influence in the Levant and the friction that was causing across the Channel.

The tumultuous year of 1944 was not yet over. On 10 December de Gaulle was in Moscow, being received by Stalin and other high government officials. On 16 December Hitler scraped together sufficient forces to launch the last great German offensive of the Second World War. In what became known as the Battle of the Bulge, von Rundstedt's Fifth and Sixth Panzer Armies burst through the forests and hills of the Ardennes in a two-pronged attempt to deny the crucial port of Antwerp to the Allies. To find reinforcements for General Patton's sector of the front, which was bearing the brunt of the attack, on New Year's Day Eisenhower ordered a retreat from the recently liberated city of Strasbourg. De Gaulle immediately requested him not to abandon to the enemy so important a city, whose citizens would be subject to brutal reprisals, and asked Churchill's and Roosevelt's support in this. In Washington, the president did nothing, but Churchill did intervene by immediately setting out for Eisenhower's HQ in France, although tired from a stressful visit to Greece. Before then, relations between the Allied Supreme Commander and his French subordinates, ordered by de Gaulle to stand firm on Strasbourg, had worsened to the point of Eisenhower threatening to stop supplies of fuel and ammunition to the French forces. In return, de Gaulle threatened to halt the transportation of American supplies across France.[21]

When de Gaulle arrived at Eisenhower's HQ in St Germain on 3 January, he found Churchill arguing in his favour with Bedell-Smith. For a combination of reasons, including French intransigence, Eisenhower that day ordered the successful counter-offensive against von Rundstedt's forces, whose impetus was running out due to over-stretched lines of communication and exhaustion of supplies. Both Churchill and de Gaulle were thus able to claim in their memoirs the credit for saving the people of Strasbourg.

The next summit conference took place early in February at Yalta on the Crimean peninsula. Photographs of the Big Three taken there show Stalin in rude good health beside Churchill, looking old and tired, and Roosevelt, who had been suffering from advanced arteriosclerosis since the beginning of 1944, looking near to death – as indeed he was. De Gaulle had not been invited to Yalta, and said bitterly, 'The Americans will commit all imaginable stupidities, and even some that are unthinkable.' Globally, he was right, for Roosevelt was outmanoeuvred by Stalin. However, largely thanks to Eden's subtle pressure on his prime minister, Churchill and he represented French interests on the grounds that a strong France would be important for European stability after the war.

When the question of the French zone of Germany was raised at the first plenary session in the Livadia Palace, Roosevelt spoke neither for nor against the idea, it being understood that the British were dividing their own zone to share with the French, so that neither Russian nor American interests were directly affected. Stalin, however, objected that the French had done little fighting in 1940 and were still doing little enough – apart from the Normandie-Niemen squadron of Fighting French airmen flying Yak-3 fighters that had downed 273 Luftwaffe aircraft in some of the worst fighting on the eastern front. If France were given a slice of German territory, he asked rhetorically, what was to stop Belgium, Holland and other countries damaged by the German attack from asking for one as reparations? As to the French sitting on the Three-Power Control Commission that was to govern Germany after the war, he did not want to see French representatives making it a four-power entity because that would leave his representatives heavily outnumbered.

But Churchill stuck to his guns, arguing that the French had useful experience of occupying Germany after the First World War and that, if they did not sit on the Control Commission, there would be no way of controlling the administration of the zone the British intended giving them. When Roosevelt gave as two years the duration he foresaw for the American occupation, Stalin had all the more reason for keeping the French out. He knew that French troops occupying any part of Germany would not go home so fast and leave their eastern frontier unprotected. So, if he could prevent the French from getting a zone, after the

British and Americans pulled out, the field would then be wide open for him to arrange a 'spontaneous' reunification of the eastern and western Länder, leaving Moscow in control of the whole country.

On the unresolved question of the French zone being referred to the separate Foreign Ministers' meeting, Eden suavely but obstinately refused to give way to Soviet Foreign Minister Vyacheslav Molotov and Cordell Hull's successor Edward Stettinius – with the result that at the eighth plenary session it was finally agreed de Gaulle would have his zone, with representatives sitting on the Control Commission. The news reached Paris before the end of the conference, but left him rightly convinced that Roosevelt had let Stalin get away with far too much in Eastern Europe. Adding insult to injury was the American president's invitation to meet him while stopping over at Algiers on the way home – an offence to de Gaulle's prickly sensibilities and an infringement of diplomatic protocol. How dare an American president 'invite' the leader of the French provisional government to a meeting on French soil?

Three weeks before the end of the war in Europe, Leclerc's troops were ordered to halt their advance into south-west Germany in order for an ALSOS team to arrive first at a German nuclear facility at Hechingen in Baden-Württemberg. On 23 or 24 April Captain Boris Pash of ALSOS seized the German scientists there, together with a large quantity of heavy water and more than a ton of uranium cubes that had been buried in a field outside the town – all of which were wafted across the Atlantic to new homes.[22]

The war in Europe ended on 8 May 1945 with the unconditional surrender signed by Admiral Doenitz, briefly Hitler's successor as head of the Reich. The war against Japan was, of course, continuing in the Pacific, but France's interest in it was peripheral. The Vichy Government had concluded an agreement with Tokyo that 'guaranteed' French sovereignty in Indochina but gave certain occupation rights to the Japanese. On the evening of 9 March 1945 disarmed French soldiers all over the country were brutally massacred by Japanese occupation troops. Roosevelt having expressed the opinion that France had milked Vietnam for a hundred years and 'the Vietnamese people deserved better than that',[23] it came as no surprise to de Gaulle when the chiefs of staff in Washington refused air support for the French and French colonial soldiers fighting for their lives against the common enemy in Indochina.

Harry Truman, who had replaced Henry Wallace as Roosevelt's running mate in the 1944 presidential elections, took the vice-presidential oath of office on 20 January 1945, but in the eighty-two days before the president died on 12 April, he was accorded only two meetings with the sick old man clinging to power in the White House, whose health deteriorated until the cerebral haemorrhage that ended his life. Truman therefore became president of the United States on the same day, unbriefed on anything except some domestic matters, and prudently decided to let foreign affairs continue as before, rather than make mistakes due to his own ignorance. At the Potsdam summit conference that followed the end of the war in Europe and lasted from 17 July to 2 August 1945, Stalin held most of the cards in a three-handed poker game against Truman, uncertain of his position on major issues, and Churchill, shattered by losing a general election that saw him replaced in mid-conference by his wartime deputy Clement Attlee, whose Labour Party had won a crushing victory at the polls in May. As at previous summit conferences, de Gaulle was not invited to witness the Soviet leader consolidate his hold on Eastern Europe, grabbing the Baltic states and a large portion of the Balkans.

On October 1945 a general election in France returned 159 communists, 146 socialists and 152 *deputés* of Bidault's Christian-Democrat-Resistance Mouvement Républicain Populaire (MRP).[24] With Roosevelt dead and Churchill removed from power, although continuing to raise his voice in the House of Commons, de Gaulle was exclusively occupied with governing France in the immediate aftermath of the Allied victory in Europe. Yet, to the surprise of everyone in London and Washington, he showed no interest in publishing a manifesto and presenting himself as a candidate in the formal election by the Consultative Assembly of a permanent head of government on 13 November 1945.

Ambassador Duff Cooper had warned Prime Minister Attlee that an unofficial visit to Paris on that day by Winston Churchill could be the spark in a powder keg. He could not have been more wrong. De Gaulle received his old ally and sparring partner warmly and showed no interest in the proceedings of the Assembly. He told Churchill with disarming honesty, 'They'll take me as I am or not at all.'[25] Wearing a blue business suit, which Duff Cooper noted in his diary as becoming him better than uniform, de Gaulle was far more deferential to his visitor that day than when he had been prime minister. Churchill's diary recorded the atmosphere thus: 'One would have thought [de Gaulle] a country gentleman living a hundred leagues from the capital. Not an interruption, not a phone call, not a message, no coming and going of secretaries, nothing that might have indicated anything extraordinary was happening.'[26]

But it was. Almost at the same time that de Gaulle was accompanying Churchill to his waiting car the Assembly unanimously elected him head of government. Letters and cables of congratulation poured in from many countries, but de Gaulle was unimpressed. 'I knew,' he wrote, 'that the vote was a gesture of respect for my past actions, and not a promise of commitment [to my policies] for the future.'[27]

And so it was to prove. Hardly had he formed his Cabinet than all the old schisms between parties and personalities reappeared to fragment the temporary alliance against the occupiers and collaborators. Making no alliances – he actually went so far as to forbid his followers from using his name or the adjective 'Gaullist' for themselves – the General found it impossible to conceal his disdain for the pettiness of politicians, despising equally the negative stance of the socialists, the naked revolutionary ambitions of the communists, the venal ineffectiveness of the Right, the radicals' suspicion of everyone else, the endless intrigues in the Assembly and the civil unrest stirred up by trade unions which had done so little for so long.

One of his first actions was to announce a referendum to determine a new constitution for a *fourth* republic, to be held as soon as the 2 million POWs and deportees could be repatriated. This massive migration was largely completed by midsummer, whereupon he scheduled a combined referendum and election for the month of October, in which Frenchwomen were to enjoy the right to vote for the first time. By an overwhelming majority – approximately 96 per cent of votes cast – the war-weary nation rejected a return to the pre-war regime of the Third Republic. As in Britain at the time, there was a thirst for change and for a 'better life', epitomised by the number of *résistants* elected at the expense of some of the Old Guard politicians who had voted total power to Pétain in 1940. As in post-war Britain, the balance of power lay with the Left: three-quarters of the *députés* were communists, socialists or former Christian Democrats who now supported the MRP.

However, a common background in the Resistance did not mean unity because opinion was sharply divided over the form the new republic should take. With Pétain's government-by-decree a painful memory, the communists and some socialists favoured the idea of a one-house legislature, with all members directly elected by the people, and the role of the president reduced to that of a figurehead and the Cabinet made subordinate to the Assembly. De Gaulle remained aloof from this and all other controversies, while letting it be known that he favoured a strong executive and stable presidency to drag France out of the poverty and instability that were the legacies of the Occupation spoliation. On 26 December 1945 the franc was devalued from 50:$1 to 120:$1 and from 200:£1 to 480:£1. Economists worked out that, by comparison with other countries, France was eighty-four times poorer than in 1914.[28] While it is often so difficult to interpret statistics, of which many accept President Truman's definition as 'damned lies', it was obvious that the French economy had been, not damaged, but ruined by the invasion of 1940, the Occupation and the war of liberation.

On 3 January 1946 the General's daughter Elizabeth married Major Alain De Boissieu of Leclerc's 2 DB, after which the bride's parents went to Cap d'Antibes for a few days of peace and quiet in which to think about the future after the socialist *députés* had demanded a reduction of 20 per cent in the defence estimates during the 1946 budget debate on the first day of the New Year. Exasperated by this repetition of a major error of the Third Republic that had left France unable to defend herself in 1940, de Gaulle resigned as head of government on 20 January 1946, half expecting a groundswell of protest in the population at the behaviour of their politicians to bring him back to power with a mandate to impose his constitutional ideas for the future of France. Instead, the public was stunned into inaction at what it had done and the politicians, as always, moved swiftly to take advantage of the moment by choosing one of their own – the socialist Félix Gouin – to replace him. British Ambassador Duff Cooper commented dryly that, on the eve of the anniversary of the execution of Louis XIV, France's first post-war head of government had 'cut off his own head and passed into the shadow-land of politics'.[29]

The man who had been his country's conscience for five and a half years retired to the life of a private citizen in his modest home at Colombey-les-deux-Eglises, 300km from Paris in the Champagne-Ardennes region. It seemed to most of his compatriots that the man with the voice they knew from all the wartime broadcasts, the man who had told Madame Monnet in June 1940, 'I have come to save the honour of France' – and one of the few who continued to believe in the honour of France – was destined for a peaceful old age, far from the in-fighting of the political scene.

They could not have been more wrong.

Notes

1. *2194 Days of War*, London, Windward, 1979, p. 572
2. A. Beevor & A. Cooper, *Paris after the Liberation*, London, Hamish Hamilton, 1994, p. 58
3. See also D. Boyd, *Voices from the Dark Years*, Thrupp, Sutton, 2007, p. 253
4. Beevor & Cooper, *Paris after the Liberation*, p. 37
5. L.R. Groves, *Now It Can Be Told*, New York, Harper & Row, 1962, p. 234
6. Beevor & Cooper, *Paris after the Liberation*, p. x
7. Ibid., pp. 20, 39 and 117
8. F. Kersaudy, *de Gaulle et Churchill*, Paris, Perrin Tempus, 2003, p. 283
9. Ibid., p. 384
10. ed. M. Jullian, *de Gaulle – Traits d'esprit*, Paris, Cherche-Midi, 2000, p. 122
11. H. Nicolson, *The Harold Nicolson Diaries*, London, Orion, 2004, p. 338
12. De Gaulle, *Mémoires de Guerre: Le Salut*, Paris, Plon, 1959, p. 338
13. C. Hull, *Memoirs*, London, Hodder & Stoughton, 1948, Vol. 2, pp. 1642–3
14. G. Bidault, *D'une Résistance à l'autre*, Paris, Presses du Siècle, 1965, p. 72
15. De Gaulle, *Le Salut*, pp. 359–60
16. Ibid., p. 51
17. W.S. Churchill, *The Second World War*, Vol. 6, London, Penguin Classics, 2005, pp. 218–19
18. Ibid., pp. 219–21
19. De Gaulle, *Le Salut*, p. 52
20. Beevor & Cooper, *Paris after the Liberation*, p. 39
21. Ibid., p. 36
22. B. Pash, *The Alsos Mission*, New York, Award House, 1969, pp. 200–12
23. D. Boyd, *The French Foreign Legion*, Thrupp, Sutton, 2006, pp. 285–91
24. Beevor & Cooper, *Paris after the Liberation*, p. 253
25. De Gaulle, *Le Salut*, p. 273
26. A.D. Cooper, *Old Men Forget*, London, RH Davis, 1953, p. 358
27. De Gaulle, *Le Salut*, p. 274
28. Beevor & Cooper, *Paris after the Liberation*, p. 26
29. Ibid, p. 261

PART 3

FIGHTING FOR THE FUTURE

16

CITIZEN DE GAULLE

Of the two wartime allies, Winston Churchill was at least still able to voice his opinions from a seat in the House of Commons, albeit on the Opposition benches, while Charles de Gaulle was a private citizen devoid of any political power except his own solitary vote. Supporters? When one well-wisher boasted of having a wife who was an ardent Gaullist, the General replied wryly, 'So is mine, I think, but it depends on the day.'[1]

The draft constitution of the Fourth Republic was rejected by a national referendum in May 1946 and a new Assembly was elected to prepare a revised draft, which it approved on 29 September after a little window-dressing. Not essentially different from the first draft, it was adopted by a narrow margin in a referendum on 13 October. The Preamble was admirable enough, reaffirming the original Declaration of the Rights of Man as set out by the National Assembly in 1789 and guaranteeing freedom of religion and equality to all citizens, whatever their origin. Women, who had not previously had the vote in France, were declared equal in all respects to men but were in effect still disadvantaged in many areas of activity and not allowed to open a bank account of their own, if married. As in Britain in the immediate post-war period, a major step forward was the institution of a national health care system and the framework of a welfare state.

The Constitution proper began with a declaration that France was an indivisible, secular, democratic and social republic with its national flag once again the familiar Tricolore and the national anthem *La Marseillaise* to be sung on all official occasions. The old revolutionary legend *Liberté, Egalité, Fraternité* replaced Pétain's *Travaille, Famille, Patrie* on all official documents.

And yet, to de Gaulle's cynical eye, the 1946 Constitution was a time bomb containing the seeds of the destruction of the Fourth Republic. He had no qualms about denouncing it as unworkable because it had no provisions for the strong executive that he considered vital to drive the impoverished and demoralised nation through the difficult years of reconstruction that lay ahead. In this, he would be proven right, but at the time its adoption was another defeat for him.

Like Churchill, a prolific writer in his wilderness years, de Gaulle spent long hours each day seated at the desk of his study on the ground floor of the hexagonal tower he had had built for the purpose at La Boisserie in Colombey-les-deux-Eglises. Originally *la brasserie* – the village brewery – it was a modest home for himself, his wife Yvonne and their handicapped daughter Anne. Lacking the money to buy dressed stone for the construction of the tower extension, he had local masons build it in *moellon* – random stone from cleared fields – and planted a creeper to unify the result with the rest of the house.

Colombey had been selected by him as a suitable place for a soldier's home because it was halfway between the War Ministry in Paris and the garrison towns on the north-eastern frontier, and also because he loved the views over the rolling countryside of the Champagne-Ardennes region stretching away uninterruptedly for 15km or more. The study is light and airy, with generous windows on three walls, from which he watched not only the course of the seasons changing the colours of the vegetation, but also the political scene beyond the horizon in Paris. In bewildering succession, the lower House, now termed L'Assemblée Nationale in reflection of its increased power, brought down a series of largely opportunistic coalition cabinets where many of the same old names from the Third Republic replayed their game of musical ministries in each other's administrations.

Between de Gaulle's resignation in January 1946 and June 1958, when it was laid to rest by him none too soon, the shaky Fourth Republic justified every gloomy doubt he had entertained at the moment of its birth. It managed in those twelve years to kill off no less than twenty-three governments under seventeen first ministers, four of whom served twice, while one managed three terms. Many administrations lasted only a few weeks, with the record going to Robert Schuman's second stint in 1948, which lasted only six days. As ministers came and went with no time to introduce their vaunted policies, France became a country run by its civil servants, while the population became ever more disillusioned about its elected leaders. Some political newcomers forged in the Resistance movements also took their place in political life, big business and the powerful state bureaucracy, where they urged social reconstruction and endeavoured to reassert France's lost international prestige, but had not enough weight to counter the politicking that sapped the strength of France like a cancer in the body politic.

As spokesman for all his compatriots who felt disgusted at this betrayal of all the blood spilled and suffering endured during the five years of the Occupation and the anguished months of the Liberation, de Gaulle made a speech at Bayeux denouncing the basic defects of the Fourth Republic and arguing that the president of France should have more power to counteract the squabbling of the parties. So many of his compatriots agreed with him that, in April 1947, he founded Le Rassemblement du Peuple Français as, literally, a rallying point for the French nation. In the local elections of October that year, this entirely new political party received nearly 40 per cent of the votes cast. It was a stunning grassroots endorsement of what he had been thinking, saying and writing since his resignation. In the general election of 1951 the RPF won more seats in the National Assembly than any other single party but, such was the resistance of the established parties, it could neither form a government nor force a modification of the constitution. In 1953, after a series of defections by RPF deputies hungry for more power than their party could give them, de Gaulle abandoned the RPF and retired again in disgust to his study at Colombey-les-deux-Eglises, emerging to speak on many issues, including Franco-German reconciliation, an enthusiasm shared with his old wartime ally north of the Channel. The General even put forward the idea of a political union between France and Germany on the model of Jean Monnet's stillborn Anglo-French union of 1940.

The French economy was slow to recover from the five years of industrial looting by the Nazis and the drain of Pétain's and Laval's collaborationist policies and from the considerable destruction wrought by the war fought across much of its economically most important territory for almost a year from June 1944 onwards. On 5 June 1947, US Secretary of State George C. Marshall paved the way in a commencement speech at Harvard for what became the European Recovery Programme, better known as Marshall Aid. The aim was to kick-start war-damaged economies in seventeen European nations as a way of preventing their communist parties manipulating their way to power through the leverage of poverty and high unemployment and also to found and nurture new markets for American industry and commerce. Aid was originally offered even to countries under military occupation by the USSR, but Moscow swiftly placed these and its whole sphere of influence out of bounds to the American initiative. For half a century the Iron Curtain was to divide the democratic states of Western Europe from the countries in the eastern half of the continent with whom they had shared for centuries a common political heritage before they were reduced to the status of Moscow's satellites.

Ironically, considering how Washington had shunned him and done de Gaulle down throughout the war, the high-ranking American diplomat John Foster Dulles approached him in December 1947 when President Truman's administration feared that France was going communist. Implying that massive American support would be available, Dulles asked whether the General would be prepared to mount a *coup d'état* to grab power in that eventuality. De Gaulle's reply is not on record but it is unlikely that he enthused over any action dependent on US support. At the same time, under a covert programme entitled 'Gladio', Washington was setting up in a number of European states including France a network of 'stay-behinds' – sleeper agents trained to remain in place after a communist takeover. Each had a sub-network of right-wing contacts and was equipped with quantities of weapons and explosives cached at strategic points ready for use. The true aim behind Gladio was to cause civil unrest on a scale that would justify American intervention 'to restore order', but the less cynical of the agents believed they had a glorious patriotic destiny before them. In the event, Gladio slumbered on, except in Italy where various outrages were perpetrated with arms and explosives from its stores. In France, despite all the francophobe Jonahs in the State Department, the communists did not come to power, despite no other party having a clear majority in the country or in Parliament.

As in Britain, the painfully slow period of industrial recovery immediately after the Second World War developed into a radical expansion in most branches of the economy by the mid-fifties, thanks to France's share of the $13 billion injected into Europe under Marshall Aid. Yet 47 per cent of the French people considered that the Marshal Plan was an American update of the Trojan Horse, and the slogan *US GO HOME* was painted on walls all over the country.

Although France's rate of growth speeded up to rival that of Germany and exceed that of most other European countries, her short-lived coalition Cabinets were unable to check the serious inflation that progressively devalued the franc to a low of 1,400 to the pound sterling. Economic cooperation was one thing, but the General in retirement at Colombey-les-deux-Eglises was particularly hostile to the abandonment of sovereignty implicit in France's signature of the Treaty of Brussels on 17 March 1948, which established inter alia the European Defence Community, tying France to the United Kingdom, Belgium, Luxembourg and the Netherlands. To de Gaulle, whose knowledge of history gave him every reason to mistrust treaties of alliance, the only certain defence of France was a French defence.

On 4 April 1949 twelve nations from Western Europe and North America signed the North Atlantic Treaty in Washington, DC. Under Article 5 the signatory states agreed that 'an armed attack against one or more of them in Europe or North America shall be considered an attack against them all'. And so the European Defence Community was replaced by NATO, with General Eisenhower as its first Supreme Commander and British Field Marshal Viscount Bernard Montgomery as his deputy. There was a certain kudos for France in the siting of the purpose-built headquarters of Supreme Headquarters, Allied Powers in Europe (SHAPE) in Rocquencourt, near Versailles.

Citizen de Gaulle was not the only European to recall how slow Washington had been to join the European conflicts that became the First and Second World Wars. As a professional soldier, his analysis of NATO was that it was the Pentagon's tool to ensure that the European signatory states were to serve as the battleground over which any military expansion by the USSR could be fought with both conventional and nuclear weapons. However, at the time, with the perennial Russian hunger for territorial expansion having swallowed up half of Germany – and adding Poland, Czechoslovakia, Hungary, the Baltic republics, Bulgaria and Romania after the end of hostilities – there seemed no alternative to Western Europe forming an alliance with the one state that was industrially and militarily strong enough to resist the further growth of the only empire founded in the twentieth century.

By today's criteria, none of the European colonial powers – Britain, France, Holland, Belgium and Portugal – divested themselves with honour of the empires they had built up in previous centuries, so it is invidious to single out any one for especial criticism. In France, the desire to expunge the humiliation of the Occupation led successive French governments of the Fourth Republic to spill more and more French and colonial blood in the futile effort to regain and hold the pre-war empire.

The Constitution of October 1946 had renamed it 'L'Union Française' and gave the colonial peoples some local autonomy, plus a small representation in the French Parliament, but the same overseas colonies which had provided de Gaulle's first power base for Free France and later furnished an important share of the resources and manpower of the French war effort, now demanded a new relationship with the parent country. Although some politicians saw the long-term advantage of making concessions, most regarded as unacceptable the prospect of giving independence to the colonies. They justified this attitude by the self-fulfilling argument that the native peoples lacked the necessary education and experience for self-government, so that the departure of the existing French administrations would be an open invitation to the Comintern to foment ostensibly spontaneous takeovers by dissidents trained in the USSR.

In Indochina, the French protectorates of Laos and Cambodia were declared independent monarchies to preserve French cultural and commercial influence there, but the situation in Vietnam was the shape of things to come in the former Dutch East Indies, British Malaya and other Asian colonies. Japan's defeat in August 1945 and subsequent withdrawal from Vietnam had enabled France – with some hindrance from American and British commanders in south-east Asia – to regain temporary control of the southern half of the country. North Vietnam, however, was the heartland of Ho Chi Minh's Viet Minh guerrillas. Commanded by General Vo Nguyen Giap, armed and trained by American agencies, they alone had been harassing the Japanese occupants and had no intention of letting their former French overlords return after VJ Day. Negotiations between the two sides broke down in December 1946, leading to an eight-year-long war of atrocities on both sides, of which the first major one was a bombardment of the northern port of Haiphong by French naval vessels under the command of Carmelite Admiral Thierry d'Argenlieu that allegedly killed 6,000 civilians. The bombardment of civilian targets is a fact; only the number of casualties is disputed.

After the final defeat of French forces by the Viet Minh at Dien Bien Phu in May 1954, French premier Pierre Mendès-France sued for peace at the Vietnam conference in Geneva, which signalled the beginning of the end of the French Empire. He had little else in mind except to extricate France from the morass and 'bring the boys home'. Thousands of them never made it back to Europe, having died of untreated wounds or malnutrition on long death marches on a starvation diet. Others were interned for various reasons by the Viet Minh and released only after specific campaigns by former comrades who knew they were still alive. The least lucky were those who had caused their captors most trouble. They did not return until five, ten or more years later.

Although various exploratory talks were held between the American and French general staffs during the French war in Vietnam, domestic politics inhibited Presidents Truman and Eisenhower from sending troops while the US was heavily committed to the United Nations' action in Korea. After that ended in the summer of 1953, hundreds of US military 'advisers' began covert and overt actions against the Viet Cong irregulars even before the French had withdrawn from the country. De Gaulle viewed with a dispassionate professional eye how the end of the Korean War was followed by the rapid build-up of US forces in Vietnam, where American generals made the same mistakes as their French predecessors but on a larger scale.

Many of the French and Foreign Legion POWs in Viet Minh hands whose lives were saved by Mendès-France – and especially the colonial troops raised in Indochina, Algeria and West African colonies – were informed by their *can-bo* political indoctrinators before release that the next step in the Comintern plan to dismantle the French Empire would be taken in North Africa. Just over six months after the defeat in Vietnam, a hard core of Moscow-trained dissidents launched the Front de Libération Nationale (FLN) and its underground armed branch, the Armée de Libération Nationale (ALN), which began a nation-wide terrorist campaign to drive the French out of Algeria by a programme of sabotage and assassination. Although most of the country's Arabic and Berber-speaking inhabitants were disenfranchised and had no particular reason to love their French overlords, it was necessary for the ALN to mount a secondary campaign of assassination and torture directed against native mayors, doctors, teachers, policemen and even postmen to drive a wedge of terror between the *colons* and the indigenous population.

As in Indochina, fears that the rebellion against French rule might spread to neighbouring states led to the French protectorates of Tunisia and Morocco being granted sovereign status in 1956. Obedient to the Comintern, the French Communist Party supported the FLN and many party activists became directly involved, thinking themselves less likely to be caught by the security services than native Algerian activists when transporting funds to purchase arms that had been raised, often by compulsory subscriptions, from the hundreds of thousands of North Africans working in France. If caught, these European 'suitcase carriers' of both sexes were subjected to particularly vicious interrogation, many simply disappearing afterwards without trace.[2]

For the next six years France was fighting, not a remote colonial skirmish in which professional soldiers and local levies died but a full-scale war with universal male conscription and recall of reservists sending more than a half a million men across the Mediterranean. In a hopeless attempt to stem the tide of history, they used fighter aircraft, napalm, heliportered troops and radar-guided artillery against small bands of *fellaghin* armed with nothing heavier than light machine guns. Twin barriers of electrified wire and minefields stretched for hundreds of kilometres on both eastern and western frontiers, but failed to prevent *les fells* returning from their training camps safely sited in Tunisia and Morocco to join the struggle.

The determination of successive French governments to hold on to Algeria had several factors. The country was home to, and run by, nearly 1 million French-speaking settlers whose families had come from France, Italy, Spain and the Levant over a span of 130 years. They had no homes in Europe to which they could retreat, and were as 'Algerian' as their Arabic-speaking neighbours because the country had only been created in the nineteenth century by France from an amorphous collection of tribal areas in the north, over which the Ottoman Empire had suzerainty, and to which were added by force of arms vast stretches of the Sahara and the sub-Sahara, where nomadic tribes had previously recognised no overlords. Having created the country and given it a name, the French had made Algeria an integral part of France itself, comprising three administrative *départements* represented in the National Assembly in the same way as the metropolitan *départements*. Well, not quite. The vast majority of Muslim Algerians had no vote because they failed to qualify educationally.

If history was the political justification for holding on to Algeria, the commercial reason for denying the country independence lay under the sands of the Sahara in the far south of the country, where substantial oil and natural gas reserves had been discovered. The French Sahara was also the ideal place to test nuclear weapons. Already in 1945 de Gaulle's provisional government had set up the Commissariat à l'Energie Atomique (CEA) to examine both civilian and military possibilities of nuclear energy. One reason was that the world was then divided into the USA and Britain, who had the Bomb, and all other countries. For France to restore itself to the first rank among nations, it was necessary to have the Bomb too. Second, since it was inevitable that the USSR would also have the Bomb sooner or later, de Gaulle believed that the United States could not be entrusted with the defence of Europe in any situation where there was a conflict with its own perceived interests; therefore France must have its own nuclear deterrent.

These latter suspicions were confirmed by the negative attitude in Washington to the joint British and French military intervention in Egypt in December 1956. Both before and after that misadventure, the General's unofficial access to the corridors of power enabled him to continue arguing for an independent French nuclear deterrent. As he rightly said, there was no need to aim to rival the United States or the USSR in numbers of nuclear weapons. Since no attacker wanted *any* nuclear retaliation, it was sufficient for France to have a small number of warheads deliverable by its own independently commanded strike force. To this end, the CEA was responsible for a research programme to build both weapons and a prototype nuclear submarine as the most effective delivery system. Under its aegis, a number of nuclear development laboratories, including a centrifuge for separating nuclear isotopes, were constructed at and around Pierrelatte in the Rhône valley.

De Gaulle made no secret of his worldview, telling *New York Times* columnist C. L. Sulzberger on 20 February 1958:

I would quit NATO if I were running France. NATO is against our independence and our interest. Our membership ... is said to be to protect France against a Russian attack, but I don't believe that the Russians will attack at this time. [NATO] is a subordination ... we cannot expect a superior power to be responsible for us.[3]

To any American argument that proliferation of nuclear weapons was a threat to world peace, he retorted that proliferation was inevitable.[4] In this, time has proven him correct.

That same month of February 1958, he startled his old wartime collaborator Maurice Schumann by showing that he was already thinking ahead to ending the war in Algeria. 'The solution,' he said, 'lies in one of three possibilities: *francisation* and integration, some kind of link with France or secession.'[5] More than any other single factor, it was the long drawn-out struggle in Algeria, characterised by torture, rape, robbery and murder routinely practised by both sides,[6] that brought down the government of Pierre Pflimlin and destroyed the Fourth Republic, whose last head of government he was. With the political Left in France favouring a negotiated settlement with the FLN and the Right wing blaming everything on the weakness of the Fourth Republic, moderate eyes turned towards peaceful Colombey-les-deux-Eglises.

As the army in North Africa grew more independent of metropolitan control, it seemed by the spring of 1958 to an increasing number of people of many political shades that the man who had been France's conscience through five long years of the Second World War and had never compromised his principles even to stay in power was the only alternative to a civil war. Their memories were long enough to recall the Spanish Civil War, in which General Franco had brought his troops from North Africa to Europe and ripped his country apart to the tune of half a million dead, plus uncounted tens of thousands more who died of malnutrition, starvation and sickness as the infrastructure of Spanish civilisation was destroyed.

In April, Washington despatched to Paris none other than de Gaulle's old opponent Robert Murphy. Accompanied by US Ambassador Amory Houghton, he delivered to French premier Félix Gaillard a situation note on the unrest in Algeria, with an oral warning that action must be taken before Maurice Challe, the senior French general in North Africa, emulated Franco and marched on Paris. Shortly afterwards, a misty organisation termed the Allied Co-ordination Committee (ACC) met at its HQ in Brussels on 29 and 30 April to work out the logistics of reactivating the Gladio stay-behinds in France. On the overt political front, John Foster Dulles' initiative in contacting de Gaulle in December 1947 was also reactivated, with a number of centre and right-wing figures organising demonstrations at which the General was hailed as the country's only hope. On 9 May, Dulles himself stopped over in Paris on a journey between Washington and Berlin, not to meet French politicians but to check out the Gladio network.

Asked by Sulzberger whether he would accept power, if offered it, de Gaulle replied, 'Why not? I've already organised two *coups d'état* in my life. In June 1940, when I launched our movement in London, that was a *coup d'état*. And, in September 1944 I carried out a *coup d'état* in Paris by setting up a government. I was the government.'[7]

The final straw that broke the back of the Fourth Republic came when yet another new Cabinet was about to present its programme to the National Assembly on 13 May 1958. Incoming head of government Pierre Pflimlin ordered the dissolution of the right-wing organisations that had been demonstrating in the streets, but felt too insecure to do anything about French-Algerian extremists in Algeria, supported by a number of right-wing politicians from Paris, who used the platform of a large assembly protesting at the assassination of three Europeans by the ALN to take control of the city of Algiers and declare an emergency government with the backing of a number of army units in the area. Enthusiastic crowds chanted, '*L'Armée au pouvoir!*' – all power to the army.

The leaders of the insurrection in Algiers compared themselves to those Romans who had rescued the infant republic in its hour of need by recalling to power the elder statesman Cincinnatus, who had retired from public life, as had de Gaulle. In Paris, all was confusion. In Washington, such were the fears that mainland France would fall into the clutches of a communist-controlled national front that the National Security Council was meeting in Washington to debate activating the Gladio network in France.

Having announced to the nation on 15 May that he was prepared to return to power if called on to do so, Citizen de Gaulle gave a full-scale press conference on 19 May. To a journalist who said that 'certain people' feared his return to power would result in the curbing of civil liberties, he replied, 'Have I ever done that? On the contrary, I restored them after they had been lost [under Pétain]. Does anyone think that I'm going to begin a career as dictator at the age of sixty-seven?'[8]

For two weeks the voice of the government had been drowned by the chanting in the streets and the clamour of threats from the rebels in Algiers. Veteran politician and Opus Dei member Antoine Pinay called on his head of government and president of the Republic René Coty to bring back de Gaulle. In Paris, half a million people marched from the Place de la Nation to the Place de la République, chanting anti-government slogans. Across the Mediterranean, former Governor General of Algeria Jacques Soustelle persuaded the rebel Committee of Public Safety to announce that it 'firmly intended to put in place a ... government presided over by General de Gaulle, to ... reform the institutions of the Republic.'[9]

On 24 May, Premier Pflimlin appealed by radio for the population to support the government, but by then a majority of France's politicians had accepted that their game of musical chairs had to end, and conceded that the retired general in Colombey was the only alternative to civil war. On 27 May de Gaulle broadcast a speech insisting on the legality of his response to the appeal to form a new government and setting out the measures he would take, which included requiring the rebels in Algeria to return to their barracks and execute the orders of their legitimate commanders, with whom he intended swiftly to confer.

De Gaulle was manoeuvred back into power to end the war in Algeria and nothing more, the Gaullists having received no more than 4 per cent of the vote at the previous general election.[10] The following day, Pflimlin formally resigned, but de Gaulle had the measure of the situation and took his time. Refusing to present himself as a candidate for office to a National Assembly he despised, he wrote instead to President Coty that he was aware of certain opposition to his return to power, but:

in Algeria and in the army, such is the attitude of those who resist my proposals, that it risks breaking down the last barriers and overwhelming the commanders. The people who, through a sectarianism that is incomprehensible to me, would prevent me from saving the Republic once again while there is yet time, will bear a heavy responsibility.[11]

In an interview of 29 May in *The Times* in London, General Jacques Massu spoke for the Committee of Public Safety when he declared that de Gaulle had only to say the word for the army to restore him to power by force. With battle-ready troops on the streets of Paris, this was no idle offer. When the National Assembly voted on 1 June to give Charles de Gaulle a mandate to form a new government, among those who refused to vote for him was one of his wartime supporters. Pierre Mendès-France protested at the 'blackmail' of the National Assembly being obliged to conduct the affairs of government under the threat of military intervention. Claiming that it had nothing to do with his personal respect for de Gaulle, he declared that in his opinion the Assembly's vote, one way or the other, in such circumstances was invalid. Such sentiments sound fine in isolation, but at the time they were just another symptom of the Fourth Republic talking itself to death.

Two days later, on 3 June the National Assembly invested France's new Cincinnatus with full powers for six months. As the photograph of him sitting alone on the government bench shows, it was a lonely moment, with a majority of the cynical politicians in the chamber expecting to see him fail and a sizeable minority hoping that he would. The session ended with the president of the Assembly announcing that its next meeting would be held 'at an unknown date'. Thus, under the threat of armed intervention but with no bloodshed, did the Fourth Republic commit suicide as de Gaulle had prophesied it would from the beginning. Its passing came just in time, with several thousand paras on Corsica and in North Africa at readiness to jump on Paris and mount a military coup – to take power by force of arms.

With the paras stood down and his political opponents reduced to impotent mutterings in the background, the citizen-general appealed to the nation to give him its support in a radio speech of blistering simplicity: 'It was very dark yesterday,' he said, 'but this evening there is some light. Frenchwomen, Frenchmen, help me!'[12]

Notes

1. ed. M. Jullian, *de Gaulle – Traits d'esprit*, Paris, Cherche-Midi, 2000, p. 83
2. See General P. Aussaresses, *Services Spéciaux Algérie 1955–1957*, Paris, Perrin, 2001 and *Pour La France*, Paris, Rocher, 2001
3. C.L. Sulzberger, *The Last of the Giants*, New York, Macmillan, 1970, pp. 61–2
4. D. Rusk, *As I saw it*, London, Tauris, 1991, p. 287
5. C. Cogan, *Oldest Allies, Guarded friends: The United States and France since 1940*, Westport, Praeger, 1994, p. 116
6. See Aussaresses, *Services Spéciaux Algérie 1955–1957*
7. See article by Thierry Meyssan on www.voltairenet.org/art8644.html
8. Press conference at L'Élysee Palace, 19 May 1958, viewable on www.ina.fr/ video100012921
9. Article by Thierry Meyssan on www.voltairenet.org/art8644.html
10. J. Newhouse, *de Gaulle and the Anglo-Saxons*, London, André Deutsch, 1970, pp. 3 and 18
11. Article by Thierry Meyssan on www.voltairenet.org/art8644.html
12. Jullian, *Traits d'esprit*, p. 19

17

PRESIDENT DE GAULLE

Back in power, *le général* – as he was still called by most of the population – set out to mend a few rifts by inviting politicians of various hues to join his government. Pflimlin himself became a member of the new Cabinet. However, to ensure that the Fifth Republic he was about to found would be immune to the fatal sickness that had claimed the Third and Fourth Republics, de Gaulle appointed as Minister of Justice one of France's Young Turks who had come of age politically in the Resistance.

Michel Debré had trained as a lawyer and was a graduate of the Ecole des Sciences Politiques. Captured by the Germans in May 1940, he had escaped and made his way to Morocco, where he joined the anti-Pétain movement before returning to occupied France to work undercover in the Resistance. De Gaulle first met him in 1944, making him one of the Gaullist appointees who did the sixty-day wonders out of a job. After moving to the Foreign Ministry, Debré had played a key role in devising a new status for the Saarland before being elected an RPF senator in 1947.

By virtue of his new appointment, Debré now headed the commission to draft a new constitution. As de Gaulle had wanted in 1946, executive power was to be considerably increased at the expense of the National Assembly, with the president of the Republic to be chosen by an electoral college rather than by Parliament. The president would, in turn, select the president of the Council of Ministers or Cabinet, whose title was changed to 'prime minister'. This would make him less a prisoner of the *députés* in the National Assembly than under the Fourth Republic and was a considerable step towards the strong executive de Gaulle considered essential for the future of France.

However, on a day-to-day basis, the most pressing problem confronting de Gaulle was the daily loss of lives in Algeria. Flying there without wasting any time, he stood on the balcony of the Gouvernement Général building in Algiers on 4 June 1958, raised his long arms in a giant V-sign and declared to a crowd of Europeans numbering more than a hundred thousand, '*Je vous ai compris! Je sais ce qui s'est passé ici.*'[1] The phrases, 'I have understood you and I know what has been going on here', were universally taken by his listeners to mean that he would support the war until every last FLN terrorist had surrendered or been killed. What he intended them to understand is a matter of conjecture.

There was poetic justice in the way de Gaulle proceeded to sack the civilian administrators who had let things get out of hand, replacing them with the generals and politicians who had been most instrumental in bringing him back to power and who would later turn into his sworn enemies. General Raoul Salan was given the Médaille Militaire and made Délegué Général; General Massu was given another star on his collar and named Prefect of Algiers; Jacques Soustelle returned to metropolitan France as the new Minister of Information, where his first move was to replace with loyal supporters of the General the top ten men in the state broadcasting monopoly Radio Television Française. Even the paras who had been prepared to jump on Paris were hailed as heroes, being accorded the signal honour of parading down the Champs-Élysées to the cheers of the crowds. The Left's hope of a negotiated settlement with the FLN was no longer on the agenda. On de Gaulle's return to Paris, his new Finance Minister Antoine Pinay was ordered to raise an additional 50 billion francs to bring the budget for General Salan's war to wipe out the FLN by military action to the unheard-of sum of 120 billion francs.

Among his first foreign visitors in July was President Eisenhower's Secretary of State John Foster Dulles, who alluded to the coup they might have mounted together in 1947 in the hope of impressing on France's new leader the Washington view of the world. De Gaulle rejected it piecemeal and wholemeal, denying that Communism was the motor of the USSR and trying to get through to Dulles that the export model of Marxism was simply the tool with which Stalin had gained half of Europe as a buffer zone at very little cost. On the other hand, he also warned that France would not tolerate on its soil American nuclear weapons over which it had no control, and informed the secretary of state that France already had a small number of nuclear devices ready for testing and intended to proceed to the stage of making its own nuclear bombs, with or without American help. Dulles had no remit to accept that cue. As to the Middle East, where US Marines were shortly to land in Lebanon, his host deplored the American view that the Levant – a French area of influence under the Sykes-Picot accord – was to serve as the next Cold War battleground. There was little, if any, common ground.[2]

On 4 September, Gaullist author-politician André Malraux addressed a crowd of 5,000 notables in the Place de la République, plus several million people listening to the state television and radio networks: '*Ici Paris, honneur et patrie. Une fois de plus au rendez-vous de l'histoire et au rendez-vous de la République, vous allez entendre le général de Gaulle.*' Deliberately evoking the spirit and flavour of the wartime broadcasts from London, he declaimed, 'This is Paris, honour, the fatherland! You are about to hear General de Gaulle responding to the call of history and the Republic.' The more astute listeners at home wondered at the hesitant delivery of some speeches because the microphone did not transmit the 'noises-off' produced by the restive crowds in nearby streets. Estimated by the organisers at half a million, but by the police at considerably less than that, they chanted, '*Non! Non! Non!*' in counterpoint to Malraux and the other speakers.

When de Gaulle took his place at the microphone, the chanting changed to an echo of the communist slogan in the Spanish Civil War. '*¡No pasarán!*' the International Brigades had cried in vain. When the anti-de Gaulle demonstrators chanted their less punchy '*Le fascisme ne passera pas!*', police in various uniforms and plain clothes went in with rifle-butts, truncheons and other blunt instruments, as ordered by Prefect Maurice Papon. Several hundred demonstrators were injured and the violent restoration of order seemed afterwards to many uncommitted people a justification of the Left calling de Gaulle a fascist. He, meanwhile, pressed on with his speech in favour of adopting the new Constitution, speaking to the nation and not the unconvertible in the surrounding streets making clear their views on Debré's draft.

Mendès-France was again vociferous in his protests that a referendum on a new constitution was impossible under the ever-present menace of army intervention and with a police force that broke up anti-Gaullist demonstrations. He also complained that the choice given to voters in the referendum was a simple YES or NO, with no discussion of detail. To the left of his Centrist position, the PCF grouped its sympathisers for battle, but was denied access to the state-run radio channels, on which de Gaulle's supporters repeatedly exhorted the population to make the right choice. Few people needed to be told that voting NO would plunge the country back into a worse mess than before the General had re-entered politics. Like him or not, he was the only choice for anyone who wanted to lead a normal life again, and if the price tag was a more authoritarian form of government than before, a majority of the population was happy to pay it.

In metropolitan France, the referendum vote was an overwhelming YES as 79.25 per cent voted for Debré's Constitution. Article 92 of the approved text provided for a period of four months in which to rearrange the business of government and elect both a new parliament and a new president of the Republic. The electoral college did its job, with 78 per cent of its members voting for de Gaulle. After a revision of constituencies, the newly organised Gaullist party, L'Union pour la Nouvelle République (UNR), gained many votes from disillusioned former supporters of the Left, and claimed 198 seats in the November general election. It thus became the largest single block in the new National Assembly. Representing more than 20 per cent of seats and with the Right and Centre-Right parties holding another 40 per cent, it gave de Gaulle a working majority against the seriously weakened Centre-Left and Left-wing parties. Among the casualties was Mendès-France, beaten at the polls by a Gaullist member of Opus Dei.

Washington saw de Gaulle's accession to power as it had in 1945: with him firmly in place, there was no danger of France going communist. While still not favourable to the General, internal State Department papers grudgingly ceased using sexist metaphors that had repeatedly alleged French inconsistency during the Fourth Republic was a *feminine* trait. To the State Department at least, it seems that France was now a logical and masculine country again.[3] In September 1958, de Gaulle set out his foreign policy in a memorandum to President Eisenhower and Prime Minister Macmillan that proposed extending NATO's responsibilities to cover the whole world excluding the eastern bloc, with the Alliance to be led by three equal partners: the United States, Britain and France. From London and Washington came a resounding lack of interest.

On 8 April 1958 an agreement had been signed by defence ministers Jacques Chaban-Delmas for France, Franz-Josef Strauss for West Germany and Paolo Emilion Taviani for Italy, covering a cost-sharing arrangement for the isotope-cracking research facility in the Rhône valley, with all three partner states to share the resultant technological advances. The tripartite arrangement between France, Italy and Germany was inevitably given the acronym FIG in State Department documents of the period. This cosy little cost-sharing arrangement did not suit de Gaulle's plans: he intended France to join the US-UK-USSR Bomb club and had no intention of any other states nipping in while the French foot was in the doorway – particularly not Germany. At his first Cabinet meetings in June, he had informed his ministers that the FIG agreement was to be annulled. In September, the Quai d'Orsay informed Strauss personally that Germany could keep its money and France would keep its nuclear secrets. Rome was similarly informed.

Strauss was understandably furious but de Gaulle told Chancellor Adenauer, who visited him on 14 September at Colombey, that Germany – East or West – would never be allowed by Washington to have nuclear weapons. At the end of their discussions, the General drafted in his own hand the first three paragraphs of a memorandum of understanding, which was never published. He wrote:

> The French government does not consider that the security of the free world, or indeed France itself, can be guaranteed by the NATO organisation in its present form ... The French government regards (a tridirectorate of USA, UK and France) as indispensable. Henceforth its present participation in NATO is predicated on this.[4]

It was an announcement that Paul-Henri Spaak, the Belgian Secretary General of NATO, was not alone in considering potentially destructive of the Alliance.[5] On

8 January 1959 the Fifth Republic officially began with de Gaulle assuming his presidential functions and Geoffroy de Courcel – the General's very first subordinate in June 1940 – recalled from his post with NATO to the key job of secretary general at the Élysée Palace, controlling access to the president and keeping his diary. To head the first administration of the new republic, the General appointed Michel Debré its prime minister. To combat the inflation caused by the war in Algeria, he introduced a programme of deflation and austerity that would have been impossible for any government of the Fourth Republic to impose.

If all these political developments restabilised France and weakened for good the power of the PCF far more effectively than President Eisenhower and the State Department could have hoped, the new man in the Élysée Palace now proved to the whole world in a single step that he did not intend to become a client of Washington. As head of state and commander-in-chief of the French armed forces, he required General Lauris B. Norstad to furnish him with particulars of what American nuclear warheads, bombs and delivery systems were stationed on NATO bases in France, and precisely where they were sited. Norstad was both commander of all US forces in Europe and also Supreme Commander, Allied Powers in Europe – and thus the boss of NATO. If he did not know the answer, nobody did.

The demand for this information was made because de Gaulle found it unacceptable that the government of France should have no say in the use of these weapons and aircraft – or even know where they were kept or when US planes were in the air above his country carrying nuclear payloads. Secondly, their use against any Warsaw Pact country, if ordered by the Pentagon, would almost certainly trigger nuclear retaliation against the launch sites, resulting in millions of French civilian deaths. Thirdly, should France one day be threatened with nuclear weapons in a situation where US interests dictated that the American weapons systems should not be used, France would be undefended unless it had its own deterrent.

When Norstad refused to disclose the whereabouts of the US-controlled NATO nuclear arsenal on French territory to the head of the French state, de Gaulle ordered its removal. As a result, 200 US aircraft took off from French bases en route to new locations in Britain and West Germany, from where use of their bombs and nuclear warheads would not implicate France.

The next step in de Gaulle's clarification of his relationship with NATO and its American controllers was more convoluted. In December 1957 President Eisenhower had offered to sell a nuclear-powered submarine to any NATO country. In February 1959 the General despatched a French delegation to the US to take up this offer, only to have Congress vote that such a submarine might be sold to the United Kingdom – and no other ally. To make his feelings at this rebuff crystal clear, de Gaulle then withdrew the French Mediterranean Fleet from NATO control. Thus, when President Eisenhower presented a scale model of an atomic sub to the General in the spring of 1960, this amazingly undiplomatic act was interpreted in Paris as deliberate mockery of French aspirations.[6]

On 1 May 1960 a Lockheed U-2 reconnaissance aircraft piloted by Francis Gary Powers took off in Peshawar in Pakistan, destination Bodø airport in Norway. The date was chosen because traditionally on May Day hundreds of thousands of Soviet soldiers, sailors and airmen paraded through the streets of Moscow and other major cities. It was thus thought by the CIA mission planners that air defence vigilance would consequently be low. They were wrong. Soviet radar operators had been tracking U-2 flights for some considerable time, prevented from intercepting them with fighter aircraft or missiles by the great height at which the spy planes flew. At some point in Powers' mission to photograph missile sites near Sverdlovsk and Plesetsk, attempts by Soviet fighters to intercept his U-2 again failed due to the high altitude at which it was flying, but a salvo of SA-2 Guideline surface-to-air missiles that also destroyed one of the pursuit aircraft finally got lucky, with the fourteenth rocket exploding near enough to damage the U-2.

Powers parachuted to safety, neither using his cyanide pill nor attempting escape, for which he carried survival equipment laughable in its inadequacy. Unaware of his survival and that a substantial part of the aircraft including its surveillance cameras and the film in them had been recovered intact by the Soviets, NASA issued a statement four days later to the effect that the U-2 had been on a weather reconnaissance mission and gone off course 'north of Turkey' by accident after the pilot experienced problems with his oxygen supply. To reinforce the fragile alibi, another U-2 was hastily repainted with NASA insignia and photographed by the press at Edwards Air Force base in the Mojave Desert. After a gleeful Nikita Khrushchev announced the shooting down of 'an American spy plane', President Eisenhower unwisely repeated the NASA weather plane alibi, enabling Mr K to go to town on 7 May with an announcement that Powers was alive and talking – and that his confession and the developed film proved the undeniable espionage purpose of his disastrous mission.

The CIA miscalculation could not have come at a more embarrassing time. On 14 May President Eisenhower left Washington for the planned summit conference in Paris, learning there on the following day that Khrushchev had read to Prime Minister Macmillan the text of his categorical demand that Eisenhower apologise for the U-2 mission and agree to punish those responsible; otherwise, he threatened to walk out of the summit. Eisenhower refused and de Gaulle supported the US position to the hilt,[7] remarking dryly after Khrushchev's feigned outburst, 'And do not Soviet satellites over-fly French territory several times a day?'[8] It was possibly in gratitude for this support that, on the day when John F. Kennedy was elected president in November, Eisenhower agreed to sell surplus uranium isotope 235 to France on condition that weapons thus produced be placed under NATO control.⁹ If relationships with his NATO allies were a delicate dance, the reason for de Gaulle's return to power called for all the resolution of which he had shown himself capable during the dark days of the Second World War. The speech on the balcony of the Gouvernement Général had been taken to mean that he shared the views of the settlers, whose slogan was '*Algérie française*', meaning *French for ever*. As time went by, it became clear to his associates that the General, as a professional soldier, had assessed the war across the Mediterranean as impossible to win by any form of military action that fell short of genocide. As a statesman, he saw a more important future role for France than hanging on to an overseas territory. To achieve this, it was necessary to change the country's image in the Third World, which was that of a colonial oppressor. On 16 September 1959 he guaranteed 'the right of Algerians to self-determination'.¹⁰ The unrest this caused among the *colons* in Algeria culminated in 'the week of the barricades' four months later, when the European population attempted to take control of Algiers. Undeterred, on 14 June 1960, de Gaulle was talking openly of 'an Algerian Algeria, linked to France'.¹¹ By 4 November, this had become an Algeria 'which will have its government, its institutions and its own laws' – a position approved by 75 per cent of the mainland voters in a referendum of 8 January 1961.

This was more than the army and the *colons* in Algeria could stomach. In three hours on the night of Friday 21 April, the Foreign Legion paras – 1 Régiment Etranger de Parachutistes, abbreviated to 1 REP – occupied the Gouvernement Général, the City Hall and the radio building with only one casualty. At 7 a.m. on the Saturday morning the civilian population awoke to learn that Algiers was now controlled by the army under generals Challe, Zeller and Jouhaud. In Paris, police arrested seven other leading military figures thought to be implicated in the coup. Members of the Cabinet begged de Gaulle to go on television and address the nation, but he refused to panic. In a Cabinet meeting at 5 p.m. he said, 'I shall do that, but my speech is not finished yet and, just because the situation is bad, is no reason to make a bad speech.'¹² Outside the Élysée Palace, the Left was mobilising itself, with the trade unions and the League for the Rights of Man demonstrating opposition to the right-wing coup in Algiers.

The following day, Sunday 23 April, the conspirators in Algiers were joined by General Raoul Salan. At 8 p.m. de Gaulle donned his general's uniform to speak to the nation on television:

A military rebellion has installed itself in Algeria. At its head is a quartet of retired generals, leading a group of ambitious and fanatical officers. In the name of France, I order that all means – I repeat, all means – be employed to bar the way to those men until they can be defeated. I forbid any French citizen and especially every soldier to carry out any of their orders.

In private, he said of the cabal in Algiers, 'Those generals! Nineteen stars between them – and not a single good brain among the lot!'[13]

While he preserved what seemed like an Olympian detachment, rumours were spreading that the Foreign Legion paras were emplaning in Algeria to drop on the capital. In fact, there was little risk of this because the French air force in North Africa had remained largely loyal to the government in Paris and flown back to France empty most of the aircraft that could have been used for the purpose. Debré, however, appeared on television at midnight to make a bizarre request for the population to proceed 'by car or on foot to the airports as soon as the sirens sound, in order to convince these misled soldiers of their grave error'.[14] Simultaneous meetings of most trade unions called for a one-hour protest strike next day, which was massively supported.

De Gaulle was proven right. The coup fizzled out as unit after unit that had promised to support the four dissident generals returned quietly to barracks. By Wednesday, it was all over. A friend of the author than serving in the Legion's Para regiment recalls marching back to barracks at Zeralda, with his colonel under arrest and General Challe surrendering to the civil power, as did Zeller a few days later.[15] But Salan and Jouhaud and several hundred officers and men decided that for the army to simply leave Algeria to the FLN was a betrayal of their many thousands of comrades who were buried there. They went underground with false identities, calling themselves the Organisation Armée Secrète (OAS), determined to use terrorism, including the assassination of Charles de Gaulle, to block his plans for Algerian independence. OAS gangs went on a killing spree, assassinating both FLN members and perfectly innocent non-Europeans – on one day targeting cleaning ladies and on another postmen, on the grounds that they 'knew too much' about their European employers and neighbours.

OAS commandos in France itself carried out nearly thirty attempts on de Gaulle's life, including a number of near-misses. Since the core of the OAS consisted of renegade army officers and other ranks with considerable military experience and easy access to caches of weapons, ammunition and explosives both in North Africa and France, it came to be thought by the general population as something of a miracle that he emerged unscathed from presidential cars riddled with bullets or grenade fragments. Politician Jacques Chaban-Delmas tells of going to visit the General after one of these near-misses which, in de Gaulle's professional opinion, had been quite a well-organised operation. Doubtless thinking of Caracalla and Elagabalus, the two Roman emperors who had been slain by assassins while seated on latrines, he added, nodding at the door leading to the bathroom behind his office, 'It would have been better to die there than be gunned down on the lavatory.'[16]

Notes

1. De Gaulle, *Mémoires d'Espoir*, Vol. I, Paris, Plon, pp. 51–2
2. Article by P. M. De La Gorce in *Le Monde Diplomatique*, March 2003
3. A. Beevor & A. Cooper, *Paris after the Liberation*, London, Hamish Hamilton, 1994, pp. 121–2
4. C. Williams, *The Last Great Frenchman*, London, Little Brown, 1994, p. 410
5. J. Newhouse, *de Gaulle and the Anglo-Saxons*, London, André Deutsch, 1970, pp. 15–16, 66, 69–70, 71–2
6. Beevor & Cooper, *Paris after the Liberation*, p. 125 and Newhouse, *de Gaulle and the Anglo-Saxons*, p. 100
7. W. Kohl, *French Nuclear Diplomacy*, Princeton, PUP 1971, pp. 110–11
8. J. Fenby, *The General*, London, Simon & Schuster, 2011, p. 458
9. Beevor & Cooper, *Paris after the Liberation*, p. 118
10. Fenby, *The General*, p. 442
11. Ibid., p. 460
12. ed. M. Jullian, *de Gaulle – Traits d'esprit*, Paris, Cherche-Midi, 2000, p. 76
13. Ibid., p. 180
14. His broadcast of 23 April
15. An account of 1 REP's operation can be found in D. Boyd, *The French Foreign Legion*, Thrupp, Sutton, 2006, pp. 45–9
16. Jullian, *Traits d'esprit*, p. 209

18

THE MAN WHO CAME WITH JACKIE

De Gaulle did not let the rebellion supported by a million French citizens in Algeria deflect him from the restoration of France to what he regarded as its proper place among the world powers. The defeat of 1940, the five years of the German occupation and the twelve futile years of inconsequential governments during the Fourth Republic had left the country with the title originally bestowed on the decadent Ottoman Empire: the sick man of Europe. To rid France of that stigma required internal reorganisation to merit external recognition. He was therefore looking forward to the state visit to France of 44-year-old US President John F. Kennedy and his wife Jacqueline Bouvier Kennedy that began on the last day of May 1961, when Air Force One touched down on French soil at 10.11 a.m.

The single, state-controlled television channel RTF covered the arrival, viewers having been delighted the previous day by a recorded interview in which the American president's wife replied to questions in fluent French. She was a gracious and beautiful woman who captivated people in many countries, but her pride in the French origins of her family, which had emigrated to America in 1815, ensured her a warm place in French hearts. She had also studied at the Sorbonne.

Her husband, on his way to meet Premier Khrushchev of the USSR in Vienna, had come for three days of one-to-one talks with de Gaulle, with only interpreters present. He was, however, very much on his guard from the moment of arrival at Orly airport, and acutely aware that he was a very inexperienced junior statesman compared with the only Second World War leader then surviving in a position of power. British Prime Minister Harold Macmillan, who knew de Gaulle well from their time together in wartime North Africa, had warned Kennedy about de Gaulle's habit of expressing himself in a roundabout way in order to minimise the risk of rebuff and also said that his belief that France had been hard done by in the Second World War and thus deprived of her proper place among the nations would make him ask for everything, but give little in return.

Among the briefings Kennedy had devoured during the transatlantic flight was one from the CIA, giving his host's daily routine. For a man in his early seventies, they said, de Gaulle was in excellent health. He rose early and worked from 8.30 a.m. to 7 p.m. – after which he refused to take telephone calls, except in an emergency. One of their sources, Adalbert de Segonzac, who was Washington correspondent of the largest circulation daily *France-Soir*, had described his president as religious, anti-communist, formal, secretive and extremely difficult to work for. His private secretary Pierre Lefranc worked from early morning to midnight each day for a salary about a fifth of what he would have received in commerce. Colonel Bonneval, the General's aide-de-camp, had never received any promotion during the years of his service to de Gaulle. De Segonzac's report mentioned also that de Gaulle had a warm and caring nature in private, and some of the first *résistants* told the author that *le général* always remembered anniversaries and other special occasions. Shortly before Kennedy's visit, de Gaulle had taken time to pen several handwritten letters to the governor general of Algeria, who had a Down's syndrome child like his own beloved Anne.

But that was not the side of the General which Kennedy was going to experience. It was closer to the briefing of the State Department which, under Secretary Dean Rusk, was as hostile to the French head of state as it had been under Cordell Hull. This document stressed de Gaulle's aloofness, describing his dislike of politicians' crowd-winning gestures and yet paradoxical habit of defying his bodyguards by plunging into a crowd to shake hands. In negotiations, it stressed, he was as impossible to read as any professional poker player. One of the frustrations of his associates and staff was that he argued with no one. His custom was to receive visitors with a cool '*Je vous écoute.*' And listen he did, until they ran out of steam. Having found out their thinking, he let them depart thinking that he agreed with what they had said. His philosophy was pragmatic, adapting to changed circumstances as a general would alter plans after ascertaining the enemy's movements, rather than rigidly guided by predetermined policies. Perhaps betraying the State Department's attitude to the French in general, it considered de Gaulle 'un-French' in a number of respects, justifying this by quoting a sentence from his *Le Fil de l'Epée*, published in 1932: 'The French adore logic, and that has cost the country dearly.'

Although his rule since returning to power was authoritarian, he believed in democracy and civil liberties, and respected the British parliamentary system, while realising that it could not work with the multiplicity of political parties in France. His foreign policy? It was considered by the State Department to be somewhat nineteenth century, largely because of his tendency to conclude treaties without reference to his allies and his refusal to keep France's air force under

NATO, i.e. American, control. His opinion of the United States Government? De Gaulle considered that events – and not a consciously pursued policy – had placed the US in its present role of world leadership, but considered the chief defect of American administrations to be a tendency to concentrate on immediate issues and lose sight of long-term consequences – a comment that might still be levelled at Washington fifty years later.

With all this advice in his head, Kennedy walked down the steps from Air Force One with Jackie to be welcomed by de Gaulle in English. 'Have you made a good aerial voyage?' he asked politely, translating his own rather archaic brand of French word for word. This was before the tightened security of today's airports and the crowd surged against the crush barriers chanting, 'Jack-ie, Jack-ie, Jack-ie.' Kennedy looked a little taken aback that they had come to see his wife and not him, so much so that his speech writers included a disarming little aside for his farewell press conference that ended the visit. 'I am the man,' he said with a rueful smile, 'who came to Paris with Jackie Kennedy.'[1]

De Gaulle's *politesse française* continued with red carpets and flowers, French and US flags everywhere and crowds lining the route to the Quai d'Orsay, estimated by de Gaulle for his guests at about 1 million people, all of whom were braving the 10°C winds on the chance of catching a glimpse of the glamorous Mrs Kennedy driving past. The third floor of the immense Foreign Ministry building on the banks of the Seine was allocated to the presidential couple for the length of their stay, Kennedy in what was known as 'the king's bedroom' and Jackie in 'the queen's room' at the opposite end of the building, on instructions from the White House staff, who had learned by experience to keep them well separated so that she did not see nocturnal visitors to his quarters.

At 11.30 that morning, Kennedy emerged to be driven to the Élysée Palace, where de Gaulle walked down the front steps to greet him, as was customary with heads of state. Inside, the first item on their agenda was Berlin. Allegedly in protest at the Western powers uniting their zones of occupation in Germany into one economic area, Soviet premier Nikita Khrushchev was threatening to force the West to recognise the puppet state known as the German Democratic Republic by signing a peace treaty with it and handing over to it the Soviet zone of Germany. This would force the Western powers to deal on questions of access to Berlin – which lay geographically well within the GDR – with a regime from which they had so far withheld diplomatic recognition. If the West chose to use armed force to insist in its rights of access without recognising the GDR, Khrushchev *said* that Soviet retaliation would lay waste the whole of Western Europe, leading to global war.

The real reason for Khrushchev's escalation of threats was not simply the presence of Western forces in Berlin and the intelligence activities they carried out there, in which the author played a minor role, but more importantly the total of two and a half *million* GDR citizens who had risked long terms of imprisonment for the crime of 'flight from the Republic' in order to escape to a better life in the West. This drain of manpower and particularly brainpower was to continue for another few weeks only – until the night of 12–13 August 1961 saw the first barbed-wire and minefield version of the Moscow-approved Berlin Wall, a concrete block wall cutting off any contact between GDR citizens and their relatives and neighbours in the Western sectors of Berlin.

Kennedy had announced in a televised broadcast to the nation that the West would not back down and abandon the people of the three Western sectors of Berlin to their fate. To show muscle, he had increased budgets for the armed forces and sanctioned the recall of 125,000 reservists. When he now told de Gaulle that he was willing to listen to what Khrushchev had to say on the subject at the summit meeting in Vienna, de Gaulle warned him that any show of willingness to negotiate was always taken as a sign of weakness by the Russians. He pointed out that Khrushchev had been making threatening noises over Berlin for two years, but done nothing more than that. Given the present military superiority of the United States, he was confident that the USSR did not want a war it could not win and that Mr K would back down if faced with firmness.[2]

As he had with Presidents Truman and Eisenhower, the General attempted to disabuse Kennedy of the illusion that Soviet policy had anything to do with communist theory. Having been born twenty-seven years before the Bolshevik Revolution of 1917, he considered communism as a passing phase in the evolution of Russia[3] – which Kennedy, who had been five months old at the Revolution, seems not to have understood.

The youngest-ever American president tried a number of *what if?* questions prepared by his staff. Far from just listening, de Gaulle replied unambiguously. The three Western powers who had divided Germany with the USSR after the German defeat in 1945 had a long-standing contingency plan, code-named 'Live Oak', which called for any interference with their access to Berlin to be met with an armed convoy driving up the autobahn from the west, at first in company strength, then in brigade strength, if necessary – and so on. Was de Gaulle happy about this? He was not. In his book, the Russians had to understand that *any* unilateral change they made in the status of Berlin would be met with immediate response from the three allied powers, not by a gradual escalation, but in the form of all-out war.

It was lunchtime by this point, and Kennedy did not ask his host what 'all-out war' meant in this context, because if it meant nuclear war, that could lead to an embarrassing discussion. De Gaulle had his own agenda but intended to wait until he knew his man better before broaching the topic of chief interest for him.

Just before 3 p.m. the talks recommenced with a discussion of the American position on south-east Asia. It was a difficult subject, since many French generals believed they had been badly let down by American unwillingness to help them in their struggle with the Viet Minh, who had been armed and trained by American intelligence operatives during the Japanese occupation of Indochina. In consequence, they looked with a total lack of sympathy on the steadily escalating US involvement in a war made necessary, in their opinion, by that lack of help. De Gaulle took a wider overview. To him, the escalating American involvement in Vietnam demonstrated what he regarded as the fundamental defects of US foreign policy: naïve self-righteousness, a readiness to quash smaller nations' independence and a tendency towards military action that could engulf France and the other European powers in a world war, if it were not contained.

He told Kennedy, 'You cannot succeed in Indochina. We failed and you will fail.'[4] Advising his visitor to restrain the CIA and the Pentagon hawks from digging their own graves in Vietnam, he argued that a more intelligent approach was to encourage the development of moderate political factions in south-east Asia, and not drive the population into the communists' arms by direct military intervention, as the US seemed intent on doing. The advice came with a warning that a second military defeat of a Western power in Vietnam would have long-lasting consequences throughout the whole world. Kennedy's own feelings were on a similar wavelength – so much so that many people later believed his assassination to be the work of the military-industrial complex which wanted the war to escalate and consume ever-increasing quantities of arms, ammunition and materiel. The first day's talks thus ended amicably, with de Gaulle taking the liberty of an elderly man to give the youngest president of the United States some advice. It was not to pay too much attention to his advisers or be influenced by previous policy, but to act on his own judgement.

On 1 June, the talks recommenced at 10 a.m. in the Élysée Palace. During the night, news had come in of the assassination of Rafael Trujillo, dictator of the Dominican Republic. Coming, as it did, so soon after the Bay of Pigs fiasco,[5] Kennedy had spent several hours trying unsuccessfully to find out by telephone whether the assassination was the work of the CIA or one of its protégé organisations. US army units had been placed on alert in the Dominican Republic, to intervene in the event that Cuban or other communist forces took advantage of the power vacuum there to mount a *coup d'état*, but Kennedy was hesitant about ordering them on to the streets, since the world would then class the United States with the USSR, which had used armed forced in 1956 to suppress the Hungarian rebellion.

As to Cuba, de Gaulle suggested that economic sanctions should be enough to cause the downfall of Castro, to which Kennedy replied that when the US stopped buying Cuban sugar, Moscow had stepped in and bought the whole export crop. He refrained from telling de Gaulle that the CIA was still under orders to achieve the overthrow of Fidel Castro in Cuba by covert means, and then had to listen to de Gaulle's view of Latin America and how all the Latin-American countries resented the Big Brother posture of successive administrations in Washington.

Kennedy next tried to persuade de Gaulle to moderate Portugal's policy in Angola, to which he received a straight rebuff. No way, said de Gaulle. Any weakening of Portuguese President Salazar's regime could lead to a communist coup, which nobody wanted in the Iberian peninsula. Not surprisingly, when he led the conversation round to the idea of a standing committee of three men to sort out world problems – he meant the president of the US, the British prime minister and himself – Kennedy was no more in favour than his predecessors had been.

After luncheon, the conversation moved on to the two most prickly subjects on the agenda: de Gaulle's obsession with building a French bomb and France's membership of NATO. France's main contribution was the two divisions occupying the French zone of Germany, but she also had on her soil some 60,000 US personnel. De Gaulle had many times voiced his support of the NATO alliance, but did not accept the American domination of the command structure of the integrated forces, of which the French contingent could thus become automatically involved in actions that suited American policies, but not those of France. He preferred to have an independent response to any threat from the east – the so-called *force de frappe* – and, of course, his own nuclear arsenal to replace the American nuclear weapons formerly based in France.

In 1959, de Gaulle had asked Eisenhower to take into account the cost to France of her war in Vietnam and the Algerian conflict and make available US research to reduce the cost of producing her own nuclear weapons. Estimates later made for President Kennedy were that going it alone in the attempt to move on from basic nuclear technology to an H-bomb would cost France the equivalent of several billion dollars. Eisenhower had replied that his hands were tied by the 1946 Atomic Energy Act, known as the McMahon Act, which expressly forbade the sharing of US nuclear secrets with *any* foreign power. An exception had been made to enable Britain to benefit from US research. Since what de Gaulle was asking for was no more than to be treated on a par with Britain, he refused to believe that an American president could not change the law. After all, as he told Kennedy, he himself had changed the constitution of France – not once, but twice. Eisenhower had argued that Britain's exception to the Act was due to the fact that she had passed to the US all her own nuclear research and supplies, and was sufficiently advanced in the field of research to profit from a pooling of information. By contrast, France at the time was not even in the race. Kennedy knew all this history but did not wish to go down the same road, preferring to demonstrate that a French bomb was superfluous, given the existence of NATO. Supposing, he asked, that Germany was invaded by the Soviets. Would France use her Bomb then? 'Look at it this way,' said de Gaulle, 'the Rhine is a lot less wide than the Atlantic.'[6]

That night, while the American president and his wife were the guests of honour at the Opéra Royale in Versailles, seated in the presidential box with de Gaulle and his wife Yvonne, Kennedy's team of advisers was desperately trying to come up with the right argument to reassure the General that he did not need a French bomb. Next morning, told by Kennedy that he could rest assured American weapons, both nuclear and conventional, would be used to defend the countries under threat in the event that the USSR launched an attack on Western Europe, de Gaulle asked, was there a line in the sand?

Kennedy explained the pre-conditions for use of US nuclear weapons: either a conventional Russian attack that could not be held by NATO's conventional forces or the imminent threat of a nuclear initiative from the other side, directed against Western Europe or the USA. Naturally enough, de Gaulle queried the first: would the Pentagon really order US missiles to nuke targets in the USSR before a single Soviet missile had been launched? Kennedy's reply was a categorical *yes*. And supposing they blockade Berlin? de Gaulle queried. It was the first of several what-ifs, by the end of which he had found the flaw in Kennedy's bland assurances: the fact was that the president of the United States was unclear at what point in an armed confrontation he would, in fact, authorise the launch of American missiles.

The United States' European allies had for some time been aware that the US-controlled NATO nuclear umbrella had holes in it, and might in fact not be deployed at all for reasons that made perfect sense in Washington and yet saw Bonn, Paris or Rome wiped off the globe. During the presidency of Dwight Eisenhower, it had been economically impossible to match the Soviet capacity for conventional war and thus logical to rely on nuclear deterrence, in which the United States enjoyed an evident superiority. After the rearming of West Germany under the Truman administration in 1955 – with its embargo on German control of nuclear, biological and chemical weapons – the Bonn Government sought reassurance that its Western allies would not trade German soil for negotiating time in the event of attack by the signatories of the Warsaw Pact,[7] but retaliate immediately with nuclear weapons against any infringement of the Federal Republic's eastern frontiers.

The other European members of NATO went along with this because it saved them the expense of large-scale conventional forces, and they did not believe that the USSR would risk nuclear war just to gain more European territory. However, simple equations went out of the window with the introduction of tactical battlefield nuclear weapons such as the Honest John rocket. The American NATO commanders argued that these new weapons were not strategic, but conventional, weapons. But supposing the other side did not agree was the question asked in Western European capitals. A few war games later, it was obvious to everyone else in the know that use of these weapons against an invader already on Western

European territory would result in an unacceptable level of collateral death and destruction to the civilian population. The illusion of 'limited nuclear war' was therefore revealed for what it was.

Kennedy's defence advisers argued that, since it was impossible to foresee exactly when a US president would use strategic nuclear weapons, the exclusively nuclear deterrent was no long credible, either to America's allies or to Moscow and its Warsaw Pact armies. It was therefore necessary to envisage thresholds of risk, below which exclusively conventional forces would react to conventional aggression. Seen from Washington, that made sense, but the European NATO partners, over whose territory a limited conventional war would be fought with immense destruction and loss of life, had an understandably different perspective.

What came to be called the US doctrine of flexible response made good sense to Pentagon planners, but made it difficult for America's European partners to believe that the nuclear umbrella would be in place when and if Warsaw Pact tanks rolled across the borders and a hostile sky began to rain bombs and artillery shells. De Gaulle was not the only national leader to realise the impossibility of predicting the nature of a flexible response *because everything would depend on Washington's perception of American interests at the time*, so long as final control of the umbrella was in exclusively American hands.

In the meeting with Kennedy, he therefore took the opportunity to press again his idea for a tridirectorate, or council of three – in this case to make the decision whether and when to use nuclear weapons in defence of Europe. Since the US had thousands of nuclear devices already in service and Britain had hundreds, it was sheer nerve on his part, because France had conducted only four nuclear explosions at the testing grounds at Reggane in the Algerian Sahara and had no workable weapon as yet.

Kennedy wriggled out of this by observing that a standing committee of three would be an open invitation to other interested countries to insist on representation, and that would create a parallel or alternative NATO. His only 'concession' was to suggest three-way 'consultation' to explore the idea. De Gaulle knew from bitter experience what 'consultation' meant in the State Department's vocabulary. The only conclusion he could draw was that he had been right all along to press on with France's own nuclear deterrent, against the day when American interests precluded use of the NATO deterrent.

However, it was by now time for their advisers to join them, to end the meeting with a press announcement, in which de Gaulle sought to imply that more had been achieved with his committee-of-three idea than was the case. To avoid an open disagreement, Kennedy declared that, as Eisenhower had undertaken to consult the British Government before using nuclear weapons anywhere in the world, except in a case where the survival of the United States was at immediate risk, so he would extend this consultation to the French head of state.

Kennedy's time in Paris was running out, but in the hope of converting this concession to something more concrete, de Gaulle suggested one extra meeting that afternoon before *Air Force One* left for Vienna. At this meeting, when Kennedy raised the question of Britain's application to join the Common Market, which de Gaulle was blocking, the General explained that Prime Minister Macmillan wanted the advantages of being European for the United Kingdom, which had phased out its anti-European system of imperial preference with the countries of the Commonwealth only to replace it with the 'special relationship' with the US. This, he said, was not in keeping with the letter or the spirit of the Treaty of Rome. It was in part pressure by Kennedy and his successor that confirmed de Gaulle's belief that the UK was too tied to American policies to be sincerely European and that Washington wanted Britain inside the Market's councils as the means for America to manipulate the development of the Common Market.[8] Nothing happening to change his mind, he continued to veto the British application as late as 14 January 1963.[9] A subsidiary reason for his resistance was that Britain had shown no preparedness to accept economic integration with the Six during the original negotiations in 1956 and 1957.[10] If he needed another reason, it was that a British Government in London which dumped its Commonwealth partners to join a European customs union was equally capable of dumping Europe, too, when that suited it.

It was Kennedy's fourth rebuff from the General. Effectively, he had wasted three days which might have been better spent preparing for his coming confrontation with Khrushchev. To salvage what little he could, he asked de Gaulle not to make any announcement implying dissatisfaction with NATO until the summit meeting had ended. De Gaulle went further, agreeing to make no such announcement before the Berlin crisis had been resolved. The two heads of state parted for the last time, with the General more determined than ever to have his Bomb. Only then, he was sure, would the American Government treat France as the great power he believed his country to be. De Gaulle's next visit to Washington would be for Kennedy's funeral in November 1963, two months before which he said in a speech at Lyon:

> For us, the question was ... to know whether we would possess this deterrent *and this ferment of economic activity* ... or whether we should give up to the Anglo-Saxons on the one hand our chances of life and death and on the other *certain aspects of our industrial potential.*[11]

So, behind what seemed to some de Gaulle's obsession with a French Bomb was not only an appreciation of its importance in France becoming again a major power, but also his awareness that not sharing US nuclear technology meant that French industry would be forced to buy peaceful applications of this technology from the United States – which could be withheld at the whim of the man in the White House or the State Department, or any other part of the American political machine. To de Gaulle, such a position was unacceptable: the French nuclear programme must therefore press on.

Notes

1. J. Fenby, *The General*, London, Simon & Schuster, 2011, pp. 471–2
2. A. Beevor & A. Cooper, *Paris after the Liberation*, London, Hamish Hamilton, 1994, p. 126
3. Ibid., p. 245
4. Ibid., p. 140
5. This was a CIA-sponsored landing on 17 April 1961 at the *bahia de los cochinos* of an invasion force of expatriate anti-Castrists, which failed disastrously.
6. Notes of the Kennedy–de Gaulle discussion, 1 June 1961
7. Signed 14 May 1955
8. W. Kohl, *French Nuclear Diplomacy*, Princeton UP, 1971, p. 136
9. D. Rusk, *As I Saw It*, London, Tauris, 1991, p. 240
10. Sir M. Palliser, '*Cent Ans d'Entente Cordiale*' in *Espoir*, Paris, Institut Charles de Gaulle, 2004, 2e trim., p. 24
11. A. Passeron, *de Gaulle Parle*, Paris, Fayard, 1966, p. 220 (author's italics)

19

150 BULLETS AND FOUR BURST TYRES

One of the lesser-known organisations spawned in Washington by the Cold War was the Air Force Tactical Application Center, known by the acronym AFTAC. Its title was deliberately chosen to confuse, because AFTAC's business was nuclear espionage using all means available. These included high-flying U-2 spy planes and fake meteorological balloons sent up to take samples of air from high altitudes, as well as ships to sample sea water, both of which could then be tested for radioactivity. The aircraft and balloons had sufficed to measure French nuclear progress for the first four tests at Reggane starting on 13 February 1960,[1] when devices were exploded on 100m-high towers in the desert, producing enormous quantities of contaminated dust at high altitudes, from which the balloons and planes could take their samples. However, the fallout that was so useful for AFTAC was a source of concern for countries neighbouring Algeria, on whom it fell.

Their protests to the UN led de Gaulle to change tack and press on with tests in underground caverns hollowed out of solid granite beneath the sands of the Sahara, and thus reduce to a minimum the fallout. On 26 July 1961, AFTAC informed the State Department that a 'reliable source' inside the French Government had confirmed that there was to be a series of eight or ten underground tests of increasingly powerful devices, culminating in one producing 75–100kt early in March 1962.[2] To monitor these tests, AFTAC planned to install a permanent network of underground seismometers in Mali, Niger or Libya, backed up by additional sensing devices when HUMINT sources indicated a test was imminent.

At a meeting in the State Department in Washington on 4 August 1961, Mali was ruled out because the government was too involved with the Soviet bloc and had many Russian and other east European technicians in the country. Niger was also eliminated because there were too many French citizens there, including counter-espionage officers. That left Libya, where US military cartographers were mapping previously unexplored territory and several US oil companies were prospecting. Either could serve as cover for the implantation of the permanent sensors and bring in the temporary ones when required. Although no declassified papers confirm this, it appears that Washington monitored the French underground tests in this way for the following five years, using the results to confirm intelligence from HUMINT sources inside the French Government.

While AFTAC was working out the best way to spy on America's French allies, President Kennedy was exploring the newly constructed shelter at his home on Cape Cod for use by his family and close aides in the event of a nuclear attack being launched on the United States while he was in residence there. In retrospect, he need not have worried, because de Gaulle was right: all the blustery threats from Khrushchev were window-dressing. So efficient was the KGB's espionage in the West and that of the Soviet military intelligence organisation GRU that his generals had a very good idea of the balance of nuclear power. The equation was simple: if Moscow's policy over Berlin or any other issue triggered a war with NATO, nuclear retaliation from the USA could wipe out every major city and military installation in the USSR. Soviet missiles could cause devastation in Europe and some retaliation would reach American targets, but American civilisation would survive, while 'the Socialist sixth of the world' would be, as the current phrase went, nuked back into the Stone Age.

The efficiency of the Soviet espionage networks was, in a sense, the reason why the Cold War stayed cold. At all levels, its penetration of Western governments confirmed that the West was united in regarding West Berlin as the line in the sand. From Paris, it also confirmed that de Gaulle was resolutely opposed to *any* negotiation.

A few hours before Kennedy's briefing about his nuclear shelter, a meeting in Moscow of the heads of state of the Warsaw Pact member countries was listening to the complaints of GDR leader Walter Ulbricht that the open border in Berlin was bleeding his country to death. The frontier between the GDR and West Germany was already barred with minefields and wire but in Berlin people could walk across a street or take the S-Bahn surface railway to cross between sectors. For several years, his government had been planning a remedy to this situation that was blisteringly simple. He wanted to build a wall with minefields and watchtowers all around West Berlin, and allow only a few heavily policed crossing points, where GDR citizens would not be allowed to cross.

Khrushchev gave the green light to Ulbricht, but at the same time warned him that the wall — at first just barbed-wire fences erected during the night of 12–13 August — must not encroach by one centimetre on the Western sectors. Such a barrier was nevertheless in flagrant contravention of the four-power agreement governing the occupation of Berlin signed in 1945. Authorising the

Wall was Khrushchev's way of testing the resolve of the West and seeing how much of a split de Gaulle's reservations about NATO had caused within the alliance. Would NATO react by implementing Operation *Live Oak*, or not?

The news reached Kennedy while he was boating off Cape Cod. He called Dean Rusk for the details, and Rusk confirmed that, while GDR citizens were now prisoners in their country, there was no interference with Bundesrepublik citizens or foreigners who wanted to visit the Soviet sector of Berlin. Kennedy rang off and continued to enjoy his sailing, without even consulting his closest ally, Prime Minister Harold Macmillan, who was in Scotland for the grouse-shooting. Ah! Those were the days!

Ulbricht had chosen his moment well. It was a hot August Sunday. Trying to reach Kennedy and Macmillan from his own home in Colombey, de Gaulle was furious, considering that the first barbed-wire barriers should have been crushed into the ground by Western tanks. As the hours ticked by in the study where he had written so many thousand words about the defence of France and the West, he was confronted with the real answer to his proposition for a council of three.

Although 'informed opinion' in Washington blamed him for causing the rift in NATO, it became apparent that he had been right. In October, US and Soviet tanks faced each other for several extremely tense hours across the demarcation line between the Western sectors of Berlin and the Soviet sector. Soviet troops at the agreed border crossings used by Berlin-bound military traffic from the Western zones delayed and hampered British, French and American access without actually stopping it outright.

In Paris, the OAS No. 1 target pushed ahead with his search for a settlement with the FLN that would combine Algerian independence with guarantees for the safety of French colonists and their property in the country. It was an impossible goal. In Algeria, nothing could stop the violence, which spilled across the Mediterranean into France itself. With twenty-two of his Paris policemen murdered by ALN terrorists in a few months, Prefect of Police Maurice Papon[3] imposed a totally unconstitutional curfew during the hours of darkness on all adults whose identity papers declared them to be of North African origin. On 17 October 1961, after left-wing organisations had organised a peaceful demonstration by several thousand unarmed immigrants, Papon's police beat up many hundreds and killed a large number. The exact figure is still disputed, but the favourite method used was to throw North Africans unable to swim from bridges into the River Seine, where they drowned. Their only offence had been to donate funds to the FLN voluntarily or under duress.

The best that could be obtained at the peace conference between French representatives and the FLN in the spa town of Evian on the southern shore of Lake Geneva was a relatively dignified withdrawal of all French troops and independence for Algeria. The agreement was signed on 18 March 1962. To the *pied noir* settlers, this was the ultimate betrayal, but a referendum in April showed that more than 90 per cent of the war-weary French voters approved the agreement ending the war that had cost every family the life of either a relative or a close friend. The Algerian settlement brought France a respite after sixteen unbroken years of colonial warfare. In a referendum held on 1 July the population of Algeria overwhelmingly endorsed the Evian agreement, with independence being declared on 3 July.

No sooner had the agreement been signed at Evian than a flight for life began in Algeria. Knowing the excesses of the ALN all too well, the *colons* had good reason to believe the OAS warning daubed on walls all over Algeria: *La valise ou le cercueil!* The suitcase or the coffin was, in truth, their only choice. Each adult fleeing to safety in France was allowed to take a single suitcase. The diehards who declared their intention to stay in Algeria had no legal way of guarding their farms, businesses or homes, since firearms were now forbidden to Europeans. Their most likely end was in a coffin.

With almost a million European refugees flooding across the Mediterranean into France in the space of a few weeks, such was the desperation to get out before it was too late that one refugee ship's captain stopped his engines just outside Algiers harbour and refused to get under way again until all the stowaways emerged and declared themselves. According to one of them, non-paying passengers outnumbered the legitimate travellers by two to one. Most of the refugees settled in Corsica and along the axis Bordeaux–Ventimiglia, where property was cheap and life, at least in the summer months, was not unlike what they had been accustomed to on the other side of the Mediterranean. The compensation for the loss of their homes and businesses in Algeria was derisory, and never paid in full. Nor did they receive a warm welcome from their new neighbours who had competed for decades against the low prices of Algerian exports produced with cheap native labour.

De Gaulle had made himself a million enemies, but the vast majority of French people supported the architect of this disengagement from a war that could not be won, thus ending sixteen years of colonial blood-letting that had cost France dearly in taxes and lives. An uncommitted observer might think that this would make him the flavour of the month – as the saying then was – with the State Department and in the White House. Not so.

On 12 December 1961 a meeting in Paris of the Foreign Ministers of the USA, Britain, the Bundesrepublik and France was deadlocked by the refusal of French Foreign Minister Couve de Murville to agree that the State Department should negotiate with Moscow on their joint behalf in an attempt to resolve the Berlin situation. Finally, Dean Rusk asked de Murville to telephone de Gaulle and request fresh instructions. De Murville's answer was, '*Non!*' To Rusk, this was intolerable, so he called the White House and asked Kennedy to call de Gaulle direct.

A hot line had been installed more than a year previously for use at just such a moment but had never been used, although de Gaulle had tried it once and been kept on hold by the White House switchboard – at which diplomatic slight he was furious. This time, with a State Department interpreter beside him, it was Kennedy's turn to find that there was no one at the other end of the hot line, forcing him to use the public telephone system to reach the Élysée Palace.

De Gaulle was not in the best of moods, being unprepared for the call and having to rely on Kennedy's interpreter, having none of his own to hand. During a half-hour of awkward discussion – Kennedy and his interpreter were sharing one handset in the Oval office – the General repeated what he had said during the president's visit to Paris: that the West had to stand firm and refuse to negotiate *anything* because there was no real threat of Moscow going to war. He was also making the point, which seemed to escape Kennedy entirely, that he had proposed a council of three and been snubbed. Why, therefore, should he bend over backwards to change his alternative policy of refusing to deal?

Kennedy insisted that it was important for NATO to present a united front to Moscow. The conversation degenerated into a word game, logged stage by stage by McGeorge Bundy, his special assistant for national security affairs, aimed – in Washington at least – at finding a text that could be issued by the four foreign ministers. It failed. There was a vague promise to continue the conversation next day, which was not followed up. Instead, Kennedy called Macmillan over the Washington–London hot line, which was regularly used, in an attempt to get him to put pressure on de Gaulle.

There was nothing Macmillan could do, so the problem was passed back to the foreign ministers in Paris who issued a vaguely worded document that was all wallpaper and no wall. In the two years that ended with his assassination, Kennedy never forgave de Gaulle and the two leaders never spoke to each other again. A letter to the French president from the White House dated 31 December 1961 was as near a slap in the face as one head of state can deliver to another. After referring to the negotiations with Moscow 'without the direct help of the French [whose] presence would add to the force and influence [of the NATO side in the negotiations]', Kennedy made it crystal clear that his administration had no intention of giving any assistance to the creation of an independent French strike force or to de Gaulle's plans for a French bomb. This latter was justified by the spurious logic that doing so would encourage the Germans to demand similar facilities, which would be unthinkable.[4] A few days later, de Gaulle replied in writing, rightly protesting that three German invasions of France in seventy years – two of which had been repulsed at some cost in American lives – made nonsense of Kennedy's pretence of having to treat the two countries as equal allies, whatever the temporary *Realpolitik* of the Cold War.

To understand his policies at this time requires an appreciation of the world as seen from the Élysée Palace in 1962. With the exception of the USSR, the whole planet was becoming increasingly Americanised, with *all* other cultures being drowned in a flood of Pepsi, Coke and Procter and Gamble detergents, bearing with it a flotsam of Hollywood films, Y-Fronts, Playtex bras, Levi jeans and Kellogg's and Nabisco cereal products. Later would come the irresistible cultural tsunami of transatlantic television series and the implantation worldwide of multinational companies able by secret boardroom decisions to avoid paying taxes and destabilise national economies. In 1962, however, it seemed to Charles de Gaulle that there was still time for France and the French-speaking countries to build a cultural/linguistic coffer dam around themselves and keep at bay this threat to their continued independent political, cultural and commercial identities.

Francophonie is a word coined as far back as 1880 to mean the sense of community imparted by speaking French, and came by extension to mean the bloc of nations including both France, Quebec and those parts of Belgium and Switzerland where French was the first language, together with the countries where it was the second language used for commercial and cultural exchanges by a French-educated middle class – such as the Levant, south-east Asia and large tracts of the African continent. De Gaulle's plan was to unite the fifty *francophone* countries virtually spanning the alphabet from Belgium, Benin and Burkina Faso all the way to Togo, Tunisia, Vanuatu and Vietnam in a bloc where common cultural and economic interests could be protected from what he saw as an Anglo-Saxon conspiracy to dominate the entire planet.

Taking for granted the convenient pre-eminence of their language, English-speakers forget that Arabic script is the second most widely used in the world and Spanish the first language of 250 million people. Mandarin Chinese has 800 million first-language speakers and is used as a second language by millions more, but if we were compelled to master even a modicum of 15,000 Chinese characters in order to use our computers, we would see the world differently. These few examples give a measure of how disadvantaged French speakers are and why de Gaulle wanted to re-validate what had been the language of diplomacy, respected worldwide for its precision.

In the early sixties, it seemed to de Gaulle that the francophone bloc could reduce some of the tensions in the dangerously polarised Cold War, whose principal players in Washington and Moscow manipulated smaller countries by commercial, political and military means like pawns on a global chessboard, with each such move and counter-move by either side potentially a step on the path to global conflict. To reduce the possibilities of French and Belgian withdrawals from their African and other colonies being exploited by either side for its Cold War ends, de Gaulle believed that France could become a force for peace by offering an alternative to intervention by either side in francophone countries wishing to become clients of neither power bloc. Having expunged the stigma of 'colonial oppressor' attaching to 130 years' armed occupation of Algeria, France was at last in a position to fulfil this new peacekeeping role.

The Constitution of the Fifth Republic envisaged increasing measures of autonomy for countries of the Union Française and things progressed so fast that virtually all the French territories in black Africa had achieved independence by 1961. To keep as allies those who had been colonial subjects, de Gaulle shrewdly embarked on a programme of military support and economic aid to France's former colonies, devoting to them most of his foreign-aid budget. To pre-empt American or eastern bloc intervention in military emergencies in these countries, he decided not to abolish the most famous colonial army in the world – the French Foreign Legion, which had never been allowed to set foot on French soil except in the darkest hours of the Franco-Prussian war and the two world wars.

The Legion's para regiment (1 REP) was disbanded in punishment for its role in the revolt against him but all other units were moved to new headquarters and permanent bases in France for the first time since its foundation in 1831 and a new para regiment (2 REP) was created and based on the island of Corsica.[5] A war-weary France thus had a permanently available peacekeeping force that could be deployed and sent into action in the former empire without spilling French blood or losing French votes.[6] Having become an embarrassment to de Gaulle because of his initially outspoken sympathy for the Algerian settlers, Michel Debré resigned the premiership and was replaced in April 1962 by Georges Pompidou, who had been de Gaulle's chief negotiator at Evian and would become the General's right-hand man in the years ahead, to the point of being satirised in *Le Canard Enchaîné* as the president's *pompier* or fireman, kept on standby to be despatched whenever and wherever his master chose to send him.

At this stage, things get complicated. The youngest American major general since George Armstrong Custer, James Gavin was a very popular former para commander who had jumped into Normandy at the head of 82nd Airborne Division. As his reward for being Kennedy's campaign manager, and because he had known de Gaulle during the war, he was given the prestigious appointment of US ambassador to France – this despite his known disapproval of the US policy of dependence on nuclear weapons. He enlisted an old comrade-in-arms, General Maxwell Taylor, who was the president's military adviser, to help present de Gaulle's case anew to Kennedy. These two senior military men spent a weekend at the president's Cape Cod retreat, where he listened to their arguments but remained unconvinced. Kennedy also listened to advocates of the other side, including Jean Monnet who, although sometimes supportive of de Gaulle, disliked his autocratic style of government and had always taken a more pan-European view than the man in the Élysée Palace.

This hearing of both sides culminated in a meeting in the White House on 16 April 1962. Whether de Gaulle was aware of it or not, Ambassador Gavin had been arguing hard in favour of a change of policy – and he was not alone. It has to be said that Gavin was not betraying his duty as an envoy of the United

States Government; what he was seeking was to avoid open confrontation with France. The meeting in the Oval Office was precipitated by the intelligence that, although still more than a dozen years behind the US in nuclear research and lacking any delivery system that could reach Moscow even when it had a bomb, France was about to test its first operational nuclear device, designated AN-11.

Putting the arguments against France was Dean Rusk, who disliked the General personally and regarded Britain as America's 'best friend' in Europe. Speaking for the advantages of keeping France on-side was Secretary for Defence Robert McNamara, who did not want to rock the NATO boat. MacGeorge Bundy's function was to weigh the two arguments, keep the minutes and record what was intended to be Kennedy's final decision on the matter. If that sounds a reasonably fair way of handling the matter, it is a matter of record that the president regarded the non-proliferation of nuclear weapons as a sort of Holy Grail and saw no reason why the nuclear Big Three should have any company, certainly not in the shape of a maverick like de Gaulle, who could not be trusted to do what the incumbent of the White House told him, if he thought it conflicted with French interests.

Savvy as ever, Rusk opened the batting by asking what reasons the president had for changing the policy on which he had decided in December – an opening which is so often a winner. He then launched into a recapitulation of the reasons why de Gaulle was not acceptable as a member of the nuclear club. They were: he was not open to negotiation; preferential treatment for France would cause complications with other European countries, especially Germany; giving American technology to a medium-class power like France would invite every other country of similar standing to ask for the same facilities; an independent nuclear force – by that he meant one not controlled by Washington – was a danger for the whole world; lastly, why should America help a European head of state who had, since his return to power in 1958, refused to obey Washington's dictates and thus dimished the authority in Europe of the United States?[7]

Against this, McNamara argued that de Gaulle would press on and have his bomb and a French-made delivery system sooner or later. Helping him now would save France enormous expenditure and that could be used as a bargaining chip to offset French reluctance to have American nuclear weapons on French soil and/or to persuade him to augment France's contribution to NATO ground forces. That may seem simplistic but arguments at the top are always reduced to the minimum, as expressed by Churchill's credo that every issue could be reduced to one page.

Kennedy, who had probably made up his mind in advance, stuck to his decision to give de Gaulle nothing, although Gavin and McNamara did subsequently persuade him to sell to France a dozen KC-135 in-flight refuelling tankers that permitted French Mirage IV fighter-bombers to deliver a bomb-load on Soviet territory – but this apparent concession was only made because the tankers were useless for American strategic purposes at that time. Whether the bomber pilots could ever have made it home or were to be expended in kamikaze missions was never made clear.

Less than a month later, an unusual approach was made to Kennedy by Gaullist author André Malraux. Jackie Kennedy was a fan of his, attracted to this intellectual who had taken part in the Spanish Civil War and been in the Resistance. A morning spent with her in the National Gallery of Art was followed by a luncheon at which Malraux's eloquent and flattering speech ended with a toast to the president and people of the United States, which he hailed as the first country in history to achieve world leadership without having sought it by military means.

By the time of the meeting that afternoon in the Oval Office there was no trace of the oil he had poured on troubled water. Kennedy's opening shot was yet another attack on de Gaulle for resisting British entry into the Common Market. His second was a thinly veiled warning that the United States would not continue to aid Europe's defence if continental leaders rejected White House policy. However that was supposed to be interpreted, he added that the US had no desire to dominate Europe. When Malraux attempted to compress the history that dictated de Gaulle's policies for France and pointed out that the high numbers of American forces were stationed in Europe to keep the Russians out and not as an act of disinterested generosity, Kennedy showed no understanding of de Gaulle's concern, but inferred openly that his attitude was a delayed revenge for the unmerited enmity of President Roosevelt during the Second World War. The meeting ended with a warning simile for Malraux to convey to the General when Kennedy likened himself to a man doing all the work (for Europe), while the people whose burden he was carrying did nothing but criticise him.

James Gavin was an honest man. Having used all the weapons in his armoury in the endeavour to get US support for France's defence policy in order to avoid a permanent rift between the White House and one of the three major European states, he resigned his post in Paris and retired from diplomatic life.

At 8.30 p.m. on Wednesday 22 August 1962, de Gaulle's cortège was driving at speed through the Parisian suburb of Petit-Clamart en route to the airbase at Villacoublay, where he and his wife were to take a helicopter to Colombey for a break from the heat of the capital, deserted by most of its regular inhabitants and given over largely to tourists. Without warning, three OAS men armed with sub-machine guns opened fire on the Citroen DS transporting the General, his wife and son-in-law. Afterwards, 150 cartridge cases were recovered at the site of the attack that lasted seconds. De Gaulle thrust his wife down to the floor, but remained sitting upright. In the front passenger seat, his son-in-law yelled at the president's regular driver not to stop. Far too well trained to do anything of the sort, he regained control of the car despite four punctured tyres and accelerated away to the safety of the airbase.

There, de Gaulle remarked to an aide, while inspecting the fourteen bullet-holes in the bodywork of the Citroen DS, 'They can't shoot for toffee. But it's just as well that the men trying to kill me are more stupid than those whose duty it is to protect me.'[8]

After the OAS commando had been ruthlessly hunted down by the Action Service, using every means both legal and illegal, the commander of the Petit-Clamart operation was identified as Lieutenant Colonel Jean-Marie Bastien-Thiry. Arrested in September, he was sentenced by court martial to death. De Gaulle's reasons for refusing clemency were that it was not merited by an officer who had planned an attack on a car carrying a female passenger and also because Bastien-Thiry had planned the operation but chosen not to share the physical risks of the three men who carried it out. Despite a legal defence that he was on anti-depressives at the time and therefore had diminished responsibility, he was shot by firing squad at dawn on 11 March 1963 in the fort at Ivry, less than 10km from the scene of the failed assassination, thus earning the distinction of being the last man to be legally executed in France.

With party leaders also plotting against the General in autumn 1962, in their case to force an amendment to the Constitution of the Fifth Republic that would give more power to them in the National Assembly, de Gaulle used subtler means than were called for with the OAS. Exploiting the groundswell of public sympathy for him after Petit-Clamart, he wrong-footed them by proposing a very different amendment to the Constitution, which would enable direct election of the president by *all* voters in France. When his political enemies denounced as unconstitutional this move to deprive the parties of any say in the presidential election process, he deprived them of a platform by dissolving the National Assembly and calling a referendum on the issue. On 28 October, 62 per cent voted for the amendment and the November elections saw a clear majority for the Gaullist UNR. Pompidou was reappointed prime minister.

Notes

1. J. Newhouse, *de Gaulle and the Anglo-Saxons*, London, André Deutsch, 1970, p. 11
2. V. Jauvert, *L'Amerique contre de Gaulle*, Paris, Seuil, 2000, p. 36
3. As Secretary in the Prefecture of Gironde, he had sent the Jews of Bordeaux to their deaths at Auschwitz, but continued his civil service career and was not prosecuted for half a century.
4. Jauvert, *L'Amerique contre de Gaulle*, pp. 43–7
5. D. Boyd, *The French Foreign Legion*, Thrupp, Sutton, 2006, pp. 295–303
6. In fact about half of legionnaires were French, but had to declare they were not in order to enlist. Called collectively *les gaullois*, they claimed to be Belgian or Swiss to account for their fluency in the French language.
7. Jauvert, *L'Amerique contre de Gaulle*, p. 54
8. ed. M. Jullian, *de Gaulle – Traits d'esprit*, Paris, Cherche-Midi, 2000, p. 58

20

THE WORLD ON THE BRINK OF WAR

Under the regime of its dictator Fulgencio Batista, the island of Cuba, lying only 160km south of Key West, Florida, had been treated by the CIA as its own backyard for nearly three decades while American Mafia bosses controlled the extensive gambling, drugs and prostitution activities that milked the *gringo* tourists on the island. After Fidel Castro came to power in January 1959 and subsequently revealed that his promises of ridding Cuba of Batista's corrupt regime had been a cover to conceal the extent of his communist sympathies, the USA retaliated by breaking off diplomatic relations to bring this difficult neighbour to heel.

When it also ceased to buy Cuba's sugar crop, the move presented the ideal cue to Soviet Premier Nikita S. Khrushchev. Stepping into the breach as purchaser, he also promised to defend the only communist country in the western hemisphere with Soviet arms, in the event of it being attacked by the United States. His first move in that direction was to send to Cuba medium-range ballistic missiles (MRBMs), to be based there 'for defensive purposes'. Such missiles could reach targets in much of the eastern United States within a few minutes of being launched from Cuban sites.

Officially, the United States took no action. After all, Cuba was a sovereign state and its government had every right to conclude alliances with whomever it chose, and to buy or be given whatever weaponry it wanted. The fact that a state is equipped to wage war is not in itself a *casus belli*. Washington's retaliation to what it regarded as an intolerable state of affairs was therefore initiated in the shadowy world of the CIA. In a document dated 18 January 1962, an operation code-named *Mongoose* was launched with Kennedy's sanction. Its expressed objective was 'to help the Cubans overthrow the communist regime from within Cuba and institute a new government with which the United States can live in peace'.[1] The scale of the operation was such that *Mongoose* was to mobilise nearly

4,000 of the agency's employees and agents, with uncounted Cuban émigrés on the payroll.

To avoid a repeat of the appalling miscalculations that led to the failure of the CIA-sponsored invasion of Cuba at the Bay of Pigs by anti-Castro émigrés in April 1961, *Mongoose* needed sources of HUMINT inside the target country to augment the high-altitude photography carried out by U-2 spy planes. With the former eyes and ears of the CIA in Cuba locked up in Castro's prisons and likely to stay there for many years, a few days after the abortive invasion at the Bay of Pigs, veteran US spymaster Allen Dulles called a long-term resident of Washington's intelligence community and asked him to make a trip to Havana and report back everything he saw and heard.

Philippe Thyraud was a former Gaullist *résistant* who still used his wartime cover name, de Vosjoli, but was referred to as 'Lamia' by his contacts inside the CIA. Officially, Lamia was a vice-consul in charge of visa applications at the French embassy in Washington. His real work, for the past ten years, had been liaison between the CIA and the Service de Documentation Extérieure et de Contre-Espionnage (SDECE), which was then the main French intelligence service. Anyone observing Lamia's lavish hosting of his contacts in expensive restaurants around Washington and in his own luxurious home might have thought that SDECE operatives were very well paid, but Lamia's lifestyle was all window-dressing and bait. Like many intelligence operatives, he always had several irons in the fire and favours owing to him, which could be called in if his masters in Paris should cease to find him useful. Since the end of the Second World War, he had kept up contact with a number of Cuban factions. Among those on the island, his friends included top army officers and Castro's sister Juanita. He was happy to oblige so important a contact as Dulles, and his report – that of a trained intelligence officer – was considered very useful on his return to Washington.

The CIA next asked Lamia to set up a small, top-level spy network in Cuba. Lamia knew he was on a winner when the price for his help was named. The McMahon Act of August 1946 forbade the passing of US nuclear secrets to other powers, but said nothing about passing on other people's secrets, and the CIA claimed to have a store of valuable nuclear intelligence gleaned from Soviet sources that was not covered by the Act. If Lamia would set up a *permanent* espionage network in Cuba, the CIA would, in return, arrange a continuing feed of this intelligence. When Lamia passed this news to his SDECE boss General Paul Grossin, the deal was agreed and Lamia conveyed the acceptance to CIA Director John McCone. On Grossin's retirement, Lamia persuaded his successor, General Paul Jacquier, to continue the arrangement whereby the CIA Cuban network was controlled by a cipher clerk at the French Embassy in Havana. The somewhat James Bond scenario had not taken into account the clerk's homosexual entanglements, in which the jealousy of a jilted Cuban lover led to the clerk's betrayal to agents of Castro's security service. With him declared *persona non grata*, French ambassador in Havana Roger Robert du Gardier took over direct control. A man of many parts, he was not above welcoming incoming dissidents from Miami when they landed at midnight on remote beaches and hiding them and other people sought by Cuban security on embassy premises.

On 18 August 1962 du Gardier passed to Washington reports on the arrival of Soviet missiles, together with 4,000 technicians to construct missile-launching facilities. He also confirmed that top Cuban army officers were having intensive Russian-language lessons. The intelligence from the Lamia/du Gardier network was so highly valued that the French ambassador in Washington was asked by Dean Rusk to pass on to French Foreign Minister Couve de Murville the Kennedy administration's appreciation of the help being given in Cuba. In the other direction, however, it seems that the CIA's feed of Soviet nuclear technology was very second rate, which did nothing to raise opinion in Paris of the Kennedy administration. The CIA–SDECE deal never made the headlines at the time because it suited Washington to pretend that all its intelligence about the Soviet missiles in Cuba came from superior American technology, especially U-2 reconnaissance photography.

By 29 August 1962 military construction and the presence of Soviet technicians on the island was confirmed by US high-altitude photo-reconnaissance missions over the island. When this was reported in the American press, Kennedy announced that the Soviet missiles in Cuba were for defensive purposes only. Early in October he received intelligence that the Soviet presence on Cuba included a number of MIG-21 aircraft capable of delivering nuclear bombs. On 9 October, after photographs had been taken of Soviet freighters bound for Cuba with crated IL-28 bombers as deck cargo, Kennedy authorised a further U-2 reconnaissance mission over Cuba itself, which clearly revealed the presence of medium-range ballistic missiles (MRBMs) with a radius of action close to 1,100 miles, as well as Soviet technicians constructing launch sites. Two days later, he was briefed by National Photographic Interpretation Centre (N-PIC) that Khrushchev had upped the stakes in the Cuban poker game from 'defensive' MRBMs to 'offensive' intermediate-range ballistic missiles (IRBMs) with a range of 2,200 miles. These missiles could reach all the continental United States except the Pacific Northwest and had warheads of five megatons' yield – twice the power of the MRBMs'.[2] No such missiles had so far been sighted but N-PIC was certain that two launch sites near Guanajay, which would be completed and launch-capable in six to eight weeks, were intended for IRBMs.

By 20 October 1962, Kennedy was looking in the Oval Office at pictures that photo-interpreters explained as showing assembly areas and launch pads for sixteen ready-to-go SS4 rockets, capable of delivering two- or three-megaton warheads. In addition, the French HUMINT feed reported an ongoing programme of construction of more launch pads for missiles, of which it estimated that only a dozen or so were already in Cuba.

Of Kennedy's advisers, it was Secretary of State Dean Rusk whose analysis of Soviet motives came closest: he connected this new threat in America's backyard with the presence of American Jupiter missiles and nuclear-capable aircraft in Italy and Turkey. Rusk also highlighted the danger of the US isolating itself within NATO – as the British and French had done at the time of Suez – by precipitate action.

This was the era of MAD – the acronym for 'mutually assured destruction' – which argued that neither side in the US–USSR power struggle could afford to strike first, since to do so would result in such retaliation that both countries would become radioactive wastelands. When on maximum alert, the US Strategic Air Command, whose motto was *Our profession is peace*, could put an average of 180 aircraft in the air with nuclear weapons on board, kept circling at their fail-safe points by mid-air refuelling as they awaited the orders to proceed to destroy strategic targets all over the USSR. At one point in the conversations on 22 October, Kennedy had to ask what the letters EDP meant, and was told they stood for European Defence Plan, a euphemism meaning nuclear war in Europe![3] Defence Secretary Robert McNamara thought that Italy would happily give up its status as a NATO nuclear base but the Turks would be more bullish. There was a further note of realism when Secretary of the Treasury Douglas Dillon averred that the Jupiter missiles in Italy and Turkey had only been sent there as a sop to their respective governments because their liquid-fuelled systems were unreliable and obsolete!

After considering the alternatives ranging from an immediate seaborne invasion of Cuba, limited air strikes to taking out the missile sites, or further diplomatic manoeuvres – all of these had their proponents in the various committees – Kennedy opted for a naval blockade to prevent further Soviet shipments of missiles reaching Cuban ports. Rusk suggested calling it a 'quarantine' in the attempt to get around the awkward fact that interfering with the free passage of ships in international waters during peacetime is a flagrant contravention of international law. Kennedy announced the 'quarantine' on 22 October and warned that US ships would seize 'offensive weapons and associated materiel' that Soviet vessels might attempt to deliver to Cuba. During the next few days, Soviet ships bound for Cuba altered course to avoid the quarantine zone while messages were exchanged between Kennedy and Khrushchev amidst mounting tension on both sides.

Also on 22 October US armed forces were moved from Defence Condition (Defcon) 5 – the normal peacetime configuration – to Defcon 3. Defcon 1 was nuclear war. On 23 October, and for the only time in the Cold War, SAC went on to Defcon 2 with more than 1,400 B-28 bombers on immediate readiness to take off and bomb military and civilian targets all over the USSR. It remained in this heightened state of readiness until 15 November. In addition troops had been

airlifted to bases in the south-east of the United States in readiness for an invasion of Cuba.[4] With SAC on Defcon 2, the world was a single command short of
nuclear war.

In the midst of all this tense manoeuvring, on 22 October Kennedy decided
that it was time for the United States to reverse its embargo on giving nuclear
technology to France.[5] It is true that UK Prime Minister Harold Macmillan was
being kept advised of each move in Washington, as befitted the much vaunted
'special relationship' between Britain and the United States. It is true that the State
Department and US embassy staffs worldwide were working hard to build support
for the US position in case worse came to worst. This was especially true, not only
vis-à-vis the NATO allies, but also with all the co-signatories of the Rio Treaty – a
western hemisphere forerunner of NATO which not only debarred the United
States from invading Cuba, but theoretically should have called all the other signatories to Cuba's defence if the US or any other country did so. It is true that Adlai
Stevenson, US ambassador to the United Nations Organisation, was working tire-
lessly there to undo the blatantly false arguments of Soviet delegate Valerian A.
Zorin that there were no 'offensive' Soviet weapons on Cuba. All that is true. But
it seems that Kennedy's willingness to offer American nuclear technology to de
Gaulle was a measure of the usefulness of French HUMINT from Cuba.

With Charles E. Bohlen, the experienced diplomat replacing Gavin as ambassador to France, on board a ship in mid-Atlantic en route to take up his post
in Paris, Secretary Rusk telephoned a previous secretary of state, who was also
a major architect of the American stance in the Cold War. Dean Acheson had
been an advocate of aid to France during its Vietnam war and was held in some
respect in Paris. Rusk was now asking Acheson to fly to Paris immediately, brief
President de Gaulle and obtain his continued support for the American initiative.

An accomplished diplomat, who preferred to test the water before jump-
ing in, Acheson hesitated before accepting. At his last meeting with de Gaulle,
after Kennedy was elected, the water had not been warm. To his suggestions that
France should tie itself more closely to the United States, as Britain had done in
the hope of future favours, de Gaulle had quoted Lord Palmerston's aphorism.
To be exact, Palmerston said that a nation has no allies, only interests. De Gaulle
expressed the same idea rather more poetically. 'Treaties,' he said, 'are like roses
and young girls, they last as long as they last.' When Acheson explained US plans
to convert NATO into a political framework, de Gaulle replied dismissively that
this was illogical and would never work.[6]

Like an old gundog hearing the shots, 69-year-old Acheson could hardly not
agree to Dean Rusk's request to go to Paris. It was, however, a Saturday and he
had only $7 in cash on him, no valid passport and no clothes packed. During his
updating at the State Department, staffers passed round the hat and collected
$50 for the president's envoy to use on the trip. The passport department was

hurriedly opened and a new passport issued. And so it was with mixed feelings that Acheson took off in Air Force One in the morning of 21 October 1962, heading for Paris. On board was also the No. 3 man in the CIA, Sherman Kent. A specialist France-watcher, Kent had persuaded Kennedy that the General's days in the Élysée Palace were numbered. The OAS attempts on his life were just one reason to think this, and Kent was not alone in believing that the General's firm intention to alter the Constitution so that future presidents would be elected by referendum was his swansong. The first such referendum was due to happen in less than a week, after which it was Kent's estimate that de Gaulle would have to retire within the year. Also on board Air Force One that morning was a representative of the State Department charged with showing Macmillan, who was already *au courant* with Kennedy's intentions via the much-used London–Washington hot line, copies of the photographic evidence on which the White House had decided in favour of a blockade. After dropping him in Britain, Air Force One continued to the US Air Force base at Evreux, 80km to the west of Paris.

At this point, the James Bond ambiance returns. In the absence of an ambassador at the US Embassy, the task of arranging a meeting with de Gaulle fell to *chargé d'affaires* Cecil Lyon. At breakfast time, he reached Etienne Burin des Roziers, the current secretary-general at the Élysée Palace, and persuaded him to rejig the General's appointments diary to fit in a secret meeting with Acheson and Kent at 5 p.m. Shortly before then, he and they with two other CIA officers were driven in an unmarked car flying no flag into the Élysée Palace and shown into the building by a normally unused door and thence conducted along unfrequented corridors to a waiting room outside de Gaulle's office. Shown inside, Acheson and Lyon were confronted by the French president standing by his desk. Acheson advanced and shook hands, at which de Gaulle said, 'Your president does me a great honour in sending so eminent an envoy,' before waving him to an armchair.

Kennedy's letter was handed over, together with the text of the speech he was to make announcing the blockade. Both were in English, which was hardly diplomatic, but de Gaulle made no comment. The letter read, 'We have irrefutable proof … that the Soviets, despite my warnings of last month and their assurances, have installed offensive nuclear missiles in Cuba.' After announcing the intention to blockade, Kennedy warned that his action could provoke Khrushchev to take some retaliatory action in Berlin, and ended, 'We in the West must be ready for a real test of our determination. It is of the highest importance that we keep in very close contact during the critical moments ahead of us.'[7]

De Gaulle passed over the irony of a US president asking for close contact with a head of state to whom he had denied contact for so long. To avoid any doubt about the purpose of Acheson's mission, de Gaulle came to the point immediately by asking him, 'Am I to understand that your president has sent you to inform me of decisions that he has already taken, or are you here to consult me on decisions that he will have to make?'

'I have come to inform you,' replied Acheson.[8]

He then proceeded to brief de Gaulle in detail on the thinking in Washington, emphasising that the major part of the launch pad construction had been done in the past week.

Listening both to him and to the translation by a French diplomat from the Quai d'Orsay, de Gaulle made the pertinent observation that this was the first time the United States had felt itself under the direct threat of nuclear attack – a situation its European allies had been living with for more than a decade. As to France supporting Kennedy's position, his response was oblique: France would make no objection, inasmuch as it was normal for a country to defend itself when its security was threatened. He doubted whether the blockade would prove effective as a way of bringing the Cubans to heel, but did not believe Khrushchev wanted all-out war. Should Moscow apply pressure in, say, Berlin, France would side with the United States. De Gaulle's reading of Khrushchev's mind was right: the whole Cuban adventure was a successful tactic to force the US to remove its missiles from bases in Turkey and Italy that were too close for comfort to strategic targets in the USSR.

Acheson mentioned that the photographic evidence from the U-2 over-flights was available in the outer office. De Gaulle replied that he had no need to see it because Kennedy would hardly have sent so illustrious an envoy to misinform him. This was him being diplomatic; in fact, he was up to date on the HUMINT passed to Washington by Lamia's people in Cuba. However, the three CIA men were then brought in with the enlarged photographs, which completely covered the General's desk. As a military man, he had no difficulty following the presentation covering the missile launch sites, the surface-to-air defence installations protecting them and parts of Ilyushin-29 strategic bombers awaiting reassembly. Impressed by Kent's estimate that the Soviet initiative in Cuba had upped by 50 per cent the likelihood of a successful Soviet first-strike, he delighted Acheson's ears by telling him that France would support Kennedy in every way during the crisis.

Looking ahead, he asked how Kennedy intended to act if Khrushchev did not break the blockade, nor remove the missiles, nor take any other measures. This had not been covered at the State Department, so Acheson had no idea. He took a guess and said smoothly, 'We shall tighten the blockade.' De Gaulle approved.[9]

The meeting had lasted an hour when the Americans were shown out, delighted with the success of the mission. None of them knew that Kennedy had offered significant assistance for the French nuclear programme in return for de Gaulle's support over Cuba. Rusk had decided – on his own initiative and apparently because he believed Kent's cleverly argued but deeply faulted analysis of de Gaulle's chances of staying in power – not to inform Acheson of Kennedy's offer when briefing him for the flight to Paris. In the short term, he had hooked his president's fish without losing the bait; in the long term, another chance of building a 'bridge of friendship' between Washington and Paris had been lost.

In the elections of 25 November de Gaulle showed that he was so far from a beaten old man not worth courting by an American administration that Kennedy had his new ambassador in Paris compile an in-depth report on his electoral techniques with a view to learning something for his own re-election campaign. This boiled down to the General's unashamed use of the single, state-controlled television channel to make five broadcasts to the nation. The real reason was that he had given the nation the choice between keeping him in power or going back to the futile in-fighting of the Fourth Republic. Despite many voters disliking his authoritarian style of government, an overwhelming majority preferred de Gaulle, warts and all, to a return to the chaos that had preceded his coming to power in 1958. Little could be learned that would be any use in an American election and no one in Washington, it seems, reflected that this was the moment to reward an ally who had stood by America in its moment of need – and who was likely to remain in power for some years to come.

For that short-sightedness, there would be a heavy price to pay.

Notes

1. Entitled 'Program Review by the Chief of Operations, Operation Mongoose (General Lansdale). Source: Department of State, Central Files, 737.00/1-2062 and see U.S., Department of State, *FOREIGN RELATIONS OF THE UNITED STATES 1961–1963*, Volume X Cuba, 1961–62 Washington, DC. Headed 'Top Secret; Sensitive' the attached distribution list indicates that fourteen copies were prepared. Copies were sent to the President, Robert Kennedy, Taylor, Rusk for Johnson, McNamara for Gilpatric, McCone, Murrow, Woodward for Hurwitch, General Craig for the JCS, Helms, and Wilson. Three copies were kept by Lansdale.
2. E.R. May & P.D. Zelikow, *The Kennedy Tapes*, New York & London, Norton, 2001, p. 76
3. Ibid., p. 150
4. Ibid., p. 224
5. Ibid., pp. 135, 141
6. J. Chace, *Acheson, the Secretary of State who created the American World*, New York, Simon & Schuster, 1998, p. 388
7. V. Jauvert, *L'Amerique contre de Gaulle*, Paris, Seuil, 2000, pp. 78–9
8. A. Beevor & A. Cooper, *Paris after the Liberation*, London, Hamish Hamilton, 1994, p. 128
9. Chace, *Acheson*, pp. 401–2

21

ESPIONAGE, ASSASSINATION AND GOLD

There is an element of farce about the next stage in the deterioration of Franco-American relations in the early sixties. President Eisenhower had agreed to sell 500 Skybolt missiles to Britain but, after taking office, Kennedy terminated the Skybolt programme on the grounds that it was too expensive and because the missile had a range of only 1,600km. Instead, Britain was to be offered the new Polaris missile with three times the range of Skybolt. However, not even America's closest ally, it seems, could be trusted entirely. The condition to the Polaris offer was that British submarines equipped with the new missile must be part of an integrated command structure.

Confronted with this condition at a meeting with Kennedy in Nassau on 19 December 1962, Macmillan was stunned. Effectively, it meant asking Washington's permission each time a Polaris was to be fired. All his ploys, including his invoking of the 'special relationship' between the two Anglo-Saxon powers, were of no avail until he threatened to 'go European' and join de Gaulle in producing an alternative nuclear delivery system without American help. At that point, Kennedy backed down a notch and agreed that the secret accord over the supply and use of Polaris should have an escape clause granting the British independence of action 'in the event of (British) national interest' being involved. Clutching this implausible straw, Macmillan flew home from Nassau pretending for public consumption that the negotiations had been successful and unaware that de Gaulle had already been sent a copy of the Polaris deal while he was still in the air.

With that copy went Kennedy's personal offer to conclude the same deal with France. From Paris came ... silence. A week passed, then two. On 3 January 1963 British ambassador Sir Pearson Dixon was at the Élysée Palace, trying to persuade de Gaulle to withdraw his veto against British entry into the Common Market. De Gaulle's reason for the veto – that the true orientation of the United Kingdom, now divested of its empire, was towards the US rather than its European neighbours – seemed entirely justified by Dixon's movements after the meeting. He went straight to the US Embassy and related the substance of his conversation to American ambassador 'Chip' Bohlen. One response of de Gaulle's worried them both. To Dixon's question what the French president intended doing about the American offer, de Gaulle had retorted, 'What offer? I haven't had one.'

On the following day, it was Bohlen's turn to be received by de Gaulle, who pointed out to him that, although Britain had submarines capable of delivering a Polaris missile with a nuclear warhead, France had not – as Rusk very well knew. Bohlen's deduction was that the General's remark of the previous day to the British ambassador meant he had not received an offer from Washington that had any practical application for France, and was awaiting one that did.

On 12 January 1963 Kennedy was mulling over with Rusk, McNamara, Bundy and McCone and other advisers whether America should offer France Polaris-capable submarines and warheads on condition they were deployed within NATO's integrated command structure. Rusk was vehemently against this, arguing that France had let down the US at every possible turn. To give an ally as difficult as de Gaulle these facilities, he maintained, would be as good as telling all America's allies that they could have everything they asked for from Washington *and* keep their independence. No, the price must be total support for the USA – or no deal.

They were all on the wrong tack, because the French president had told his Cabinet even before Bohlen's audience that he had no intention of assigning the defence of France to an American-dominated multinational force. Sooner or later, he promised the Cabinet, France would move from having her own A-bombs capable of being delivered by French-made Mirage IV fighter-bombers to the level of having her own H-bomb deliverable by a French rocket from a French submarine. The British, he said dismissively, were obsessed with the hi-tech nature of the missiles they were to receive under the Nassau accord, and seemed not to take into account the degree of dependence on Washington that came with them. France was lagging behind, but would eventually catch up *and* have the advantage of being in full control of its nuclear deterrent. As to the words in Macmillan's piece of paper that the agreement would be voided in the event of 'national interest', that was a load of eyewash. If an American key had to turn in the lock before a Polaris was fired, how could the British get hold of that key, in addition to their own? And supposing British 'national interest' conflicted with America's interests, what then?

The question posed by historian Vincent Jauvert and others is this: if de Gaulle wanted a better offer from the White House, why did he not simply say so to Ambassador Bohlen? The answer to that one is that Washington was playing diplomatic games with the General and he was, in return, testing Washington's goodwill – or absence of same. When, in 1963, the French Government tightened up rules for foreign investment, US direct involvement in French industry fell from

$210 million in 1963 to $149 million in 1966. In Western Germany, the figure rose from $304 million to $646 million.[1]

Anticipating that no better offer would be forthcoming which did not carry an unacceptable price tag in limiting French freedom of action, de Gaulle also gave instructions to the SDECE to initiate a dangerous initiative. Spying on one's enemies is always hazardous; to be caught spying on one's friends can be very embarrassing. General Jacquier summoned Lamia to Paris and ordered him to set up and run a spy ring in the United States with the sole aim of stealing as many nuclear secrets as possible in order to speed up French research. There was nothing orginal in this: the Americans had got the Manhattan Project off to a flying start on the back of previous British and other research; the USSR had stunned Washington by successfully detonating its first nuclear device in 1949 – a decade or so before the time predicted by the physicists at Los Alamos – by deploying its deepest-cover spies to steal American secrets.

Lamia, however, would have nothing of this. He had been working closely with the CIA for too long, and was too aware of the security surrounding US research in the aftermath of the trials of Soviet agents like Julius and Ethel Rosenberg and Klaus Fuchs[2] to believe that a French spy ring set up from scratch would have much chance of obtaining any really useful material. It was more likely, in his view, to be detected and cause a further rift between the United States and France. Another case officer was therefore appointed to direct a small number of French 'students', due to spend study periods in the United States after being carefully briefed by General Jean Thiry, director of the Centres d'Expérimentation Nucléaires, on what they were to look for. The principal targets were miniaturisation technology, triggering mechanisms and production of heavy metals. It does not seem that naval secrets were on the list, although the first French nuclear submarine *Redoutable* was launched in 1967.

At the same time, de Gaulle was saying openly that his reason for opposing British entry into the six-member Common Market was largely to stop the United States, which already controlled much of Europe's defence, pushing its way into commercial and political dominance of the whole continent. In seeming corroboration of his suspicions, Washington launched a massive diplomatic campaign to persuade the other five countries in the Common Market to manoeuvre France into letting Britain join at the next meeting of the Six on 28 January 1963. The tone of these instructions from the State Department to US diplomats in European embassies implied that mere Europeans had no right to decide who could join their club. Typically, to the US ambassador in Brussels Dean Rusk wrote: 'you must ask [Belgian Foreign Minister] Spaak to support us totally.' Another US diplomat was ordered to speak to (president of the European Commission) Walter Hallstein 'and make him understand the importance we attach to a rapid and positive conclusion to these negotiations'.[3]

Six days before the meeting of the six Common Market leaders, de Gaulle thumbed his nose at Washington by signing a bilateral defence treaty with West German Chancellor Konrad Adenauer. There was no reason why he should not and, to an objective observer, it was commendable that the wartime leader of France should achieve a rapprochement with the powerful neighbour state under which his country had suffered in three recent invasions. Yet a kind of panic seized some sectors of what de Gaulle saw with some reason as the Anglo-Saxon conspiracy. The British Secret Intelligence Service MI6 passed to the CIA details of another secret deal de Gaulle was preparing – this time with Moscow. Allegedly originating from an MI6 source in the Élysée Palace, the deal was for the USSR to withdraw its occupation forces from the East German Republic, after which German reunification with free elections would be followed by both Germany and France leaving NATO. In the course of this, the long-term post-Second World War Pentagon scenario of fighting a sub-nuclear and even nuclear Third World War on Battlefield Europe would go out of the window.

It has to be said that, although many in Washington wanted to believe this apparent proof of de Gaulle's ill will, saner counsel prevailed. It was at one point mooted that Kennedy should write to de Gaulle and ask him whether the intelligence was true. The president refused, considering such a move to be too humiliating. As he said to the National Security Council, he had only two weapons in such a case: to withdraw financial aid and to back out of defence obligations. Since France was receiving no aid and was happy to go it alone, neither could be used in this case.

Instead, the CIA was tasked with securing all possible information on the alleged Paris–Moscow negotiations and the James Bond scenario was off again, this time with the part of Bond played by Lamia. In disgrace with his masters in the SDECE, Lamia was now persuaded to become the CIA's mole in the French embassy in Washington! Although he later denied this, many people in the Washington intelligence community noted the way he would stay late at night in the embassy, allegedly to photograph documents himself and to facilitate the entry on to embassy premises of covert operatives à la Watergate. The plot thickens with Lamia fleeing to Mexico to avoid retribution from his French employers. There, a chance meeting between him and mega-selling author Leon Uris resulted in some details of the operation being used in Uris' novel *Topaz*. And thickens again with the establishment of a major invasion of CIA personnel under cover in every possible US agency in France, from NATO HQ to Radio Free Europe, with the aim of penetrating security at the Élysée Palace. This did not pass unobserved by the French counter-intelligence organisation Direction de la Surveillance du Territoire (DST) and complaints were made to American diplomatic representatives. Passing through Paris, veteran OSS boss Alan Dulles promised Foreign Minister Couve de Murville to see that the number of American intelligence operatives on French soil was reduced. It was not.

Finally, sanity supervened even at the temple of paranoia in Langley, Virginia. A number of sources tended to indicate that the MI6 material which had sparked off the 'emergency' was false – whether fabricated in London to increase tension between Washington and Paris, or palmed off on MI6 by its source, was never officially revealed. Some maintained that the whole affair was connected with British double agent Kim Philby, whose defection to the USSR aboard a Soviet freighter kept waiting for him in Beirut harbour came within twenty-four hours of the MI6 report reaching the CIA. Another school of thought was that MI6's 'reliable source' in the Élysée Palace was a double agent planting a delayed-action bomb in the knowledge that CIA reaction would be over the top and provide yet another reason for de Gaulle's eventual refusal to tolerate American defiance of French sovereignty. In the wilderness of mirrors, anything is possible. So, the CIA now set about resuscitating an old canard that it had flown in May, to the effect that de Gaulle had renewed the offer to West Germany of a partnership in the nuclear facility at Pierrelatte between Orange and Montélimar in eastern France.

Five months later, the agency was trying to convince Kennedy that the French head of state was a dangerous wounded animal, liable to turn on anyone. Why was that? Because he had suffered several setbacks: first, America had outbid him in courting the Bundesrepublik and its new Chancellor, Ludwig Erhard; second, the French economy was stagnating; third, he was increasingly isolated in a Europe more and more dominated by American foreign policy; fourth, before France had even got a deliverable A-bomb – let alone an H-bomb – the USSR and USA had agreed to sign a nuclear non-proliferation treaty.

The first multinational non-proliferation treaty was signed by sixty-one states on 1 July 1968, but France would continue to show resentment about exclusion from the nuclear club by not signing until 1992, by which time its status as a nuclear power was indisputable. Back in October 1963, the CIA's conclusion, based on its own interpretation of raw intelligence, was that de Gaulle would make a desperate effort to wean West Germany away from American influence by offering to share with the new Chancellor details of the independently produced French nuclear deterrent, such as it then was.

Both this autumnal alarm and the scare in May were transparent to anyone who had seriously studied de Gaulle's thinking. Rapprochement with Germany was something he earnestly desired for multiple reasons, but equipping the past enemy with the weapons of the future was not on his agenda. On the other hand, developing relations with the powers of the future was. Since the United States shunned him, he turned to its enemies. Where else would he find friends?

In September 1965 Ambassador Bohlen passed on to the State Department intelligence from a highly placed source in the Quai d'Orsay, indicating that de Gaulle was about to take steps against NATO in the very near future. So seriously was this taken in Washington that President Johnson ordered a complete review of plans to evacuate American troops from France. Even so, on 18 October Washington was stunned to hear that de Gaulle had such a poor opinion of the United States' chances of justifying its increasing commitment to the war in Vietnam ending in victory that he had sent veteran politician and former Prime Minister Edgar Faure to Beijing.

Whether Faure was actually sent or was asked to act as a sounding board during a trip he had planned for personal reasons hardly matters. Either way, the CIA station in Paris pressed the panic button in Washington because it was a feature of de Gaulle's administration that he tended to give instructions to his ministers, rather than consult them, and Faure's trip revealed how closely to his chest the General held his cards. Since none of the CIA sources inside the French Government had heard so much as a whisper in advance about the trip, it was decided at high level to bribe or otherwise corrupt an official high in the hierarchy of the Élysée Palace or Quai d'Orsay to become Washington's permanent eyes and ears.

On the same day that Faure left Paris, Ambassador Bohlen was reassured by the Quai d'Orsay that France had no intentions of recognising Communist China, having exchanged ambassadors with Chiang Kai-shek's Kuomintang Government on Formosa as representing China. This was not deliberate disinformation; even at the top level in his Foreign Ministry, no one knew what was in de Gaulle's mind until they had been told. Ordered to go back and ask the General himself, Bohlen did so on 5 November. As delphically as Roosevelt had answered him twenty years earlier, de Gaulle said only that he had, on learning of Faure's intention to make the trip, asked him to make a general report on his return.

On 22 November 1963 the thirty-fifth president of the United States was shot dead in Dallas, Texas in circumstances never elucidated, and a statistically improbable number of witnesses died shortly afterwards. Two days later, de Gaulle arrived to represent France at the state funeral, held on the following day. Greeted by his old enemy Dean Rusk, he said, 'Don't thank me for coming.' The FBI and Secret Service were on tenterhooks at having on their patch a head of state who had been the target of so many assassination attempts, but de Gaulle refused to ride in a bullet-proofed limousine in the funeral cortège, insisting on walking behind the widowed Jacqueline Kennedy.[4]

That evening, de Gaulle was the first foreign head of state to speak with Kennedy's successor, Lyndon Baines Johnson. What might have been a fresh beginning was blighted from the start. Someone in the CIA or State Department fed to Johnson shortly before the meeting a purely anecdotal report that de Gaulle had warned a neutral diplomat in Washington that one could not necessarily count on US support in the hour of need. As Simon and Garfunkel put it in their 1970 hit song *The Boxer*, 'A man hears what he wants to hear, and disregards the rest.' Johnson thus made no overtures, except vaguely to agree they should meet again in the near future. It was not to be. De Gaulle considered that, as the West's senior statesman, he should not have to go to Washington to meet LBJ. He offered to meet in the French West Indies, but this was turned down by the White House.[5]

The security services heaved a collective sigh of relief when the French president's aircraft took off for Paris, where he summed Johnson up to his close associates as a careerist wheeler-dealer, who reminded him, at that early point in his presidency, of the French politicians whose internecine plots had destroyed the Third and Fourth Republics.

A week in politics is a long time, as Harold Wilson said. Ten weeks after Ambassador Bohlen had been told that France had no intention of recognising Communist China, Foreign Minister Couve de Murville calmly informed him that, because de Gaulle considered US refusal to recognise the most populous nation on earth as ridiculous and potentially dangerous, Paris and Beijing would shortly be exchanging ambassadors.[6] There was nothing Johnson's administration could do to change de Gaulle's mind because it gave France nothing that could be withdrawn as a mark of disfavour. With diplomatic protocol inhibiting any country from accrediting two ambassadors representing the same state, President Johnson used the only weapon in his armoury. He leaned heavily on Chiang Kai-shek in Taiwan not to withdraw his ambassador in Paris out of understandably injured pride. His regime kept in power by subsidies from the United States, Chiang did as he was told, but when, on 27 January 1964, the Quai d'Orsay formally recognised the Beijing regime with only a few hours' notice to Washington, Chiang's pride could stand it no longer. On 10 February, he broke off relations with France – after which, nothing stood in the way of Paris and Beijing exchanging ambassadors.

Few people thought that the rift between Paris and Washington could get any wider – until, in March 1964, the General announced that he was to visit Mexico at the invitation of President Lopez Mateos.

To *los yanquís de Washington*, this was another intrusion into their backyard. What right had the president of France to accept an invitation to Mexico? To an outsider, it is incredible that there still lingered in educated minds in Washington what was known in the nineteenth century as the Manifest Destiny of the United States to occupy *all* the North American continent. In 1845 the American Government annexed the Republic of Texas, at which the Mexican Government broke off diplomatic relations. US President James K. Polk then claimed that US territory ended, not at the Nueces River, but much farther south at the Rio Grande – and despatched American troops to occupy the intervening territory. In April 1846 skirmishes there between them and Mexican forces enabled Polk to claim that American blood had been spilled on American territory. Congressman Abraham Lincoln from Illinois was among the saner spirits who requested Polk to state exactly where on American territory this had happened, but Polk carried a gung-ho Congress with him in declaring war on Mexico that month. And so, the first colonial war of the United States began against Mexico.

After a *coup d'état*, the new president south of the border, Antonio Lopez de Santa Anna, led his army against US General Zachary Taylor. Much blood on both sides was spilled at the battle of Buena Vista on 23 February 1847, after which it was decided to teach the Mexicans a lesson they would never forget. A new US expeditionary force marched on Mexico City, which was taken on 14 September 1847, causing another change of government south of the disputed border. When the peace treaty was signed on 2 February 1848, the United States paid Mexico $15 million for 1.36 million square kilometres of territory – now the states of (northern) California, Nevada, New Mexico, Utah and Texas.

It is quite conceivable that the Manifest Destiny would have gobbled up the whole of Mexico and the rest of Latin America, had not the American Civil War intervened. With the Unionist North busy fighting the Confederate South, however, exiled Mexicans in France persuaded Emperor Napoleon III to help them construct a political buttress protecting all the Catholic, Romance-language countries of the New World against the expansionist greed of the Protestant, Anglo-Saxon United States by sending military support to install the puppet 'emperor' Maximilian as ruler of Mexico. The details of his resulting, short-lived 'empire' would fill a thick volume,[7] but it seems that a paranoid delusion within the American intelligence community 100 years later misinterpreted as an aggressive move de Gaulle's natural interest in a country with which France had this historic link, and with which it shared a common attitude to the new American colonialism.

What had the most powerful nation on earth to fear, except de Gaulle's role model as a head of state who owed nothing to either power bloc in the Cold War? He himself told his architect of the Fifth Republic, Michel Debré, that he was going to Latin America for reasons of instinct, by which he may have intended Debré to understand that the tour – now expanded to embrace ten countries, spread over nearly a month – was a gesture of political sympathy with their governments of various political hues, all of whom had also been, and would continue to be, under pressure from Washington. His welcome in Mexico was ecstatic, although the CIA station in Buenos Aires delightedly reported back to Langley that only half as many *porteños* turned out to line the streets as had done so for Kennedy's visit to Argentina in 1961. Sour grapes? Residents of BA at the time told the author that the crowds' welcome was very warm. One wonders how many more have turned out to see other contemporary European politicians, such as Britain's Prime Minister Harold Wilson or German Chancellor Erhard.

In or about March 1964 the CIA finally found, close to the top level in the Quai d'Orsay, the mole it had been desperately seeking. According to this source, debriefed on a visit to London in May 1965 at the US Embassy in Grosvenor Square, de Gaulle was planning to withdraw France from NATO. President Johnson's advisers had various plans to counter this threat, which ranged from withdrawing US and other NATO troops from bases in France first – and thus avoiding the humiliation of being told to go – to telling the American command in NATO and the CIA in France to be very discreet and keep a low profile that would not give de Gaulle any excuse to wind up the leases of the NATO bases on his soil.

Desperately seeking dirt with which to smear de Gaulle, the CIA now began spreading rumours that his recognition of Communist China and diplomatic activity in Indochina was part of a policy that included clandestine support of the Viet Cong. Not until June 1964 was Johnson informed that any contacts between French expat businessmen in Vietnam and the Viet Cong – with whom they had to deal on the level of local blackmail if they did not want their business premises blown up and their employees murdered – were made on their own initiative and not part of any Machiavellian plot in Paris.

On 6 June 1964 de Gaulle surprised his advisers by turning down an invitation to be present at a ceremony in Normandy to mark the twentieth anniversary of D-Day. 'You want me to go there to commemorate *their* landing, which was the prelude to the second occupation of our country?' he retorted. As a result, President Johnson, Ex-President Eisenhower, Prime Minister Harold Wilson and Field Marshal Montgomery refused to attend.[8]

NATO aircraft based in West Germany regularly over-flew French territory on training flights. In the same way that they 'accidentally drifted off-course' and crossed the eastern frontiers of the Bundesrepublik to test the defences of Warsaw Pact countries, NATO also used these training flights across France to make photographic reconnaissance. It seemed that one of these flights had gone too far on 16 July 1965, when an RF-101 reconnaissance aircraft based at Ramstein, less than 30km north of the French frontier, was intercepted by a French fighter and requested to identify itself while in the forbidden air space designated P-59 above a plutonium-enrichment facility at Marcoule, near Orange. When the news leaked, details were confused and the US pilot was supposed to have been forced to land in France.

At 12.30 Washington time on 17 July the duty officer in the Situation Room beneath the White House briefed the president to the effect that the training flight had not trespassed into zone P-59, and had not been forced down, but landed back at Ramstein – after which the flight plan and a can of film said to have been exposed during the flight were handed over to the French authorities. Whatever the film actually handed over was, it included no pictures of Marcoule, but did have twenty frames exposed over the nuclear facility 25km to the north, at Pierrelatte. The sky above Pierrelatte was not forbidden airspace, but standing flight regulations limited over-flying aircraft to heights above 3,000ft, and the RF-101 had been detected flying at 2,500ft. It seemed a marginal error, for which the State Department apologised a week later.

All allies spy on each other, for who knows how long an alliance will last? However, wanting no repeat of an action that was widely interpreted as showing that American forces stationed in Europe, theoretically for its own protection, also spied on the host countries, Johnson gave instructions that no covert or overt actions which might upset French sensibilities were to be initiated for the following six months. The departments of State and Defence and the CIA, USIA and other agencies were required to draw up a list of activities in France that could be prejudicial to Franco-American relations. The list included, 'espionage targeting French citizens or foreigners in France' and, more revealingly, 'clandestine subsidising of political parties, associations and news media [and] presence of American nuclear weapons on French territory'.[9] On 10 September, McGeorge Bundy was able to summarise for the president the replies to the questionnaires. Those released under the US Freedom of Information Act passed during Johnson's presidency on 4 July 1966 are pretty anodyne, but that of the CIA has unsurprisingly not been declassified.

Ironically, the next act of overt hostility to France came not in France itself, but in the White House, where Bundy was at the centre of this downturn in Franco-American relations. On 12 November he was considering an order from the Commissariat à l'Energie Atomique for two IBM and two Control Data Corporation super-computers that were roughly ten times as fast as any non-American computer. It was up to Bundy to decide whether the order came within the embargo on selling to France *anything* that could be used in its nuclear programme. Previously forbidden articles included specialised oscilloscopes and RB-5 aircraft that could have been used to collect samples of high-altitude dust. The order for super-computers landed on his desk because the CEA had already ordered one CDC super-computer, which had been delivered only to avoid repercussions on American companies trading in France and on condition that it be used for non-military purposes. On his return to the United States, the engineer responsible for supervising the installation of the Control Data machine was interrogated by the CIA and reluctantly admitted what his company had known all along – that it was in a military base and not a civilian facility, as stated on the order.

In favour of accepting the new order – and, indeed, of *encouraging* the French to buy expensive equipment like super-computers – was the alarming build-up of French dollar reserves. The Bretton Woods agreements of 1944 which laid the basis for the World Bank and International Monetary Fund obliged each country to maintain the exchange rate of its currency within plus or minus one per cent in terms of gold. At the time, this suited the United States, which held the largest gold reserves of any nation, amounting to around 60 per cent of total world reserves. However, by 1965 the Banque de France was one of many central banks to calculate correctly that a number of factors including the costly US military involvement in Vietnam would soon force the Federal Reserve Bank to devalue the dollar against gold. De Gaulle naturally set about converting France's dollars into gold at the Bretton Woods rate before this could happen.[10] As proof that the nation was behind his American policy, the 1965 French opinion polls showed 53 per cent of the adult population in favour and only 5 per cent against it.[11]

Notwithstanding the increasing pressure on the dollar, Bundy was angry at having been outwitted over the first CDC sale and vetoed the new order. The decision made headlines in French newspapers. It was one thing for the United States to veto the sale of arms and military materiel to hostile or non-aligned countries; refusal to sell four super-computers to an ally was in every sense of the word an insult.

In the following month, Charles de Gaulle was re-elected for a second presidential term in the first election since 1848 where the people of France could directly choose their president. In the second round he beat future president François Mitterand by 55 per cent to 45 per cent of votes cast. Factors that influenced the voting were the greatest stability in government that any living French citizen had known, France's continuing economic growth and a firm currency. In addition, many people voted for the man who had extricated them from the Algerian war without provoking a civil war. Very importantly, de Gaulle's decision in April 1944 that women should be given the vote bore fruit in the shape of 61 per cent of women voters ticking his name on their ballot forms.

For all these reasons, Charles de Gaulle had won seven more years in power. A respected elder statesman, he was widely regarded in France as a sort of elected monarch. With France deriving more benefit than expense from the European Common Market, most sectors of the population accepted his paternalistic style of government as the price of stability, and opinion polls continued to show a majority in support of his policies.[12]

Notes

1. A. Beevor & A. Cooper, *Paris after the Liberation*, London, Hamish Hamilton, 1994, p. 152
2. Julius and Ethel Rosenberg were executed by electric chair on 19 June 1953. Klaus Fuchs was deprived of his acquired British nationality and given the maximum sentence of fourteen years for espionage for 'a friendly power' in March 1950, but released in June 1959 and allowed to return to his native Dresden, then in the Soviet-controlled German Democratic Republic.
3. V. Jauvert, *L'Amerique contre de Gaulle*, Paris, Seuil, 2000, p. 105
4. D. Rusk, *As I Saw It*, London, Tauris, 1991, p. 269
5. Beevor & Cooper, *Paris after the Liberation*, p. 137
6. Ibid., p. 139
7. For more details of the French campaign, see D. Boyd, *The French Foreign Legion*, Thrupp, Sutton, 2006, pp. 117–37
8. ed. J. W. Müller, *Memory and Power in Post-War Europe*, Cambridge, CUP, 2002, p. 62
9. Jauvert, *L'Amerique contre de Gaulle*, pp. 134–9
10. See F. William Engdahl's essay in *Current Concerns* titled 'Iraq and the Hidden Euro-Dollar Wars' on www.richardheinberg.com/museletter 149
11. Beevor & Cooper, *Paris after the Liberation*, p. 138
12. J. Newhouse, *de Gaulle and the Anglo-Saxons*, London, André Deutsch, 1970, p. 305

22

'DEAR MR PRESIDENT, GO HOME!'

McGeorge Bundy's refusal in November 1965 to allow IBM and Control Data Corporation to sell super-computers to France triggered a new downturn in Franco-American relations. With his success in the presidential elections demonstrating a national endorsement of his policies, de Gaulle ordered all French officers at NATO HQ to terminate their attachments and return to their own army, air force and naval units on 21 February 1966. At this, there was a certain numb incomprehension among planning officers on both sides of the rift. The fundamental justification for NATO's existence was that the Cold War might at any moment turn hot, leading to conventional or nuclear hostilities. If this were to happen, there would in future be no integrated plan to move both French and NATO troops and logistics along the same rail and road system heading towards the front in central Europe. The result would be one huge uncoordinated tangle, from which only the enemy would benefit. As a career soldier, de Gaulle was as well aware of this as anyone. However, having accurately foreseen the major events of the Second World War and that it would end in the Cold War, he was now 100 per cent certain that MAD – mutually assured destruction – ensured neither the USA nor the USSR would initiate direct hostilities in Europe, but would have to content themselves with proxy wars in Asia, Africa and Latin America, as proved to be the case.

Two weeks after all French officers left NATO, on 7 March 1966 the newly appointed French ambassador in Washington Charles Lucet took to the White House a handwritten letter from de Gaulle to Lyndon Johnson. It was handwritten to make the point that this was not the result of advice but the writer's personal decision. It was also brief, courteous and to the point. The most important paragraphs read:

Dear Mr President,

Our Atlantic Alliance will end its first term in three years' time [*sic*]. I must tell you how France appreciates the extent to which (NATO's) unified defence system contributes to the security of the fifteen free Western member nations, and particularly the essential role played by the United States of America in this. Consequently, France plans at present to opt, at the end of the ten year period to remain a party to the treaty signed in Washington on 4 April 1949. This means that, unless events of the next three years should radically change relations between East and West, France would remain determined in 1969 and afterwards to fight beside her allies, should one or other of them be the object of unprovoked aggression.

However, as far as France is concerned, the changing situation in Europe, Asia and elsewhere since 1949, and the developments in its own political situation, no longer justify the military arrangements made when the Alliance was set up, whether under multilateral agreements or by bilateral agreements between the French and American governments. France therefore proposes to re-establish complete sovereignty within its territory, currently diminished by the permanent presence of allied military elements and by the habitual use of its airspace, and to end its participation in the integrated command structure, and to withdraw its forces from NATO.

The bombshell of a letter ended:

Dear Mr President, my government will therefore contact yours regarding all these points. However, in the spirit of openness and friendship between our two countries and, permit me to add, between yourself and me, I wished firstly to convey to you personally the reasons for, and the purpose and the extent of, France's need to modify the form of our alliance without destroying its basis.

Respectfully yours,[1]

De Gaulle's first sentence refers to the original Treaty signed in Washington on 4 April 1949, of which Article 12 bound the signatory powers for ten years only, so that the 'first term' actually ended in 1959. Meeting in Washington 2–4 April 1959 the foreign ministers of the signatory powers agreed that the current military/political situation justified continuing the Alliance.

His letter of 7 March 1966 was the diplomatic equivalent of a notice for *all* American forces to get out of France. After all the build-up, it can hardly have come as a surprise to such a savvy politician as Johnson – whose policy throughout his administration was never to act on advice from the State Department to 'deal with' the difficult president of France. In any case, a draft of the letter had been leaked four days previously to the White House via Ambassador Bohlen or the CIA station in Paris, sourced as coming from the Mole in the Quai d'Orsay. The main difference was that, in the draft Monsieur X had given his American handlers, de Gaulle demanded that France be given control over NATO forces within her territory, including the American contingent – presumably because the inevitable refusal from the White House would give him a reason to kick them out. The final text was more honourable. As president of France, the General sought no excuse, because none was needed. What was at issue was French sovereignty.

Why now? the Mole was asked by the handlers desperate for an in-depth analysis. His answer was a rationalisation: de Gaulle was approaching his seventy-sixth birthday and, having undergone one operation for prostate cancer, he was feeling that there was much to do before he retired finally from political life. Ending the American 'occupation' of France was top of his list.

The notice to quit could not have immediate effect. Negotiations dragged on for several months. The Americans wanted several safeguards built into the massive relocation involved. The three main ones were the right to use French airspace for training and other purposes, the right to return to the bases in France in the event of war, and the continued use of the oil pipeline that ran right across France from Donge on the Atlantic coast to Metz in Alsace, which was vital for US troops in Germany. In return, the French negotiating team was instructed to secure a continuing feed of information from NATO radar defences in West Germany and the future NATO 'Dewline' early warning system. Perhaps as a bargaining counter to be renounced for a quid pro quo, they also demanded that France be allowed to keep the American nuclear weapons issued to French forces in Germany since 1961.[2]

The negotiations ended unsatisfactorily for both sides. The French, of course, were not allowed to keep the nuclear weapons in Germany and the Americans did not succeed in obtaining an automatic right to return to their bases in France in the event of war. The only success that could be claimed was a secret agreement signed in August 1967 by NATO's General Lyman Lemnitzer and the Chief of the French General Staff General Charles Ailleret setting out in detail the role to be played by the two French divisions in Germany on NATO's southern flank, should the Soviets cross the border between the two Germanies. By the end of July, the NATO Secretary General's office had moved from Paris to Brussels; Supreme Headquarters Allied Powers in Europe had relocated from Rocquencourt to the west of Paris to a new home in Casteau, Belgium; and Allied Forces Central Europe had moved from Fontainebleau to Maastricht, with the NATO Staff College re-established in Rome. Although France had not abrogated the Treaty and continued to sit on the NATO Council, with a liaison mission at the new NATO HQ, it made new bilateral agreements with the Bonn Government regarding its ground forces in West Germany. The considerable cost of relocating 30,000 NATO servicemen and 60,000 dependants, starting on

30 June would be a bone of contention for years between the Élysée Palace and the White House, the bill remaining unpaid for eight years until a modest contribution was made under President Pompidou to settle the matter.

With President Johnson refraining from open comment, de Gaulle's many enemies in Washington made common cause against him. Dean Acheson was only one major figure who accused the president of France both in Congress and on the media of 'making the Russian bed'. This he did with the specific aim of being reported in France and thus panicking French voters at the next general election in 1967 into believing that their country would be unprotected in the event of war with the Soviet Union, thanks to their president's misguided policies. From Paris, Ambassador Bohlen urged that strong action be taken to show de Gaulle the error of his ways. According to his despatches, less than half the French electorate supported their president's anti-American stance. Yet happily in the Washington aviary there were both hawks and doves, who argued that Lyndon Johnson should take no directly hostile action against a president of France who had recently been re-elected for a seven-year term. The wiser counsels prevailed, with Johnson ordering the secretaries of state and defence on 4 May 1966 to get on with the important task of rebuilding NATO-without-France as rapidly, economically and effectively as possible – and not go looking for trouble.

Et voilà! The White House found that de Gaulle had done it a favour. One year after his famous letter to LBJ, Secretary of Defence Robert McNamara informed President Johnson that the relocation and reorganisation would result in savings of $50–60 million per year – without any weakening of NATO![3]

In June 1966 de Gaulle was the first foreign head of state to be honoured by accommodation inside the Kremlin on his state visit to Moscow for talks with the Brezhnev-Kosygin-Podgorny triumvirate then in power. He was given the full treatment, including a visit to the secret city of science Akademgorodok and the space centre at Baikonur to witness the launch of a Soviet rocket, and streets lined with cheering crowds. In Washington the White House and State Department waited anxiously for news of what the maverick president of France was actually doing or saying during the visit. Sure enough, the Mole passed to Bohlen the official account after de Gaulle's return, from which it was learnt that he had not made any unilateral promises over Berlin, German reunification or any other issue that affected NATO. The only concrete result appeared to be the inauguration of a telex hot line between Paris and Moscow.

As far as the French nuclear deterrent was concerned, the separation from NATO – it was not actually a complete divorce so long as France kept its seat on the Council – accelerated the development of de Gaulle's long sought *force de frappe*. This all-French strike force was initially composed of sixty-two Dassault Mirage IVA supersonic strategic bombers capable of reaching Mach 2 to deliver 60kt nuclear bombs within a radius of action, enhanced by in-flight refuelling by the American KC-135 jet tankers, that included Moscow. Whether the pilots could ever have made it safely home from such a mission is a moot point.

In July 1966 a Dassault supersonic Mirage IV successfully dropped for the first time an all-French AN-II nuclear bomb at Fangataufa in the Pacific Ocean test zone. U-2 spy planes painted in the colours of the 'Office of Naval Research' had been keeping tracks on the construction there over the past two years. The first generation of US spy satellites also provided photographs. Once the tests began, AFTAC launched Operation *Skin Diver*, later becoming *Cold Skin* and then *Cold Chuck*. The aim was to monitor the French air-burst explosions and, by analysis of the radioactive dust, determine exactly how far the French were advancing towards the goal of home-produced thermo-nuclear bombs and warheads.

The logistics of *Skin Diver* were impressive. Four bases were established – at Lima-Callao airport in Peru, at El Plumerillo in Argentina, at Howard airbase in Panama and at Pago-Pago in mid-Pacific. Painted with the insignia of 58th Meteorological Reconnaissance Squadron, four specially adapted KC-135s, three high-altitude RB-57 Fs and eventually two U-2s also scooped up high-altitude dust downwind of the test sites, which was then transported in lead-lined boxes by USAF officers in civilian clothes aboard civilian flights from their several bases back to Panama, whence they were transported by military aircraft to an AFTAC base in California.

The analyses gave no cause for alarm. Even in 1968 when the first French H-bomb was detonated at Mururoa, AFTAC's conclusion was that the device had been far too large to fit into a submarine-launched missile or the warhead of an ICBM. But still, France had done it. Without significant help from either side of the Cold War divide, it had managed to jump almost all the technological hurdles and was indisputably in the Bomb-qualifying race, with only the US, USSR and Britain ahead in the field. In 1967 the first French nuclear submarine was built, followed in 1968 by the detonation at the Mururoa test site of the first French H-bomb. Later plans also gave priority to the development of all-French ballistic missiles, which did not become operational until 1971, with thermo-nuclear warheads only available in 1976. From that moment, de Gaulle's vision of France as a country capable of defending itself, whatever the future shape of alliances, was a reality.

But before then came one of the strangest moments in his political career. On 24 July 1967 he was in the town hall of Montreal, capital of the French-speaking province of Quebec. No especial public ceremony had been planned and only the forceful last-minute intervention of his chief bodyguard had produced a microphone on the balcony outside, below which surged a crowd of the people who made up the largest *francophone* community outside France.

Allegedly because the Canadian Government had expressed its nervousness about the visit and placed certain difficulties on his arrival by air, de Gaulle had decided to cross the Atlantic aboard the cruiser *Colbert*. This permitted him to throw in a visit on the way to the islands of St Pierre and Miquelon, liberated by Admiral Muselier in December 1941. The *Colbert* continued its voyage up the St Lawrence estuary and moored in the harbour of Quebec city, where the General mentioned in his after-dinner speech how the province had been 'wrested from France' two hundred years before as though this was a temporary aberration of history. He then referred to the importance of safeguarding Canadian independence from the 'colossal state which is their neighbour'.[4] This diplomatic faux pas touched a chord in the hearts of Quebeckers, who feel disadvantaged in predominantly English-speaking Canada.

Continuing by car the following day to Montreal, the capital of this province of nearly 6 million French speakers, he had been greeted everywhere by jubilant crowds and spent the last miles standing up in a convertible limousine returning the acclamations of an estimated half-million excited Quebeckers, eager to demonstrate to the greatest Frenchman of his time that they were as one with him, in their Frenchness and their mistrust of their Anglo-Saxon neighbours. The omission of a microphone at the evening reception in the Hôtel de Ville of Montreal may well have been deliberate but there was no stopping the General now. Deeply affected by the exuberant reception, which reminded him of the welcomes all over France during the Liberation, he approached a hastily rigged microphone on the balcony and made a speech ending, '*Vive Montréal! Vive Québec!*' The crowd roared back, '*Vive de Gaulle!*' Waiting for a lull, he ended, '*Et vive le Québec libre!*' The cheering climaxed into a storm of applause, of which the political echoes reached well into the Canadian federal capital, Ottawa, where Prime Minister Lester Pearson declared publicly that de Gaulle's behaviour was 'unacceptable' – as indeed it was, coming from a visiting head of state. De Gaulle was invited to Ottawa to find some way out of the embarrassing situation he had caused, but decided instead to return by air to Paris.

Back in France, de Gaulle's enthusiasm for the liberation of Quebec was not shared by the people or the press, because it made no sort of economic sense. His Cabinet ministers, waiting to greet him when his plane touched down at Orly airport at four o'clock in the morning, were overheard muttering rebellious comments ranging from 'He's gone too far this time' to 'He's mad'.[5]

Shortly after the visit to Quebec, Secretary of State Dean Rusk told German Foreign Minister Willy Brandt that the State Department was worried about de Gaulle's inappropriate behaviour. 'Has he,' Rusk asked, 'gone off his mind?' Having met the General only a few weeks before, Brandt shook his head. 'No, he's as sharp as ever. You'll have to put up with him for another few years yet.'

So what was in de Gaulle's mind? It seems that he was not letting himself get carried away by the enthusiastic welcome and humouring the long-felt desire of Quebeckers to end their domination by the English-speaking provinces, so much as exploiting the desire of the crowds to demonstrate their difference from the millions of English-speaking North Americans in order to worry Washington with the, albeit remote, possibility of seeing Quebec secede from the Canadian federation. And why not? Washington had done enough to worry him over the years, and since the Johnson administration was doing France no favours, perhaps it was time to raise his nuisance value.

Notes

1. C. de Gaulle, *Lettres, Notes et Carnets (juin 1964 – juin 1966)*, Paris, Plon, 1987, pp. 261–2

2. V. Jauvert, *L'Amerique contre de Gaulle*, Paris, Seuil, 2000, pp. 150–1

3. Ibid., pp. 151–6

4. J. Lacouture, *De Gaulle*, Vol. 3, Paris, Seuil, 1984, pp. 517–18

5. C. Williams, *The Last Great Frenchman*, London, Little Brown, 1994, pp. 454–5

23

BEWARE THE IDES OF MAY!

The Liberal peer Lord Gladwyn, who was British Ambassador in Paris 1954–60, knew the Fourth Republic at first hand and was personally acquainted with President Charles de Gaulle. He remained an acute observer of French political life, and spoke of '*les événements de mai '68*' some years later to the author – then a BBC assistant television producer – as 'the turning point for Europe'. By that he meant a radical change in the way dissidents – especially the young – found they could ignore the ballot boxes of democratic process and apply disproportionate political leverage to force government action by causing social unrest which confronted the authorities with the choice of being tolerant and seeming to have lost control of law and order or of acting firmly and appearing to the ever-present cameras of the media age to have been brutally repressive. The newspaper images of CRS riot police beating up unarmed students in Paris during May 1968 especially come to mind.

No two historians agree exactly about the causes of *les événements*, as they are still called In France. Their overt beginning was in a succession of noisy student demonstrations during January 1968, which many people in France choose to believe were incited by unspecified 'foreign interests'. Trouble was not confined to the universities. Since the beginning of the year many thousands of secondary school pupils had also been demonstrating in the streets against the Vietnam War. The unrest continued through February, March and April. Certainly, there was a heavy far-Left influence driving the student movement, where the principal ringleader Daniel Cohn-Bendit was known as 'Danny le Rouge' – Red Danny.

Born in April 1945 at Montauban in south-west France to a French mother who had had a German lover during the Occupation, he attended school in Oberhambach, Germany, and thus avoided growing up in France with the stigma of being taunted by classmates as a *fils de Boche* – as were so many children born in France during and after the war, whose fathers were German.[1] Was Danny French or German? The decision being complicated by his part-Jewish origins, Cohn-Bendit could not make up his mind until he became liable for military service in France at the age of 18. He then decided to take German nationality. Thus safe from conscription, he returned to France on a German Government study grant and enrolled as a student of social sciences at Nanterre University in Paris with a decidedly ambivalent attitude to his mother's native country. A charismatic and persuasive public speaker, he rapidly became a student leader and focus of discontent that placed him at the centre of the 'events of May'.

It would be hard to imagine a greater contrast between any two men than between the loquacious, photogenic 22-year-old dissident Red Danny and the ageing, aloof, autocratic soldier-politician in the Élysée Palace, to whom he threw down the gauntlet of rebellion in a classic scenario of youth versus age and authority. The only thing de Gaulle and he had in common was the unshakeable belief of each that he knew what was best for society.

Certainly, American foreign policy was a gift to student dissidence that year, with banners in many countries condemning American imperialism and demanding an end to the US involvement in Vietnam drawing into the maelstrom many otherwise politically inactive young people, who swelled enormously the numbers of the hard-core Left at demonstrations. In France, the Paris offices of an American bank and American Express were early targets in a phase intended by the organisers to give a taste for the heady excitement of vandalism and defying the forces of order to the maximum number of students – many of whom would thereafter be prepared to go further against different targets.

Psychologists point to the erosion of parental authority as a key factor in the 'events', but that was not peculiar to France at the time. However, neither was student unrest, which was disturbing the authorities on both sides of the Iron Curtain and both sides of the Atlantic: students in Washington, DC, appalled at the civilian casualties of American weapons in south-east Asia, were parading past Lyndon Johnson's White House chanting, 'Hey! Hey, LBJ! How many kids did you kill today?'

De Gaulle had little respect for the social sciences that Cohn-Bendit was supposed to be studying, but he did recognise the attraction that dogmatic communism held for young people searching for a philosophy which gave them what sounded like scientific answers to the moral and social questions of the time. They were, he thought, looking for ideals and hope – neither of which they could find in the materialistic consumer society of late 1960s France or in its patriarchal president who, for some years, had been planning a reorganisation of French universities, which were overcrowded with discontented and confused students and run by academics out of touch and out of sympathy with those students. Empathy for youth, he had. But it was impossible for a career soldier like him to sympathise with disorder aimed at bringing down the very institutions that sheltered them. His own rebellions against inept superiors between the wars had always been conducted openly and with the aim of strengthening France's armed forces, not destroying them. He therefore recommended his ministers to deal firmly with the unrest in the streets – after which, he believed, mature reflection would lead to some solution.

On 2 May, as Pompidou flew off on an official visit to Iran and Afghanistan, the students occupying Nanterre University and the Sorbonne were evicted by police, lectures were suspended and the universities closed. The Latin Quarter around the Sorbonne now saw increasingly angry confrontations between police and students in the streets, with classic pictures in the media of helmeted CRS riot police beating unarmed young men and women with batons – and rifle butts on occasion – that aroused popular sympathy for the students, more adept by far at exploiting media interviews than was the government. The climax came with a massive turnout for a march of students and trades union members through the streets of Paris on 7 May, during which the demonstrators managed to cross the Seine and confront a slender security cordon guarding the immediate sur-roundings of the Élysée Palace. Had de Gaulle been personally less courageous, this would have frightened him into ordering an immediate crack-down on the ringleaders, but he did not do so.

In an attempt to restore calm, Minister of Education Alain Peyrefitte announced the reopening of the universities on 8 May. Although Nanterre reopened the fol-lowing day, the Sorbonne stayed closed, leading the famous 'night of the barri-cades' on 10 May, when the police took no action for hours while demonstrators smashed shop windows, overturned cars and buses and set them on fire. Student leaders immediately accused undercover police *agents provocateurs* of throwing the Molotov cocktails, but there was no evidence of this. On Pompidou's return to France the following day, de Gaulle's only instruction to him was that his job, as prime minister, was to deal with the unrest. Pompidou chose the soft path of negotiation. Reopened on 13 May, the Sorbonne was immediately occupied again by the militant students. The trades union leaders, fearing that their more militant members would become uncontrollable if they did not appear to give a lead, issued strike calls.

Incredibly, de Gaulle saw no reason to postpone a state visit to Romania, as guest of dictator Nicolae Ceauşescu. As though his departure from the country was a capitulation, and not a gesture of disdain, the strike movement spread with occupation of the Renault factories and that of Sud-Aviation in Nantes. Between 17 and 20 May sympathetic strikes spread like a rash across the map of France until the whole country was paralysed. Rioting spread to the provinces and, with petrol and diesel fuel unobtainable, transport ground to a halt, preventing even deliveries of food. By 20 May the rumours of an imminent civil war or communist revolution were reaching the CIA and DIA (Defense Intelligence Agency) daily from sources inside French security organisations.

By now disgusted with the chaos, the silent majority began on 23 May to form *Comités pour la Défense de la République*. After his return from Romania, on 24 May de Gaulle made a broadcast speech to the nation, but his talk of strong action to put an end to the unrest was out of synch with the indecisiveness of the authorities until then. On Saturday 25 May, Pompidou met with trades union leaders in the Ministry of Social Affairs on the rue de Grenelle in Paris and made important concessions, known as the Grenelle agreements, which, however, were rejected by their rank-and-file membership with more public demonstrations. These, in turn, led to a counter-movement by the silent majority, which planned a massive counter-demonstration for the following Thursday. However, by Tuesday 28 May things had gone so far that future president François Mitterand announced himself prepared to take over the presidency if it should become vacant. Pierre Mendès-France and other leading politicians made similar declarations.

De Gaulle refused to believe that a few thousand noisy and irresponsible students could destroy the Fifth Republic and bring down its elected president. He said famously at one point, '*La réforme, oui. La chienlit, non!*'[2] ('Evolution, yes. But disorder, no!'). Oddly enough, the communist and other left-wing union leaders did their best to limit the unrest, fearing that, if it escalated, many of their followers would desert to extremist anarchistic movements, to the detriment of their own power. Even among the working classes, there was by now a noticeable groundswell of hostility to the students and militants as people saw the fabric of their society disintegrating.

After the broadcast that day, de Gaulle discussed with his inner circle three courses of action. Should he return to Colombey and make a speech to the nation saying haughtily that he would only return to Paris when order had been re-established? Or take the government with him to a provincial city well away from the agitators in Paris and there continue to govern the country, supported by the armed forces? Or disappear by helicopter from the capital to leave everyone wondering what he was up to?

In the event, he chose the last course. The following day being a Wednesday, when by tradition the Cabinet met at the Élysée Palace, ministers arrived and parked in the forecourt as usual, to be informed that their president had left. In fact, he departed a little later, but that is what they were told. Later, the news filtered back to the ministries that the General had travelled by helicopter to Baden-Baden in Germany, where he held a ninety-minute conference with General Jacques Massu, commanding the two French divisions in Germany. What they talked about is a mystery, although at the time it was bruited that Massu had agreed to move his troops into France to restore order if necessary. In fact, no general alert was issued to Massu's units and armoured formations normally stationed near Paris remained far away on manoeuvres, not returning to base until the planned date – by road, because all the railways were out on strike by then. Even the paramilitary Gendarmerie Mobile was not called out.

At the postponed Cabinet meeting on the afternoon of Thursday 30 May, de Gaulle informed the assembled ministers that he was dissolving the National Assembly. With a massive counter-demonstration organised for that evening by the Committees for the Defence of the Republic, there was insufficient time to set up a television broadcast beforehand, so he acceded to his supporters' pleading and announced his decision to the nation on sound radio only in a dramatic four-minute broadcast from the Élysée Palace, in which he made it clear that he had no intention of resigning, nor sacking his prime minister. He appealed to the partisans of law and order and presented himself as the only barrier to anarchy or communist rule. Loyal Gaullists and nervous citizens rallied round him, with the extremists becoming more and more isolated after the PCF leadership refused to back their demands for an open revolt against the forces of law and order.

That evening, an estimated 1 million of the normally silent majority marched through the streets of Paris behind Malraux, Debré and Schumann in support of their president and the rule of law. This was followed by the Committees for the Defence of the Republic organising similar marches in all main cities the next day. By the end of the first week of June, France was getting back to normal with factory workers and those in the public services back at their jobs. In a televised interview on 7 June, the General spoke of the 'events' as a breakdown of civilisation and announced specific remedies for a number of social problems. Taking this as a victory, on 11 June the students demonstrated again but, with the shift in public sympathy, Cohn-Bendit's rebellion was fizzling out. The National Assembly was dissolved and general elections announced for the end of the month. There were still some clashes with the police, notably by left-wing activists at the Renault and Peugeot car factories, but by the third week of June these and the steel industry were working normally.

In the general election, de Gaulle's Union des Démocrates pour la République (UDR) gained 29.3 per cent of votes cast, and with their allies won 270 of the 456 seats in the Assembly. After this victory over the far-Left, the General reappointed Pompidou as prime minister. Pompidou's resignation on 10 July, ostensibly because he was unable to form a Cabinet, came as a surprise to many. Conflicting reasons were advanced. Those who sought scandal everywhere repeated wild stories about 56-year-old Madame Claude Pompidou, who was said to have been photographed in compromising positions while participating in a sex orgy. The more rational found sufficient reason for his resignation in her husband's ambition to become president himself and de Gaulle's wariness of Pompidou as a serious rival.

De Gaulle instructed the loyal Couve de Murville to form a new government, which made a wide-sweeping series of concessions: higher minimum wages;

improved working conditions; education reforms that promised to give teachers and students a voice in running their institutions. The economy having suffered profoundly from the upheaval, austerity measures were needed to stabilise things, including the reintroduction of exchange control, which had only been abolished the previous year.

With the nation having pulled through what might have turned into a revolution, if handled differently by the authorities, by the time of his seventy-eighth birthday in December 1968, almost any leader except Charles de Gaulle would have played it safe for what could have been the triumphal last five years of his second term. But he saw the reform of the Senate and a devolution of power in favour of the regions as a vital step in equipping France politically for a Europe to which it would be progressively committed. Announced in a speech at Quimper in Britanny on 2 February 1969, his proposals aroused the immediate opposition of the political parties, who preferred to keep things the way they were. Future president Valéry Giscard d'Estaing was one of many leading politicians who announced they would vote against the proposals. In order to carry these reforms through against the will of the parties, de Gaulle therefore decided once again to short-circuit them by going to the country in a referendum.

Enter Richard Nixon ...

The manner of his going, after the Watergate scandal, overshadows commentators' opinions of his administration, but he was the first president of the United States to genuinely attempt to bridge the abyss that Roosevelt and Hull had dug between Washington and Paris. Closing a tour of European capitals with his arrival in Paris at the end of February, America's new president was treated to a state banquet on 1 March at the Élysée Palace, which was 'sumptuous' in the words of Henry Kissinger and 'magnificent' according to the guest of honour. Kissinger made no secret of the fact that he considered the policy towards de Gaulle pursued by the Kennedy and Johnson administrations both insensitive and politically wrong. Nor was Nixon's speech the normal diplomatic safe talk; he went overboard in praising de Gaulle as 'a rare leader ... who has restored to France its proper place in the world ... and a giant among men'.[3]

The praise could not have come at a better moment. De Gaulle's public standing had taken a severe knock after the events of May '68, the French franc was low, the long-promised *force de frappe* was way behind schedule and the General's policy of rapprochement with countries of the eastern bloc was discredited since Red Army tanks had rolled into Prague in August 1968, revealing the Warsaw Pact countries for what they were: Russia's buffer states, invasion of which by NATO would give Moscow time to mobilise the vast resources of the Soviet Empire. As if de Gaulle needed another problem, Pompidou had just declared, without warning his patron, that he would contest the presidency at the next election.

In the ups and downs of American politics, Nixon had known his own wilderness years and thus had both sympathy for de Gaulle personally and a high opinion of what he had managed to achieve for France, not least because he knew the odds that had been stacked against him. In the ten hours of private discussions during the visit, de Gaulle impressed his visitor with his clear-cut views on world affairs. The two presidents often agreed and often agreed to differ, but with a show of respect and understanding on the American side that had never been there before. End the Vietnam war as I ended the Algerian war ... Recognise Beijing, as I have done. De Gaulle had no hesitation in giving advice, while Kissinger, the arch negotiator who would go secretly to Beijing two years later as midwife of US diplomatic recognition of Communist China, listened and interjected here and there.

The most significant breakthrough in the Paris talks came with two sentences of Nixon's. He said to de Gaulle, 'I have nothing against France possessing a nuclear force. On the contrary, I think it would be useful.'[4]

At the end of the three-day visit, seeing off his guest at Orly airport, de Gaulle promised to pursue the talks in Washington the following year. The two presidents were to meet sooner than planned, due to the death of ex-President Eisenhower at the end of March 1969. Attending his funeral in Washington provided de Gaulle with the ideal opportunity to continue talks with Nixon. In return, it seems, for his gesture in not leaving NATO at the end of the agreed period, Nixon set in motion on 21 April a top secret re-evaluation of America's military relations with France, particularly in the domain of nuclear technology. On 1 September 1970 National Security Study Memorandum No. 100 signed by Henry Kissinger set in process the possibility of nuclear technology sharing.

In the event, the American team at the secret negotiations that followed found French security procedures very close to their own. As matters progressed, National Security Decision Memorandum (NSDM) No. 103, dated 29 March 1971 and also signed by Kissinger, permitted IBM 370/165 super-computers to be sold to France's Commissariat à l'Energie Atomique. To get around the congressional bar on selling these advanced machines to any foreign country, they were neatly redefined – in the case of France alone – as something less than 'advanced'. Finally, NSDM No. 104, signed by Kissinger on the same day, went a giant step further by sanctioning exchange of information on nuclear safety.

Two years of delicate bridge-building led, on 7 March 1973, to the Nixon White House instructing the Pentagon to pass specific information on aspects of nuclear delivery systems ranging from construction of IBM launch silos to the heat shields necessary to prevent ballistic missiles burning up on re-entry into the atmosphere.[5] Finally, under President Gerald Ford, NSDM 299 of 23 June 1975 took the step of assisting France to conduct underground explosions at the Mururoa test site in the Pacific.

DECLASSIFIED
E.O. 12958, as amended, Sect 3.5
NSC/Soubers & Smith 9/06/2002
By *LfL* Date *01/30/07*

NATIONAL SECURITY COUNCIL
WASHINGTON, D.C. 20506

~~TOP SECRET/SENSITIVE/EYES ONLY~~

September 1, 1970

National Security Study Memorandum 100

TO: The Secretary of State
             The Secretary of Defense
             Director of Central Intelligence

SUBJECT: Military Cooperation with France

1. The President has directed that a study be prepared to review all the various areas of current and potential military cooperation with France. The study should include:

   a. a status report on bilateral and multilateral areas of cooperation with France relating to NATO (SACEUR), and, specifically, alternative ways to encourage French association with the NPG; future problems and policy choices should be identified;

   b. a status report on Franco-American military Research and Development projects under consideration or proposed in the recent meeting of the Steering Group in Paris; potential problems should be identified;

   c. a status report on technical discussions thus far with French on their requests for assistance in their missile programs, a discussion of alternative courses of action in providing assistance, including an analysis of areas of potential conflict with a possible SALT agreement;

   d. an evaluation of prospects for Anglo-French nuclear collaboration and alternative postures that the US might adopt;

   e. a discussion of alternatives in regard to dealing with the French request for a relaxation of restrictions on the use of US computers and computer components in the French nuclear weapons program, including as much factual detail as necessary on the status of the program, the contribution of computers and the pertinent legal and political factors involved in our restrictions.

~~TOP SECRET/SENSITIVE/EYES ONLY~~

Charles de Gaulle did not live to see these fruits of his defiance of six US presidents. Within a month of his second meeting with Nixon came the referendum on his planned reform of the Senate and regional government. As in the past, he had already announced that he would accept the will of the people and resign, should the voting go against him. With the opinion polls progressively more gloomy, the Cabinet met at the Élysée Palace on 23 April in a farewell mood, complemented by the president's instruction that evening to his private

```
  DECLASSIFIED
E.O. 12958, as amended, Sect 3.5
NSC/Soubers to Smith 09/08/2002
By  LT    Date 02/14/09        NATIONAL SECURITY COUNCIL
                                   WASHINGTON, D.C. 20506


    TOP SECRET/SENSITIVE            March 29, 1971


    National Security Decision Memorandum 104

    TO:          The Secretary of State
                 The Secretary of Defense

    SUBJECT:     Cooperation with France on Nuclear Safety


    The President has directed that discussions with the French Government
    concerning nuclear safety be reopened.
```

secretary that all his personal files should be removed from his office there and taken to Colombey. At midday on 25 April he recorded a broadcast confirming his resignation in the event of defeat in the referendum and departed Paris for La Boisserie. In the morning of Sunday 27 April he walked from his home to the little village church for Mass, ignoring the reporters and cameramen, and walked into the village again in the afternoon to register his vote in the little Mairie. At 8 p.m. his secretary called from the Élysée Palace to say that the first results were looking bad. Two hours later, Charles de Gaulle knew he had lost his last gamble in politics.

The constitutional amendments he had proposed were defeated by a 53 per cent vote against him. Formally announced by the Constitutional Council on 2 May, the figures were: voters registered – 29,392,390; votes recorded – 23,552,611; valid votes – 22,908,855; YES – 10,901,753; NO – 12,007,102. The defeated president did not wait for the formal announcement. Once the count was in, he issued a brief communiqué from his home in Colombey-les-deux-Eglises at just after midnight on 28 April: 'I am ceasing to exercise my functions as president of the Republic. This decision will take effect at midday.'[6]

The announcement was typically Charles de Gaulle: spare and unapologetic. Without fuss or ceremony, he exchanged the glare of the spotlights for the peace and quiet of village life in Colombey. There in his study he turned once again to the writing of his memoirs. In June, he left France with Yvonne for a holiday in Ireland, where his mother's family had relatives, in case his presence in France complicated the presidential elections to select his successor.

Pompidou made it into the Élysée Palace by defeating in the second round the Centrist Alain Poher, who had been acting president of the Republic in the interim by virtue of his office as president of the Senate. On 20 June, in his acceptance speech, the new president paid homage to his mentor:

At the very moment of officially accepting the responsibility of the President of the Republic, for which I have been designated by the people of France, I first call to mind General de Gaulle. It is he who has bequeathed our country those institutions that have given us ten years of political stability, steered us through several very grave crises, and at the last assured a transmission of presidential powers without mishap. During those ten years, General de Gaulle has represented France here [in the Élysée Palace] with unprecedented authority. His example serves as a model to me.

The transition from head of government to private citizen in 1947 had been difficult for Charles de Gaulle. To step down from the elevated status of head of state was even more difficult. For the depression that assailed him, as it always had after a setback, his antidote was writing his memoirs. Rarely has a room been put to better use than his light and airy study at La Boisserie. He spent the day of 9 November 1970 working there. Among the many pages penned on that writing desk was his will.

The last wills of statesmen are sometimes revealing. What does that of Charles de Gaulle tell us about the man who was stigmatised by his enemies as a fascist and a power-hungry dictator? Did he leave instructions for a spectacular state funeral, which lesser men and women have been granted? Did he ask for room to be made for his remains to lie beside Napoleon Bonaparte's marble monstrosity of a tomb at Les Invalides? For his body to be placed within the confines of the Ecole Supérieure de Guerre would have been appropriate for the general who had done so much more for France than Napoleon – who was a loser twice over, bringing his country low and costing the lives of millions.

Not so. In the will written in the sunlit study of La Boisserie, looking out over the countryside he loved so well, we read:

I wish my funeral to take place at Colombey-les-deux-Eglises. Should I die elsewhere, it will be necessary to bring my body home without the least public ceremony. My tomb shall be the one in which my daughter Anne already rests and where my wife will also rest. Inscription: Charles de Gaulle 1890- … Nothing else. The ceremony will be arranged by my son, my daughter and my daughter-in-law, assisted by my personal staff, and shall be extremely simple. I wish to have no state funeral. No president, no ministers, no officials or official bodies. Only the French armed forces may participate officially, but this must be on a very modest scale, without band, fanfare or bugle calls. No speech may be made, either at the church or elsewhere. No funeral address in Parliament. No space reserved during the ceremony except for my family, my fellow members of the Ordre de la Libération and the town council of Colombey. Men and women of France and other countries may, if they wish, honour my memory by accompanying my body to its last resting place, but I wish it to be taken there in silence. I hereby refuse in advance all distinctions, dignities, awards and honours, be they French or foreign. If any such should be made, it would be in violation of my last wishes.

Was this modesty the voice of an old man sulking in withdrawal from the modern world? It was not. The will was dated 16 January 1952 and signed, Charles de Gaulle.[7] In almost nineteen years since that date, the General had no second thoughts.

Pompidou could not resist organising a solemn Mass at Notre Dame Cathedral, attended by heads of state, after which some hundreds of the General's faithful followers braved a torrential downpour to march up the Champs-Élysées to the Arc de Triomphe. At the funeral in Colombey, however, apart from the silent crowd of mourners, the only indication that the object of their grief had led a life in any way extraordinary was the scout car with turret removed, on which the coffin was brought to the churchyard at the pace of a slow march.

Since then, the little village in Champagne-Ardennes could have become a tourist trap, with cafés and ice cream stalls everywhere battening on the steady stream of visitors come to pay their respects. Yet, the village has not changed very much since the General walked down the main street to Mass each Sunday when he was in residence.

Atop the hill overlooking the village now stands a modern visitor centre with an immensely tall Cross of Lorraine that dominates the countryside from afar. Even there, the atmosphere is sober and respectful, for the visitors are more pilgrim than tourist. They walk down the hill into the village to visit La Boisserie and the grave in the little churchyard, which is simplicity itself. Beneath a white stone cross is a single slab of the same stone, on which is engraved just *Charles de Gaulle 1890–1970* and the names of his daughter Anne and wife Yvonne, who are also buried there. Nothing else.

Notes

1. This theme is treated at length in D. Boyd, *Voices from the Dark Years*, Thrupp, Sutton, 2007, pp. 141–2, 146–7, 180, 214–17, 248, 256–8
2. See television interview at www.inafr/video/109167762
3. J. Fenby, *The General*, London, Simon & Schuster, 2011, p. 620
4. V. Jauvert, *L'Amerique contre de Gaulle*, Paris, Seuil, 2000, p. 180
5. Ibid., pp. 178–82
6. Presidential communiqué of 29 April
7. de Gaulle's will reads:

   Je veux que mes obsèques aient lieu à Colombey-les-Deux-Eglises.
   Si je meurs ailleurs il faudra transporter mon corps chez moi, sans la moindre cérémonie publique.

Ma tombe sera celle où repose déjà ma fille Anne et où reposera ma femme. Inscription: Charles de Gaulle (1890 –…). Rien d'autre.

La Cérémonie sera réglée par mon fils, ma fille, mon gendre, ma belle fille, aidés par mon cabinet, de telle sorte qu'elle soit extrêmement simple. Je ne veux pas d'obsèques nationales. Ni président, ni ministres, ni bureaux d'assemblées, ni corps constitués. Seules les armées françaises pourront participer officiellement, en tant que telles; mais leur participation devra être de dimensions très modestes, sans musique, ni fanfare, ni sonneries.

Aucun discours ne devra être prononcé, ni à l'église, ni ailleurs. Pas d'oraison funèbre au Parlement.

Aucun emplacement réservé pendant la cérémonie, sinon à ma famille, à mes compagnons membres de l'ordre de la Libération, au Conseil Municipal de Colombey.

Les hommes et les femmes de France et d'autres pays du monde pourront, s'ils le désirent, faire à ma mémoire l'honneur d'accompagner mon corps jusqu'à sa dernière demeure. Mais c'est dans le silence que je souhaite qu'il y soit conduit. Je déclare refuser d'avance toute distinction, promotion, dignité, citation, déclaration, qu'elle soit française ou étrangère. Si l'une quelconque m'était décernée, ce serait en violation de mes dernières volontés.

Charles de Gaulle 16 janvier 1952

APPENDIX A

Text of letter from Prime Minister Churchill to President Roosevelt dated 8 December 1940

10 DOWNING STREET, WHITEHALL
   December 8, 1940

My dear Mr. President,

1. As we reach the end of this year I feel you will expect me to lay before you the prospects for 1941. I do so with candour and confidence, because it seems to me that the vast majority of American citizens have recorded their conviction that the safety of the United States as well as the future of our two Democracies and the kind of civilisation for which they stand are bound up with the survival and independence of the British Commonwealth of Nations. Only thus can those bastions of sea-power upon which the control of the Atlantic and Indian Oceans depend be preserved in faithful and friendly hands. The control of the Pacific by the United States Navy and of the Atlantic by the British Navy is indispensable to the security and trade routes of both our countries, and the surest means of preventing war from reaching the shores of the United States.

2. There is another aspect. It takes between three and four years to convert the industries of a modern state to war purposes. Saturation point is reached when the maximum industrial effort that can be spared from civil needs has been applied to war production. Germany certainly reached this point by the end of 1939. We in the British Empire are now only about half-way through the second year. The United States, I should suppose, is by no means so far advanced as we. Moreover, I understand that immense programmes of naval, military, and air defence are now on foot in the United States, to complete which certainly two years are needed. It is our British duty in the common interest, as also for our own survival, to hold the front and grapple with the Nazi power until the preparations of the United States are complete. Victory may come before two years are out; but we have no right to count upon it to the extent of relaxing any effort that is humanly possible. Therefore I submit with very great respect

for your good and friendly consideration that there is a solid identity of interest between the British Empire and the United States while these conditions last. It is upon this footing that I venture to address you.

3. The form which this war has taken, and seems likely to hold, does not enable us to match the immense armies of Germany in any theatre where their main power can he brought to bear. We can however, by the use of sea-power and air-power, meet the German armies in regions where only comparatively small forces can be brought into action. We must do our best to prevent the German domination of Europe spreading into Africa and into Southern Asia. We have also to maintain in constant readiness in this Island armies strong enough to make the problem of an oversea invasion insoluble. For these purposes we are forming as fast as possible, as you are already aware, between fifty and sixty divisions. Even if the United States were our ally, instead of our friend and indispensable partner, we should not ask for a large American expeditionary army. Shipping, not men, is the limiting factor, and the power to transport munitions and supplies claims priority over the movement by sea of large numbers of soldiers.

4. The first half of 1940 was a period of disaster for the Allies and for Europe. The last five months have witnessed a strong and perhaps unexpected recovery by Great Britain fighting alone, but with the invaluable aid in munitions and in destroyers placed at our disposal by the great Republic of which you are for the third time the chosen Chief.

5. The danger of Great Britain being destroyed by a swift, overwhelming blow has for the time being very greatly receded. In its place there is a long, gradually-maturing danger, less sudden and less spectacular, but equally deadly. This mortal danger is the steady and increasing diminution of sea tonnage. We can endure the shattering of our dwellings and the slaughter of our civil population by indiscriminate air attacks, and we hope to parry these increasingly as our science develops, and to repay them upon military objectives in Germany as our Air Force more nearly approaches the strength of the enemy. The decision for 1941 lies upon the seas. Unless we can establish our ability to feed this Island, to import the munitions of all kinds which we need, unless we can move our armies to the various theatres where Hitler and his confederate Mussolini must be met, and maintain them there, and do all this with the assurance of being able to carry it on till the spirit of the Continental Dictators is broken, we may fall by the way, and the time needed by the United States to complete her defensive preparations may not be forthcoming. It is therefore in shipping and in the power to transport across the oceans, particularly the Atlantic Ocean, that

in 1941 the crunch of the whole war will be found. If on the other hand we are able to move the necessary tonnage to and fro across salt water indefinitely, it may well be that the application of superior air-power to the German homeland and the rising anger of the German and other Nazi-gripped populations will bring the agony of civilisation to a merciful and glorious end.

But do not let us underrate the task.

6. Our shipping losses, the figures for which in recent months are appended, have been on a scale almost comparable to those of the worst year of the last war. In the five weeks ending November 3 losses reached a total of 420,300 tons. Our estimate of annual tonnage which ought to be imported in order to maintain our effort at full strength is 43 million tons; the tonnage entering in September was only at the rate of 37 million tons, and in October of 38 million tons. Were this diminution to continue at this rate it would be fatal, unless indeed immensely greater replenishment than anything at present in sight could be achieved in time. Although we are doing all we can to meet this situation by new methods, the difficulty of limiting losses is obviously much greater than in the last war. We lack the assistance of the French Navy, the Italian Navy, and the Japanese Navy, and above all of the United States Navy, which was of such vital help to us during the culminating years. The enemy commands the ports all around the northern and western coasts of France. He is increasingly basing his submarines, flying-boats, and combat planes on these ports and on the islands off the French coast. We are denied the use of the ports or territory of Eire in which to organise our coastal patrols by air and sea. In fact, we have now only one effective route of entry to the British Isles, namely, the Northern Approaches, against which the enemy is increasingly concentrating, reaching ever farther out by U-boat action and long-distance aircraft bombing. In addition, there have for some months been merchant-ship raiders both in the Atlantic and Indian Oceans. And now we have the powerful warship raider to contend with as well. We need ships both to hunt down and to escort. Large as are our resources and preparations, we do not possess enough.

7. The next six or seven months [will] bring relative battleship strength in home waters to a smaller margin than is satisfactory. *Bismarck* and *Tirpitz* will certainly be in service in January. We have already *King George V*, and hope to have *Prince of Wales* in the line at the same time. These modern ships are of course far better armoured, especially against air attack, than vessels like *Rodney* and *Nelson*, designed twenty years ago. We have recently had to use *Rodney* on transatlantic escort, and at any time when numbers are so small a mine or a torpedo may alter decisively the strength of the line of battle. We get relief in June, when *Duke of York* will be ready, and shall be still better off at the end of 1941, when *Anson*

also will have joined. But these two first-class modern 35,000-ton [should have read nearer 45,000 tons] 15-inch-gun German battleships force us to maintain a concentration never previously necessary in this war.

8. We hope that the two Italian *Littorios* will be out of action for a while, and anyway they are not so dangerous as if they were manned by Germans. Perhaps they might be! We are indebted to you for your help about the *Richelieu* and *Jean Bart*, and I daresay that will be all right. But, Mr. President, as no-one will see more clearly than you, we have during these months to consider for the first time in this war a fleet action in which the enemy will have two ships at least as good as our two best and only two modern ones. It will be impossible to reduce our strength in the Mediterranean, because the attitude of Turkey, and indeed the whole position in the Eastern Basin, depends upon our having a strong fleet there. The older, unmodernised battleships will have to go for convoy. Thus even in the battleship class we are at full extension.

9. There is a second field of danger. The Vichy Government may, either by joining Hitler's New Order in Europe or through some manoeuvre, such as forcing us to attack an expedition dispatched by sea against the Free French colonies, find an excuse for ranging with the Axis Powers the very considerable undamaged naval forces still under its control. If the French Navy were to join the Axis the control of West Africa would pass immediately into their hands, with the gravest consequences to our communications between the Northern and Southern Atlantic, and also affecting Dakar and of course thereafter South America.

10. A third sphere of danger is in the Far East. Here it seems clear that Japan is thrusting southward through Indo-China to Saigon and other naval and air bases, thus bringing them within a comparatively short distance of Singapore and the Dutch East Indies. It is reported that the Japanese are preparing five good divisions for possible use as an overseas expeditionary force. We have to-day no forces in the Far East capable of dealing with this situation should it develop.

11. In the face of these dangers we must try to use the year 1941 to build up such a supply of weapons, particularly of aircraft, both by increased output at home in spite of bombardment and through ocean-borne supplies, as will lay the foundations of victory. In view of the difficulty and magnitude of this task, as outlined by all the facts I have set forth, to which many others could be added, I feel entitled, nay bound, to lay before you the various ways in which the United States could give supreme and decisive help to what is, in certain aspects, the common cause.

12. The prime need is to check or limit the loss of tonnage on the Atlantic approaches to our island. This may be achieved both by increasing the naval forces which cope with the attacks, and by adding to the number of merchant ships on which we depend. For the first purpose there would seem to be the following alternatives:

(1) The reassertion by the United States of the doctrine of the freedom of the seas from illegal and barbarous methods of warfare, in accordance with the decisions reached after the late Great War, and as freely accepted and defined by Germany in 1935. From this, United States ships should be free to trade with countries against which there is not an effective legal blockade.

(2) It would, I suggest, follow that protection should be given to this lawful trading by United States forces, i.e., escorting battleships, cruisers, destroyers, and air flotillas. The protection would be immensely more effective if you were able to obtain bases in Eire for the duration of the war. I think it is improbable that such protection would provoke a declaration of war by Germany upon the United States, though probably sea incidents of a dangerous character would from time to time occur. Herr Hitler has shown himself inclined to avoid the Kaiser's mistake. He does not wish to be drawn into war with the United States until he has gravely undermined the power of Great Britain. His maxim is 'One at a time'.

The policy I have ventured to outline, or something like it, would constitute a decisive act of constructive non-belligerency by the United States, and, more than any other measure, would make it certain that British resistance could he effectively prolonged for the desired period and victory gained.

(3) Failing the above, the gift, loan, or supply of a large number of American vessels of war, above all destroyers, already in the Atlantic is indispensable to the maintenance of the Atlantic route. Further, could not the United States Naval Forces extend their sea control of the American side of the Atlantic so as to prevent the molestation by enemy vessels of the approaches to the new line of naval and air bases which the United States is establishing in British islands in the Western Hemisphere? The strength of United States Naval Forces is such that the assistance in the Atlantic that they could afford us, as described above, would not jeopardise the control of the Pacific.

(4) We should also then need the good offices of the United States and the whole influence of its Government, continually exerted, to procure for Great Britain the necessary facilities upon the southern and western shores of Eire for our flotillas, and, still more important, for our aircraft, working to the westward into the Atlantic. If it were proclaimed an American interest that the resistance of Great Britain should be prolonged and the Atlantic route kept open for the important armaments now being prepared for Great Britain in North America, the Irish in the United States might be willing to point out to the Government of Eire the dangers which its present policy is creating for the United States itself.

His Majesty's Government would of course take the most effective measures beforehand to protect Ireland if Irish action exposed it to German attack. It is not possible for us to compel the people of Northern Ireland against their will to leave the United Kingdom and join Southern Ireland. But I do not doubt that if the Government of Eire would show its solidarity with the democracies of the English-speaking world at this crisis a Council for Defence of all Ireland could be set up out of which the unity of the island would probably in some form or other emerge after the war.

13. The object of the foregoing measures is to reduce to manageable proportions the present destructive losses at sea. In addition, it is indispensable that the merchant tonnage available for supplying Great Britain, and for the waging of the war by Great Britain with all vigour, should be substantially increased beyond the one and a quarter million tons per annum which is the utmost we can now build. The convoy system, the *détours*, the zigzags, the great distances from which we now have to bring our imports, and the congestion of our western harbours, have reduced by about one-third the fruitfulness of our existing tonnage. To ensure final victory not less than three million tons of additional merchant shipbuilding capacity will be required. Only the United States can supply this need. Looking to the future, it would seem that production on a scale comparable to that of the Hog Island scheme of the last war ought to be faced for 1942. In the meanwhile we ask that in 1941 the United States should make available to us every ton of merchant shipping, surplus to its own requirements, which it possesses or controls, and to find some means of putting into our service a large proportion of merchant shipping now under construction for the National Maritime Board.

14. Moreover, we look to the industrial energy of the Republic for a reinforcement of our domestic capacity to manufacture combat aircraft. Without that reinforcement reaching us in substantial measure we shall not achieve the massive preponderance in the air on which we must rely to loosen and disintegrate the German grip on Europe. We are at present engaged on a programme designed to increase our strength to seven thousand first-line aircraft by the spring of 1942. But it is abundantly clear that this programme will not suffice to give us the weight of superiority which will force open the doors of victory. In order to achieve such superiority it is plain that we shall need the greatest production of aircraft which the United States of America is capable of sending us. It is our anxious hope that in the teeth of continuous bombardment we shall realise the greater part of the production which we have planned in this country. But not even with the addition to our squadrons of all the aircraft which, under present arrangements, we may derive from planned output in the

United States can we hope to achieve the necessary ascendancy. May I invite you then, Mr. President, to give earnest consideration to an immediate order on joint account for a further two thousand combat aircraft a month? Of these aircraft, I would submit, the highest possible proportion should be heavy bombers, the weapon on which, above all others, we depend to shatter the foundations of German military power. I am aware of the formidable task that this would impose upon the industrial organisation of the United States. Yet, in our heavy need, we call with confidence to the most resourceful and ingenious technicians in the world. We ask for an unexampled effort, believing that it can be made.

15. You have also received information about the needs of our armies. In the munitions sphere, in spite of enemy bombing, we are making steady progress here. Without your continued assistance in the supply of machine tools and in further releases from stock of certain articles, we could not hope to equip as many as fifty divisions in 1941. I am grateful for the arrangements, already practically completed, for your aid in the equipment of the Army which we have already planned, and for the provision of the American type of weapons for an additional ten divisions in time for the campaign of 1942. But when the tide of Dictatorship begins to recede many countries trying to regain their freedom may be asking for arms, and there is no source to which they can look except the factories of the United States. I must therefore also urge the importance of expanding to the utmost American productive capacity for small arms, artillery, and tanks.

16. I am arranging to present you with a complete programme of the munitions of all kinds which we seek to obtain from you, the greater part of which is of course already agreed. An important economy of time and effort will be produced if the types selected for the United States Services should, whenever possible, conform to those which have proved their merit under the actual conditions of war. In this way reserves of guns and ammunition and of aeroplanes become interchangeable, and are by that very fact augmented. This is however a sphere so highly technical that I do not enlarge upon it.

17. Last of all, I come to the question of Finance. The more rapid and abundant the flow of munitions and ships which you are able to send us, the sooner will our dollar credits be exhausted. They are already, as you know, very heavily drawn upon by the payments we have made to date. Indeed, as you know, the orders already placed or under negotiation, including the expenditure settled or pending for creating munitions factories in the United States, many times exceed the total exchange resources remaining at the disposal of Great Britain.

The moment approaches when we shall no longer be able to pay cash for shipping and other supplies. While we will do our utmost, and shrink from no proper sacrifice to make payments across the Exchange, I believe you will agree that it would be wrong in principle and mutually disadvantageous in effect if at the height of this struggle Great Britain were to be divested of all saleable assets, so that after the victory was won with our blood, civilisation saved, and the time gained for the United States to be fully armed against all eventualities, we should stand stripped to the bone. Such a course would not be in the moral or economic interests of either of our countries. We here should be unable, after the war, to purchase the large balance of imports from the United States over and above the volume of our exports which is agreeable to your tariffs and industrial economy. Not only should we in Great Britain suffer cruel privations, but widespread unemployment in the United States would follow the curtailment of American exporting power.

18. Moreover, I do not believe that the Government and people of the United States would find it in accordance with the principles which guide them to confine the help which they have so generously promised only to such munitions of war and commodities as could be immediately paid for. You may be certain that we shall prove ourselves ready to suffer and sacrifice to the utmost for the Cause, and that we glory in being its champions. The rest we leave with confidence to you and to your people, being sure that ways and means will be found which future generations on both sides of the Atlantic will approve and admire.

19. If, as I believe, you are convinced, Mr. President, that the defeat of the Nazi and Fascist tyranny is a matter of high consequence to the people of the United States and to the Western Hemisphere, you will regard this letter not as an appeal for aid, but as a statement of the minimum action necessary to achieve our common purpose.

A table was added showing the losses by enemy action of British, Allied and neutral merchant tonnage for the periods given.

APPENDIX B

The 'fourteen points' of President Woodrow Wilson, published on 8 January 1918

I. Open covenants of peace, openly arrived at, after which there shall be no private international understandings of any kind but diplomacy shall proceed always frankly and in the public view.

II. Absolute freedom of navigation upon the seas, outside territorial waters, alike in peace and in war, except as the seas may be closed in whole or in part by international action for the enforcement of international covenants.

III. The removal, so far as possible, of all economic barriers and the establishment of an equality of trade conditions among all the nations consenting to the peace and associating themselves for its maintenance.

IV. Adequate guarantees given and taken that national armaments will be reduced to the lowest point consistent with domestic safety.

V. A free, open-minded, and absolutely impartial adjustment of all colonial claims, based upon a strict observance of the principle that in determining all such questions of sovereignty the interests of the populations concerned must have equal weight with the equitable claims of the government whose title is to be determined.

VI. The evacuation of all Russian territory and such a settlement of all questions affecting Russia as will secure the best and freest cooperation of the other nations of the world in obtaining for her an unhampered and unembarrassed opportunity for the independent determination of her own political development and national policy and assure her of a sincere welcome into the society of free nations under institutions of her own choosing; and, more than a welcome, assistance also of every kind that she may need and may herself desire. The treatment accorded Russia by her sister nations in the months to come will be the acid test of their good will, of their comprehension of her needs as distinguished from their own interests, and of their intelligent and unselfish sympathy.

VII. Belgium, the whole world will agree, must be evacuated and restored, without any attempt to limit the sovereignty which she enjoys in common with all other free nations. No other single act will serve as this will serve to restore confidence among the nations in the laws which they have themselves set and determined for the government of their relations with one another. Without this healing act the whole structure and validity of international law is forever impaired.

VIII. All French territory should be freed and the invaded portions restored, and the wrong done to France by Prussia in 1871 in the matter of Alsace-Lorraine, which has unsettled the peace of the world for nearly fifty years, should be righted, in order that peace may once more be made secure in the interest of all.

IX. A readjustment of the frontiers of Italy should be effected along clearly recognizable lines of nationality.

X. The peoples of Austria-Hungary, whose place among the nations we wish to see safeguarded and assured, should be accorded the freest opportunity to autonomous development.

XI. Rumania, Serbia, and Montenegro should be evacuated; occupied territories restored; Serbia accorded free and secure access to the sea; and the relations of the several Balkan states to one another determined by friendly counsel along historically established lines of allegiance and nationality; and international guarantees of the political and economic independence and territorial integrity of the several Balkan states should be entered into.

XII. The Turkish portion of the present Ottoman Empire should be assured a secure sovereignty, but the other nationalities which are now under Turkish rule should be assured an undoubted security of life and an absolutely unmolested opportunity of autonomous development, and the Dardanelles should be permanently opened as a free passage to the ships and commerce of all nations under international guarantees.

XIII. An independent Polish state should be erected which should include the territories inhabited by indisputably Polish populations, which should be assured a free and secure access to the sea, and whose political and economic independence and territorial integrity should be guaranteed by international covenant.

XIV. A general association of nations must be formed under specific covenants for the purpose of affording mutual guarantees of political independence and territorial integrity to great and small states alike.

FURTHER READING IN ENGLISH

Note: *All translations in this book are by the author, unless otherwise attributed.*

All reasonable steps have been taken to clear copyright material. If any copyright has been inadvertently infringed, please write to the author, care of the publisher.

D. Acheson, *Present at the Creation*, New York, Norton, 1969

G. Ball, *The Past has another Pattern*, New York, Norton, 1992

A. Beevor & A. Cooper, *Paris after the Liberation*, London, Hamish Hamilton, 2004

C. E. Bohlen, *Witness to History*, New York, Norton, 1973

D. Boyd, *Voices from the Dark Years*, Thrupp, Sutton, 2007

McG. Bundy, *Danger and Survival*, New York, Vintage, 1988

D. Campbell, *The Unsinkable Aircraft Carrier*, London, Collins/Paladin, 1986

J. Chace, *Acheson, the Secretary of State who created the American World*, New York, Simon & Schuster, 1998

L. Chang & P. Kornbluh, *The Cuban Missile Crisis 1962*, New York, New Press, 1992

W. S. Churchill, *The Second World War Vols I–V*, London, Penguin Classics, 2005

C. Cogan, *Oldest Allies, Guarded Friends: The United States and France since 1940*, Westport, Praeger, 1994

F. Costigliola, *France and the United States, The Cold Alliance since World War II*, New York, Twayne, 1992

L. Freedman, *Kennedy's Wars*, Oxford, OUP, 2000

J. Haswell, *The Intelligence and Deception of the D-Day Landings*, London, Batsford, 1979

R. H. Jackson, *That Man – An insider's portrait of Franklin D. Roosevelt*, Oxford, OUP, 2003

J. Keegan, *Churchill's Generals*, London, Cassell, 1991

K. Kelley, *Jackie Oh!*, New York, Ballantine, 1978

W. Kohl, *French Nuclear Diplomacy*, Princeton, PUP, 1971

P. Mangold, *The Almost Impossible Ally – Harold Macmillan and Charles de Gaulle*, London, Tauris, 2006

E. May & P. Zelikow, *The Kennedy Tapes*, New York & London, Norton, 2001

J. Newhouse, *de Gaulle and the Anglo-Saxons*, London, André Deutsch, 1970

J. Prado, *Presidents' Secret Wars*, Chicago, Elephant Paperbacks, 1996

D. Reynolds, *Rich Relations – The American Occupation of Britain 1942–1945*, London, HarperCollins, 1995

H. Rousso, *The Vichy Syndrome*, London, Harvard, 1994

D. Rusk, *As I saw it*, London, Tauris, 1991

W. Thornton, *The Liberation of Paris*, London, Rupert Hart-Davis, 1963

P. Thyraud de Vosjoli, *Lamia*, Boston, Little Brown, 1970

B. Turner, *Countdown to Victory*, London, Hodder, 2004

A. Verner, *Assassination in Algiers*, London, Macmillan, 1990

R. Vinen, *The Politics of French Business*, Cambridge, CUP, 1991

C. Williams, *The Last Great Frenchman*, London, Little Brown, 1994

W. A. Williams, *The Tragedy of American Diplomacy*, New York, Dell, 1972

INDEX

If you enjoyed this book, you may also be interested in...

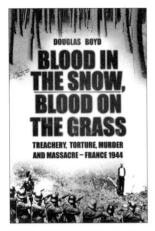

Blood in the Snow, Blood on the Grass: Treachery, Torture, Murder and Massacre – France 1944
DOUGLAS BOYD

Nearing D-Day, Allied intelligence used RAF airdrops to send Allied liaison officers down with supplies to the thousands of young men hiding in France's forests and hill country. Here the officers defied the two principles of guerrilla warfare: never concentrate your forces or risk a pitched battle. They assembled small armies of untrained civilians but in reality they were being used as bait – to draw German forces away from the invasion beaches. Douglas Boyd, a former international businessman and BBC television producer, personally interviewed hundreds of survivors of the German occupation.

978 0 7524 7026 9

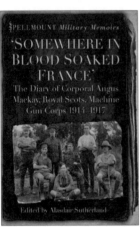

Somewhere in Blood Soaked France: The Diary of Corporal Angus Mackay, Royal Scots, Machine Gun Corps, 1914–1917
ALASDAIR SUTHERLAND (ED.)

From the heat and dust of the Dardanelles to the mud of the Western Front, Corporal Angus Mackay had one constant companion: his diary. He wrote of the battles and campaigns he fought in, names that would go down in history: Gallipoli, the Ypres Salient, the Somme and Arras. Part of the Spellmount Military Memoirs series, *Somewhere in Blood Soaked France* is a previously unpublished account of the First World War, complete with historical context, orders of battle and extracts from official war diaries.

978 0 7524 6446 6

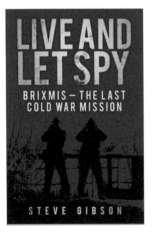

Live and Let Spy: BRIXMIS – The Last Cold War Mission
STEVE GIBSON

BRIXMIS (The British Commander-in-Chief's Mission to the Group Soviet Forces of Occupation in Germany) is one of the most little-known elite spying units of the British Army. They were dropped in behind 'enemy lines' ten months after the Second World War had ended and remained operating their intelligence-gathering missions until October 1990 and then covertly until 1993, long after the fall of the Berlin Wall in November 1989. During this period Berlin was a hotbed of spying between East and West. This book is a unique history of this most elite of units.

978 0 7524 6580 7

Visit our website and discover thousands of other History Press books.

www.thehistorypress.co.uk